Emily D. West and the
"Yellow Rose of Texas" Myth

ALSO BY PHILLIP THOMAS TUCKER

*Westerners in Gray: The Men and Missions of the
Elite Fifth Missouri Infantry Regiment*
(McFarland, 1994; paperback 2007)

EDITED BY PHILLIP THOMAS TUCKER

*Cubans in the Confederacy: José Agustín Quintero,
Ambrosio José Gonzales, and Loreta Janeta Velazquez*
(McFarland, 2002)

Emily D. West and the "Yellow Rose of Texas" Myth

PHILLIP THOMAS TUCKER

Foreword by Mario Marcel Salas

McFarland & Company, Inc., Publishers
Jefferson, North Carolina

LIBRARY OF CONGRESS CATALOGUING-IN-PUBLICATION DATA

Tucker, Phillip Thomas, 1953–
Emily D. West and the "Yellow Rose of Texas" myth /
Phillip Thomas Tucker ; foreword by Mario Marcel Salas.
p. cm.
Includes bibliographical references and index.

ISBN 978-0-7864-7449-3 (softcover : alkaline paper) ∞
ISBN 978-1-4766-1328-4 (ebook)

1. West, Emily D., 1801– 2 West, Emily D., 1801– —Legends.
3. Yellow rose of Texas. 4. Free African Americans—Texas—Biography.
5. African American women—Texas—Biography. 6. Free African Americans—
Connecticut—New Haven—Biography. 7. African American women—
Connecticut—New Haven—Biography. 8. Alamo (San Antonio, Tex.)—
Siege, 1836. 9. San Jacinto, Battle of, Tex., 1836. 10. Texas—Biography. I. Title.
F390.W47T83 2014   976.4′04092—dc23   [B]   2013048079

BRITISH LIBRARY CATALOGUING DATA ARE AVAILABLE

© 2014 Phillip Thomas Tucker. All rights reserved

*No part of this book may be reproduced or transmitted in any form
or by any means, electronic or mechanical, including photocopying
or recording, or by any information storage and retrieval system,
without permission in writing from the publisher.*

On the cover: illustration of Emily West by Sarah Fox;
Alamo illustration © 2014 Clipart.com

Manufactured in the United States of America

*McFarland & Company, Inc., Publishers
Box 611, Jefferson, North Carolina 28640
www.mcfarlandpub.com*

To Teri Tucker-Posey, for all of her kind support
and assistance over the years.

Contents

Foreword by Mario Marcel Salas	1
Preface	5
Introduction	7
Chapter I: Emily D. West, The Popular Myth and Legend	19
Chapter II: Emily D. West's Birth in New Haven	34
Chapter III: A New Life and Adventure Beckons	64
Chapter IV: Texas Bound	79
Chapter V: Slaughter at the Alamo	111
Chapter VI: Muddy Roads Leading to San Jacinto	122
Chapter VII: Climactic Showdown at San Jacinto	160
Chapter VIII: Popular Myth-making and the Creation of "The Yellow Rose of Texas"	195
Chapter IX: Emily After the Fiery Storm of San Jacinto	217
Epilogue	229
Chapter Notes	233
Bibliography	253
Index	261

Foreword

by Mario Marcel Salas

As a professor of political science and a life-long resident of Texas, specifically San Antonio, I have been subjected to an array of historical falsehoods concerning Texas history. I first became aware of the "other Alamo story" as a result of being a civil rights activist in SNCC (Student Non-Violent Coordinating Committee) for many years. As a child I was told of the heroic action taken by the Alamo defenders and how they fought against a Mexican tyrant. It was later that I came to discount that idea, and that those "heroes" were actually unapologetic slave owners or pro-slavery men that came to San Antonio to institutionalize slavery on soil that did not belong to them. I had a modicum of facts to back up my beliefs, but it was not until Dr. Phillip Tucker published his important work *Exodus from the Alamo: The Anatomy of the Last Stand Myth* that I had access to important primary source material clearly showing that the Texas war with Mexico in 1836 did not happen as I and millions of others had thought.

I have also been the victim of another bogus story—that of Emily Morgan (Emily West). Over the course of my teaching career I have tried to convey the facts which refute these historical inaccuracies, but time constraints on other research projects often only afforded me use of secondary material on this subject. With the historical data produced from previously overlooked and purposely ignored primary documents, Dr. Tucker has given Texans a concrete basis to question the racial fiction that has infected the state since the defeat of Mexico. Dr. Tucker dissects the racial underpinnings of Texas myth and brings us to a greater understanding of the calculus used to reinforce historical fraud. The important message in this new book is for historians and readers of history to dig below the surface to see the method of entrapment used by bigoted or pusillanimous writers of history.

In understanding the works of Dr. Tucker, it becomes necessary to know that one of the main features of the virus of white supremacy in America, and indeed heretofore the fashion of all conquest, is the calculated loss of memory by those that conquer. It is a force used to devise and create invented historical authenticity, and hammer into others, from birth to death, to accept as confirmed reality an embroidered labyrinth of invention that displays history as if it began with their victories, allowing for a fabricated historical loftiness and mythology totally out of sync to the reality sustained by the historical record. Historical reality is condensed into half-truths, omissions, lies, distortions, and erasures. It is the brick and mortar of a matrix of fabrication that is spread to the population via educational institutions, literature, and repeated by people whose human spirit of inquisitiveness has been betrayed; for it is a foundational web of falsehoods that has infected our educational system and everyday narratives; it operates in the foreground and in the background to sustain a status quo of sugar-coated myth that often has a racial component. It is an Alamo account, or an Emily Morgan fairy-tale, a counterfeit narrative, that was designed to convey an invented reality to bolster and sustain a very biased and altered copy of history.

It is thus crucial that an analysis of the connectivity of racial myth and historical agency be constructed to illustrate how myth is used to hammer into millions an invented reality synced in place as a historical prop for white supremacy. Racial myth must be identified and confronted with data mined from the historical record in order for our country to grow beyond its racial colonialist past. Dr. Tucker has accomplished this in his other works and has done so again in this study.

I first was made aware of the Emily Morgan story from an African American friend who found it strange that a supposed slave woman, or a free one for that matter, would want to help Anglo slavers that came to construct a slave empire in Texas. The story was doubtful in his mind and mine as well, for I was familiar with a parallel myth concerning the fabrication that blacks fought freely for the Confederate States of America during the Civil War. It is entirely illogical that slaves would have been trusted with any weapons since every southern state had some type of law severely punishing any black in possession of a weapon. Why then were a small number of pictures manufactured of blacks in Confederate uniform brandishing weapons? It was my conclusion, at that time and now, that virtually no black ever enthusiastically fought for the slave owners. It has since been confirmed by credible historic evidence that blacks were often used as grave diggers, trench diggers, runners, cooks, and in other roles of a non-combat nature. In fact, blacks were sometimes forced into these roles or they would be killed or tortured, family members murdered, or returned to harsher plantation life. In some instances, blacks were forced into taking pictures by means of old daguerreotype photography so that southern propagandists could make claims that blacks supposedly were "happy" being slaves and servants to a "superior race." As explained by Dr. Tucker, the Emily Morgan myth is but another invented reality used to construct racial fiction.

Racial narratives are invented to sustain the forced idea that non-whites do not possess morals and integrity, in order to sync barbaric treatment with ready-made justifications. This can be seen in the narratives that have provided bogus explanations for the defeat of Mexico and to the racial moorings of white supremacy that are attached to non-whites. These ideas are dissected by Dr. Tucker, leaving little wiggle room for the accepted versions of San Antonio and Texas history.

It has been my experience to take note of the fact that it is an old and much-used device of white supremacy to decorate deceitful inventions of racial superiority with a veil of sanitized historical holiness through hero worship and through stabbing, belittling narratives, to give the appearance of truth to historical smoke and mirrors. This method of systematic deception is at the crux of much of the existing educational literature concerning the Battle of the Alamo and San Jacinto, and still manages to find acceptance in our educational system. There is a host of pre-meditated calculations that assemble a false history designed to bury the dignity of non-whites and elevate a load of invented Eurocentric interpretations up a racial pyramid that holds no credibility. When history is taught in this way, millions are infected. The infection spreads from generation to generation, and on one level plays psycho-ideological havoc on the unconsciousness mind to develop, day after day, narratives that pander to overt and subtle racial thought that is just below the surface. In this work, Dr. Tucker leaves the reader stunned by the stinging weight of facts that refute the bigoted versions of history.

Racial myth even has tourist value. In San Antonio, this has taken the form of naming a hotel after Emily Morgan, an idea that reinforces the other myth—that of the Alamo, for the hotel is directly across the street. Racial myth remains an almost permanent structure of thought that is transmitted from one generation to the next, carried in a mental Trojan horse, hibernating, embedded in the minds of millions, and hidden in bedtime stories and old grandpa tales that are highly infectious and are sometimes transferred to place names. In modern times, myth making along racial secular lines was utilized, and religious dogma was replaced or reinforced with "logical constructs" that developed scientific racism and justifications for viewing non-whites as inferior and subject to an array of foundational racial exaggeration. In the 1700s, Carolus Linnaeus and Johann Friedrich Blumenbach, two racialized scientists, paved the way for the prototype of what we now call scientific racism, or racial permutations, to justify white superiority. Linnaeus developed taxonomies for plants, which he later tried to transfer to human beings by creating broad geographical definitions of human populations that would be eventually contorted into physical characteristics and skin color. He then pinned personalities on these invented groups: Indigenous People were said to be "quick tempered, choleric, and eager," Africans were labeled "slow and negligent," while whites (Europeans) were described as "swift, clever, and inventive." Soon thereafter, these falsehoods were refined by Blumenbach, who created the unsubstantiated race models of Negroid, Caucasoid, Mongoloid, and others that provided a scientific cover for racial thinking. This provided a ready-made mold to churn out principles about the inferiority of blacks and other non-whites. These classifications were used to construct a hierarchical structure with white Europeans on top and all others below.

Dr. Tucker, in fine specificity, professionally steers us to understanding racial thought and philosophy. Black men were described as sexual monstrosities in much the same way one would describe an animal. Black women were given the role of being sexually promiscuous and seducers. But in this theater of racial fiction there loomed the possibility of using it to detail historical events along lines that prescribed an outcome of white perfection. Dr. Tucker points us in the direction that Emily Morgan was used for such a purpose in a multifaceted fashion. She could be used to reinforce the idea of the "animal instincts of blacks" and the "heathen instincts of Mexicans." The supposed Santa Anna rendezvous with Emily Morgan was designed on the plains of an accepted racial belief system that was constantly being manufactured or simply morphed to explain away universal humanity. Mexicans were seen as "mixed-race heathens" infused with an "Indian" love of the natural world which had to be tamed. The formulaic black female, drawn from the canvas of slavery, as a creature of "extreme sexual desire," would meet the "natural sensual lust of the Mexican" in the supposed encounter between Santa Anna and a black woman in a pictographic racialized Garden of Eden. Here the stage was set for the victory of white supremacy, in that this sexual passion provided the "clear mind of the white" with an opportunity to gain victory over Mexico as punishment for abolishing slavery in 1829.

Using this analogy, it could be proclaimed that Antonio López de Santa Anna Saldana ate the racial fruit and suffered the fall at the hands of a superior and focused race. It was but another twist upon the myth that non-whites cannot effectively govern themselves and that for the non-white lust or passion (negligence or choleric temperament) comes before responsibility, or unlike the sham idea that the genetic traits of swiftness and the clever temperament of whites were not transmissible to non-whites. Mexico sinned in the eyes of most white settlers of that day by freeing blacks from slavery, and to substantiate that it was a mistake, an incident was to be manufactured to prove it. What better way than to invent a sexual rendezvous between "passion and negligence," between a Mexican and a black, allowing for the "swift" white to conquer the day.

All of Dr. Tucker's books should be kept on the shelf where they can readily be seen and utilized. This book is worth what I would call a physical Socratic effort, in that I plan to literally carry the book into the Alamo and share with others, and along the banks of the San Antonio River, and into the shops and eateries along its course, and to conduct educational seminars for public and private institutions. There are many levels in the house of white supremacy, and each dreadful yarn is connected to the overall imaginary calculus of non-white inferiority. Non-whites are expected to ignore the racial curtain that covered the Americas, and speak as if racism was just a passing phenomenon and not wedged like a petrified stake in the minds of millions. Inventions of a white racial character bestow a squinting stare that does not speak to truth, but to following the code of racial conduct.

The author herein mines the data and traces the development of the creation of the Emily Morgan myth, a myth that serves to paint a very shrewd picture which underpins the illogical pre-mediated design of racial superiority which is often repeated, not just by bigoted historians, but by a crowd of faint-hearted academicians whose intellectual laziness has contributed to the derailing of the historical evidence. There are many racial walls that need tearing down, and Dr. Phillip Thomas Tucker has added his name to those whose academic knowledge, integrity, and courage is unquestionable in removing these obstacles.

Mario Marcel Salas is a retired professor of political science. He also served as a councilman for the city of San Antonio, and was very active in the Civil Rights Movement for many years. He has authored several textbooks, including Foundation Myth in Political Thought: The Racial Moorings of Foundation Myth *(Kendall Hunt, 2011).*

Preface

The story of the famed "Yellow Rose of Texas" has become a legend and enduring part of not only Texas history but also American history. No scholarly work has been devoted to the remarkable life of this free black woman named Emily D. West, who has been most readily identified and celebrated as the "Yellow Rose of Texas." And perhaps no chapter in Texas history has been more distorted by fiction and myth. Therefore, this work has been focused on presenting the true story of the "Yellow Rose of Texas."

This work was a collective effort. I would like to thank countless historians, librarians, and advisors across the United States. With grace and a high level of professionalism, they have contributed their time, expertise, and assistance to make this work possible. One of the foremost contributors was Doris B. "Deb" Townshend, the capable and ever-helpful Center Church historian in New Haven, Connecticut. And I would like to also thank the good people at the New Haven Museum and Historical Society, New Haven, Connecticut, for their efforts.

Introduction

Only one African American woman has been celebrated for playing a key role in the creation of a nation conceived in violent revolution. Her name was Emily D. West, the alleged famed "Yellow Rose of Texas." By any measure, "The Yellow Rose of Texas" has become one of the most popular folk legends in not only Texas history but also American history.

Her story has been one of the most sexually-charged and sensational tales in American history. This is no small distinction given the turbulent times and unruly lives of so many dynamic men and women of frontier Texas, strong, unforgettable personalities, fiery revolutionaries of the heroic mold, and legendary sinners and epic hell-raisers of an untamed, tempestuous frontier second to none on the North American continent.

West became a folk heroine of Texas because of her supposedly influential sexual role in winning the new republic's independence—which had to be reaped on the battlefield—in what was very much a rough-and-tumble, southwestern frontier reprise of the American Revolution. A much-embellished almost commercial product created in the mid-twentieth century, the mythical Emily of "The Yellow Rose of Texas" fame has evolved into a legendary folk heroine in no small part because of a nineteenth century song made popular across America during the mid–1950s.

In a rather remarkable development without precedent, a woman of color has been placed at center stage of the Texas creation story and the decisive battle of San Jacinto, where Texas' independence was won in a climactic confrontation on the afternoon of April 21, 1836. Although too often overlooked or ignored because of the dominance of traditional and conservative history in Texas, the Lone Star State in fact has one of the richest multi-racial and most vibrant multi-cultural histories in all America. Free black men and women were longtime residents of this bountiful, fertile, and picturesque land known as Tejas long before the colonizing effort of the first hopeful Anglo-Celtic migrants from the United States—Stephen Fuller Austin's colonists, or Texians, who settled in Texas in the early 1820s. Nevertheless, the dramatic story of the African American experience, especially that of free blacks (the most forgotten Texians), has long been the most thoroughly neglected chapter of not only Texas history but also American history.

General Sam Houston's climactic victory on the coastal plain of San Jacinto opened the door for America's eventual acquisition of half of Mexico and the westward push of the American people all the way to the golden shores of the Pacific, thanks to Mexico's crushing defeat in the Mexican-American War of 1846–1848. This bitter conflict between neighboring republics had been sparked by the 1845 annexation of Texas by the United States and because Mexico refused to acknowledge the loss of Texas. In this dramatic setting, relatively recent recognition has been bestowed upon this remarkable black woman named

Emily D. West, who allegedly played a key role at San Jacinto that shaped the course of American history.

Long mistakenly thought to have been a lowly slave with the common slave name of Emily who possessed her master's last name of Morgan, Emily D. West was in fact the real name of the alleged "Yellow Rose of Texas" of romantic legend and myth. But the real Emily was no slave. In fact, she never had been enslaved. In truth, Emily D. West was one of the first free black women to migrate from the United States to the land west of the Sabine River, sharing in the traditional challenges, trials, and dangers of the western frontier experience along with other Texians, both males and females.

This woman who decided to migrate to Texas on her own free will and with high hopes for a better life has been long erroneously known and widely misidentified as a slave named Emily Morgan who was owned by James Morgan. Despite the fact that absolutely no contemporary (either in 1836 or the decade of the 1830s) account or primary evidence (especially letters or diaries) of Emily's alleged role at San Jacinto has been found or are known to exist, since the 1950s she has become a legendary figure.

The central mystery of "The Yellow Rose of Texas" story was the fact that no mention of Emily, or her supposedly legendary sensual role at San Jacinto, has appeared in any of the first published treatments—books, pamphlets, or memoirs—of the decisive battle of San Jacinto, one of the most important clashes of arms in American history to alter the destinies of three nations. Even more, Emily D. West was not a native Texan or from the South. Instead, she was a New England–born free black and New Yorker by the mid–1830s. In fact, Emily only lived in the Gulf Coast region of east Texas for barely a year, from December 1835 to early 1837.

Her legend has far superseded even the legendary Jane Long, the "Mother of Texas," whose notable contributions to Texas history and the Texas Revolution have been long verified. The southern Maryland–born Jane Herbert Wilkinson-Long, the wife of Mississippi physician, revolutionary dreamer, and ambitious filibuster James Long and an authentic Texas revolutionary heroine in her own right, was never involved in high-level sexual intrigue and scandalous behavior that allegedly changed the course of Texas and American history.

Emily's enduring recognition and fame has stemmed from what allegedly happened between her and General Antonio López de Santa Anna, the great arch villain of Texas history, in secret intimacy inside the Mexican encampment at San Jacinto on April 21, 1836. This sexual escapade allegedly took place in the Mexican commander's large field campaign and headquarters tent just before General Sam Houston unleashed his frontal attack across the grassy, open coastal plain of east Texas to catch Santa Anna by surprise and reap his great victory.

But if the enduring romantic legend of "The Yellow Rose of Texas" perhaps can be yet verified by any reliable primary documentation, then Emily might truly deserve the authentic renown as the real "Mother of Texas" for her role at the decisive moment. According to the romantic myth, Emily planned and played a leading role in paving the way for Houston's remarkable success by utilizing her sexual skills and ravishing beauty to distract the Mexican commander from military matters at the most critical moment, when Houston unleashed his surprise attack. If this scenario was indeed the case, then Emily should be recognized as the African American woman who had the most dramatic impact on the course of Texas history.

But did this most celebrated incident in Texas history really take place? Is there any truth at all to the most sensational, sexually-laden and embellished legend in Texas history that so suddenly came to life in the 1950s and then reached its zenith during the "patriotic" fervor of the 1986 Texas Sesquicentennial? Have multiple layers of romance, myth, and folklore simply obscured the real truth about Emily that was much less sensational and dramatic?

After all, how can we really know what happened in Santa Anna's headquarters tent on the field of San Jacinto that hot afternoon of April 21, 1836, just before Houston ordered his attack across the plain of Hyacinth (San Jacinto), especially if no contemporary accounts, especially letters or diaries, or even later-day memoirs on any side (Texan, American, Tejano, and Mexican) have told of her alleged sexual role at San Jacinto that helped to pave the way for Houston's remarkable success to save the life of the seemingly doomed infant Texas republic?

In the American consciousness and popular imagination, the American West was historically a land of myth and enduring romance, with larger-than-life characters and personalities that have only grown even larger over time. And no part of the American West has been more mythical and romantic than the history of Texas. Texas has long served as a colorful, dramatic stage for the rise of legendary historical figures and sagas. And in much the same way, no woman in all Texas history has been more a subject of romance, legend, and myth than the fabled "Yellow Rose of Texas." According to the myth, Emily's timely carnal contribution (thanks allegedly to her highly-developed skills in the sexual art of seduction and irresistible beauty that made Santa Anna little more than an unthinking sexual slave) to Texas history set the stage for the winning of Texas liberty at San Jacinto.

The real Emily was in truth a rather ordinary, hard-working, and humble woman of African American descent and lower class origins from the North. Nevertheless, especially since the mid–1950s, she has been transformed by a good many imaginative journalists, popular writers, and historians (mostly white) into a Texas patriot and heroine of mythical proportions not unlike the most famous central players of the Texas Revolution, especially the Alamo triumvirate of James Bowie, David Crockett, and William Barret Travis.

As if created from the vivid imagination of a gifted Hollywood script writer who made a career out of penning dramatic stories for the big screen, Emily and her alleged carnal role on that warm April afternoon in Santa Anna's headquarters tent at San Jacinto has been embellished, fictionalized, and sensationalized without any accordance to the facts. Larger than life and almost mystical in regard to legend-creating, Texas history has been long defined by popular myths, colorful tales, and excessive romanticism. Indeed, all newly formed nations, including the United States, required a romanticized creation story that called for a mythical past and larger than life personalities, like the founding fathers in regard to the United States, to legitimize their birth, existence, and uniqueness on the world stage, especially if recently forged in the throes of violent revolution and if stemming from complex, contradictory causes.

Emily's alleged role on April 21, 1836, certainly deserves more serious investigation and analysis because the battle of San Jacinto was one of the most decisive in American history, with far-reaching consequences for the future of the United States and Mexico. On the blood-stained field of San Jacinto, the fate of the fledgling Texas republic was decided in record time. In only eighteen minutes of brutal combat that swirled across the Gulf Coastal Plain, Houston's improbable success in thoroughly vanquishing Santa Anna's force in one of the most one-sided victories in American history saved an infant republic lingering near extinction.

Mexico's loss of Texas led directly to annexation by the United States in 1845, which sparked the Mexican-American War the following year. As a result of America's flexing of its nationalistic muscle in its first foreign war from 1846 to 1848, Mexico lost half its national territory, while the American nation fulfilled its lofty, idealistic Manifest Destiny–inspired vision: a vigorous, youthful republic spanning to the Pacific and from sea to shining sea. And according to the romantic legend and enduring myth, a single, lowly woman of African descent named Emily played the key role in triggering this remarkable chain of events, shaping the course of history like no other woman in the annals of Texas history.

But the intoxicating spirit of America's Manifest Destiny that reached a zenith at San Jacinto in fact disguised and hid a much darker reality that has been often overlooked by Texas historians who glorify Houston's victory. The Emily Morgan myth has been romanticized almost as if for the express purpose of disguising the ugly truths and horrors of what really happened at San Jacinto. More of a massacre than a conventional clash of arms, the battle has been long trumpeted as a morality play of superior Anglo-Celtics vanquishing an allegedly inferior people of mixed race, as epitomized by Santa Anna's dramatic fall from grace.

A close look at the real Emily D. West will illuminate a forgotten saga of the trials, hardships, and sacrifices of the ordinary African American women who migrated to Texas in search of a brighter future outside of the United States' physical and racial boundaries. In following her dream to carve a life for herself on the western frontier of Texas, Emily became unwittingly caught amid the ebb and flow of a people's revolution against Mexico, a war for independence, a civil war, and a struggle for survival.

Searching for a brighter future like so many other hopeful immigrants during the 1820s and 1830s, Emily migrated to Mexico's northern province of Tejas (Texas), a yet undeveloped frontier, in late 1835. But contrary to the myth, this adventurous and ambitious New England–born woman had never been a slave like the majority of blacks living in Texas at this time. In this sense, Emily was representative of early women settlers who not only helped to create a civilization in the wilderness but also forged a new nation, the Republic of Texas.

Departing from the relative comfort the eastern United States and the environments of both small town (New Haven, Connecticut) and major city (New York), this enterprising free black woman first migrated to this seemingly boundless land of promise as a contract worker. As both a free woman and a black newcomer to Texas, Emily was not the typical immigrant. Few free black women journeyed toward the setting sun and so far from relative safety to become part of the Texas Revolutionary experience, especially on their own without husband or family.

Contrary to the myth, Emily D. West was a proud, independent-minded, and resourceful woman who has been often misidentified with the last name of her mythical "owner." James Morgan was in fact Emily's employer in Texas and not an owner or master. Worst of all, Emily is erroneously long thought to have been the subject of the popular antebellum song "The Yellow Rose of Texas." This jaunty tune, originally an old slave song, became a popular anthem for the Lone Star State and the people of Texas during the mid–twentieth century. The song's immense popularity has a large part in the romantic legend and myth surrounding Emily D. West, despite no existing evidence of this dubious claim.

Thanks in part to the song's popularity beginning in the mid–twentieth century, the identity of Emily Morgan and Emily D. West mistakenly merged, becoming one and the same. However, a simple reading of the words of "The Yellow Rose of Texas" song has clearly revealed absolutely no connection to Emily—either Emily Morgan or Emily D. West—the Texas Revolution, or the battle of San Jacinto.

In truth, the words of "The Yellow Rose of Texas" tell the romantic tale of a lovesick male slave longing to join his beautiful mulatto (or "high yellow") female lover, who was "the sweetest rose of color." During the antebellum period, this particular slave woman featured in the song had evidently escaped slavery in Texas, like a good many other Texas slaves, to find a safe haven in the neighboring republic. Nestled in Mexico's northeast corner, the old commercial city of Matamoros, located on the south bank of the Rio Grande River, was where this light-skinned beauty "walks along the river" known as the Rio Bravo, or the Rio Grande, according to the popular song. But this beautiful woman of African descent was certainly not Emily D. West, who never saw Mexico or even got close to the Rio Grande River.

Therefore, the true story of this resilient free black woman from the North named Emily D. West has long been not only shrouded in romantic myth and legend, but also tainted by a host of negative sexist and racist stereotypes that have tarnished her role, character, and place in Texas history. Based upon long-existing racial stereotypes, the overall image of Emily D. West has been considerably distorted by the myth of "The Yellow Rose of Texas," deviating extensively from the facts and the less sensational reality.

She has been most often portrayed in an overall negative light. Emily has been most often seen as just another lowly black woman, driven by mostly base, dark passions in keeping with an alleged racial inferiority; an artful, bewitching seductress with a penchant for sexual indiscretions, based solely upon her color and the accompanying racial stereotypes. But the truth and the historical record has revealed a far different person and much more complex Emily, and one far beyond the many unflattering racial stereotypes.

Instead of the fabled slave woman named Emily Morgan, or the "The Yellow Rose of Texas," who has been portrayed as a young seductress and conniving mulatto beauty (based upon white societal standards of beauty—light-skinned, long straight hair, and Caucasian features), Emily was actually more of an average-looking middle-aged African American women.

The real Emily certainly possessed more ordinary looks and probably acted with a measure of dignity, confidence, and grace in keeping with her varied life experiences, northern background, education, and an active life as a free black woman of spirit and with connections to some of the leading abolitionists in America. Emily was surely proud of her New England background and heritage, African roots, northern abolitionist influences, and coveted free status.

The real Emily D. West, who was raised born and raised in New Haven, Connecticut, little resembled the mythical Emily—the sexy, adulterous slave of master Morgan, of the San Jacinto legend—in any way, shape, or form. The entire basis of "The Yellow Rose of Texas" story has come from a single and highly-questionable source, written years after the battle of San Jacinto, that cannot be corroborated by any existing contemporary (especially in 1836) account on either side.

As recently ascertained by historian Jim Lutzweiler, Sam Houston himself was in fact the previously unidentified writer of the controversial "Emily" paragraph in the William Bollaert Papers, housed in the Newberry Library in Chicago: "The Battle of San Jacinto was probably lost for the Mexicans owing to the influence of a Mulatta Girl (Emily)." At first glance and without careful or serious contemplation, Houston's alleged words from a now nonexistent letter to an unidentified friend, that William Bollaert marked as "private," has seemed almost beyond reproach or question to many Texas historians, because "Old Sam" had commanded the victorious Texas Army at San Jacinto.

But upon more careful reflection, Houston's words from a private letter, never meant for publication, must be carefully analyzed in the context of the times and within a relatively narrow cultural framework.

It was quite ironic and even strange (perhaps a case of projection) that Houston should have relayed to William Bollaert such a sexually-charged story about the downfall of his most hated opponent from the beauty or sexual wiles, or both, of a most alluring woman of color. Houston's own greatest personal disgrace and political downfall as the Tennessee governor was thanks to a disastrously short marriage to a much younger woman. Houston was also widely criticized for his well-known penchant for Indian women. He even took an Indian wife, Tiana Rogers.

One of the great sinners of the Texas frontier—like so many other new migrants to Texas, which shielded them from United States laws and creditors, including the most famous commander of the Alamo, William Barret Travis—Houston was never guilty of discrimination or excessive color-consciousness when it came to the art of love-making. He had taken lovers of all races and classes by the time of the Texas Revolution. In perpetuating the "Yellow Rose of Texas" story, Houston seemingly projected his own considerable weaknesses, follies, and failings upon his opponent, Santa Anna, in relating the Emily story.

All in all, what Houston relayed in his alleged letter, which cannot be found today or verified as even authentic, to an unidentified friend was in fact nothing more than a humorous, racial stereotype-ridden bawdy tale—Texas frontier gossip and a sensational yarn—that had made the rounds among white males in the smoke-filled saloons, and brightly-decorated, dingy whorehouses across Texas by the early 1840s. In spreading an authentic Texas tall tale, even though the story was untrue, the grizzled, roughhewn Houston almost certainly was merely exploiting the naïveté and gullibility of an over-educated, dandified Englishman, Bollaert.

The popularity of this sex-infused story of an interracial liaison stemmed from its reaffirmation of a host of long cherished Anglo-Saxon cultural values based upon concepts of racial and cultural superiority. The story of the alleged Emily–Santa Anna tryst at San Jacinto was most of all a white male tale about the folly of an opponent of a different race and religion and the fatal sexual indiscretion of the most thoroughly-despised foreign leader in Texas history; a bawdy tale that only reaffirmed a plethora of deep-seated racial identities, values, and stereotypes to bolster a greater sense of white superiority, while making Mexicans and blacks objects of even greater scorn and ridicule, if that was possible.

Like fellow Tennessean David Crockett, who was America's most famous western frontier teller of tall stories before meeting his grisly end at the Alamo on the early morning of March 6, 1836, Houston was a marvelous story teller whose tall tales and whoppers were well-known throughout Texas. After all, imaginative story-telling, the most colorful and sensational the better, was a primary source of entertainment and popularity—especially for a politician—on the western frontier. This popular frontier form of entertainment was only part of the Celtic oral tradition that continued to thrive, especially among the Irish and Anglo-Celtic settlers, on first American, especially in the South, and then Texas soil. This endearing quality of telling colorful whoppers was one secret of Houston's popularity among the Texians. Drawing upon the central tenets of some of the best known stories and moral cautionary tales from the Bible almost certainly to gain much-needed popular support in the United States during the early 1840s for the annexation of Texas, which was opposed by anti-slavery advocates in Congress in Washington, D.C., Houston evidently spun what was essentially a spicy, racially-charged Samson and Delilah morality tale that has evolved into the popular folklore known as "The Yellow Rose of Texas." Since the mid–twentieth century, this tale then became a permanent part of the Texas creation myth.

As the first president of Texas (elected on September 5, 1836), Houston also sought to calm the fears about the unnerving prospect of another invasion from Mexico. Therefore, the Santa Anna–Emily liaison story, which first surfaced in the early 1840s, emphasized Mexican military incompetence at the highest level to reassure Texians, who faced an omnipresent threat from a Mexico that refused to concede the permanent loss of Texas to the norteamericanos.

Part of the core audience for the sexually-explicit Emily–Santa Anna tryst story were the slave-owners of Texas. The fact that a good many slave-owners, in both the South and Texas, maintained sexual relations with female slaves allowed them to relate in a very personal way to a humorous tale of a fatal sexual indiscretion that doomed Santa Anna, while holding him up as a prime object of public ridicule for alleged racial liabilities and weaknesses.

All of these diverse factors gave Houston a number of valid motives to have created the Texas tall tale and to write his letter, which came into Bollaert's possession by some unknown means to an unknown friend for personal amusement and certainly not for publication. Therefore, demonstrating sound judgment, Bollaert wisely considered the letter not only private but also of no consequence or historical significance. He correctly considered the Emily–Santa Anna liaison story as nothing more than a Texas tall tale with no real credibility, and hence undeserving of publication. Bollaert almost certainly realized that Houston, like some good-natured Texas frontier jokester, had only merely attempted to pass off idle gossip, a bawdy tale, and a fanciful story to a non–Texian and Englishman unfamiliar with Texas humor and cultural norms, especially in regard to slavery.

Indeed, if the alleged Santa Anna-Emily liaison had actually occurred and had played such a vital role in Santa Anna's defeat at San Jacinto, then it would have been certainly mentioned by the many Mexican officers and soldiers, especially Santa Anna's many diehard enemies, including subordinate officers, who wrote extensively about what happened at San Jacinto during the postwar period. But this was certainly not the case. No Mexican sources of the day even remotely hinted at the most infamous sexual tryst in Texas history. Indeed, the most revealing sources that could have verified Houston's brief words about the most celebrated interracial liaison in Texas and American history (after Thomas Jefferson and Sally Hemings at Monticello) would have come from the writings of Santa Anna's own men, especially the generalísimo's many haters among the Mexican officer corps. Lieutenant Colonel Enrique de la Peña, who authored the controversial David Crockett execution paragraph in his journal-memoir, made no mention of the alleged liaison.

Mexican officers who survived San Jacinto's slaughter wrote extensively and explored in great detail how and why they had suffered the worst one-sided defeat in Mexican military history at San Jacinto. But not a single word about the alleged Santa Anna–Emily tryst was ever forthcoming from anyone, military or civilian, from Mexico. This was a most unusual development because the Mexican government, army, and people all condemned and blamed Santa Anna for the loss of the nation's most prized possession and richest northern province—Texas. After all, the disgraced Mexican president, who saved his own life only by signing an illegal treaty (without the consent of the Mexican Congress) that recognized an independent Texas, became a national whipping boy for the loss. Modern Mexican historians have long maintained that Santa Anna had conspired with Texas and United States leaders to deliberately hand Texas over to the norteamericanos.

Almost everyone in Mexico, especially many of his top lieutenants, placed all blame for the San Jacinto disaster squarely on the shoulders of Santa Anna. However not a single person, from Mexican officers and soldiers who somehow survived the terrible bloodletting at San Jacinto to modern Mexican historians, have ever mentioned anything about their disgraced commander having dallied with a slave woman in his headquarters tent at the moment that Houston launched his attack. Indeed, the easiest way for his many enemies to have thoroughly disparaged Santa Anna was to have written about the folly of any ill-timed sexual escapade that brought his downfall at San Jacinto.

Santa Anna in fact represented an abolitionist nation, more enlightened in racial matters compared to the United States and Texas. Mexico had abolished slavery in mid–September 1829 and Santa Anna liberated slaves across Texas in 1836. His forgotten role as liberator of Texas slaves gained for Santa Anna acclaim in the United States from anti-slavery Americans. Even more during his 1836 Texas Campaign, Santa Anna was determined to eliminate Anglo-Celtic Texas, whose robust economy—principally resting upon cotton—was based upon slave labor, before he met his Waterloo at San Jacinto, where the Texians fought in no small part to defend their social order whose foundation was slavery.

The idea that slavery played an important role in early Texas history and in the Texas Revolution has long seemed almost a fantastic concept to the average reader, because of its notable, glaring absence from the historical record and the dominance of Texas romantic myths, including the story of the Alamo. What has been most forgotten about the story of the Alamo was the fact that Santa Anna's attackers were fighting in part for human freedom and against slavery, while the band of defenders of the old Franciscan mission were mostly pro-slavery.

Contrary to the words penned by Houston in his long-lost letter and despite the popularity of "The Yellow Rose of Texas" myth, the improbability of the supposed sexual liaison between Emily and Santa Anna at San Jacinto could not be greater. After all, why would the decisive victory at San Jacinto—one of the most complete routs in the annals of American military history—have been explained in such simplistic terms devoid of any military skill or tactical genius by none other than Houston himself, who was most responsible for reaping that amazing April success on the Gulf Coastal Plain?

It makes no sense for Houston to have seriously written such a paragraph that so thoroughly disparaged his own tactical ability and the quality of his own generalship—which was already under severe attack from his many political enemies for having withdrawn before Santa Anna's relentless advance east across much of Texas before reaching San Jacinto.

Had Houston, a slave-owner himself with deep-seated Southern roots and cultural values, merely assumed that Emily had been a slave and hence was traditionally readily available (in the Deep South planter tradition of using slave women to quench carnal desires) to be sexually exploited simply because she was in Santa Anna's encampment, along with a number of slaves liberated from the Texians? Or had Mexican prisoners taken at San Jacinto, who feared execution and knew of the Texians' disdain for people of color, only passed along a fantastic story about their commander, now humiliated before the world, in an attempt to win favors by describing Santa Anna's sexual folly with a black woman to merely confirm long-existing Anglo-Saxon stereotypes? Was this mysterious letter, which cannot be found today nor has been seen by anyone alive today, really written by Houston at all?

Like David Crockett's controversial death at the Alamo as described by de la Peña in his memoir, the story of Emily Morgan and the "Yellow Rose of Texas" has become one of the great unsolved mysteries of the Texas Revolution and American history. In his 1994 work *Texian Iliad: A Military History of the Texas Revolution*, author Stephen L. Hardin, one of the most respected Texas Revolutionary period scholars, concluded before the relatively recent discovery that it had been Houston himself who had penned the controversial "Emily" paragraph that was first included by the editors in the reprint of Bollaert's book as a mere note: "There is not a scintilla of primary evidence to support the oft-reported myth that Santa Anna was engaged in a tryst with mulatto slave girl Emily Morgan." But given the recent discovery of the paragraph's authorship from an alleged Houston letter, does Hardin's emphatic conclusion yet ring true? This heated debate continues among scholars in the much-contested field of Texas Revolutionary historiography, where passions yet run high. Therefore, this present work attempts to settle the persistent riddle of "The Yellow Rose of Texas" once and for all.

Most telling of all and a factor long overlooked by Texas historians and popular writers, generations of modern Latino historians have continued to remain noticeably silent and absent in the "Yellow Rose of Texas" controversy. Mexican scholars have concluded that the alleged Santa Anna–Emily tryst was not even worthy of serious consideration, and that it was not debatable or even a legitimate controversy, because the liaison story has been deemed too fantastic and fictional: just another Texas tall tale, and a race-based one at that.

After all, like other white Texian males on the frontier, Houston certainly enjoyed sexually explicit, entertaining bawdy tales, and his tantalizing paragraph from the mysterious letter that Bollaert obtained by some unknown means certainly verified as much. Therefore, what Houston communicated was primarily a racially- and culturally-cultivated tale, if not part sexual fantasy centered on the Anglo societal sin of miscegenation.

From the beginning, the Santa Anna–Emily liaison story was created and circulated to convincingly demonstrate the moral, cultural, intellectual, and racial superiority of whites to darker-hued people, which helped to justify the longtime oppression of blacks, Tejanos, and Mexicans in Texas. Such physical, economic, social, and cultural domination over people of other darker races was founded upon the premise of Anglo moral, biological, racial, and cultural superiority, and Houston's brief paragraph provided additional concrete evidence and a highly-visible example of the alleged inferiority of both blacks and Mexicans in the most important of settings.

The liaison story was steeped in a large dose of Protestant, almost Puritan, moralism, providing an Old Testament–like cautionary tale to not only warn whites about the dire consequences of interracial unions but also to remind blacks (considered heathens), Tejanos (Catholics), and Mexicans (Catholics) of the folly of ever attempting to mix with or unite as one against the dominant ruling class in Texas, because disaster would inevitably result: a classic case of the old axiom of divide and conquer.

It is now time to go beyond the seemingly impenetrable multi-layers of popular myths, romance, and stereotypes to discover the authentic Emily, the actual person instead of the romantic legend of "The Yellow Rose of Texas." Like nursery rhymes, myths have long provided comfort and affirmation to peoples and nations around the world, and the history of Texas has been especially excessive and almost limitless in this regard. But the truths of Texas history even without the multiple layers of mythology, romance, and embellishment can yet provide us with some of the best stories in the America saga. Looking beyond the myth of "The Yellow Rose of Texas," the true story of Emily D. West has been far more beneficial and meaningful by provoking seldom-asked questions about hidden, untold aspects of the Texas frontier and revolutionary experience, especially in regard to complex and overlooked matters of race.

What were her experiences in not only her native New Haven and later in New York City, but also on the untamed frontier Texas before the war reached New Washington? And what hardships and challenges did Emily D. West face on the western frontier when on her own without a husband or family beside her during difficult situations, especially in a wartime environment? Who was the real Emily D. West and what combination of factors can explain the strange, twisting, and unpredictable course of her life, as opposed to the more mundane life of a lowly slave woman of the "Yellow Rose of Texas" fame? And why was the Emily of San Jacinto readily, but belatedly, transformed into the best known of all Texas heroines?

Instead of the romantic myth and legend of "The Yellow Rose of Texas," Emily was very much only an average, ordinary person (although exceptional in many ways, especially in terms of resiliency, perseverance and survival skills), who was determined to get ahead in life and to succeed, but not at the high cost of her personal values or dignity. Therefore, the story of this free black woman was one of a constant struggle against the odds and all types of adversity beyond what was experienced by the average white woman of the day. As a free black woman living in a racist society, she was forced to provide for herself as best she could. Despite her free status, Emily struggled to survive outside of the mainstream world of white women, who were generally well provided for and protected by their men, especially husbands, during this period.

Very few free black women dared to venture so far from home and into the hazardous environment of this strange, almost exotic foreign land (owned by Mexico) known as Tejas, where slavery thrived along with vibrant cotton production, because of the obvious risks involved in a free black getting kidnapped into slavery, not to mention the typical dangers of the western frontier experience, epidemics of disease, nature's unpredictable wrath, and possible Indian trouble in an untamed land far from civilization.

Therefore, to fully appreciate the life of this daring free black woman in Texas—a story not yet told in full, realistically, or with fairness, it is important to look much deeper into Emily's background, especially her hometown experiences in New Haven and New York City. Emily D. West had a full and eventful life, including close connections with northern abolitionists. Most of all, it is important to take a look at the daily lives other free blacks, especially women, and explore the evolution of the abolitionist movement in New Haven and New York City in order to understand not only Emily's life but also the very essence of the black experience, both free and slave, in America and frontier Texas during the early and mid–1830s. In this way, the real person of Emily D. West finally can be revealed, understood, and fully appreciated.

After all, what has been almost always left out of the traditional histories of Texas are the forgotten lives, struggles, and achievements of ordinary, but heroic, women. Consequently, the story of the free black experience, especially forgotten African American women, in frontier times has remained one of the greatest voids and most overlooked chapters in all Texas history. Therefore, this true story of Emily D. West has been written not only to solve a central mystery but also to fill two large gaps in the historical record by focusing on the little-known experiences of a dynamic free black woman and other free blacks in early Texas.

By 1835, when Emily arrived 1,500 miles from the place of her birth with such high hopes for the future, almost all blacks in Texas were slaves, who were either recently brought west across the Sabine River, the Louisiana border with Texas, from the United States, where they were not taught to read or write according to law, or transported in ships from Cuba and other Caribbean sugar islands by slave smugglers. Therefore, memoirs, remembrances, and accounts by black women and their stories about the challenges and difficulties of life on the early Texas frontier are virtually non-existent. Quite simply, the stories of the sacrifices, contributions, and accomplishments of black women, both slave and free, in early Texas have not been told, leaving a large gap in the historial record.

As Emily's case has clearly demonstrated, however, free black women played their part in shaping the history, culture, and society of early Texas. The many challenges on the Texas western frontier brought about a timeless, universal theme as applied to the overall struggle of women, both black and white, against adversity and artificial barriers imposed by society's dictates and paternal authority. In relative terms black women faced the dual obstacles of racism and sexism, encountering even more daunting challenges and handicaps than the average white pioneer woman.

The entire life of Emily D. West, and not just her relatively belief Texas period (late 1835 to early 1837), offers a rare inside look at the long-ignored and forgotten experiences of a single, free black woman. Therefore, as much as possible, the human side of Emily D. West will be explored to reveal what has not previously been seriously investigated by generations of Texas historians who focused primarily on the famous men (such as Houston, Crockett, Bowie, or Travis) and only briefly the black experience in slavery. Consequently, this work will have a singular focus on the many upheavals and twists and turns in the life of a free black woman on a wartime frontier, providing a much needed chapter of early Texas history.

The story of Emily D. West will perhaps demonstrate that she and other long-overlooked African American women made their own distinct, notable, and multiple contributions to the creation of Texas. These almost always unknown women of color were part of the rich fabric of a multi-cultural and multi-ethnic story of early and revolutionary Texas.

The popular Old West adage that "When the legend become fact, print the legend" has certainly applied without doubt or equivocation. Unfortunately, this genuine Texas tall tale has only managed to obscure and overshadow some forgotten historical gems, especially in regard to the life of the real Emily D. West and a good many other ordinary, but quite remarkable, women in the ever-fertile, but too often mythical, field of Texas history, while only perpetuating old, tired stereotypes, fantasies, and fairy tales at the expense of the historical facts and the dignity of sturdy, persevering people of both sexes. At last, it is time for the fanciful story of "The Yellow Rose of Texas" to be laid to rest.

Chapter I

Emily D. West, the Popular Myth and Legend

Perhaps no part of America's story has been more romanticized than the Texas Revolution and its key players, William Barret Travis, Sam Houston, Jim Bowie, and David Crockett, who have become legendary, almost mythical figures. Perhaps the most popular relatively recent myth is the story of "The Yellow Rose of Texas." By the time of the 150-year anniversary of the Texas Revolution in 1986, Emily Morgan (Emily D. West) was bestowed recognition as a true Texas patriot and heroine, the most famous Texas Revolutionary legend among white, black, Tejano, Indian, or Mexican women during the birth of a new nation conceived in violent revolution.

As the popular "Yellow Rose of Texas" legend goes, Emily helped to win Texas independence by occupying General Santa Anna in his tent while General Houston's ragtag army was only a short distance away hidden in the thick cypress and oak forest along the dark waters of Buffalo Bayou. This liaison allowed the golden opportunity for Houston's frontal assault in the late afternoon of April 21, 1836, to catch the Mexicans by surprise and easily defeat them on the most decisive day in Texas history: a situation and scenario, if true, that was little more than miraculous, especially in regard to precise timing. The belief has developed that the Republic of Texas sprang "symbolically from her womb," because of Emily's alleged unorthodox but timely contributions to victory at San Jacinto.

The image of Emily has been transformed by several generations of popular writers, journalists, and historians into a Texas cultural icon almost as sacred as the legendary Travis, Bowie and Crockett, the famed Alamo triumvirate who became martyrs at the old Franciscan mission on the bloody morning of March 6, 1836. Today, the picturesque gulf coastal community of La Porte, Texas, has proudly embraced the romantic legacy of the "Yellow Rose of Texas" with gusto. As featured prominently on the city's welcoming sign to greet visitors from far and wide, the words "Home of the Yellow Rose of Texas" have helped to keep the myth alive.

Even the most grand and stately hotel in San Antonio has been named the Emily Morgan Hotel to honor the popular heroine of San Jacinto. Located just across the street from the Alamo and bordering its hallowed grounds on the north, this massive high rise dominates Alamo Plaza to overlook the old mission, which has been described as the "Cradle of Texas Liberty." The Emily Morgan Hotel towers over the most sacred ground in all Texas, seemingly watching over the shrine of the Alamo in symbolic fashion, almost as if to reinforce the myth that Emily Morgan had ensured that the diminutive Alamo garrison had not died in vain by her alleged sexual activities in Santa Anna's headquarters tent at San Jacinto. A plaque in the hotel's lobby perpetuates a cultural, state and national myth that has been generally accepted without serious scrutiny or investigation by historians: "Were it not for the heroics of a beautiful mulatto slave Emily Morgan, Texas may to this day have remained [the state of] Coahuilla y [and] Texas, Republic of Mexico.... Santa Anna's eye for women and Emily Morgan's allegiance to Texas proved to be a fatal combination for Mexico."[1]

As historian James W. Loewen has emphasized in his fine book *Lies Across America: What Our Historic Sites Get Wrong*, such historical plaques and markers have been notoriously guilty of perpetuating myths. Enthusiastic, agenda-driven local leaders have been guilty of falsifying history across America without serious academic scrutiny, as Loewen has emphasized with his on-target analysis.[2]

Nevertheless, the sheer romance and popularity of the Emily Morgan legend and mystique has continued to enchant new generations not only across Texas but also America. In *Three Roads to the Alamo: The Lives and Fortunes of David Crockett, James Bowie, and William Barret Travis*, premier Civil War historian William C. Davis, who warmly embraced the history-rich environment of San Antonio and the historical aura of the Alamo and Emily Morgan with some passion, wrote, in the beginning of his widely respected 1998 book: "There is a fair bit of irony about the writing of this book.... The last chapter was finished in the Emily Morgan Hotel in San Antonio in a room overlooking the Alamo itself, on March 6, 1997, the anniversary of the battle."[3]

The Emily Morgan Hotel represents the most public recognition of how the real life story of Emily D. West has grown into a romantic legend second only to the mythical Alamo, obscuring the free black woman who was never a factor in the San Jacinto battle. Emily has been long described as a ravishing beauty, as emphasized on the hotel's plaque, who helped to ensure decisive victory at San Jacinto, perpetuating a common racial stereotype of Emily as little more than an exploited sexual object or a seductress (the dual stereotypes of the black woman). Thus, both Emily and Santa Anna have been conveniently reduced to the lowest common denominator by this popular Texas myth to provide a representative example of the old racial stereotypes of blacks and Latinos as excessively sensual beings who allowed their lust and weaknesses to dominate their intelligence and rational thought.

And today the fact that the high-rise hotel's name has not corrected Emily's real name—West instead of Morgan—is also significant in perpetuating the myth, after the discovery of the real person of Emily D. West in the historical record. This example has demonstrated how the enduring myth has continued to possess a more powerful hold on the public consciousness and popular imagination than the real, or historical, Emily D. West. However, perhaps this development has been inevitable because the western frontier has always served as America's mythical land of historical romance and pure fantasy in both films and books, with its central players—be them pioneers, revolutionaries, gunfighters, lawmen, or bandits—becoming legendary figures.

Therefore, as the old adage goes in John Ford's *The Man Who Shot Liberty Valance* (1961), when the historical facts contradicted the myth in a significant way, "This is the West, sir. When the legend becomes fact, print the legend!" This certainly has been the case in regard to "The Yellow Rose of Texas," and, of course, the story of the Alamo as presented in the 1960 John Wayne film, basically a Cold War propaganda film. Wayne's *The Alamo*, which emphasized "better Tex than Mex," deviated from the truths of the Alamo to a degree unseen in perhaps any other historical film. While the Ford film explores how myths of the West are created and evolved, the Wayne Alamo film itself has played a leading role of the myth-making process itself in regard to the Alamo's story. Wayne's film laid a sturdy foundation for the traditional core concepts of the mythical Alamo: a classic case of bringing the greatest distortions of the legend rather than the facts to the big screen, an unfortunate development that has been mirrored in the writing of Texas history for generations.

Consequently, the popularity of the highly-charged, interracial sex-laden myth of the Emily–Santa Anna liaison and the emphasis on her slave status has almost completely erased the real free black woman from New England. In the evolutionary myth-making process not unlike that explored in great detail in Ford's *The Man Who Shot Liberty Valance*, this enduring popular myth has bestowed upon Emily D. West not only the wrong name of Emily Morgan, but also the wrong recognition as "The Yellow Rose of Texas."

However, the many myths and romance of the Texas Revolution, including the story of Emily D. West and as in the glaring case of Wayne's *The Alamo*, have overlooked and completely ignored the complex issues of race and slavery in the Texas creation story. Indeed, no issues have been more overlooked than the complexities of race, especially in regard to slavery, and Mexico's abolitionist stance. This has developed in part because Texas has been seen as more western than southern, when in fact Texas of the revolutionary period was nothing more than an extension of the Deep South in terms of demographics, culture, cotton cultivation, and the robustness of the institution of slavery.

Contrary to the myth, Emily D. West never had been a slave. She was born a free woman in New Haven, Connecticut, in 1801, and basked in her free status. Emily enjoyed a free status like the flood of white pioneers, consumed with "Texas Fever," who crossed the Sabine and Red Rivers and poured into the northern Mexican province of Texas from the United States during the 1820s and early 1830s.[4]

Perhaps the greatest irony in regard to the Emily D. West story has revolved around the institution of slavery in Texas: that a free black woman has been erroneously identified and long portrayed as a slave. This land of promise, unlimited potential, and plenty was as dominated by slavery and cotton cultivation as in the Deep South. In fact, the Texian economy, society, and culture—merely as extension of the Deep South—rested solidly upon the institution of slavery. However, the popular misconception persists today that slavery played no significant role in Texas history or in regard to the Texas Revolution, when in fact it was extremely important, serving as the early foundation of Anglo-Celtic settlement made successful by cotton cultivation and playing a leading role in causing open warfare.

It was known as the "Empire State of the South" during the antebellum period, populated by the early 1830s largely by Southerners, especially from the Deep South. It has since lost its southernness and a great silence has developed about Texas' southern antecedents and roots, allowing the image of the Old West to dominate. Mirroring the longtime efforts of Hollywood, which found its greatest expression and success in the Western films, generations of historians, especially those from Texas, have embraced a narrow western orientation and laser-like focus on the romance of the Old West rather than the original southernness that most of all distinguished Texian culture and society by the time of the Texas Revolution.[5] Just as much of Texas history has lost southern qualities and distinctiveness, the true Emily D. West story has been silenced and lost.

Instead, as utilized by popular writers, she has served as little more than a symbolic pawn employed in the name conquest—racial, economic, social, moral, and physical—in the domination of the Anglo-Celtic people over Tejanos, Mexicans, Indians and blacks, by playing her celebrated alleged heroine role in the triumph of Manifest Destiny in Texas. By imaginative writers having transformed her into a Texas revolutionary heroine second to none because of her alleged role at San Jacinto, Emily D. West has been viewed in the popular imagination not as a free black woman, but as a seductress and sexually-charged slave whose immorality ensured Santa Anna's fall from grace. In this way, Emily's mythical image fit neatly into the ethnocentric dominant culture and the overall Anglo-Celtic revolutionary experience.[6]

Therefore, with writers, journalists, and historians not seriously taking into account the complex issue of Texas slavery, the free black experience, and her distinctive ethnic and cultural identity, Emily has been transformed into a sanitized Texas heroine with hardly a hint of African features, heritage, or cultural qualities of any kind. This seamless transformation to Texas Revolutionary heroine was made plausible by her alleged white blood that bestowed an "Anglo-derived beauty" and her alleged pro-revolutionary sentiment, causing her to faithfully serve white Texians and the Texas cause of wresting the land from its rightful owners. Emily's identity as a proud, individualistic woman and a northern free person, who was closely linked with northern abolitionists and almost certainly possessed abolitionist views, has been neatly transformed into an advocate for slavery's defense and expansion in Texas.

What has been most of all silenced in the Emily Morgan myth was the key role played by slavery and the importance of "King Cotton" on Texas soil in leading to the Texas Revolution's outbreak, and the fact that Santa Anna headed a liberating army that freed slaves across Texas. Therefore, would not Emily D. West, as both a free and black woman from the northeast and with strong abolitionist ties, have been more sympathetic toward a slave-free, abolitionist Mexico—and even toward Santa Anna himself—rather than supporting slave-owning Texians, who wanted to make slavery permanently safe and secure in Texas, which meant breaking away from an abolitionist Mexico in one of the biggest and most audacious land grabs in history? Most historians have long chosen not to investigate such important issues, ignoring the complexities of the Texas Revolutionary experience in regard to slavery.

Emily possessed strong ties with leading abolitionists in both New England and New York City. She was part of the overall flow of progressive thought of the civilized world, led by Great Britain, which permanently ended slavery in 1834—two years before the dramatic showdown between the band of defenders and Santa Anna's Army of Operations at the Alamo. Therefore, Emily D. West was anti-slavery in the progressive abolitionist tradition, and hardly supportive of Texas independence that resulted in stealing a large chunk of the Mexican nation and from a more enlightened, largely mixed-race republic that had abolished slavery in the previous decade. As traditionally portrayed by white writers and historians, the mythical Emily Morgan betrayed not only her heritage and racial identity, but also relinquished her hatred of slavery, abolitionist views, and hence, central identity as a proud free black woman from New England. The real Emily was anything but a diehard Texas patriot willing to play a leading role at San Jacinto in ensuring that Texas remained part of a vast slave empire and all the way until the Civil War's conclusion.[7]

Not only have Emily's abolitionist connections and roots been minimized by historians to serve the special requirements of the romantic myth of the seductive slave woman and self-sacrificing Texas heroine, but even her African physiology and personal characteristics have been de-blackened, or whitened, to support the myth. Historical writers and journalists have gradually created an ever-whiter Emily to bestow more credence upon the myth and gain wider popular appeal, conforming to the physical requirements of white perceptions and standards of beauty. From the imaginative pens of historians, writers, and journalists, she has been bestowed with lighter skin, long flowing hair, and a ravishing beauty without a hint of characteristically African features—a cleansing and popularizing process to create a more attractive image of Emily based more upon sexual fantasies of white men and their own and society's standards of beauty rather than the real person. Consequently, Emily has been described as "Latin-looking" and "light-skinned" rather than black and distinguished by distinct African features. But in truth, the racial background and heritage of Emily D. West is not known, in part because the United States census did not designate any blacks with white blood as "mulattoes" until the Census of 1850.

She was not youthful or a teenager. The real Emily was in her mid–thirties. She was most likely not only a typical woman of the working class, but also one with quite ordinary looks compared to the Latin-looking fantasy of the breathtaking physical beauty, who dazzled and captivated men, including Santa Anna.

Of course, such a thorough beautification of Emily's popular image by way of an overall whitening process has played a role in denying the real Emily D. West her racial identity and African heritage. From the imaginations of white writers, journalists, and historians, Emily has been transformed into what she never was, "a golden-skinned seductress" without African features, who used her ample charms to seduce Santa Anna, who was unable to resist her at San Jacinto. Of course, this systematic whitening of Emily's image was based upon the dominant cultural and societal concept that lighter-skinned women were the most beautiful, appealing, and attractive. With a thorough, complete transformation brought about by the beautification, whitening, and sexualization of the mythical image of Emily, she has evolved into an alluring sexual object in the popular consciousness and imagination: the central foundation of the "Yellow Rose of Texas" myth and the alleged liaison between her and Santa Anna at San Jacinto, which has made the tale more believable, understandable, and acceptable to the American public, and perhaps even to Houston himself back in the early 1840s. Houston employed the image of Emily's alleged intoxicating beauty—the key "influence" in Houston's polite, evasive language—as a basis for the Emily–Santa Anna tryst paragraph because it made for a much better story.

Some historians have even gone so far as to say Emily was really the wife of the Mexico-born Lorenzo de Zavala, who was interim vice president of the Texas revolutionary government. This most recent speculation is an ill-founded attempt to discover the real Emily and has been based upon the faulty premise that a much younger Miranda West de Zavala, whose husband changed her first name to Emilia, or Emily, upon marriage, was not only a woman of color but also that she was actually the mythical "Yellow Rose of Texas." This recent speculation also denies the real Emily D. West her African heritage, identity, and free status.

The possibility that the wife of the esteemed vice president of Texas was a mulatto from upstate New York (like the free black Solomon Northup, who was kidnapped in Washington, D.C., and then sold into slavery and sent to the Deep South) has been covered up not only by Mrs. Zavala herself, but also by leading white Texas military and political men, who knew her well and were enchanted by her captivating beauty. In a strange twist of revisionist history, the real Emily D. West, from a town (New Haven) and area where large numbers of free blacks hailed, has been denied acknowledgment and recognition according to the tenets of this speculative theory, while bestowing a presumed African heritage upon a woman from upper New York State, where relatively few free blacks and mulattos were found living so close to the United States border with Canada, which had long served as a haven for escaping slaves.

This relatively recent speculation has been based largely upon the flimsy premise that Mrs. Zavala was especially attractive and distinguished by dark features, brown eyes, and dark hair. But in truth Mrs. Zavala was most likely not a "mulatta" of any black blood, but of Indian blood. After all, upper New York State, including the Albany area, was the ancestral homeland—or Iroquoia—of the five tribes and nations of the old Iroquois Confederacy or League. In 1775, American colonial officials held conferences with Indians at Albany, from where Mrs. Zavala hailed, in the hope of keeping them from siding with the British. Thanks to relentless pressures of westward expansion and the stealing of Indian lands by the unremitting push of American settlers toward the setting sun, the majority of the Iroquois remained Great Britain's most powerful Indian ally during the American Revolution. Most importantly in regard to more properly ascertaining the probability of Mrs. Zavala's background, the people of the Iroquois Confederacy were "the true assimilationists of early America," including mixing of races. Unlike among xenophobic and race-obsessed white Americans since before the nation's founding, marriage to an Indian by a respected male of mostly Spanish blood and even high rank was fully acceptable in a more racially tolerant Mexican society (a largely mixed race—or mestizo—society of Spanish and Indian) This explains Mrs. Zavala's early and easy acceptance in the highest levels of Mexican society. After all, Spanish Conquistadors and settlers early mingled with native people, both Aztecs and Mayans, and to a lesser degree Africans, to create a mixed-race nation—the antithesis of United States society.

This most recent revisionism has been as ill-founded as it has been misleading. The authentic Emily was around 10 years older than Vice President Lorenzo Zavala's wife, who was the mother of three. And while Emily was born in the port city of New Haven, Connecticut, Mrs. Zavala was born in the Albany, New York, area in the Hudson River country north of New York City. And while the free black woman from New Haven was a relatively homespun and ordinary person of the working class, Mrs. Zavala was an aristocratic, sophisticated, and world-traveled social climber, if not elitist, with fine tastes and upper class standards and proclivities. Emily was a person of little means and with hardworking and religion-based values stemming from a society originally forged by Puritan New England. While Mrs. Zavala's husband was the vice president of the Texas government (by mid–March 1836) and a leading investor and land speculator of the New Washington Association, Emily D. West was an employee of the association bound by a one-year contract, accounting for the fact that they traveled together (hence the shaky premise that Mrs. Zavala was the real "Yellow Rose of Texas") on the same steamboat, the *Flash*, to Texas in late 1835, after Emily boarded at New York City and Mrs. Zavala at the port of Baltimore, Maryland. The two women both left Texas in 1837—Mrs. Zavala returning to her native New York state in March after her husband's death, Emily D. West returning to New York City in the summer, her one-year-contract to work in Texas having expired some months eariler and New Washington, where she worked, having been destroyed by Mexican troops just before the showdown at San Jacinto.

But more important, Mrs. Zavala was not a mulatto and no evidence has placed her on the field of San Jacinto as in the case of Emily D. West. But this relatively recent speculation that Mrs. Zavala and Emily D. West were in fact the same person and not two distinct individuals has left out the most vital information: her distinctive New Haven, abolitionist, and free black aspects and roots. In addition, the respective signatures of the two women have clearly indicated two different hands.[8]

Though allegedly a Texas heroine and in a historical paradox that exemplified the double-standards in regard to race that has persisted to this day to create two separate societies—one black, one white—in America, the character of the mythical Emily has been tarnished because of racism. This development has been all but inevitable, because America has been long obsessed with the issue of race. Therefore, Emily has been described as "a gal on the make" without decency, morals, or Christian values. To support the unproven speculation that she seduced Santa Anna, Emily has been labeled as a loose, promiscuous woman with an "unsatiable love for, and a certain expertise, at, the art of sex."[9]

But absolutely no primary evidence or documentation has verified any of these assertions. In a glaring contradiction, she is held up as a heroine and scorned as a seductress, a paradox that mirrors the story of the United States, which was founded upon the concept of human liberty while simultaneously maintaining a vibrant institution of slavery. But this Faustian bargain was required for national unity. Therefore, the slave-owning South united with the North for the creation of the American nation and Constitution. This was America's "Dark Bargain," in the insightful words of gifted historian Lawrence Goldstone.

The heart of the story of Emily D. West was as much about what happened in the North before she migrated to Texas in late 1835. The abolition activities and progressive ideas of the day profoundly shaped Emily's life, thinking, and ambitions, and now provide us clues about what exactly led her to Texas in the first place. Most of all, the truth of Emily D. West's story has contradicted and contrasted sharply with the popular, romanticized version of the "The Yellow Rose of Texas." After all, it is based primarily on a few words never intended for publication and never published as part of the Englishman William Bollaert's colorful narrative of his travels in Texas from 1842 to 1844. Bollaert wrote,

> I beg to introduce the following given to me by an officer [General Houston] who was engaged in it—given in his own words: "The Battle of San Jacinto was probably lost to the Mexicans, owing to the influence of a Mulatta Girl (Emily) belonging to Col. [James] Morgan who was closeted in the tent with General Santana, at the time the cry was made, 'The enemy! Them come!' They come! & detained Santana so long that order could not be restored readily again.

Allegedly as copied by Bollaert, these are Houston's own words describing a situation—especially the exact words from the mouths of Santa Anna's soldados on April 21, 1836—that he could not have possibly heard or known about, since he was twice de-horsed and wounded in the ankle during the attack and never saw the moment of surprise in Santa Anna's encampment on the smoke-wreathed field of level ground that hampered visibility. And why Bollaert never identified Houston as the writer has also indicated that the astute, erudite Englishman considered the story simply too fantastic and unbelievable to an intelligent reading public of Great Britain.

No one, not even Bollaert, took this bawdy barroom story seriously, and very likely not even Houston himself. Bollaert's obscure, ever-so-brief reference first appeared as the editor's footnote in a modern edition and not in the original narrative. The original Bollaert reference to "Emily," with no last name revealed, which alluded to a slave status, had been written in the margin of the page of the original Bollaert manuscript. Bollaert was a gossipy English ethnologist, prolific writer and promoter of sensational stories, and not a professional historian. Like Houston and other Texians, therefore, he almost certainly delighted in this racy story, but nevertheless found it beyond belief and without either credibility or substance.

Bollaert's work was first published in 1956 as *William Bollaert's Texas*, edited by W. Eugene Hollon and Ruth Lapham Butler. In a 1989 reprint, Hollon explained why the Santa Anna–Emily reference had been included only in a footnote and not in Bollaert's narrative, explaining how he, as "the editor ... has omitted some delightful, even gossipy, tidbits from the heavy cache of Bollaert's manuscripts," a scholarly, prudent, and correct decision that separated fact from fiction which even Bollaert recognized, because he never meant to publish it. These conscientious editors from academe were correct in their evaluation that the

Emily–Santa Anna liaison story was nothing more than idle gossip, and unworthy of publication in the Bollaert narrative.[10]

The Historical Emily D. West

The birthplace of Emily D. West, a free black woman, was also the ancestral home of the revered "Father of Texas," Stephen Fuller Austin. Elijah Austin was a leading citizen and merchant of New Haven, Connecticut, by the end of the Eighteenth Century. He hailed from a most enterprising, distinguished New England family who embodied the entrepreneurial spirit and meaning of the Puritan ethic that played a part in taming the land and bestowing prosperity in the New World.[11]

Elijah Austin was the enterprising oldest of the four sons of Elias Austin, a successful tailor who had migrated southwest to New Haven from Durham, Connecticut. Elijah and his brother Archibald then became leading New Haven merchants, whose brisk trade across the Atlantic and patriot efforts in the struggle for liberty, including the outfitting of wide-ranging privateers sailing from the port of New Haven to attack British merchant vessels, reached new heights during the American Revolution. The youngest brother, Moses Austin, made his livelihood in mining lead amid the Blue Ridge Mountains of southwest Virginia, where his son, Stephen Fuller Austin, the future founder of the first colonization of United States settlers in Texas, was born in early November 1793.[12]

Located in southeast Connecticut on the eastern shore of Long Island Sound that separated Long Island from the mainland's expansive fields and forests and about halfway between New York City to the south and New London, Connecticut, to the north, New Haven grew into a prosperous port city, thanks to nature's gift of a wide, beautiful harbor. Nestled between Massachusetts to the north and New York to the south, Connecticut was blessed with more than a hundred miles of coastline running along the north side of east-west Long Island Sound. A number of excellent harbors lay at the mouths of a host of navigable rivers. By the mid–1600s, Connecticut had been the western frontier for the religiously-inspired Puritans of Boston and the Massachusetts Bay Colony, which had been established primarily for the freedom of worship and to create a "New Jerusalem."

Like an untamed Texas in the 1820s and 1830s, the fertile lands, abundant game, and the pristine beauty of the north-south running Connecticut River Valley, west of the port of Boston, early drew eager settlers southwest from the congested, urban environment of Boston. Beginning a pattern of western expansion that continued for hundreds of years, these first west-moving pioneers, of sturdy English stock, had tired of the strict rules and regulations of an autocratic theocracy and moved toward the setting sun. They journeyed west along the narrow thread of Indian and game trails that cut through primeval woodlands of virgin timber, despite the threat of the formidable Pequot.

Between 1790 and 1830 and thanks to the steady flow of commerce and plentiful jobs generated by a brisk trade across the Atlantic, the population of New Haven doubled, along with the general prosperity. As long as sailing ships traded at its busy port town northeast of booming New York City, prospects for future growth and wealth seemed limitless. Despite the bay's relative shallowness at New Haven, this embayment of Long Island Sound, situated at about Connecticut's midpoint along the coast, easily accommodated the largest sailing vessels from around the world. After all, the town had been first established by opportunistic

Puritan founders with commerce and lavish profits in mind, and that ambitious economic vision had been fulfilled.

Located on the site of a former Indian village, a number of fresh water streams and the Quinnipiac, Mill, and West Rivers flowed from the lush, heavily-forested interior and into the ever-expanding width of New Haven harbor. These fast-flowing watercourses provided a bountiful supply of fresh water to a fertile coastal plain, covered with a luxurious growth of tall, majestic elms that stood along the shore in guardian fashion. Less than 40 miles east of New Haven, the Connecticut River entered Long Island Sound, ending its lengthy north-south journey through a pastoral countryside that promised bounty and the expansion of an agricultural empire to yeomen farmers.

At the town's busy center, a park-like expanse of sixteen acres added a picturesque touch to the layout of New Haven Green. This commons had been laid out not long after the town's founding by freer-thinking Puritans, who had migrated to a new promised land to seek freer worship and more autonomy about eighty miles southeast of the Massachusetts Bay Colony, safely away from a rigid, intolerant Boston, in 1638. As envisioned by ambitious city planners, New Haven Green lay in the city's busy heart, pulsating with vibrant urban life from the steady flow of maritime commerce.

For these Puritans, the idealistic, utopian dream of New Haven was not fulfilled by the Massachusetts Puritans' strict, autocratic vision espoused by Massachusetts Governor John Winthrop in 1630 of a tightly-controlled "City on a Hill," but by a newfound, bustling town in a low-lying coastal plain along a splendid natural harbor on the Long Island Sound. Therefore, the town's name derived from the harbor, or haven. The flow of westward expansion in upcoming decades fueled New Haven's economic growth. The town's enterprising merchants, savvy men who seamlessly combined religious worship and an aggressive pursuit of profits, reaped their riches from providing goods from trade and local manufacturing for settlers, who pushed west and toward their own vision of a better future for themselves and their families.

New Haven prospered from a steady flow of ships sailing into port from the east and settlers moving west with the setting sun in their eyes to start a new life. After the American Revolution, New Haven increased its commercial fleet from a single sloop, a single-masted, fore-and-aft rigged vessel, in 1783 to sixty ships by 1789. Among these merchant sailing ships were vessels owned by the Austin brothers. A risk taker but also a visionary, Elijah Austin was the first New Haven merchant to break into the China market (1793) after dispatching one of his sailing ships on a successful mission to Canton in southern China. Besides the busy commercial traffic and the spirit of a robust entrepreneurialism in the air, what most dominated New Haven life was the vibrant intellectualism and free thinking spirit of Yale College. Diminishing the usual pervasive provincialism and localism even of a thriving port, the university helped to early create a liberal yet aristocratic atmosphere compared to most other Connecticut communities in the interior.

By 1830, Yale College, which boasted the nation's leading medical department and a focus primarily on teaching the traditional classics, had become not only the largest but also the premier institution of higher learning in America. Hard-working Noah Webster, tall and thin and looking every inch the scholar and known as "America's Schoolteacher," authored the first American dictionary, and called New Haven home. A wealthy merchant class and a respected clerical and college elite developed early to govern the town of sturdy common folk, who were mostly employed in the shipping industry. This coastal clerical-mercantile aristocracy—a long-existing ruling class system that had been transferred seamlessly from

England—of New Haven was as elitist as the Deep South's ruling planter class. Here, in picturesque New Haven, this situation led to broad class divisions that were eventually tempered with the rise of liberalism.

Most of New Haven's early industry was connected with the booming shipping industry, including a lengthy row of busy shops, where sail-makers, ship builders, ship carpenters and even bakers of a ship bread bakery worked at a brisk rate along the noisy waterfront. Whalers, manned by hardy black and white sailors in the integrated New England tradition, also sailed in air-filled canvas sails from New Haven. These whalers pursued the principal source of fuel in Eighteenth and early Nineteenth Century America, whale oil, which was the day's petroleum.

A thriving trade with the West Indies sugar islands and the lucrative sugar boom brought sugar and molasses, which was then distilled into rum, back to New Haven in exchange for what the high-yield farms among the Connecticut hinterlands, despite relatively poor and rocky soil except along the fertile Connecticut River Valley, produced—corn, pork, beef, and oats. Not raised on the islands, these products sustained the planters and vast numbers of slaves on the Caribbean's sugar plantations. Therefore, a large rum distillery at New Haven was most productive. By 1830, this lucrative West Indies trade was New Haven's very lifeblood that fueled the town's economy and general prosperity. However, relatively little traditional trade went back and forth to Europe after the sugar boom.

Quite simply, New Haven's trade, like New England in general, rested largely in directly supporting the vast slave system and plantation economics, the sugar-producing machines that generated lavish wealth. In consequence, the profitable Caribbean islands, especially England's most prosperous colony and largest Caribbean island, Jamaica, devoted little precious acreage to grain crops or livestock. The raising of sugar cane on Jamaica and other British Caribbean islands like Barbados was just too profitable to grow anything else. England's most lucrative colonies in the Americas early ensured the rise of a large planter class, including John Winthrop's son, who was one of the first arrivals from England to Barbados, that steadily grew more wealthy and powerful.

New Haven's economy touched the most remote corners of both America and the Caribbean. By the antebellum period, a good many slave-masters of sprawling cotton fields across the South drove fine wooden carriages made in New Haven. Gangs of slaves on Southern plantations used farm implements manufactured in New Haven. And slaves also drove teams of horses or mules with harnesses made in New Haven. This direct economic connection between New Haven manufacturers and merchants—and to a lesser degree the common farmers—to the South's plantation system and slave regimes, and the lucrative Caribbean sugar islands, thrived. Many aristocratic sons of leading Southern planter elites attended Yale College and brought their slave servants with them, as if they were yet in the sunny South.

New Haven also benefited considerably from the northeast's industrial boom, fueled in no small part by the institution of slavery and the vast profits it produced throughout the antebellum period. Most important to the South's development as a cotton empire was an invention by Yale graduate and schoolteacher Eli Whitney. His cotton gin literally changed the course of history, first economic and then political, in the United States. After the American Revolution, the South's agricultural focus on growing staples had initially floundered, with the market dropping for tobacco, rice, and indigo. Cotton had not yet become a major crop in large part because of the time-consuming process of slaves separating the cotton seed, buried deep in the layers of fiber, from the closely-intertwined cotton fiber. But with the invention of Whitney's cotton gin, seed could be separated from fiber some fifty times faster and more efficiently than manual labor and without losing the precious fiber ("white gold"), especially when horsepower was employed to turn the cotton gin.

Thanks to young Whitney's groundbreaking 1794 invention, two years after his graduation from Yale, and its spread west in conjunction with slavery's expansion and across the Deep South's new lands blessed with more fertile soil and ample sunshine, the South's economy was dramatically transformed. Cotton became the foundation of the Southern economy and instigated the bondage of millions of blacks. Across the Deep South, therefore, cotton became king and southern plantations provided most of the world's cotton to an insatiable market.

A gun factory, the New Haven Arms Company, initiated a dramatic revolution in gunmaking. Here in New Haven's free-thinking environment that allowed creative minds and technical innovation to soar, the six-shot automatic revolver was developed by Samuel Colt in 1836. But Whitney's cotton gin had the most far-reaching and longer term repercussions in shaping the course of American history, fueling slavery's expansion and viability across the South, while helping to pave the way to an inevitable war over slavery in not only 1835 in Texas but also across the United States as it existed in 1861.[13]

Thanks partly to egalitarian traditions and Yale College's liberalism, New Haven and other parts of Connecticut were more progressive in social matters, including race. Ironically, however, New Haven's prosperity resulted in wealthy citizens acquiring black household servants, who functioned primarily as status symbols to impress the neighbors, before the American Revolution. During the American Revolutionary period and inspired by the Age of Enlightenment ideal that all men are created equal, as penned by Thomas Jefferson, the sage of Monticello, in the Declaration of Independence, blacks in colonial Connecticut demanded that the General Assembly grant them equal rights. In diplomatic tones, as not to offend white sensibilities, they reminded Connecticut's revolutionary leaders that it was time for them to live up to their own declared egalitarian principles or prove hypocrites to the day's most progressive thought.

Some enlightened whites in Connecticut, including distinguished Yale graduates, echoed these revolutionary calls for black equality. In 1784 immediately after the revolution's end, the state of Connecticut passed a gradual emancipation act. This act proclaimed that black children born of slave parents after March 1, 1784, were to be granted freedom at age 25, or in 1809 at the earliest. In the American nation's first census in 1790, a total of 5,500 blacks lived in Connecticut, with about half free and the other half slave. The black population had grown since 1760, when Connecticut's estimated black population stood at around 3,800 (more than 2.5 percent of the total population). Thanks largely to the American Revolution's enlightened legacies, Connecticut possessed an early free black tradition, ensuring that most free blacks remained in the state rather than moving west.[14]

However, the earliest tradition of black equality in Connecticut, and New England in general, was seen in the region's lengthy seafaring tradition. Out on the ocean's waters far from shore, New England men were judged more on how well they could perform as seamen rather than their African ancestry. Embracing a "rough egalitarianism" aboard ship, black sailors—wearing gold earrings, their dark hair in queues, and moving with a well-deserved swagger—manned New England's sailing ships and whaling boats for generations. This distinguished legacy of black seamanship was faithfully continued during the American Revolution, when the Connecticut state navy recruited as many black sailors and gunners as possible in the fight against Great Britain.[15]

By any measure, the struggle for liberty brought forth new progressive ideas and enlightened thinking about matters of race among many northern whites, especially those men who fought beside zealous black revolutionaries. The fact that free blacks and slaves from Connecticut served with distinction beside their white peers in revolutionary armies, including General George Washington's Continental Army, had bestowed many Connecticut whites with the firm belief that blacks deserved equality, especially after they had demonstrated courage on the battlefield. More than 5,000 African American soldiers served year after year in patriot armies, including in the ranks of Washington's well-trained Continentals, or regulars, across America during the American Revolution. Washington, the tobacco planter and large slave-owner from Mount Vernon, Virginia, on the banks of the Potomac River, was initially shocked to see so many New England blacks serving in the ranks when he first took command of America's first volunteer army just outside Boston during the summer of 1775. One Connecticut regiment contained such resolute African American soldiers as Sharp Liberty, Dick Freedom, Pomp Liberty, and Jeffrey Liberty.

But in fact, the black military role in America's defense far predated the American Revolution. African American soldiers of New England fought in the most famous American combat unit of the French and Indian War, Major Robert Rogers' Rangers. Wearing green uniforms that blended in with the dense pine and spruce forests, these tough frontier rangers excelled at irregular warfare in the northeastern wilderness along the Canadian border. They served as a source of inspiration for British commanders and both English and colonial troops. Donned in Indian-like garb and utilizing the savvy ways of Indian and guerrilla warfare, these New Englanders were mostly Scotch-Irish and originally hailed from the green, rolling hills of Ulster Province. These hardy frontiersmen and yeomen farmers came from remote log cabins and settlements situated along the Merrimack River Valley and other frontier regions of New Hampshire. Known for their combat prowess, Rogers' Rangers became more than a match for the Indian, Canadian, and French opponents they faced in savage (including no quarter) wilderness warfare, often in the deep snows and freezing winter temperatures of the north country.[16]

But among the most resolute of New England's black soldiers were those ebony warriors who served in one of Washington's most legendary commands during the crucial year of 1776, when the dismal course of the revolution was reversed in late December, Colonel John Glover's seamen and fishermen from the shipping and whaling port of Marblehead, Massachusetts. As members of the elite Fourteenth Massachusetts Continental Regiment, these reliable Marbleheaders served as trusty infantrymen in what was essentially an amphibious regiment, and Washington's most versatile command. Indeed, after the crushing American defeat at the battle of Long Island on August 27, 1776, Glover's resilient men saved much of Washington's army by transferring it from its doomed position on Long Island back across the East River to New York City's safety. Then, in one of the war's boldest offensive operations Glover's resourceful, highly-disciplined mariners rowed Washington's main strike force across the icy Delaware River in Durham boats during the wintry blackness to catch an entire Hessian brigade by surprise on the cold morning of December 26, 1776, at Trenton, New Jersey, reversing the revolution's course in dramatic fashion.[17]

Then, on September 6, 1781, at the battle of Groton Heights, immediately outside Groton, Connecticut, just across the Thames River from New London, more than one black soldier stood firm beside their white patriot neighbors at the parapet of the large earthen fort perched atop a commanding hilltop overlooking the wide river. In fighting for liberty and defending their New England homeland, these two African American soldiers from

Connecticut under arms were Jordan Freeman and Lambo Latham. During the overpowering British infantry assault, both of these fighting men of African descent were fated to die either in the ensuing combat that swirled inside the fort, or in the massacre of many garrison members who surrendered to the enraged British and Loyalists in one of the war's forgotten atrocities.

When the cheering British troops poured like a flood into Fort Griswold, commanded by Colonel William Ledyard, who was killed when he handed over this sword to a Loyalist officer in a futile attempt to surrender, one black soldier rose to the challenge. He killed Major William Montgomery before he himself fell to the wrath of Benedict Arnold's forces in scarlet uniforms. Such inspiring examples of African American courage in battling for a new nation's freedom gave a sense of pride to free blacks across Connecticut and New England during the antebellum period.[18]

With patriotism running high, Captain David Humphreys raised a full company of black soldiers from the port of New Haven, Connecticut, which sent its black sons off to war nearly a century before the famed Fifty-fourth Massachusetts met its rendezvous with destiny in the assault on Fort Wagner, South Carolina. Unlike the African Americans who served in integrated Continental regiments in Washington's Army, this all-black unit served in the Connecticut regiment of Colonel Return Jonathan Meigs, Sr., who was born in Middletown, Connecticut, in 1740. This command fought with distinction against the British until the war's end. Captain Humphreys later functioned capably as an aide-de-camp to General Washington during the war years, when America's future often looked especially dark and the bold experiment in nationhood and republicanism seemed at an end.[19]

Why would African Americans, especially those in New Haven and Connecticut, fight for a new nation that yet supported slavery and against a British army that not only liberated slaves on American soil, especially in the South, but also eagerly enlisted them in the struggle against the American rebels? For one, anti-slavery traditions among whites existed in Connecticut, including in New Haven, even before the American Revolution's beginning. Two distinguished Congregational ministers of New Haven, Jonathan Edwards and Ebenezer Baldwin, published fiery sermons that demonstrated that slavery was against Christianity's core values and the epitome of man's sinfulness, signifying his fall for grace. They proclaimed that slave-owners were the worst of all sinners for holding fellow human beings in bondage against God's word and will. This enlightened, progressive thought stemmed partly from the teachings of the religious revival known as the Great Awakening that brought people closer to God by inspiring individual worship outside the strict confines and ancient rituals of the established church, while challenging the moral authority and supremacy of the Church of England, or the Anglican Church. As John Locke had earlier advocated political separation from Great Britain and Old World immorality, so Edwards early emphasized the importance of a spiritual and moral separation and moral regeneration in the new land of America. Significantly, Edwards' anti-slavery sermons were later employed as effective propaganda by the most militant abolitionists in attacking the South's entrenched system of slavery, continuing Locke's and Tom Paine's own strong anti-slavery advocation. Paine's anti-slavery pronouncements played a key role in the formation of the world's first anti-slavery society in Philadelphia on April 14, 1775, before the signing of the Declaration of Independence in the "City of Brotherly Love."[20]

Paine early denounced the hypocrisy of Christian justifications for slavery by way of bestowing religion to so-called heathens from Africa. He asked in a typically hard-hitting, powerful essay: "Is the barbarous enslaving [of] our in offensive neighbors, and treating them like wild beasts subdued by force, reconcilable with all these *Divine precepts*?[21] The eccentric, outspoken transplanted Englishman reminded white colonists and revolutionary leaders of Philadelphia and across the thirteen colonies not long before the Declaration of Independence's signing, "Forgot not the hapless African?"[22] But, of course, blacks were forgotten by a rapidly-developing America that benefited from the cheapest and permanent of all labor.

Perhaps more important as an explanation why blacks picked up arms and marched off to war against the British, Hessians, Indians, and Tories—Connecticut was their native homeland and it needed to be defended against the invader. After all, blacks had called New Haven their home since the early colonial period. After the first group of "Old Settlers" of African heritage came to New Haven, black immigrants from the British West Indies, especially Jamaica, and even black Portuguese migrated to the town from other parts of New England. Wealthy New Haven merchants purchased black slaves like other members of the aristocratic social elite across New England, especially in the port cities. For generations, ship captains who traded for slaves to the West Indies brought Africans back to New Haven for either sale or to be used as domestics in their own homes.

For generations, large numbers of New Haven's free blacks served on vessels that sailed the seas, or worked in the shipping or whaling industries. Most served as common seamen and worked beside white sailors, while others went to sea as cooks. The number of blacks in New Haven was 4 percent of the state's population in 1790. By 1820, New Haven's continued prosperity resulted in the town containing a large black population, which was nearly 8 percent of the total number of African Americans residing in Connecticut.

Both Connecticut and New Haven possessed an early abolitionist tradition, emerging long before the national trend during the antebellum period. In 1790, the "Connecticut Society for the Promotion of Freedom and for the Relief of Persons Unlawfully Holden in Bondage" was created. Annual meetings were held thereafter in New Haven and Hartford. Thanks to the enlightened principles of the revolutionary period, widespread freedom was bestowed to slaves when the state legislature enacted the Gradual Emancipation Act of 1784, three years after the American Revolution's end. This act mandated that the children of slaves born after March 1, 1784, were to be freed at age twenty-one. These free people of color then became citizens with full legal rights, at least in principle.[23]

However, free blacks in Connecticut soon discovered that lofty theory of the Age of Enlightenment was considerably different from the harsh realities of everyday life in a contradictory white world, where race was yet far more important than flowery words. Free Connecticut blacks remained separate but unequal from whites. Discrimination and racism were almost as strong in New England as in the South. For instance, free blacks were legally denied the right to vote during the War of 1812. This injustice occurred at the exact time when the young American republic was struggling to maintain freedom from England's domination, while large numbers of blacks, including seamen and cannoneers from Connecticut, served on the nation's warships and privateers, and with the merchant fleet. While these African Americans fought for their country in the expectation of more inclusion into the mainstream of society because of their heroic contributions and sacrifices against the British, discrimination against free blacks became a lawful feature of the Connecticut state constitution in 1818.[24]

Because of such discouraging legal setbacks, the central dilemma faced by America seemed to revolve around the permanent place of blacks in society, and the ultimate solution seemed to many white Americans to lie in transporting blacks back to Africa in ambitious colonization schemes. Meanwhile, a vibrant abolitionist tradition that was anti-colonization and instead sought to find a permanent place for blacks in American life and society, if the ever-contradictory nation would only live up to its egalitarian principles as so proudly proclaimed in the Declaration of Independence, continued to survive in New Haven. After the American Colonization Society was formed 1816, an auxiliary society was established in New Haven in 1820. The growing sympathy for the welfare of slaves and free blacks among influential liberal citizens in New Haven was destined to have a dramatic effect on the life of a young free black woman named Emily D. West in the near future, forever altering the course of her destiny.[25]

CHAPTER II

Emily D. West's Birth in New Haven

In 1801, less than eight years after Elijah Austin's trading vessel returned to the safe harbor of New Haven from the lengthy trip to China, an infant daughter by the name of West was born in New Haven, Connecticut. Her black mother of unknown name added another member to the town's large free population. The infant was named Emily. In Gothic terminology, the name Emily meant the industrious one: a name appropriately bestowed by Emily's mother, because her daughter's life in later years clearly demonstrated that this name was a perfect fit. And in Latin, the name Emily meant the winning one, which also came to summarize Emily's life in many ways in future years.

Because Emily's mother was a free woman, so her daughter was also born with the coveted status of free. If Emily had been born of a white master and slave woman in America, the "land of the free," then she would have been a slave according to law. It cannot be determined with primary documentation, but either Emily's mother yet carried her own father's name of West, or she was married to a man named West, who fathered Emily. The 1830 United States census records for New Haven revealed but a single free black family, a couple, including a woman named Jane, married in 1825, by the name of West. However, the last name of West is very common today among African Americans in New Haven.

Evidently, Emily's father was a free black, and perhaps even an American Revolutionary War veteran from Connecticut. He might have won his freedom in that conflict, as more than 5,000 blacks, including quite a few from Connecticut, fought for American liberty from 1775 to 1781. Or Emily's father might have been free for what a distant ancestor had achieved in the colony's defense during the French and Indian War or earlier. As early as 1672 and more than a century before the American Revolution, the colony of Connecticut had allowed blacks to serve in the militia, especially in defense against Indian attacks. Therefore, one of Emily's earlier ancestors might have even served in Connecticut's colonial militia long before the first shots were fired at Lexington and Concord in April 1775.

However, if Emily was indeed a mulatto, as so often portrayed in the Yellow Rose of Texas myth, then the distinct possibility also existed that her father was white. Her birth might have even resulted from his marriage with Emily's mother, but more likely she was born out of wedlock if her father was indeed white. And it is not known if her father or her grandfather had been a white master, which would have explained how she and her mother became free. For good reason, Emily often carried her "freedom papers," or "free" papers, in her words, or manumission papers that proved her free status if necessary, especially to avoid kidnapping and an ugly entry into the nightmarish world of slavery for the first time in her life.[1]

In 1800 and about the time that Emily was born, New Haven contained barely 5,000 people. About 4.8 percent of New Haven's population was black, consisting of 166 free blacks and 82 slaves. Ten years later, the population of New Haven had grown to nearly 7,000, with 371 free blacks, or more than double the number ten years before in 1800. When Emily was around 10 in 1810, the number of slaves in New Haven dropped to 18, indicating that slavery was fading away, unlike in the Deep South.[2]

Unfortunately, almost nothing is known of Emily's early life, because little, if any, documentation was maintained about the lives of free blacks in New Haven. But life for a young free black girl was relatively good in New England and especially in a small town like New Haven compared to the much larger New York City, and, of course, in the South. And Emily and her New Haven family were most thankful that they never experienced the horrors suffered by enslaved African Americans across the South.

Here, in relatively cosmopolitan New Haven, Emily's family most likely lived in a segregated black section of town. Naturally, the town's blacks lived a good distance from where the Elijah Austin, the wealthy merchant, and his family, including a precocious daughter named Mary, had long lived in a fine mansion on Whiting Street. The existence of the West family was comparable to that of other blacks. New Haven's lower-class and oldest section was situated near the harbor in the town's factory district, in New Haven's southeast corner and east on the Long Island Sound. Most of New Haven's blacks lived in this isolated, segregated community to the southeast of Yale College, the pleasant New Haven Green, and the fashionable, stately two-story homes of the town's white elite.

Across the North, and New Haven was no exception, free blacks faced considerable discrimination in regard to housing, which reduced them to living in squalid quarters of ramshackle shanties, because white owners simply did not want African American tenants. In addition, free blacks faced the threat of harassment and racial violence, which forced them to stay together for safety's sake. This hostile and discriminatory environment forced free African Americans to reside in the worst part of town, where rents were often inflated to exploit them further. One black family was forced to live near New Liberia along the water in part of New Haven's black section of town on the southeast and east in a half-underground room, more of a cellar than a house, that was structurally unsound and unsafe.

And in 1829 when New Haven possessed a population of more than 500 free blacks, one ramshackle building in the lower class section of town housed 70 people, including twelve black families, along with boarders and renters, which might well have included Emily and her family. Here, in the shanty town of New Liberia, free blacks "lived and died by candlelight in spare, unplastered rooms, and warmed by the half-heat of fireplaces" that provided inadequate warmth and comfort during the bitter New England winter. Denied legal rights, free blacks across the North, including those in New Haven, did not find life easy. Exclusion from white schools and the ballot box ensured a permanent poverty-stricken, second-class status from cradle to grave in America's caste system above the Mason-Dixon Line.

The most run-down, oldest housing was on the town's eastern and southeastern outskirts in an area known as New Guinea. This area was named for the West Africa nation Guinea, which was located just north of the equator, and had long served as the center of slave trading (beginning with the Portugese) along the low-lying Guinea coast. Because of poverty and mirroring the situation of free African Americans in major American cities across the North, New Guinea had a rougher, vice-filled neighboring black community situated just to the northeast, New Liberia. The most infamous hell-raising establishment in New Liberia and in all New Haven was the notorious Liberian Hotel. Here, all nature of vices flourished and ample amounts of good corn whisky and rotgut flowed freely, while interracial couples made love, drank, and shocked the pious citizens, both black and white, by their flagrant breaches of social and traditional customs.

Emily probably lived with her mother. As a teenager, she very likely worked as a domestic in a white home like so many other black females. In such domestic occupations, African Americans of New Haven, a quarter of whom had no home of their own, lived as domestics in the houses of white families, occupying a small single room.

The northern edge of New Guinea extended north until it lay across, or northeast of, from Yale College and the neat, manicured public square of New Haven. Here, the northern part of the black community, which had recently grown economically stronger by the arrival of more prosperous African Americans, who had fled the crime, squalor, and vice of New Liberia and so-called "Poverty Square" by 1830, was centered along the so-called "Negro Lane." Later named State Street, Negro Lane ran northeast from the town's center and toward the commercial-agricultural community lining the Connecticut River, Middleton, Connecticut. During the 1830s, most black families, which very likely included Emily and her family, were concentrated around Negro Lane northwest of town and Sodom Hill to New Haven's southwest and directly west of New Guinea. However, like the area around Poverty Square, the land on both sides of Negro Lane was particularly infertile, eroded, and poorly drained: quite simply land not desired by whites. Hence, the perfect place for free blacks in the white community's estimation. Therefore, African Americans were left with relatively little opportunity to grow their own food in small gardens for subsistence, as was usually the case if they had resided in more favorable areas.

Despite having escaped the squalid misery of New Liberia to the southeast, blacks yet lived in a bewildering collage of primitive, but yet ingenious in many ways, wooden shacks and shanties situated along the ribbon of dirt, or mud, depending on the weather, known as Negro Lane. These shabby dwellings had been constructed of anything that the resourceful, often desperate, black builders could lay their hands on to create barely livable structures for themselves and their suffering families.

The structures along Negro Lane consisted of a menagerie of hand-built dwellings that differed sharply in size, style, and shape. Some black homes were described as small wooden "sheds" and "hovels." Another problem for free blacks was the lack of decent drinking water, because too few wells were located in the area, guaranteeing poor sanitation and health. Despite their being locked into a discriminatory caste system of America's apartheid, an enterprising spirit yet existed among the free blacks. Some made homes in abandoned buildings or dragged entire sheds or outbuildings from town, setting them up along Negro Lane not only to house families but also to rent out.[3]

Free blacks of New Haven learned early a painful truth about everyday life in America, because "one was never looked at but was simply at the mercy of the reflexes the color of one's skin caused in other people."[4] As much apart of America as mom and apple pie, this omnipresent racial hostility, including living under the threat of violence, led to an unofficial policy of segregation and independent black communities across the North, including New Haven, even in the midst of prosperous white urban areas and amid a land of plenty. Faced with legal discrimination at all levels, large numbers of New Haven's blacks lived in an infamous area known as early as 1800, about the time of Emily's birth, as Sodom Hill. Where no self-respecting white person dared to tread, at least in daytime, Sodom Hill was situated in southwestern New Haven, and just north of Mount Pleasant.

Thanks to the North's grim racial realities and pervasive discrimination, Sodom Hill was one of the unhealthiest places in New Haven. There in fact was no hill at this notorious location, only a slight rise of ground that was as bleak as the disease-ridden, low-lying areas. Consisting of poor soil lacking nutrients and eroded by heavy rains that prevented productive subsistence gardening for desperate black families living in poverty, this slight elevation rose gently amid a low-lying salt marsh—only partly drained—surrounding West Creek. Along West Creek's muddy banks and brackish waters, a lengthy row of filthy tan-yards stood amid the squalor. Here, workers processed cattle and hides for export to the vast sugar plantations of Jamaica. Rotting piles of beef waste byproducts polluted the marsh and creek, contaminating the area and contributing to the squalor and misery for the hard-pressed free black families. Polluted waters and raw sewage spread fatal diseases, like malaria, dysentery, and typhoid fever, among the African American populace without proper access to physicians and medicine. Consequently, the death rates for free blacks in New Haven soared at a rate much higher than for whites.

One section of Sodom Hill was the Trowbridge Square neighborhood. Here, free black males engaged mostly in the daily drudgery of menial and common labor, because they could find no other employment in a racist society, where discrimination of every kind was rampant. Beyond the strict racial boundaries of segregation in a New Haven that nevertheless widely boasted of Yale's enlightened and progressive thought, African American women worked as domestics for rich white families, including taking care of children. Other black women labored as laundresses, maidservants, dressmakers, and hair dressers. Emily's mother, and perhaps even herself when Emily became older, might have been employed in such typical menial occupations.[5]

For African Americans, both slave and free who were a diasporic people much like the Jewish people who had suffered under Egyptian slavery in ancient times, nothing was more important in the overall health and life of the black community than religion to maintain hope for a better future: an emotional, psychological, and spiritual refuge from the harsh realities of living and existing in a harsh world dominated by oppression, hostility, and prejudice.[6]

Religion provided a sturdy foundation for enslaved blacks across the South to persevere and endure slavery's horrors. One visitor to the South never forgot how the "doctrine of the Savior comes to the negro slaves as their most inward need, and as the accomplishment of the wishes of their souls."[7] For both slaves in the South and free blacks in the North, religion offered a much-need "alternative to hopelessness." Therefore, blacks were among the most religious people in America, in part out of need to survive and to maintain hope for a better day. Religion served as the central glue that united and sustained the black community, both slave and free, while bolstering black self-identity that provided a sturdy foundation for the creation of a distinctive people in America.

Religion was equally vital in the lives of free blacks, who struggled for daily survival. Free blacks of New Haven embraced the fiery evangelical Protestantism that grew out of the Great Awakening, which had early spread through rural America to break down the strict formalities of ritualistic religious instruction to allow individuals, including blacks, to worship on their own. Most importantly, this passionate style of worship was based upon a more democratic religion that proclaimed all people as equal. The Great Awakening unleashed an exhilarating new sense of equality that emphasized how black souls were as important as those of whites. This new enlightened religious thought challenged the pro-slavery view that the peculiar institution was actually good for blacks, because it was allegedly sanctioned in the Bible, and was a manifestation of God's ordained natural order. Outside of New England, the rise of Methodism, thanks to Englishman John Wesley's tireless efforts in spreading the faith, promised equality for one and all, allowing blacks to join the church as equal members. Symbolically, the first two people baptized by Wesley were black female slaves in Georgia.[8]

In the face of outright hostility from whites who viewed blacks as undeserving of even religious equality, these courageous white Methodist men of God sought to save black souls, which they viewed as the same as white souls. One of the primary founders and leaders of the Methodist Movement, Gloucester, England-born Rev. George Whitefield, the slender, Oxford-educated son of a wine merchant, asked Southern planters the bold question in a hard-hitting anti-slavery pamphlet: are your children "in any way better by Nature than the poor Negroes?"[9]

Unknown to Emily, a young, pious white man in New Haven was destined to have a dramatic impact one day on her life and the lives of a good many other free blacks. Undistinguished-looking, modest, and humble, he hardly looked the part of a person who could change lives in a dramatic way. Indeed, Simeon S. Jocelyn "was spare and frail-looking" as an adult. But Jocelyn's ordinary appearance masked a brilliant mind, an unbounded humanitarian spirit, and compassion for all people, especially African Americans.

Simeon S. Jocelyn was born to an enlightened and religious middle class family in New Haven on November 21, 1799. Simeon and Emily were near the same age, and their destinies would intersect and be connected in unusual, unexpected ways in the years ahead. Like Emily, he was raised in the town situated along the north side of Long Island Sound. Jocelyn had a heightened compassion for people of color not often seen in the white community, even of New Haven. He obtained a general education in New Haven's fine common schools, and then became a hard-working artisan of note. Entering into a partnership in a successful commercial engraving business with his brother Nathaniel, Jocelyn was creative and enterprising. He became a masterful engraver known for his ability and skills, which promised a bright future.

But wanting to accomplish more for the welfare of people, Jocelyn was an extraordinary man of vision, destined for greater things in the future. Not content with the selfish, narrow concerns of an engraver's life in a dusty little shop, Jocelyn felt a much higher calling. After becoming more prosperous but more conscientious, perhaps he became unsettled by the sad plight of impoverished free black families around him, including Emily's family, especially during the harsh New England winters that caused widespread suffering. At some point in his daily existence in New Haven, Jocelyn might have even passed by Emily, very likely ill-clothed, on the snow-covered streets, or saw her family's small tenant house or shack, where blacks huddled together for warmth in the biting cold. Most African Americas lived in the poorest section (the factory section) of town near the harbor, barely scratching out a meager existence in a constant struggle for daily survival. Whatever catalyst motivated his increasing compassion toward blacks, Jocelyn continued to work as an engraver through the week, while "stealing time for study and preaching on Sundays."[10]

Before 1820, he found his most rewarding personal fulfillment in spreading God's word to New Haven's free black population and in helping impoverished people of color rather than in selfishly reaping greater personal riches and recognition for himself. Consequently, Jocelyn gave up his lucrative business to devote himself to full-time preaching the gospel to African Americans, and improving their dismal plight. Like his abolitionist brother Nathaniel, Simeon early possessed a special empathy for African Americans in bondage that fueled his hatred toward slavery and his desire to assist free blacks as much as possible.

Despite facing white opposition, hostility, and resistance as could be expected, Jocelyn's pet project was to create of his own church for the most impoverished free blacks of New Haven, hoping to provide a permanent foundation for their "moral and society regeneration."

It is not known because so little is known of Emily D. West's early life in New Haven, but the possibility existed that the zealous white man of God might have even employed Emily in his stately home in the heart of downtown New Haven. But more likely, at an earlier date, Emily and her family were part of the black congregation of this young fire-and-brimstone preacher throughout the 1820s, when Emily was in her twenties. Even though he was only officially ordained in the ministry in 1829, after studying under the leading divinity professor at Yale College, Dr. Nathaniel Taylor, the passionate Jocelyn had preached his message of redemption to New Haven's blacks for nearly a decade by this time.

Taylor's credentials were most impressive, and he served as a key influence in Jocelyn's life. Taylor was the primary inspirational force behind the fiery religious doctrine known as the "New Haven Theology." He had served as the revered head minister at the town's most stately church—the Center Congregational Church on the Green in New Haven's urban heart—until 1822. At that time, Taylor then embarked upon a new career at Yale College, after ten years of impassioned ministry at New Haven's principal house of worship.

Here, at New Haven's most beautiful church, Jocelyn worshipped in the magnificent house of God dominated by a steeple towering nearly 200 feet. Center Church had been dedicated in the most turbulent of times when New England, unlike the enthusiastic South and West, opposed conflict with England during the War of 1812. Both Noah Webster, who served as the church's choir director, and Eli Whitney had worshipped at Center Church at the same time that Jocelyn was praising God for his mercies and blessings. By the time Jocelyn officially became a minister, thanks to Taylor's influences and inspiring teachings, in 1829, Emily was in her late twenties, as was Jocelyn. Jocelyn's brother, Nathaniel, painted a fine oil portrait of the respected Taylor in 1825, displaying a natural talent and nice artistic touch.

Like so many of New Haven's hard-working sons, Jocelyn made history in his own way by going against tradition and social norms. "Father Jocelyn was the first white pastor in this country of an exclusively black congregation" after securing his own church on Temple Street in 1824, and despite encountering opposition from some less enlightened whites. No longer would New Haven's blacks have to worship in a segregated white church: Jocelyn's former Center Church, where African Americans, almost certainly including Emily, were relegated to a second story balcony with a seating capacity of 156 people. The second balcony worshippers included both blacks and Indians and an inordinate number of youngsters. Jocelyn was determined to address this segregation and inequality in God's house.

Compared to the average white worshipper, who maintained a reverent silence in keeping with the solemn setting during worship and not hindered by restrictive Puritan legacies of a religious theocracy, blacks embraced a more expressive form of praise, with more emotion and being especially vocal. Therefore, the second balcony at Center Church early garnered a well-deserved, but misunderstood, reputation as "an ruly place, which frequently required discipline." With the establishment of Jocelyn's church on Temple Street, Emily, in her mid-twenties by 1824, was almost certainly among these devout black men and women who basked in the joy of their own house of worship.

New Haven's black population was not large at 624 individuals in 1820, or 7.5 percent of the populace. But the free black population steadily grew over the ensuing years. New Haven boasted a total population of around 10,000 in 1830, while nearly 600 blacks, or 5.3 percent of the population, lived in the town. Jocelyn served as a good shepherd in watching faithfully over this black flock, bestowing greater religious faith and fulfilling that guardian role during a most challenging time.[11]

After 1824, the congregation steadily grew to more than 100 African Americans and Jocelyn's church, simply known as the "Temple Street Church," was located just west of New Guinea. The pride and joy of Jocelyn and his enthusiastic parishioners, this first black church in New England was hardly imposing at first sight: a small, non-plastered, and thirty by forty feet wooden building that displayed no architectural gaudiness or religious splendor. And this glaring plainness of his church was exactly to Jocelyn's homespun tastes and desires. To him, the inspirational religious message was most important. Contrasting sharply with the magnificence of Center Congregational Church, Jocelyn's modest house of worship was located in New Haven's heart, only one and a half blocks southwest of the town's most revered "public square," or New Haven Green.

In this key location, Jocelyn and his African American congregation were hardly hidden from the view of New Haven's upper class whites and the political and commercial elite, worshipping God only a short distance directly south of Yale College, which hugged the square's northwest corner. None other than Arthur Tappan lived in a stately mansion on Temple Street. He was a wealthy silk merchant from New York City and perhaps America's leading abolitionist by this time, and one of the founder fathers [1833] of the American Anti-Slavery Society, a national abolitionist society. Tappan's house was next door to that of Rev. Nathaniel Taylor, who had served as Jocelyn's own personal minister at his Center Congregational Church, which was also situated on Temple Street and surrounded by mature elm and oak trees of a commanding height in a park-like setting fronting the Green, until 1822. The highly-respected Taylor now taught at Yale, continuing to bestow his considerable wisdom to eager youth.[12]

Early 1900s postcard of the "Three Churches on 'The Green,' New Haven, Connecticut."

Sketch of the Center Congregational Church on "The Green," New Haven, Connecticut (courtesy Deb Townshend, church archivist).

In his classic novel *Moby-Dick*, which was written from personal experiences in New England and at sea, Herman Melville described the unforgettable scene upon accidentally entering a black church at night and encountering an enthralled congregation in the whaling port of Nantucket, Massachusetts, about the same time that Jocelyn's church in New Haven was thriving two hundred miles to the west of the Atlantic port. Melville entered to the shock of both himself and the parishioners: "It seemed the great Black Parliament sitting in Tophet. A hundred black faces turned around in their rows to peer; and, beyond, a black Angel of Doom [minister] was beating a book in a pulpit. It was a negro church; and the preacher's text was about the blackness of darkness, and the weeping and wailing and teeth-gnashing there."[13]

Jocelyn organized the African Ecclesiastical Society, consisting of black committee members and his own parishioners, in 1824. On August 25, 1829, at a time when he was not an official reverend after his Yale College instruction and study under the inspirational Taylor, Jocelyn's United African Society was officially accepted as a Congregational church, the first Negro Congregational church. Four males and 17 females became members, possibly including Emily.[14]

This young, impassioned Congregational minister knew that his congregation of free African Americans needed to be able to read and write to advance themselves in life and to demonstrate equality with whites. Education was denied to free blacks, and Jocelyn was determined to address this crippling deficiency that ensured that his parishioners were fated to be a detested permanent underclass. Therefore, utilizing his Temple Street Church and its active congregation and supporters, he established a comprehensive Sunday school in the late 1820s.

Then, Jocelyn created the first primary school for black youth in the early 1830s. Jocelyn now oversaw a vibrant black church, a Sunday school known as the African Sabbath School, an African American educational day school, and a night school for black adults, and black temperance society, which had been established by him at his Temple Street Church in 1830: all part of his tireless efforts to raise African Americans higher and break down racial barriers in American society. Jocelyn and his Temple Street Church, which produced a new generation of inspirational black preachers by the 1840s, served as focal point for these spiritual and benevolent activities that concentrated on intellectual and moral advancement. Jocelyn's string of successes in New Haven in part revealed the close interconnection between religion and abolition, dual moral crusades that merged into one.

Emily may have attended one or more of Jocelyn's black schools, because she was literate in adulthood. Like other students in New Haven, she almost certainly learned to read with the assistance of Noah Webster's spelling book. In fact, Emily might well have seen Webster on New Haven's streets, where he often walked in silence.

At least one respected Texas historian, James E. Crisp, believed that Emily in fact lived in the Jocelyns' own home, because a free black woman of around her age was listed as a member of the Jocelyn household in the 1830 census. But he was incorrect about her age, following the popular trend of portraying Emily as a younger woman than was actually the case by the time of the battle of San Jacinto in April 1836. Emily was around age thirty in 1830. In 1830 and thereafter, Emily saw few slaves in New Haven; there were only four in the entire community at this time. This situation represented a dying institution in the North and in a world that was becoming more progressive in regard to slavery.

While Jocelyn's efforts have gained the most widespread recognition, however, the first primary schools for African Americans in New Haven had been established around 1811 and

1812. And another such school, with a six month term for black students, had functioned in New Haven as early as 1824. Emily could have attended either school for small black children.

America's foremost abolitionist by the early 1830s, William Lloyd Garrison, possessed unbounded admiration for Jocelyn and his multiple efforts in assisting New Haven's free black community. He even visited New Haven to view first-hand the success of Jocelyn's educational efforts, especially the black primary school. From the bustling town poised in picturesque fashion on the wind-swept shores of Long Island Sound, Garrison wrote with almost fatherly pride, "Thanks to Mr. Jocelyn's unselfish ministry for six years, in no place in the Union were the prejudices of the community against the blacks weaker" than in New Haven.[15] Even though he "never sought higher position than that of Pastor with the race he loved," Jocelyn's ambitions to assist long-suffering people of color knew few, if any, bounds.[16]

Around the time that Emily reached adulthood, especially if she was an orphan and had not gained steady employment, she might have received assistance not only from Jocelyn but also from two charities that were founded in New Haven before 1818, the Society for the Relief of Poor Female Professors of Religion and the Female Humane Society. Then, in the summer of 1826 when Emily was just past her mid–twenties, New Haven religious leaders, including Jocelyn, created not one but two societies to benefit people of color. These two organizations were the Antislavery Association and the African Improvement Society. Later, by the 1830s, the African Improvement Society was formed in New Haven to assist impoverished African Americans. Clearly, at some point in her life and like other free black women in New Haven, Emily certainly benefited directly from Jocelyn's many humanitarian and religious efforts, improving her overall lot in life on multiple levels.[17]

One of Jocelyn's most idealistic visions was for African Americans to successfully integrate not only economically but also socially into mainstream American life. Jocelyn envisioned blacks enjoying full rights—especially in regard to education, housing and voting—as American citizens. Therefore, he sought to create his own idealistic "city on a hill," like John Winthrop, the first governor, who had early envisioned the Massachusetts Bay Colony becoming a religious haven and a "New Jerusalem," where a "spirit of harmony and brotherliness" prevailed. To provide free blacks with an opportunity to prosper without segregation and with equality, Jocelyn became a savvy real estate developer with the natural instincts of an enterprising businessman and investor. He turned his ambitious sights on creating his own utopia for both lower class blacks and whites in an area known as Trowbridge Square in southwest New Haven.

In 1830 and thanks to his considerable profits gained from his successful engraving business that he operated with brother Nathaniel, Jocelyn formed a business partnership with Isaac Thompson to purchase fifteen acres of good land. This prime real estate was then divided into lots, creating what they optimistically christened the Village of Spireworth. An utopian and spiritual vision coming to life, this new village, as early planned by Jocelyn, was centered around Spireworth Square, a much-used, popular, and picturesque public space for the local community well into the Twenty-first Century. With Thompson serving as the project's chief architect, Jocelyn was inspired about the possibility of creating a fully integrated community, with black and whites living together in harmony and working side-by-side to reach their potential: the fulfillment of the ever-elusive dream of creating equality for free blacks in American society. Jocelyn also invested in and developed the 40-acre subdivision in the eastern part of New Haven, Franklin Square. But the integrated community of the Village of Spireworth remained Jocelyn's greatest achievement.

During the early 1830s and as planned with so much hope for creating a better future, Jocelyn populated his idealized community largely with the lowest members of New Haven society, primarily free blacks, who had long suffered from the lack of decent housing because of discrimination and segregation. Jocelyn's ambitious project represented a timely and much-needed humanitarian effort, because all black living areas in New Haven were "unsatisfactory of habitation," resulting in the spread of disease and too many unnecessary deaths, especially children. Here, in this uplifting environment as Jocelyn had envisioned with optimistic foresight, free blacks possessed the rare opportunity to reach their potential morally, economically, intellectually, and socially once free of the miserable squalor and pervasive corrupting influences, especially alcohol, that made New Liberia the vortex of vice and crime in New Haven.

New Haven's black community possessed its own esteemed leaders and activists who worked closely with Jocelyn. A free black named Scipio C. Augustus was one of the most distinguished members of Jocelyn's Temple Street Church congregation. A natural leader, he served as the only New Haven delegate who attended the all-black 1830 convention in Philadelphia, when the American Society of Free Persons of Colour was first organized to spread the abolition gospel. It is not known, but by the early 1830s Emily might well have lived in this close-knit community of hard-working men and women that was the fulfillment of yet another one of Jocelyn's utopian visions, the interracial Village of Spireworth.[18]

Year of Turmoil, 1831

As America matured as a young republic and grew stronger and more confident in its prosperity, so increased the nation's inherent internal complexities, turmoil, and contradictions, especially in regard to race and slavery, which tore at the nation's fabric and inner soul during the traumatic year of 1831. Fueled by an increase in popular religious thought and zeal among people across the North, a new sense of righteous reform swept the land, promising to change America in fundamental ways. And, of course, no budding reform movement promised more revolutionary internal change than the movement advocating the abolition of slavery. Jocelyn was hardly a lone idealistic and progressive voice crying out in a darkness for change, but a representative example of the rise of America's most radical reformers and uncompromising abolitionists, who hailed mostly from New England.

Jocelyn and William Lloyd Garrison, America's foremost abolitionist leader, hated slavery with a passion, believing that blacks were equal to whites in every way, if only bestowed with freedom, equality under the law, and a decent education. Garrison called for equal rights as American citizens to be bestowed to free blacks across the North. For his militant abolitionist efforts that even outraged the conservative North, which yet remained anything but progressive in racial matters, the outspoken Garrison had been once placed in jail for "denouncing slavery in a free country." Fellow abolitionist Lewis Tappan, with ample resources and deep pockets, bailed Garrison out. Creating America's most influential abolitionist newspaper, Garrison published the first edition of *The Liberator* in Boston on January 1, 1831. As proclaimed in his first edition that revealed no exaggeration in regard to the irrepressible determination of a true crusader, Garrison threw down the gauntlet by announcing his determination to promote emancipation at any cost: "I am in earnest [and] I will not retreat a single inch."[19]

Invoking the enlightened egalitarian concepts of the Declaration of Independence to support his shrill demands for the immediate emancipation of slaves, Garrison denounced the United States Constitution, America's most revered document, because it not only legally protected slavery, but also allowed for its expansion in the West, potentially all the way to the Pacific: the tragic result of the paradoxical "dark," but necessary politically, Faustian bargain that had been struck between North and South to create a viable national union. Garrison, therefore, sharply derided the Constitution as a "covenant with death and an agreement with hell."[20] As a discriminated-against free black woman struggling on a daily basis to survive in the North, Emily already, and of course more intimately than Garrison, knew all about the hollowness of the Constitution's lofty words and the unfulfilled promises of a hypocritical nation that yet had to fully live up to its most lofty egalitarian pronouncements.

June 1831 proved to be a turning point not only in the lives of Jocelyn and Emily but also in abolitionist efforts. In that year, Jocelyn attended the first annual Convention of the Free People of Colour at Philadelphia, where Tom Paine had been first sickened by viewing from his rented room the city's main slave auction at the Philadelphia Slave Market not long after his arrival from England. Departing New Haven, Jocelyn traveled to the City of Brotherly Love with Garrison and Arthur Tappen, Lewis Tappen's abolitionist brother who had moved to Temple Street in New Haven in 1828.

Arthur Tappen embraced Jocelyn's vision of a bustling black college, which had been endorsed by leading members of Yale College. Jocelyn, with Tappen's assistance, convinced Garrison to attend the Philadelphia convention with a larger strategic plan in mind: to combine their efforts for the creation and establishment of America's first black institution of higher learning, a college in New Haven. But this idea of the nation's premier black college was mostly Jocelyn's brainchild and burning vision as part of his larger dream for a more progressive America living up to the core principles. New Haven's black leaders had long hoped for such a school of higher learning.

But it was Jocelyn, not Garrison, who was the first to articulate his lofty vision for the American nation's first "Negro" college to be established at New Haven before hundreds of the convention's attendees at Philadelphia. At this historic convention, Jocelyn emphasized that such a ground-breaking institution of higher learning would "cultivate habits of industry and obtain a useful mechanical or agricultural profession, while pursuing classical studies." He additionally described how the proposed college, headed a majority of black trustees and a lesser number of whites, would serve as an esteemed center of higher learning "where our youth many be instructed in all the arts of civilized life." Most of all, Jocelyn advocated "a college on the manual labor system, connecting agriculture, horticulture, and the mechanic arts with the study of literature and sciences."

Jocelyn's bold "vision of racial and equality and self-improvement galvanized the entire convention." After thunderous applause in response to Jocelyn's words, convention members unanimously approved of Jocelyn's bold strategic plan for an educational institution that was essentially in conceptual terms an early Tuskegee Institute. Garrison and the boisterous convention not only endorsed Jocelyn's ambitious project but also pledged $20,000, of which Tappan offered $1,000, if the required funds could be raised in a year's time. Garrison became convinced that New Haven was the ideal place for the black college to serve as a bright beacon of hope for African Americans across America for generations. Garrison's words reflected his hope and faith: "What Yale College ... has done for the whites, may in time be done by the new college for the colored people."

Jocelyn viewed the proposed New Haven black college—in essence a black Yale—as providing the inspirational example to prove to white America the determination of blacks to aspire higher in order to fit into the mainstream of society. Quite simply, the central idea of a prestigious black college was an ambitious bid to demonstrate equality with whites for all to see. Above all else, Jocelyn hoped that this lone black college at New Haven would eventually open the door for the establishment of additional African American colleges across America. Clearly, at this time, Jocelyn's vision was not only a bold but also a most revolutionary concept that challenged the fundamental foundations of segregation, racism, and inequality to an unprecedented degree: bestowing higher education to the most despised and discriminated against members of American society, free blacks who occupied the lowest rung of the social ladder, after African Americans in slavery, of a harsh caste system. After all, American racism was based on the concept that blacks were not deserving of equality because they were allegedly inferior subspecies of humanity. Jocelyn's college would prove that blacks were worthy of full equality as American citizens.

After his heady return to New Haven from Philadelphia in soaring spirits, Jocelyn articulated his strategic plans for not only a black college but also an abolition society, based upon the model founded in England, which was now leading in world in an anti-slavery crusade, dedicated to an "immediate" emancipation of slaves. Even more, Jocelyn viewed this black college as the future headquarters of a broad-based, active abolition organization with a global reach.

Indeed, he envisioned not only a national but also, in time, a world-wide abolitionist organization and headquarters centered in New Haven, after gaining additional support and influence for his efforts. Jocelyn hoped that this international abolitionist headquarters would then serve as a magnet to draw blacks and newly-liberated slaves from elsewhere, such as those in the British West Indies, including Jamaica, who had been freed by Great Britain by 1834. Therefore, in the fertile mind of the Congregationalist minister from New Haven, Jocelyn's college would then evolve into the dynamic "center, the pillar for oppressed people of color everywhere": a bold global vision that was in accord with the day's most enlightened and progressive thought. Most significant for her own evolution in thought that negated the provincialism of small town New Haven, Emily D. West was literally in the midst of the talk and debate of potentially earth-shaking developments that were predicted for her hometown.

Feeling that he was drawing ever closer to realizing his dreams, this young minister of the unshakeable faith described his lofty vision for an inspirational black college not only to the white congregation of his Center Church on September 7, 1831, but also his own Temple Street congregation of African Americans. Therefore, if she was present and sitting in a wooden Temple Street pew on Sunday morning at the black church, Emily would have marveled at Jocelyn's ambitions plans and global vision that promised a new day for people of color.

Jocelyn was not simply an idealistic dreamer and idle talker but a man of action. By this time, he had joined forces with America's two most dynamic abolitionists who were equally dedicated men of vision and accomplishment, Arthur and Lewis Tappan. These two wealthy New York City brothers believed so strongly in Jocelyn's ambitious project that they purchased the land for the college in south New Haven near the harbor. The Tappan brothers also donated $1,000 to fuel a fund-raising campaign for the erection the college in Jocelyn's integrated community, the "Village of Spireworth" in eastern New Haven along Carlisle Street and facing Trowbridge Square. By this time, Jocelyn was confident for success and the fulfillment of his greatest dream for blacks on an international scale, with everything going according to plan.[21]

Jocelyn's intoxicating "vision of New Haven and Yale working together" to fuel his and the black college's objectives held limitless potential, or so it seemed. Most of all, he was convinced that New Haven's whites would be as enlightened and forward-thinking as himself, especially in regard to supporting his ambitious projects for uplifting the long-suffering people of color. However, this was a risky assumption. Nevertheless, Jocelyn believed that he had hit upon the right place and right time by choosing New Haven as the site of his future black college, which would serve as a worldwide beacon of hope for blacks around the world. He was convinced that "the literary and scientific character of New-Haven renders it a very desirable place for the location of the college."[22]

In truth, Jocelyn's idealistic vision was way ahead of its time, and far too progressive for the people of New Haven, or anywhere else in the United States for that matter. His bold idea was even too radical for liberal New Haven, even though this well-respected and normally open-minded community was known far and wide for an advanced degree of enlightened thought. As so often in the past, an ever-resilient racism, always just lingering just below the surface, once

Abolitionist Simeon S. Jocelyn (courtesy Massachusetts Historical Society).

again raised its ugly head at the mere thought of Jocelyn's proposed college. Nether America nor New Haven was yet ready to embrace such an advanced concept in ultra-sensitive matters of race, especially one that was perceived as offering far too much equality for African Americans and raising them to the level of whites. Therefore, Jocelyn's advocation and activities in promoting the black college resulted in severe backlash from the white community.

A heated open town meeting was held in New Haven on Saturday evening, September 10, 1831, only three days after Jocelyn spoke in detail about his all-consuming dream at his home church. Concerned city officials and civic leaders, including Yale graduate Mayor Dennis Kimberly, who had called the town meeting at City Hall, united as one in stiff opposition to Jocelyn's plan. They quickly voted down Jocelyn's revolutionary idea. Adding insult to injury for Jocelyn, the vote was a landslide of 700 to 4. And, of course, Jocelyn was one of those supportive 4 votes. The white townsfolk of New Haven had delivered a lethal blow on the premise, or excuse, that a black college would be "destructive of the best interests of the City" of New Haven.

From the beginning, Jocelyn had chosen the site for a black college specifically because of New Haven's well-known tolerance and the people's open-mindedness, or so he had once believed without hesitation. Instead, Jocelyn and Garrison were stunned to discover how quickly "a sober and Christian community [could so enthusiastically] rush together to blot out the first ray of hope for the blacks." Equally ironic, the decisive voting down of Jocelyn's ambitious college plan was based upon an obsessive and paranoid concern that New Haven might be transformed into the vortex of the most militant, if not revolutionary, abolition agenda not only on a national but also on a worldwide basis. If so, then such a global development would become a "dangerous interference with the concerns," especially to the Southern states. The inevitable hostile backlash from Southerners might well not only damage the carefully-developed images of Yale, New Haven's female seminaries, and other prestigious institutions, but also eliminate the profitable flow of bright-eyed Southern students from wealthy families of the planter and merchant elite. If so desired or planned by her now that she was in her early thirties, Emily's possible once-in-a-lifetime chance to go to a black college in New Haven, with Jocelyn's assistance and blessings, was no more, fading away in the angry community overreaction that was intolerance on an organized scale.

But the irrepressible Jocelyn was not discouraged by the unexpected setback as might be expected with a shattering of a great dream. He, therefore, only continued his anti-slavery activities with renewed energy and commitment. For instance, Jocelyn served as an influential delegate to the anti-slavery national conventions in Philadelphia, where he was a leading voice for change in America on the executive committee of the American Anti-Slavery Society in 1835. In the latter role, Jocelyn helped to raise funds for anti-slavery activities, societies, and their efforts dedicated at ending slavery in America.[23]

What other factors explained this unexpected and quite sudden reversal in public sentiment, once considered so enlightened, liberal, and religiously-inspired, in the community of New Haven? Why such a sharp rise of hostility toward Jocelyn's initiatives and free blacks in New Haven by a liberal community that had long been known for its racial tolerance and open-mindedness toward people of color? The key to what most of all transformed enlightened northern liberals of New Haven into angry, reactionary conservatives lay in what happened around 450 miles to the southwest in the humid, rolling hills of Southampton County, Virginia, and along the cypress-lined Nottoway River country in August 1831—a bloody slave uprising that shook the entire South.

The most successful slave revolt in America history was yet reported in New Haven's newspapers in the very same editions that applauded the voting down of Jocelyn's novel concept of a black college in New Haven. Jocelyn's timing could not have been worse. As a strange fate would have it and another one of American history's omnipresent ironies, Jocelyn's great dream had been unwittingly swept away by a pious black man of God, who might have been even more devout and determined that God's will should prevail than even Jocelyn. His name was Nat Turner. This diminutive, unimpressive-looking black prophet had attempted to destroy slavery at any cost and lead his enslaved people to freedom. During his desperate bid to bestow liberty to the slaves of the Virginia Tidewater, "General Nat," hoping to become the revered George Washington of his people, led his rebellious blacks on a war of liberation. After slaughtering white families along the way, Turner then attempted to capture the county seat, which was appropriately named Jerusalem, on the slow-moving, cypress-lined Nottoway River.

Convinced "that Heaven would interfere" and inspired by a number of prophetic visions that God would assist those humble souls who possessed the courage to rise up against slavery, Turner orchestrated the bloodiest slave revolt in American history with a righteous vengeance. Believing that God was on his side, Turner and his band of revolutionaries spared few whites. He was a charismatic, self-anointed preacher who had long delivered fiery inspirational sermons—not unlike Jocelyn in New Haven—to the slaves of the Tidewater tobacco country of Southampton County.

Like most revolutionaries who fought against on oppressive status quo, he was motivated by a fiery religious zeal and vivid visions of blacks and whites engaged in mortal combat. Intelligent, pious as a monk, and literate, Turner sought not only to free his oppressed people of the Virginia Tidewater, but also to spread a righteous war of liberation, or his "great work," throughout this land cursed by the moral stain of slavery. Turner and his 50 to 60 slaves slaughtered more than 50 whites during the Southampton Massacre on August 21 and 22. Indeed, with the blacks settling old scores after lifetimes of oppression under slavery, "whole families [were] butchered, thrown into heaps, and left to be devoured by hogs and dogs, or to putrify on the spot." But this disorganized band of rebellious slaves, heady over their success, was shortly crushed by the local mounted Virginia militia, before Nat and his followers reached their strategic objective of Jerusalem, where guns and ammunition could be procured to continue their rebellion against slavery.

The victorious Virginia militiamen celebrated their success in smashing the bloodiest slave revolt in American history, cutting the heads off of black rebels and planting them high atop wooden poles along the road as a grisly warning. After initially evading capture, Turner was eventually taken prisoner by a lone farmer. He was hung high from a large oak tree at Jerusalem after a mock trial. Then the rebel leader's body was dissected with morbid curiosity, as if to attempt to ascertain why any African American would desire to lead a revolt to obtain freedom for himself and his long-suffering people against such allegedly kind masters, especially those of the genteel, refined planter class. In a final desecration, Nat was then decapitated and skinned by a tough local Irishman named "Buck" Mallory, who won additional respect in the community's eyes in consequence. Thereafter, Nat's skin was tanned and sold for souvenirs to a host of eager buyers, while a reign of terror from vengeful whites fell upon African Americans, mostly innocent free blacks and slaves, across southeast Virginia.

This terrifying revolt by an obscure black prophet sent shock waves reverberating across America, especially in the Deep South, as never before. And no people were now more targeted by the severe backlash than free blacks, who were seen by whites as the promoters of slave insurrections, despite Turner's revolt having been carried out by slaves and the fact that Nat was not a free man.

Thanks to Turner's righteous wrath in far-away Southampton County, the last thing that the good town fathers and people of New Haven now desired was to have a good many out-of-state blacks, especially those from Southampton County, Virginia, and from around the world, including the first free black republic of Haiti, attending a college in their town. They conveniently ignored the fact that northern abolitionists yet advocated non-violence as the best policy for ending slavery in America.

Nevertheless, many New Haven whites feared that the sight of black college students would embolden local free blacks, who were noted to be more surly and disrespectful toward whites as of late. It is not known, but this new belligerency might have included Emily, or perhaps family members if that was the case. But most of all, the people of New Haven even feared that Jocelyn's proposed school might send forth black revolutionaries to the South to encourage other slave revolts like Turner's insurrection. Consequently, advanced education for blacks in New Haven came to be seen as an incubator for future revolutionaries, like Nat Turner, who had shaken a complacent, paternalistic confidence about what whites assumed was a benign institution of slavery and docile slaves.[24]

With prophetic foresight and offering a grim warning not only for slave owners but also northerners, Garrison predicted how Turner's revolt in that fateful August of 1831 was "but the beginning of sorrows. All the blood which has been shed will be required at your hands. At your hands alone? No—but at the hands of the people of New England and of all the free states. The crime of oppression is national. The south is only the agent in this guilty traffic [and] Wo to this guilty land, unless she speedily repents of her evil doings! .... IMMEDIATE EMANCIPATION can alone save her from the vengeance of Heaven, and cancel the debt of ages!"[25] Garrison proclaimed an awful truth with a searing logic that now haunted the American nation: "Our slaves have the best reason to assert their rights by violent measures, inasmuch as they are more oppressed than others."[26]

As could be expected, an outraged South blamed Turner's uprising not on the slavery's horrors that they had themselves and the institution created—after all they saw themselves as good, decent masters who bestowed Christianity on barbaric Africans by following God's will—but upon northern abolitionists, especially Garrison. Therefore, the Georgia Senate passed a resolution offering a reward of $5,000 for Garrison's arrest and conviction for inciting slaves to revolt. Garrison now had a price on his head.[27]

Combined with the news of Turner's bloody revolt and newly emboldened attitudes among some New Haven's free blacks, the white backlash from Jocelyn's progressive efforts to establish the first black college included an organized attempt to deny any hint of "an assurance of equality," in Jocelyn's words, for free African Americans. Some free blacks were even attacked by whites on the streets of New Haven. Venting their heightened anger, a white mob attacked both Jocelyn's and Tappan's home on Temple Street with a barrage of loud insults and a barrage of stones. Then, a mob of enraged whites surged into Sodom Hill, assaulting blacks and tearing down at least one black shanty in the race riot. Gangs of white vigilantes took the law into their own hands. They even arrested a number of whites who were engaged in carnal activities with black prostitutes in the most notorious dens of iniquity of New Liberia. Hysteria and racial intolerance among New Haven's whites reached a fever pitch, nearly mirroring the South's own backlash in the wake of Turner's rebellion.

In the agricultural community of Canterbury in east central Connecticut, white anger rose against an attempt toward black equality when a courageous white Quaker woman, Prudence Crandall, opened her boarding school exclusively to black females in 1831. This development caused quite a sensation all the way to the capital. The state legislature outlawed the latest egalitarian enterprise, but Tappan's ample pocketbook kept the case mired in the legal tangles of the court system. Then, fearing future black equality and, of course, the alleged accompaniment of amalgamation that was viewed as a pandora's box leading to society's destruction, the outraged people of Canterbury partly destroyed Crandall's home. They forced her to flee to Illinois for her life. Not only New Haven but also Connecticut—much like the North in general—was proving not to be as enlightened as once thought and hoped by idealistic abolitionists, who were viewed as too radical and as dangerous extremists even in the North.[28]

Turner's slave revolt on that hot summer in Southampton County, Virginia, was not the only event to have sweeping repercussions in 1831, so did the revolutionary activities of another defiant black man of God in the Caribbean, Sam Sharpe. This dynamic Baptist preacher, who was born in 1801, the same year as Emily D. West, led a slave revolt on December 28, 1831, at Montego Bay, St. James Parish, on Jamaica's north coast. In part inspired by the egalitarian Baptist faith of the slave community, the revolt was eventually crushed by the rapidly-aroused white militia of Jamaica. Like Nat Turner, Sharpe was captured and then executed, suffering the fate of almost all black revolutionaries, in May 1832.

But more importantly, the largest and best organized slave revolt in the history of the British West Indies convinced the British government that now was the time to abolish slavery. Government leaders feared the ugly reality of a costly epidemic of slave insurrections and the loss of sizeable investments around the Caribbean and England's other West Indian islands. Suddenly, the freeing of slaves became a matter of extreme urgency. And, of course, newly freed slaves provided plenty of cheap labor, the inexpensive fuel of the Industrial Revolution. Therefore, the Emancipation, or Abolition, Act was passed in London in August 1833. This act inspired the Tappan brothers and other abolition leaders to form the New York Anti-Slavery Society, which advocated immediate abolition. An auxiliary organization was then set up in New Haven, where Jocelyn played the leading role in this effort.[29]

Meanwhile, in 1833, the Tappan brothers, Arthur and Lewis, united their New York Anti-Slavery Society with Garrison's New England Anti-Slavery Society to form a new national organization christened the American Anti-Slavery Society. The Society of Friends, or Quakers, also combined with the Tappan brothers and Garrison to launch this new national organization dedicated to universal liberty and human rights.[30]

In the most idealistic terms that included the doctrine of non-violence, the American Anti-Slavery Society was dedicated, as penned by the idealistic Garrison, to ending slavery by way of "the overthrow of prejudice, by the power of love—and the abolition of slavery by the spirit of repentance."[31]

Despite being frustrated in his attempt to establish a black college in New Haven and the unexpected strength of white opposition, Jocelyn never relinquished his cherished dream of higher education for African Americans. After all, he had originally proposed the spread of black colleges across the United States to uplift as many blacks as possible and integrate them as equals in American society. Jocelyn attempted to address the most vexing problem facing the American nation: the place of blacks in American society. Jocelyn's solution was founded upon the premise that the United States was their home: a reality that argued convincingly against the many colonization schemes that were directed at shipping American-born blacks to Africa, which most had never seen before and knew nothing about.

Jocelyn was adamantly against colonization efforts like those of the Tappan brothers and other abolitionists. He explained:

"If we ever expect to see the influence of prejudice decrease, and ourselves respected, it must be by the blessings of an enlightened education. It must be by being in possession of the classical knowledge which promotes genius, and causes man to soar up to those high intellectual enjoyments and acquirements, which places him in a situation, to shed upon a country and a people, that scientific grandeur which is imperishable by time, and drowns in oblivion's cup their moral degradation. Those who think that our primary schools are capable of effecting this, are a century behind the age .... If we wish to be respected, we must build our moral character, on a base as broad and high as our nation itself."[32]

By 1834 when Great Britain permanently ended slavery and Jocelyn's black college now no longer feasible, Jocelyn continued his relentless efforts to improve the lives of free blacks in a covert fashion. He and Isaac Thompson quietly donated funds for a black primary school and the building, which was established as a trust for the future education of African Americans in New Haven. Filling a large void, Jocelyn's new primary school was christened the Spireworth School, located in the neighborhood that Jocelyn had created in his crusading zeal.[33]

Garrison, the editor of America's foremost anti-slavery newspaper, *The Liberator*, continued to hold the upmost respect for Jocelyn for his many efforts to improve the lives of free blacks of New Haven. He merely concluded with no small amount of admiration how "Jocelyn is full of heavenly mindedness."[34] One young free black woman in New Haven who benefited from this "heavenly mindedness" was Emily D. West. However, as fate would have it, she had missed an opportunity to have perhaps become one of the first black female college students in United States history, when the great dream of Jocelyn's black college died an early death. As later events demonstrated, Emily possessed closer associations with whites, including abolitionists and especially Jocelyn, than normally expected among free blacks.

By this time, Jocelyn had succeeded in his determined efforts to change New Haven society by creating the neighborhood known as Trowbridge Square, which was part of Sodom Hill. Here, black and white lower class menial workers and domestics lived side by side. In this environment, a good many African Americans now enjoyed overall better health, more decent living conditions, and brighter future prospects than in the segregated black communities. Given Emily's connection with Jocelyn and his efforts and her possible mixed race background, she most likely lived in this integrated neighborhood, which was largely of Jocelyn's making and the fulfillment of his vision for racial harmony with black and white living in peace together.[35]

Despite the occasional angry backlash from the white community, New Haven and Yale College remained at the center of the young, but growing, northern anti-slave movement in future years. Jocelyn and his brother Nathaniel also served as conductors of the underground railroad. Violating man's arbitrary laws but not a higher moral law, they funneled escaped slaves north to safer refuges far from those opportunists, including professional slave-catchers, who sought to capture and return blacks back to slavery for lavish profits.[36]

In time, New Haven also became the location of the famous *Amistad* trial, gaining worldwide publicity. Jocelyn played a leading role in gaining national support for the African slaves, who had rebelled against the Spanish crewmen of the slave ship, *La Amistad*, which had just departed Havana, Cuba. Fifty-three Africans from the rice-growing Mende country of Sierra Leone, in West Africa, overpowered the Spanish ship's crew in the early morning hours of July 1, 1839, and took control of the ship. They then demanded that the captured pilots take them back to their native homeland. However, the Spanish survivors instead headed the ship north, not east, and toward the United States. Captured near Long Island which New Haven overlooked, the slave ship and the West Africans, who only wanted to return home, were taken to New Haven. Here, they were tried for both murder and piracy, because of their efforts in overpowering the ship and killing crew members in their desperate bid for freedom.

But leading northeastern abolitionists came to the rescue of the seemingly doomed Africans, forming the *Amistad* Committee. The Jocelyn brothers and Lewis Tappan and other advocates for equality provided moral and financial support for the Africans, who sat in the New Haven jail for two years during the trial period. They went to great lengths to publicize the incident across the nation to garner widespread sympathy for the Africans' sad plight. Nathaniel Jocelyn, Simeon's wealthy brother, even painted an excellent oil portrait of the revolt's leader, Cinque, who was in his mid–twenties. On a daily basis to keep fit, the Africans exercised on the New Haven Green within sight of Jocelyn's Center Church and not far from his black church on Temple Street. Here, Emily almost certainly attended religious services, a logical assumption because of the later documented association and connection between Emily and Jocelyn.

Finally, the controversial case went to the Supreme Court, which freed the blacks and allowed their return to the far-away Mende homeland in the tropics of West Africa, thanks to timely support from Jocelyn and the *Amistad* Committee. Most importantly, the *Amistad* committee had masterfully employed the Africans' sad plight to garner widespread empathy for Africans and people of color, gaining additional recognition for the abolitionist movement and its merits.[37]

Meanwhile, Jocelyn's primary school continued to teach eager young students in New Haven. The Spireworth School bestowed quality educations upon African Americans well into the 1840s.[38] Most significant, Jocelyn's egalitarian and abolitionist legacies also lived on in the actions of those young men and women, including very likely Emily, who was surely inspired by his humanitarian efforts to assist free blacks in New Haven. Among these future abolitionist leaders were two men of African descent who had been inspired by Jocelyn's vision of a black college at New Haven. One was an escaped Maryland slave, James Pennington, who had eagerly listened to Jocelyn's pro-black college speech at the national convention in Philadelphia in 1831, and Cassius Clay, who graduated from Yale in 1832. Both men became activists and champions for black equality, to which they committed their lives.[39]

The Challenge of New York City

According to the best available evidence, Emily departed her hometown of New Haven and sought greater opportunities in New York City during the mid–1830s. Like Connecticut, New York possessed an anti-slavery tradition. Founding father Alexander Hamilton, despite being born and raised in the British West Indies where slavery thrived, had played a key role in founding the New York Manumission Society in 1785.

Here, in New York City, Emily found a relatively safe haven with other free blacks from New Haven who had resettled in the city, most likely with the abolitionist's financial assistance and efforts. It is not known what caused Emily to finally leave the place of her birth. But most likely, Emily departed her homeland because the New England states and Connecticut had become the most inhospitable of all states to free blacks by this time. In fact, more anti-black and anti-abolition riots swept Connecticut than any other state in New England. Even worse, and if Emily either witnessed the sight or only heard about it, she almost certainly would have never forgotten how the last slave auction had occurred in New Haven on Saturday, March 8, 1825, when she was in her mid–twenties. An unfortunate mother, Lois Tritton, and her child were sold on the auction block to the highest bidder. The auction took place before a gathered crowd of whites on the Green itself and within sight of Jocelyn's Center Church, as if mocking religion and Jocelyn's tireless efforts.

When Emily left New England (very likely for the first time in her life) for the major urban center New York City eighty miles to the southwest, it was almost certainly because the environment for free blacks in New Haven had turned more threatening. But in fact, the changes in New Haven only reflected the dark trend sweeping across the North.

Emily had become abolitionist-minded because of her race, free status, early struggles in New Haven, the egalitarianism of the local black community, and Jocelyn's inspirational influence and efforts. As Emily matured, she naturally grew disgusted by the realization that much of New Haven's economy, prosperity, and wealth had rested in no small part on the institution of slavery—not only in the South, where cotton was king, but also in the West Indies, where sugar was king.

Equally disconcerting, Connecticut passed a law that prohibited free black schools, because these "would tend to the great increase of the colored people of the state and thereby to the injury of the [white] people" of Connecticut. Worse, Connecticut amended its state constitution to even more thoroughly disenfranchise free blacks, making their lives more difficult.[40]

Like other free blacks from New Haven, Emily most likely encouraged and received funds for passage south to New York City from Jocelyn, as later events and her close connections to him and New Haven's abolitionist community clearly suggest. Jocelyn himself had relocated from New Haven to New York City in 1834. Apparently, Emily arrived in New York City with at least one other free black from New Haven or perhaps even with Jocelyn. This free black person was either one of two young free black men—George Cooper, age thirteen, and another African American named Turner who was of mixed black and white blood—or, more likely, a free woman named Diana Leonard. If Emily journeyed to New York City on her own, then she almost certainly moved in with these New Haven free blacks after they had relocated to New York City at an earlier date.

After all, Diana would also migrate from New York City to Texas in 1835 with Emily, after signing a one-year work contract with Texian James Morgan along with Emily. Diana hailed from New Haven. She was very likely Emily's friend and longtime hometown associate. Diana Leonard was also assisted by abolitionists, and naturally hated discrimination against blacks, both slaves and free, as much as did Emily D. West. As could be expected, the connection between these two free black men and two free black women from the same community was close, especially when faced with an unfamiliar, and hostile, environment. They had most likely worshipped together at Jocelyn's Temple Street Church before migrating to New York City. In time, Morgan signed the same one-year contracts with these two free black males (George Cooper and Turner), who likewise journeyed to Texas in 1835. In all likelihood and for good reason, Emily was not alone while living in the bustling urban sprawl of New York City.[41]

However, with any surviving family members yet in New Haven and herself away from most of the familiar faces and surroundings that she had known all her life, Emily was much more vulnerable in New York City than in New Haven. The greatest risk for any free black, especially a female on her own, was getting kidnapped by opportunistic whites and sold into slavery. The routine kidnapping of free blacks in the North was big business because of the sizeable profits involved. Consequently, free blacks were not only kidnapped in New York City, but also in the nation's capital, which was surrounded by the slave states of Virginia and Maryland.

A free black from upstate New York, Solomon Northup, whose father's side of the family hailed from New England (Rhode Island) like Emily's family, was one such unfortunate victim. Solomon's father, Mintus Northup, had been set free when his master died. Therefore, Solomon, born in the Essex County in northwest New York just west of Vermont in the summer of 1808, had never known slavery until after he was kidnapped in Washington, D.C., during a visit. After his kidnappers reaped their ill-gotten gains, Solomon was sent south to work in the sun-baked fields of a Louisiana plantation in the bayou country along the Red River near the Texas border.[42]

Emily was more fortunate, benefiting from her times. Humanitarianism and abolitionism were on the rise in the civilized world, led by Great Britain, which had turned against slavery. This was a religious and reform-minded period, especially in the northeast, when an growing number of influential whites sought solutions for the plight of African Americans. They had decided that colonization was the only real solution, because they knew that a racist America would not change. A colony for African Americans had been established in the early 1820s by northern abolitionists of the American Colonization Society, organized in 1816 and with an auxiliary chapter in New Haven, for free blacks.

This newly designated land for transplanted African Americans was the future republic of Liberia. Departing "our native land—to abandon forever the scenes of our childhood and to sever the most endeared connections—was the desire for a retreat where, free from the agitations of fear and molestation, we would approach in worship the God of our Fathers," wrote one black emigrant. Free blacks with common Anglo-Saxon last names like Johnson, Draper, and Hunter were dispatched across the Atlantic to West Africa because they were viewed as threats to the institution of slavery.

Emily might have felt much the same as this transplanted African American who obviously regretted departing his native homeland, having been forced to leave New Haven's and Connecticut's increasingly anti-free black environment. By the time that Emily journeyed to Texas in late 1835, blacks of Liberia were yet expanding their domain along the coasts of this tropical land and creating a transplanted homeland in the low-lying jungles. These African Americans established such communities as Marshall during the gradual process of nation-building. Liberia eventually became a republic in 1847, at the time of the Mexican-American War.[43]

Schemes for black colonization included those located closer to the United States than far-away West Africa. White abolitionist Benjamin Lundy, a young Quaker who detested slavery from his personal experiences with slavery in Virginia, and Garrison's friend, united with a former Mexican army officer, a mulatto of French heritage who had retired from active duty, Nicholas Drouett. They planned to establish a colony of free blacks in Texas with the backing of the government in Mexico City during the early 1830s. Of course, this prospect of a black colony horrified the Anglo-Celtic settlers, or Texians, in the northern Mexican province of Texas, raising the worst racial fears and paranoia. The Texas Revolution's outbreak in early October 1835 thwarted this ambitious colonization plan that in itself held the potential to spark open revolt in Texas among the transplanted settlers, mostly Southerners, from the United States.[44]

Even for a free black like Emily D. West, sprawling New York City was not only unfriendly but also alien territory. Free blacks faced even more discrimination and hostility in New York City than in New Haven, suffering as second-class citizens and competing for survival with other ethnic groups, especially the recently-arrived immigrant Irish. Free blacks were denied equality in every aspect of life. Ostracized from the mainstream of American society and without the right to vote or receive an education, the free people of color lived in the squalor of filthy boarding houses and shacks. Other free black families struggled to survive in the dark cellars of tenement slums of hellish urban ghettos. For warmth in winter and protection against the harsh, bone-chilling winds sweeping off the East River, many were forced to sleep close together in cramped quarters.

The inner city's most notorious slum—and America's worst in the Nineteenth Century—was the infamous Five Points District at the southern tip of Manhattan Island. The city's poorest immigrants, from Europe, especially Ireland, and including China, called the crowded, unruly Five Points home. Here, as in the nearby Hell's Kitchen and the Bowery, a dark, seething underworld of all manner of vice and roving, ever-opportunistic gangs thrived, along with disease and squalor.

However, New York City presented some solace to this woman from New Haven. Emily saw a good many enterprising free black females, including older women, wearing colorful madras head-scarves as in the Caribbean. These women sold vegetables, mints, and hot yams, which was a staple in their native West Africa, on busy street corners amid the seemingly endless flow of human traffic. The Five Points was largely a working class area and the unsavory residence for both black and white. Most of all, the Five Points was the most infamous urban center in all America by the time that Emily arrived in New York City. She suddenly found herself in a more threatening world than relatively gentle New Haven, despite its shortcomings in racial matters.

By 1835, the Five Points was dominated primarily by impoverished Irish immigrants and free blacks who had flooded into New York City since the early 1800s. Even though they shared a mutual hostility, the free African Americans and Irish had much in common: they were shackled and bound together by lower class status, exploited as cheap labor, stuck in poverty and menial jobs, if they worked at all, amid the filthy urban squalor of the Five Points. Emily was yet another free black woman who now attempted simply to survive in the rough-and-tumble world of lower Manhattan. Slum life was all that was affordable to a free black woman of limited means. Even more appalling than the worst tenement slums of London, England, which were infamous on both sides of the Atlantic for their depravity and crime, the Five Points had been called "the most dismal slum section in America."[45]

Thousands of free blacks lived in New York City during the early 1830s. And more free blacks were located in the Five Points than any other part of New York City by the time that Emily called this thriving city her new adopted home. Struggling and hard-working out of necessity in simply attempting to survive in their harsh urban environment, these free people of color played a key role in the city's economic and urban life. Many were descendants of the first slaves brought to America by the Dutch. The enterprising Dutch had first settled Manhattan Island and created a thriving colony, New Netherlands, until conquest by the English, who established a new government and laws in 1664.

Brought across the Atlantic by way of the Middle Passage in the slave ships of the Dutch West India Company, Dutch slaves enjoyed what resembled more of an indentured status under a more tolerant Roman-Dutch law than under the English. Black slaves were even "treated as members of the New Netherlands community," including in New Amsterdam (New York). However, this relative benevolence changed forever for blacks in Dutch bondage when English law established a permanent servitude to ensure that slavery flourished for future generations, while slave importations increased dramatically as part of westward expansion and English settlement of the interior.

The people of Connecticut, including New Haven, had long encouraged slaves to defect by land and sea from the Dutch in the 1600s and to join their Connecticut communities to the northeast. Emily's own descendants were perhaps brought from Guinea or the Gold Coast of West Africa, where Dutch slavers, who became the leaders of the Guinea slave trade in the 1660s, had long acquired their "black gold." If so, then they might have fled to New Haven from this bustling port city, escaping from slavery under either the Dutch or the English and heading north to an inviting haven.

By 1754 and barely two decades before the American Revolution's beginning, the colony of New York contained the largest slave population, more than 9,000 souls, of any English colony north of Maryland. However, fresh from New Haven, Emily probably could not have imagined or realized how much of New York City's prosperity rested upon the city's slave traders, investors, and merchants, whose fortunes had been earned in the lucrative slave trade. Some of the most respected members of New York City society, including Philip Livingston, were in fact slave traders, reaping wealth, respect in society, and elevated social status, despite their unholy transactions in human flesh. Although often either overlooked or not acknowledged by historians, the institution of slavery had long served as a vital foundation of the unprecedented growth and success of New York City as a great commercial center.

But, inspired by the Age of Enlightenment's and American Revolution's egalitarian principles, anti-slavery activities early rose in New York City. Sparking the abolition movement in New York State and elsewhere in the North at a later date, the New York Manumission Society was formed in 1785, only several years after the American Revolution's end. This abolitionist society's work included winning the release of free New York City blacks who had been tricked back into slavery by whites seeking lavish profits from selling them to the highest bidder.

Overall, New York City evolved early into a relatively safe haven for free blacks. The free black population steadily grew to the point of rendering slavery unprofitable. Abolitionists of the Manumission Society even established a school for free black children and a night school for adults of African descent. Blacks were not only taught to read and write but also a variety of vocational skills, allowing them to enter the large free black labor pool of New York City.

More than 2,000 free blacks were employed in a wide variety of occupations in New York City by 1797. Two years later, the first legal steps were taken to destroy slavery as a institution in New York with the passing of the Gradual Manumission Act. All children born of slave women after the Fourth of July 1799 were freed, when females became the age of twenty-five and men reached their twenty-eighth birthdays. Then, it was deemed by New York law that every slave born before July 4, 1799, was to be freed as of July 4, 1827, on the fifty-first anniversary of the Declaration of Independence's signing.[46]

Therefore, if Emily had been brought earlier to New York City as a slave, a possibility also existed that she could have been freed in 1827 based upon this law, or eight years before she migrated to Texas in 1835, if she had been in New York City at that time. But since she had been born in New Haven and not New York City, this possibility was highly unlikely. And no primary evidence has been discovered that she was born a slave.

By her early thirties Emily aspired higher in life. After all, she had left New Haven and migrated to New York City for a new start in life. After what she had experienced at an early age in regard to society's deeply-imbedded institutional discrimination against blacks, she wanted something better for herself and family, if one existed for Emily at this time. However, like for so many of the 14,000 free blacks who lived in lower Manhattan by 1835, New York City proved to be only yet another economic and social dead-end for Emily D. West. Because she no doubt found her new life shrouded by the chaos, poverty, and crime of an urban nightmare amid sprawl of the largest city that she had ever seen, Emily very likely early became disillusioned with New York City. And this would have certainly been the case in regard to the infamous Five Points, where she most likely lived, because of the large free black presence and pressing economic considerations. In addition, Emily evidently had no ties to bind her permanently to New York City. And she apparently had no children at this time. Emily was very likely more than ready to leave New York City for greener pastures, if a good opportunity arose elsewhere. Emily's willingness to relocate perhaps indicated the extent of her ambitions and strong inner drive to get ahead in life, despite the seemingly endless obstacles that she and other free blacks, especially women, faced at almost every turn.

Simeon Jocelyn had relocated to New York City at some point in 1834, after his own New Haven home had been attacked by an anti-abolition mob, driving him from his own hometown. He was forced to leave his beloved position as minister of his modest black church on Temple Street because of fear for his personal safety. Jocelyn had earlier warned other abolitionists that it was no longer even safe for them to visit New Haven: a clear indication that the town was equally unsafe for Emily D. West.

In New York City in 1834, Jocelyn again met with abolitionist New Yorkers Lewis and Arthur Tappan and Joshua Leavitt. Here, they united their efforts to assist black people. These abolitionist leaders laid plans to help free blacks mired in the daily misery of the hellish Five Points. Combined with the Tappan brothers' fortunes, Jocelyn's wealth also helped to operate the underground railroad, bestowing timely assistance to blacks on the run after escaping bondage. The transplanted native New Havenite also introduced New York City to the Phoenix Societies, which held annual interracial meetings and dinners, and the Dorcas Societies, which made and donated clothing and blankets for the protection of black children from the bone-numbing cold of the pitiless northern winters.[47]

Nevertheless, the daily existence for free blacks in the Five Points was so challenging that even Southerners often employed its ugly examples to defend slavery, arguing that African Americans fared better under the Southern slave-master's care than as free blacks in New York City. With conviction and righteous certitude, leading Southern spokesmen declared that not a "negro quarter" in the South compared to the "picture of vice, brutality and degradation comparable" to the misery of the Five Points.[48] In truth, this was not much of an exaggeration.

New York City Riots

As demonstrated by the thorough rejection of Jocelyn's idea for the creation of a black college in New Haven and groundswell of white opposition, including even at Yale College, that erupted so suddenly much to his surprise, one of the most persistent myths in American history was the image of the stereotypical anti-slavery and racially-tolerant North. In truth and to the disillusionment of Emily D. West and other free blacks, anti-abolitionist and anti-free black hostility and violent mob action against people of color reached new heights across the North during the so-called Turbulent Thirties.[49]

Many anti-black New Yorkers openly sympathized with the South and the Democrats' choice for president, Martin Van Buren, who embraced upper class interests and pro-slavery sentiments that were necessary to win over the South to gain entry into the White House and succeed Andrew Jackson. In Machiavellian fashion to ensure victory, northern politicians masterfully played the "race card," garnering widespread support by exploiting deep-seated racial fears and anxieties among lower and middle class whites. Anti-black feeling reached such heights that anti-slavery meetings were broken up by angry mobs in New York City and elsewhere in the North. Abolitionists were widely denounced as "traitors" across New York.

In July 1834, one of the "longest [racial] riots on record" erupted in full fury, raging through New York City with a vengeance. A notable example of yellow journalism in the early Nineteenth Century, the conservative anti-abolition press fiercely attacked Lewis and Arthur Tappan for their abolitionist activities and progressive views, especially in racial matters. Inflammatory newspaper articles were calculated to stir mob violence. Whites especially feared the abolitionists' efforts toward immediate emancipation and equality for blacks, which were viewed as a racial overturning of America's social order to their detriment: the threat of a complete reversal of their social world as they knew it.

The large white mob of New Yorkers was incensed that the abolitionists, especially

Arthur Tappan, the rich silk merchant born in 1788, and his New York associates, seemed to be determined to place blacks above them. In fact, the two upper class brothers were hated even more than Garrison and his Boston abolitionist cohorts because they utilized their New York City power, wealth, and connections to advance their cause. Whites especially feared the threat of amalgamation if equality was bestowed upon blacks, believing that abolitionists viewed racial mixing as their ultimate objective and solution to America's racial dilemma. Even worse, many people across the North were convinced that racial war would result if blacks gained freedom and equality. Abolitionists became viewed as little more than devils incarnate bent on creating the greatest of all racial nightmares, Armageddon in America. It was even rumored that Tappan had divorced his white wife for the sake of a black woman's charms, providing the anti-abolitionists with a much-publicized example of the horrors of a fully integrated America and a radical disruption of the social order.

With the fear of amalgamation reaching new heights among northern whites, who preferred colonization to rid America of blacks rather than incorporating them into society, a white backlash erupted wherever African Americans and whites freely mixed. Lewis Tappan's fine home on Rose Street was attacked repeatedly by angry mobs, as was Tappan's store on Pearl Street. Then, the riot turned into a full-fledged "racial pogrom" of the worst sort, resembling the dark legacy of centuries of pogroms against the Jews across Europe that continued a historic persecution of the Hebrew people since antiquity. The homes, churches, and businesses of free blacks in the Five Points were targeted by rampaging, mostly lower class mobs, suffering the same fate of Jocelyn's own home in New Haven. African American churches, such as St. Philip's African Episcopal Church, was almost completely torn down. And an unknown number of free blacks were killed and wounded by the mob during the greatest riot in New York City's history.

Rioting continued for three days and until well-trained New York City militiamen were called out to stop the spiraling racial violence. However, before the rioting ended, a good many black homes and churches were destroyed. The terrible summer of 1834 was a nightmare for people of color, including Emily D. West, in New York City. Instead of attacking white abolitionists, the principal source of their hatred, mostly lower class whites instead turned their wrath on the city's free black population and community. No black section of New York City was hit harder by the rampaging mob than the infamous Five Points of lower Manhattan.

Emily D. West's experience during the riots has not been documented, because she left no letters, memoir, or diary. However, as a member of the New York City's free black community by this time, she might have been threatened or might have been displaced, if her place of residence was destroyed by the mob's unchecked fury. If so, then she might well have suddenly found herself destitute without income and without a place to live. Because Emily was a proud free woman from New Haven, however, she might have received some kind of timely support from Jocelyn or other abolitionists during this time of crisis, especially if she had been a member of Jocelyn's Temple Street congregation, which was almost certainly the case.[50]

And the worst was yet to come for the free black popular of New York City. Emily remained in harm's way and in the path of the racial storm. Anti-abolitionist and anti-black mob violence against free blacks reached a high-point not in 1834 but during the broiling summer of 1835. By this time Arthur Tappan—whose seemingly inexhaustible sources of money continued to fuel his wide-ranging abolitionist efforts, including Garrison's own abolitionist work, and his associates, such as Jocelyn—had become one of the most hatred men in America, both North and South. Tappan's vital abolitionist contributions indicated in part how the New York philanthropists had gained control of the anti-slave movement in the North. However, Tappan's activities to assist blacks only incensed the South to new heights, contributing to greater polarization between North and South. Louisiana citizens of East Feliciana offered a $50,000 reward for Tappan, dead or alive. Other Southern towns offered comparable rewards for the racially enlightened New Yorker, who was not intimidated. Tappan's New York City home was under constant threat of attack by the mob, but he ignored the threats to his life and property. Instead, he continued to serve as the prime economic, political, and moral force behind the anti-colonization agitation, and Tappan took little interest or effort to disguise the fact.

At the root of the ever-increasing anti–free black anger among northern whites was the belief that the abolitionists sought immediate equality for blacks and that free blacks, like Emily, would be fully incorporated into American society with complete racial assimilation by way of the much-feared process of amalgamation. Therefore, the violent white backlash mostly centered upon free blacks and the potential "threat" that they seemed to pose in terms of racial mixing, which was common in the Five Points, to the horror of most whites of New York City. By the mid–1830s, no people in all the North were more hated than free blacks, including Emily, for nothing more than her color and for nothing that she had ever done or said, especially in the highly-combustible racial climate of New York City.[51]

More Ugly Racial Turmoil in the Summer of 1835

Hostility against Tappan and his abolitionist associates and free blacks again exploded in New York City in the summer of 1835, coinciding with top temperatures that seemed to fuel the racial rage. Since the previous summer, New York City had been a simmering powder keg which finally ignited in mid–August. To many whites, it seemed that the very foundation of their social structure was under direct assault from the wealthy abolitionists, because they continued to advocate immediate emancipation and equal rights for blacks. By this time, and ignoring the threats to themselves and their families, Tappan and his active New York abolitionists had become even more aggressive in pushing forward their agendas. Knowing the power of the circulating information with the savvy of Twentieth Century journalists, they flooded the country with more than one million pieces of free anti-slavery and abolitionist propaganda. Besides the omnipresent fear of amalgamation, conspiracy-minded whites were also concerned that America's arch-enemy, Great Britain, which made for an ideal scapegoat, was behind the aggressive, well-funded efforts of the American abolitionists.[52]

The alarming fact that the North had seemingly become increasingly more pro–South in sentiment in matters of race mocked the central foundations of America's most enlightened and progressive concepts. This harsh realization of anti–free black hostility almost certainly disheartened Emily and her hopes for a brighter future. Even Congressman David Crockett, who was strongly anti–Jackson and anti–Van Buren, was upset by the fact that New York City and New York state was seemingly becoming more thoroughly pro–Southern in sentiment. As he wrote in a letter to Charles Schultz on Christmas Day, 1834: "I have almost given up the Ship at last [because] if Martin Van Buren is elected [then] I will leave the United States [and] I will go to the wildes of Texas. I will consider that [anti-slavery Mexican] government a paradise to what this will be .... Our Republican government has dwindled almost into insignificance, our boasted land of liberty have almost Bowed to the Yoke of Bondage."[53]

The fates of Congressman Crockett, who was essentially a populist, and Emily D. West were about to be set on a course to the far southwest frontier of Texas, arriving at about the same time in part because of the Northeast's political and social upheavals.

At the same time that Crockett—dogged by nagging debts, personal failures on multiple levels, and the end of a once shining political career as a flamboyant Tennessee congressman—prepared to leave the United States for brighter prospects in Texas, so Emily faced a comparable dead-end situation in New York City that had seemingly rejected her very presence. After all, the clock of progressive thought in racial matters had been turned back in New York City not only for the privileges of free blacks but also for their very safety in the streets. Animosity became so pronounced that increasing numbers free blacks were thrown out of their occupational positions, both skilled and menial Emily also might have lost a menial job, which was almost certainly a domestic position. Since most adult free blacks now back in New Haven and those transplanted in New York City from New Haven were members of the artisan class, including skilled jobs like carpenter, mason, and blacksmith, this major racial upheaval came as a heavy blow to the fragile economic structure of the black community. Emily's husband, if married, or boyfriend, if either was the case, might have also lost his employment, causing greater hardship and diminishing future prospects for her in New York City.

Free blacks lost a good many skilled positions to white immigrants, especially the Irish, in the North's much-proclaimed "free" society. Therefore, greater numbers of free blacks were now denied the means of making a living: the bitter irony that life for many northern free blacks was worse than even for some Africans, especially house slaves, in slavery. Clearly, with the increased racial intolerance, the post-slavery lives for many blacks in the North proved to be even more challenging than under slavery.

Because of the race riots during the summer of 1835, Emily might have not only lost her job but also her New York City residence by this time. The once prevalent opportunities for free blacks across New York City were fast fading away like a hot summer evening along the Long Island Sound. In the words of historian Edgar J. McManus: "Hemmed in by hostility and pilloried by demagogues, great numbers of Negroes sank to the level of pariahs condemned to a bitter existence on the fringe of free society. Their isolation was complete. The Negroes were in a very real sense a population in quarantine, trapped in a system of racial bondage in many ways as cruel and intolerable as slavery."[54]

By the summer of 1835, economic hard times descended upon the United States, thanks to over-speculation in western lands and irresponsible banks over-extending credit and financial commitments, eventually leading to a full-blown depression in 1837. And, of course, economic hardships always fell hardest on the lowest rungs of society, especially free blacks who lived on the margins of society. Consequently, everyday life and existence certainly became harder for Emily, who suddenly found herself in a no-win situation and downward spiral that became worse than what had existed in New Haven. Perhaps Garrison said it best in regard to the sad, if not tragic, plight of free blacks across the North, including in New Haven or New York City. He lamented "the burdens under which the free people of color labor" because "you are not free [as] you are not sufficiently protected in your persons and rights."[55]

An educated, refined English traveler to America in 1831, Thomas Hamilton was appalled by what little America and its much-touted promise of liberty offered to free blacks. A horrified Hamilton described with disgust how free blacks in the North "are subjected to the most grinding and humiliating of all slaveries, that of universal and unconquerable prejudice. The whip, indeed, has been removed from the back of the Negro, but the chains are still on his limbs, and he bears the brand of degradation on his forehead. What is it but the mere abuse of language to call him *free* [because] the law, in truth, has left him in that most pitiable of all conditions, *a masterless slave*."[56]

Another astute foreign observer of the complexities and contradictions of race relations in America was French traveler Alexis de Tocqueville. He was shocked to discover that free blacks in the North "can share neither the rights, nor the pleasures, nor the labor, nor the afflictions, nor the tomb of him whose equal he has been declared to be; and he [or she] cannot meet him upon fair terms in life or in death."[57] Emily had every reason to gain an increasing desire to leave the North, and the difficult life that she knew only too well in New York City, which was now just another major American city divided by race and torn by hatred.

David Crockett and Emily West were convinced of the wisdom of migrating to Texas about the same time in part because of the unbelievable depths of depravity that they had seen in the Five Points which Crockett visited in 1834. Emily was naturally troubled by the steady deterioration of race relations in the North, which made her life in New York City more risky and precarious. By 1830, more than two million slaves labored in the largest democracy and the largest slave-owning nation in the world: the tragic paradox of American history. Slavery had long served as a sturdy foundation for the American economy, and the mid–1830s was no different.

Slave pens and auction blocks in the District of Columbia stood under the shadow of the national capitol's stately dome, conducting a brisk business to reveal the epitome of America's hypocrisy to a free-thinking, independent woman like Emily. She probably came to a new realization that was only reconfirmed with the New York City racial riots: the land of her birth, the United States, was simply no place for an enterprising and ambitious young free black woman to get ahead and prosper. She was vulnerable to mob violence and could be kidnapped and sold into slavery while merely attempting to scratch out a meager living for herself. The western frontier of Texas seemed to offer a more promising and even a secure place where a free black woman could at least retain a measure of her dignity, sense of self, and personal worth. Texas was the far-away land that offered opportunities which now existed in another country—Mexico—that promised a better life.[58]

Emily was forced to flee a place that had once been a haven for enterprising single women back when the Dutch reigned supreme in New Amsterdam. At that time, Manhattan stood at the heart of the thriving commercial colony, New Netherland, and presented unprecedented opportunities to young single Dutch women, such as the remarkable Margaret Hardenbroeck Philipse. She became wealthy and highly respected in Dutch colonial society as one of the "she-merchants," by creating a personal empire based upon international trade, including for slaves. Indeed, Manhattan had early "welcome[d] autonomous, self-sufficient women to its shores," which presented opportunities to young single women like no other colony in the Seventeenth Century.[59]

Emily found no such inviting possibilities or opportunities as a free black woman in the ghettos of New York City. Like many people, especially blacks, left out of the mainstream of American life, Emily probably embraced a personal value system that not only rejected slavery but also America's materialism and greed at the expense of other human beings. Neither Emily's identify or self-esteem were permanently tied to the United States, which so crassly exploited people of color to increase its wealth, prosperity, and standing in the world: a most discouraging situation which likely made her look toward a new land of opportunity.[60]

Another adventurous woman of spirit and New Haven native was likewise smitten by

"Texas fever" during this period, Mary Austin Holley. She was the intellectual, gifted daughter of Elijah Austin. He was the brother of Moses Austin, whose son, Stephen Fuller Austin, was now the empresario of the thriving Anglo-Celtic colony situated along the Brazos and Colorado Rivers. Austin, a hard-working bachelor obsessed with the opportunities presented by Texas, was as smitten with his cousin, a literary talent and cultured sophisticate of fine tastes, as she was with him. But as an unkind fate would have it, their relationship never had an opportunity to blossom as planned because of the brewing conflict between Texas and Mexico.[61]

Holley's dream of the possibilities of a new life in Texas began with a January 21, 1831, letter that he wrote to "My dear Cousin." In this letter, the now widowed New Haven native explained to Austin that "with regard to my son, I have thought that I would write to you and renew our acquaintance, in order to learn what prospect Texas would offer to him ... whether it would be an object for me to take any steps with such views—securing land—etc. [and] I have thought, too, if my brothers could make it their interest to remove to Texas, we could there build up our fallen family in new hope and happiness."[62]

Holley and other Austin family members, in her own words, were now "full of Texas" and the boundless promise that this far-away, almost mystical land held to grip both heart and mind of those many Americans who fell under its bewitching spell. After all, their own cousin, the most adventurous and ambitious family member, had carved out a new world in the untamed wilderness yet undeveloped by Mexico.[63] From the colony's capital of San Felipe de Austin on the muddy waters of the Brazos River, Austin was delighted about the prospect of Holley and other family members joining him in Texas. Here, in a land of seemingly endless potential, he envisioned that they could "form a little world of our own," as he optimistically hoped and penned in a July 1831.[64] In this same letter, Austin also revealed to Holley his deepest, all-consuming passion at the time: "The credit of settling this fine country and laying the foundation for a new Nation which at some future period will arise here cannot be taken from me; and that part of my family who have ventured to follow me [to Texas] will be sufficiently provided for."[65]

Therefore, as empresario with the right to issue land grants as guaranteed by the Mexican government, Austin bestowed to his cousin a league of land, "a good tract," in Austin's understated words, on mid–June 1831.[66] Eager for a new start as a large landowner on the southwest frontier, Mary Austin Holley visited Texas in the fall of 1831 to not only take a look at her newly-granted tracts situated near the western end of Galveston Bay, but also to gather information for the forthcoming books that she planned to write about this most inviting land of Texas. After crossing the Gulf of Mexico from New Orleans to reach Texas and then pushing northwest up the Brazos, an awed Holley wrote, "There is nothing in the whole course of the Ohio and Mississippi, for quiet beauty, to be compared with the Brazos."[67]

She described the romance, spiritual power and sense of wonder that Texas inspired in her. "One's feelings in Texas are unique and original, and very like a dream or youthful vision realized. Here, as in Eden, man feels alone with the God of nature, and seems, in a peculiar manner, to enjoy the rich bounties of heaven, in common with all created things."[68]

The admiration of Mary Austin Holley, a distinguished daughter of New Haven and its merchant class society, toward her dynamic, visionary cousin never diminished for the remainder of her eventful life. As she penned in a prophetic 1836 tribute: "When, in the progress of years, the state of Texas shall take her place among the powerful empires of the American continent, her citizens will doubtless regard Gen. [Stephen Fuller] Austin as their patriarch, and children will be taught to hold his name in reverence."[69]

CHAPTER III

A New Life and Adventure Beckons

The opportunities of Texas beckoned as much to Emily as to Mary Austin Holley. After what she had experienced in regard to the prejudice, intolerance, and racial hatred across the North, Emily no doubt felt much like a frustrated Charlotte Forten, a Philadelphia-born free black woman of higher social and economic status than Emily, and the promising granddaughter of wealthy abolitionist James Forten, Jr., who contributed his efforts and ample finances to the abolitionist cause: "Again and again there rises the question, When, oh! When shall this cease."[1] Both grandfather and granddaughter Forten dedicated their lives, passions, and efforts to ending the horror of slavery in America. It is not known but Emily might also have gained comparable views about equality and a longing for a better place in life in part from her own mother. After all, Emily and her mother were part of a matriarchal society and kinship network that distinguished African American society from European influenced white patriarchal society. These were distinctive cultural qualities that had been transferred to America from West Africa.[2]

Additionally, both slave and free black families were in fact "unusually egalitarian," where women enjoyed a more equal status with males compared to white women in the traditional family of America's patriarchal society, where the male dominated family, society, and occupations.[3] Emily benefited from her mother's influence and a host of distinctive cultural legacies from West African matriarchal society, and she lived her life "very much in the pattern of their female African ancestors who had for generations stood at the center of the African family."[4]

As antagonism increased toward more than 320,000 free blacks across the United States, by 1830 Texas had gained a reputation as a land of opportunity and relatively safe haven for blacks. Here, in Tejas (Texas) under the liberal, racially-tolerant laws of Mexico, which had remained true to its egalitarian and revolutionary traditions and to the many blacks who served in the lengthy revolutionary struggle against Spain, people of color experienced far more freedom. Mexico had turned against slavery like most other civilized nations of the world. Consequently, free blacks in the neighboring republic could marry any race they chose, and own land and other forms of property. They were not restricted from their rights as a Mexican citizen by a lowly status determined only by color as in the United States. Unlike in America, where free blacks like Solomon Northup were kidnapped and sold into slavery, free blacks were safe under the liberal laws of the Mexican Constitution, which recognized them as full citizens in the Republic of Mexico.

For such reasons, free blacks from the United States migrated to Texas even before

Mexico won its independence from Spain in 1821. Neighboring Louisiana, especially lower Louisiana, contained the largest free black population in the South, which amounted to around 10 percent in the early Nineteenth Century. Greenbury B. Logan, the son of a slave mother and white master father, who was freed by his father, David, was one early free black pioneer in Texas. He migrated from the slave state of Missouri to Texas with his wife, Judah Duncan, and their five children in February 1831. Greenbury Logan, a thirty-three-year-old blacksmith, and his family made their Texas dream come true in the pristine, heavily-timbered lands along Chocolate Bayou in the lower Brazos River country, after Greenbury secured a full league of land on December 22, 1831.

Mexican law was essentially colorblind, thanks to the legacies of mixed-race priest revolutionary leaders who abolished slavery by force, in stark contrast to the law of the land across the United States. Abolitionist Benjamin Lundy visited Texas in the summer of 1834 and could hardly believe his eyes. He was astounded by the sight of the prosperous lives enjoyed by free blacks in San Antonio de Béxar, located on the sprawling central Texas plains, and Nacogdoches amid the pine forests of east Texas. Thanks to Lundy's well-publicized views about the greater equality for blacks in the Mexican lands of Texas, New England abolitionists, like Jocelyn, began to view Texas as an ideal place for free blacks to start a new life outside the United States.

On October 25, 1835, Emily's life was destined to change forever, when she made her most momentous decision. On this autumn day at "a portside coffeehouse" in New York City, Emily D. West signed an employment contract to work in far-away Texas located on the isolated northern frontier of the Republic of Mexico. Indicating that she had received some education and almost certainly through Jocelyn's teachings of free blacks in New Haven, a literate Emily signed a one-year contract of indenture in the employment of James Morgan, writing her name in a fine hand. She signed up to work for one year as a cook and housekeeper at a new hotel at a new frontier community on the Gulf Coast plain.

The New Washington Hotel was owned by a land speculation company known as the New Washington Association. This association had been founded by New York City investors (like today's venture capitalists) in mid-1834 for the express purpose of raising sizeable funds for the purchase of "a strategic, high" peninsula that overlooked the San Jacinto River at the northwest head of Galveston Bay. At the center of New Washington, the newly-built hotel stood at the tip of this fertile peninsula that jutted eastward into shining, blue waters, called Clopper's Point—today's Morgan's Point, Texas—on Galveston Bay and at the wide mouth of the San Jacinto River. Emily was only one of a number of free northern blacks who signed up to work for Morgan, who was the company's enterprising agent and manager, as laborers and artisans, such as carpenters, a common occupation of free blacks.

Jocelyn served as a witness when Emily signed the contract to work for the New Washington Association. Jocelyn even signed his own name to Emily's employment contract. It seems Jocelyn played a role in assisting not only Emily, but also other free blacks, who signed up with Morgan, in starting a new life in far-away east Texas. Clearly, by this time, Emily D. West had complete trust and faith in Jocelyn, who was from her own hometown.

The New Washington colony was located in an untamed frontier, where women were relatively scarce. Texas was a rough, harsh land dominated primarily by men who had migrated to take advantage of new economic opportunities. Emily's skills as a laundress, housekeeper, and cook were much in demand at both the New Washington Hotel and the fledgling settlement situated in a most picturesque setting that stood like a glowing promise of a New Canaan amid the Gulf Coastal Plain wilderness.

Besides Emily, also signing up for a one-year contract with Morgan were other free blacks and Scottish Highlands immigrants. Many of the newly-signed employees were much-needed skilled workers such as craftsmen and seamstresses. These Scottish Highlanders hailed from an ancient Celtic land of towering mountains that were the very antithesis of the low-lying coastal plain.

By this time, many blacks from Five Points had been displaced by the ugly race riots and the northeast's nascent industrial revolution that resulted in more mass-produced goods than handmade items crafted by free black artisans. Another who decided to journey to Texas and become part of the New Washington settlement was Diana Leonard, a washerwoman. Like Emily, she signed a one-year contract with Morgan, and hailed from New Haven. Legally, Emily and these other immigrants were short-term bonded domestic servants as opposed to long-term indentured servants in the Eighteenth Century tradition.

Formed in October 1835 and backed by $60,000 of eastern money provided by rich New York City financiers, the New Washington Association was a bold speculative venture backed especially by the wealthy chairman of the board and president of the company, Samuel Swartwout. Like other opportunistic investors, Swartwout was infected by Texas fever. Gambling at high stakes in a bold speculative venture in the hope of reaping fantastic profits once Texas land prices rose to lofty levels in the near future, they sought to get rich from New Washington's growth, development, and future prosperity. One chief principal of the New Washington Association was a Mexican aristocrat, the liberal-minded and pro-republican Lorenzo de Zavala. James Treat, the former Mexican consul in New York City, served as secretary. He and the New York City financiers had organized the company to purchase and develop Texas real estate on a massive scale. Zavala was the former Mexican ambassador to France before making an enemy of Antonio López de Santa Anna. He was destined to become future vice president of a new, independent Texas Republic.

For Morgan's part, employing free blacks was much cheaper than purchasing slaves. Morgan had been born in Philadelphia, Pennsylvania, on October 13, 1787, at a time when the city contained the largest free black population in the United States. Therefore, Morgan very likely had early associations with some free blacks. However, thanks to his North Carolina upbringing in an environment dominated by slavery, he was also a slave owner.

After he had first visited Texas in 1830, Morgan decided to open up a mercantile establishment there. He migrated from Florida to the port of Anahauc, Texas, on the northeast bank of Trinity Bay, the northeast arm of Galveston Bay. Here, he opened his store, becoming a businessman. Morgan migrated to Texas with at least sixteen slaves, whom he legally bound with indentures of ninety-nine years as required by Mexican law to circumvent the republic's legal restrictions against slavery, and with his wife, Celia Harrell, a son, and two daughters.

This seeming contradiction in Morgan's nature in matters of race reflected the paradox of the American settlement in Texas that mirrored the overall dilemma and contradiction of the United States, where reality clashed with rhetoric. From the beginning with the establishment of the colony of Stephen Fuller Austin, whose family roots extended back to New Haven and their patriarch Elijah Austin, along the fertile lands of the lower Brazos and Colorado River Valley in the early 1820s, Anglo-Celts, mostly from the South, had first settled in Texas with their slaves. Continuing the great dream of establishing a colony of American settlers in Texas began by his now deceased father, Moses Austin, Stephen was "astonished at [the] natural beauties and many valuable resources" of Texas. By 1835, Texas was an isolated northern borderland where slavery was tolerated and slave smuggling was rampant to reap high profits. Nevertheless, free blacks were treated with greater equality than in the United

States, because of the liberal laws and more enlightened social and cultural traditions of Mexico, which had abolished slavery in mid–September 1829.

Not only demonstrating empathy toward free blacks, including Emily, Morgan also shortly displayed compassion—at a time when little was forthcoming from Texians—for vanquished Mexican soldiers captured at San Jacinto in April 1836 and held in captivity on Galveston Island, which he commanded as a Texas colonel. Morgan was a complex person, both northerner and southerner. To promote his own interests and those of the New Washington Association, he maneuvered carefully and with skill between his northern employers, investors, and friends and his slave-owning Texas friends.

After all, his association with northern abolitionists like Jocelyn and free blacks explained why Emily was bound for New Washington in the near future. Reflecting the beliefs of board members and fellow stockholders from the northeast, Morgan believed that the New Washington Association would benefit from the labor of free blacks, combining an unique mix of humanitarianism and commercialism for a colonizing experiment on the Texas frontier.

In Morgan, however, Emily found a man quite unlike Jocelyn in fundamental ways. Morgan was not only the agent and a large stockholder of a speculative company but also a slave owner. With the ample funds of New York City investors he had purchased an enormous quantity of land in the Harrisburg and Liberty municipalities, and slaves were yet needed to develop this land to make it profitable and productive. Some evidence existed that he had brought as many as 30 slaves from Florida to Texas in 1830. Explaining their seemingly contradictory partnership, Morgan and Jocelyn, who were both ambitious visionaries and natural businessmen, shared a passion for exploiting new economic opportunities. These two enterprising white men, one from Connecticut and the other from Texas, separated by a distance of more than 1,000 miles, had a dramatic effect on the life of Emily D. West.[5]

The prospects for the New Washington Association improved dramatically when the Texas Revolution erupted in early October 1835. At that time, one Texian rebel declared in no uncertain terms that "the Rubicon is crossed, and it is now of vital importance in Texas that we should be immediately reinforced" by volunteers from the United States.[6] If the Anglo-Celtic colonists of Texas won their bid in breaking away from Mexico, then land prices would rise and future economic development would greatly accelerate. Therefore, on October 23, 1835, less than three weeks after the Texas Revolution's outbreak, formal articles of agreement for the establishment of the New Washington Association had been officially signed by principals.[7]

Only two days later, October 25 was one of the most important days in the life of Emily D. West. Unlike many white female pioneers in Texas, including Susanna Dickinson, a future Alamo survivor from the backwoods of west Tennessee who never received an education, Emily basked in her own educational background and literacy.[8] With fine penmanship, including the added flourish of a tight curl on the left top corner her middle initial, "D," which revealed her education, Emily signed the following contract:

> This agreement, made & entered into by and between Emily West of New Haven, Connecticut of the one part & James Morgan of Texas of the other part, Witnesseth that the said West hereby binds herself that she will go out in said Morgan's vessel [the schooner *Flash*] to Texas and there work for said Morgan at any kind of house work she, said West, is qualified to do and to industrially pursue the same from the time she commences until the end of twelve months and not to quit or leave said Morgan's employ after she commences work for him, at any time whatever, without said Morgan's consent, until the end of twelve months aforesaid, said Morgan hereby binding himself to the said West out to Texas, on board said Morgan's vessel, free of expense, and

to set said West to work within one week after she gets there, if not sooner, said Morgan agreeing to pay said West at the rate of one hundred dollars per year, said wages to be paid every three months, if required.

In witness whereof the parties have hereunto set their hands and seal in New York this 25th day of October 1835, In the presence of Frederick Platt and Simeon L. Jocelyn.[9]

According to the agreement, she would sail south on one of the company's two ocean-going schooners (the *Flash* and the *Kosciuszko*), which were swift, two-masted vessels with narrow hulls. However, this lengthy journey down the East Coast and into the Gulf of Mexico was not without risk. Like Emily in 1835, the young son of Sojourner Truth, who widely toured the North as a influential anti-slavery and feminist lecturer, disappeared at sea while sailing on a whaling voyage. Peter was never seen again, like the dream of so many free blacks who struggled in vain to get ahead in life in an unkind America.[10]

The risk was high for Emily, who most of all was now placing her absolute trust and faith in whites, a risky proposition for blacks, especially a woman. Around this time, Charlotte Forten, despite her fine education and upper class northern upbringing not shared by Emily, despite her New Haven background and having grown up in the shadow of Yale University, described the disheartening situation for free blacks in America: "Oh! It is hard to go through life meeting contempt with contempt, hatred with hatred, fearing, with too good reason, to have and trust hardly anyone whose skin is white."[11]

As specified in her binding contract of employment, Emily had other choices to make that would play a large role in her future. She could wait a full year before receiving $100 for her labors, or she could take regular payments in installments every three months. If she already had some money available or saved up from her menial work in New York City, then she would have been savvy to defer the payment of her salary for a full year so as not to pay the high costs for food and other necessary items sold by Morgan's store, where prices were high as goods were imported, at New Washington, essentially a form of debt peonage.

The contract that Emily signed in New York City recognized that she was a free woman and not an indentured servant for ninety-nine years like the large numbers of slaves that had long poured into Texas. They included blacks brought across the Sabine River by Morgan himself, under this legal loop-hole of indentured servitude to promote Anglo-Celtic settlement, because Mexico had abolished slavery in 1829. Since 1828, the state legislature of Coahulia and Texas, united in 1824, had allowed exemptions for Americans to bring their slaves into Texas by way of the indentured servitude concept.[12]

As a free black woman and unlike most blacks in America, Emily was exercising the advantages of her free status: the right to make her own decisions, be mobile, and to change employers by her own free will.[13] Most significant, Emily's decision to migrate to Texas was not only a bold one for a free black woman on her own, but also represented an utter rejection of any colonization that required United States–born blacks to forsake America for Africa. By going to Texas, she was at least staying on the North American continent, and could easily return to the northeast. Colonization was based on the concept that America was for whites only, a concept detested by blacks who had known America all their lives. Quite simply, America was their home.

Emily ruled out becoming part of any colonization effort in Africa by deciding to go to Texas. Many free blacks, perhaps even Emily herself, across the North had voiced their contempt for the Colonization Society and its efforts to transport blacks out of America forever. After all, the overall concept of colonization was more anti-black than it was anti-slavery, and even strengthened the institution of slavery by forcing free blacks from the nation's borders. Along with other abolitionists, therefore, Garrison denounced the colonization efforts to ship free blacks far away as "a libel upon humanity." Free black outrage at the concept of colonization not only indicated "the degree to which free Negroes of the country had attained self-respect," but also the universal acceptance of the fact that they were true Americans, who loved their country as much as United States–born whites and deserved equal rights in the land of the free. Like so many other free blacks, Emily believed that America was her home and not Africa.

Such a thorough rejection was voiced by blacks of New Haven during an 1831 meeting, which Emily might have attended. At that time, they formed the "Peace and Benevolent Society of African-Americans." Then these free blacks of New Haven declared in no uncertain terms: "We are Americans and any of us who goes to colonization [and Africa or elsewhere] is either weak in mind or a traitor." In much the same way, Emily demonstrated comparable "self-respect" like so many other free blacks around the United States by choosing to go to Texas rather than to Africa, which was only another strange, foreign land to her.[14]

However, Emily was now preparing to leave the United States and the land of her birth, but not in the sense of completely rejecting it, as she had only a one-year contract. Greater social advantages, overall acceptance, and economic opportunities for her beckoned in this much publicized northern province of the Republic of Mexico. Especially as a free black woman and like so many other people of color, Emily very likely felt a sense of not only disillusionment but also resentment, because of the intensity of white opposition in New Haven to Jocelyn's college and the overall concept of black advancement. Therefore, she might have felt a sense of good riddance to the United States and its hypocrisy.

A healthy, strong sense of black self-identity and "race pride" had been developed among the African American population in New Haven during her formative years. Such qualities would serve Emily well during the stern challenges posed by life in Texas. Jocelyn and other dynamic black leaders of New Haven succeeded in developing a distinct sense of race consciousness and "Negro" independence, including among young black women like Emily, who had been taught to read and write in this relatively enlightened environment.

Emily probably felt this sense of pride in herself and her distinctive African American heritage. However, like other Nineteenth Century blacks, Emily most likely emphasized her "American-ness," while minimizing the emotional bond with her African antecedents, choosing to remain in the only homeland (a community of Americans in Mexican territory and on the North American continent) that she had ever known. But after her harsh experiences of everyday life in New Haven and New York City, Emily very likely also viewed Texas as a distant place where she might be able to better preserve that individual dignity, self-respect, and a sense of pride.[15]

She had never been to another country before or beyond her native northeast. At the small infant community of New Washington, she envisioned quite correctly the start of a new life with enthusiasm and hope. The native New Englander must have felt quite excited about the prospect of a new start in life and an adventure in a land far from the slums of New York City.

Her decision to go to Texas revealed not only an ambitious quality but also a hopeful, positive outlook on life. Best of all in these tough economic times, she would reap a total sum of $100 for her one-year employment of performing "house work" at the New Washington hotel, and free passage aboard a company vessel. Land was so plentiful in Texas that perhaps she even could save her money and buy her own piece of property, becoming a proud landowner in the western frontier tradition. Such coveted opportunities were unavailable and impossible for a financially hard-pressed free black woman in New York City, especially in the dismal squalor of the Five Points.

Since the early 1820s after the first colony of American settlers was established by Stephen Fuller Austin, who had continued the colonization initiative begun by his father, Moses Austin, a flood of Anglo-Celtic hopeful migrants from across the United States, especially the South, had crossed the Sabine River, the boundary between Mexican Texas and the United States, Louisiana, to enter Texas. By 1835, only a relative handful of migrants had officially entered Texas with the Mexican government's blessings, setting the stage for eventual conflict with Mexico, because of wide political, cultural, and racial differences. Most people from the United States migrated to Texas as squatters, taking possession of land owned by Mexico where they found it and against Mexican laws. Like these opportunistic Anglo-Celtic settlers, Emily also looked toward the setting sun to fulfill her ambitions and dreams by the fall of 1835.

When she signed her employment agreement in New York City on October 25, Emily did not know that only 23 days before, the first fighting had erupted between a small but feisty band of Anglo-Celtic colonists and Mexican troops at a little western frontier town, Gonzales, just east of San Antonio de Béxar and the westernmost extension of the colonization effort. Unknown by Emily, a people's revolution, sparked by the feisty volunteers of Gonzales, against the central government in Mexico City had already begun. And this conflict, in no small part fought over the issue of slavery, was destined to thwart the lofty ambitions of the New Washington Association, forever alter the life of Emily D. West, and change the fate of Texas.

Initiating the triumph and tragedy of the Texas Revolution, this brief clash of arms near Gonzales, the westernmost Anglo-Celtic settlement in Texas, became known as the "Lexington of the Texas Revolution." Here, on the lush grasslands of the Ezekiel Williams' ranch on the warm morning of October 2, 1835, eighteen citizen-soldiers of Gonzales stood up to around 100 mounted Mexican soldados dispatched from San Antonio on a mission. These hardy Texians refused to relinquish a little cannon that had been loaned to the people of Gonzales by the Mexican government for defense against Indians. As the only Anglo-Celtic settlement on the vulnerable western frontier and west of the Colorado River and deep in hostile Indian country, the relatively few settlers of Gonzales yet needed the artillery piece for their own and the community's survival.

Like their Massachusetts Minutemen forefathers at Lexington Green, just outside Boston back in April 1775, the Texas revolutionaries' fiery defiance was best exemplified not only in retaining the small cannon for their own use but also in a most creative homemade battle-flag. Fashioned from the dress of an Irish bride, this white battle-flag was made by the women of Gonzales, including Susanna Dickinson, who was destined to lose her captain-husband, Almeron Dickinson, at the Alamo on March 6, 1836. An authentic revolutionary banner waved by defiant Gonzales settlers, who had been born in the United States, was decorated with the taunting words "Come and Take It," fluttering proudly in the summer-like breeze sweeping off the brown waters of the Guadalupe River on this foggy morning. A blast of homemade canister-pieces of scrap iron and cut-up chains from the little cannon altered the course of history.[16]

But this homespun rebellion against Mexico was much more complex than simple analogies comparing the colonists' struggle of 1835 to that of their forefathers of the American Revolution. This struggle of the Texian colonists was also very much about slavery and cotton. Cotton was among the first crops grown by the Spanish at the old Franciscan missions, including the one called the Alamo at San Antonio de Béxar, along the San Antonio River seventy-five miles to the west. When the Gonzales colonists rose up in defiance, the economy and society of Texas was dominated by slavery and cotton culture, an extension of the Deep South plantation system that had been seamlessly transferred by settlers from east of the Sabine. After the first shots were fired in anger in Gonzales, leaders implored fellow citizens to rise up or become "the menial slaves of military despotism" from Mexico City. In October 1835 after the dramatic opening clash of arms at Gonzales, Texian volunteers grabbed their smoothbore muskets, hunting rifles, and shotguns and rode off to war to contest Mexican rule over Texas, which they viewed rhetorically (rather than realistically) as "worse than Egyptian bondage."[17]

Unknown to Emily by the time that she had decided to journey to Texas, Southerners, especially those in the Deep South, envisioned the creation of "a great slave republic stretching from the Potomac to the Rio Grande." Nor was Emily fully aware of the fact that perhaps as many as 150 free African Americans, with the full rights as Mexican citizens, lived in Texas by 1835. These enterprising free blacks, mostly from the United States, had managed to carve out a distinctive life for themselves in an increasingly Anglo-Celtic land, although owned by Mexico and inhabited by a small Tejano population, because of the unrestricted flood of illegal immigration across the Sabine.[18]

A number of free blacks joined the fight to drive General Martín Perfecto de Cos, who had been dispatched north by Antonio López de Santa Anna in September 1835, and more than 1,000 of his troops out of San Antonio de Béxar. Here, with the Alamo compound continuing to stand firm for defenders regardless of race or nationality, the soldiers of Mexico had concentrated to contest the possession of Texas. Meanwhile, Texian revolutionaries rose up across Texas. The first Texas casualty of the uprising against Mexico City, which was waged in large part to protect slavery against an abolitionist Mexico, was a free black man, Samuel McCulloch, Jr. McCulloch's fall, only two days before this twenty-sixth birthday, during the October 9, 1835, attack on the Mexican garrison at Goliad was most symbolic.

After all, the first American casualty of the American Revolution was a runaway slave who was cut down during the so-called Boston Massacre, Crispus Attucks. This natural rebel with a Roman name had not only defied his Framingham, Massachusetts, master's authority but also that of the British government and military. The fifty-one-year-old Attucks led the mob in harassing the occupying British soldiers, who fired on the menacing crowd of Boston rowdies out of fear. Attucks, a powerful man who was the product of a white father and slave mother (like McCulloch) and stood six foot two inches, hailed from New England. Falling on March 5, 1770, with a handful of other colonists of the rampaging mob, this defiant black sailor for the past two decades became one of the earliest martyrs of America's struggle for liberty.

The Celtic-Gaelic last name of Attucks indicated that his white father possessed Irish roots and heritage. McCulloch had been born in 1810 in Abbeville, situated amid the rolling hills of the fertile Piedmont of northwest South Carolina, of Samuel McCulloch, Sr., and a slave mother. The McCulloch family had migrated to Texas from the cotton country of Montgomery County, in south central Alabama, in May 1835, the same year that Emily migrated to Texas. The bestowing of his own name, Samuel McCulloch, Jr., by the master was a rare acknowledgment of paternity. His son was also literate at a time when slaves in the South were denied an education by law. McCulloch had received an education, and enjoyed the benefits of literacy like his three sisters, Mahaly, Jane, and Harriet, who were also free blacks. As a single man concerned about the future welfare of his children, Samuel McCulloch, Sr., had fled to Latino Texas because it was considerably more racially tolerant than the Deep South. He settled the family in the low-lying, fertile lands along the Lavaca River, which flowed southeast into Lavaca Bay, which was an extension of Matagorda Bay, that led to the Gulf of Mexico.

Facing his baptismal fire on October 9, 1835, as a private of the Matagorda Volunteer Company, McCulloch marched forth with an ad hoc Texian force in the surprise attack on Goliad. In the foremost ranks, he took a serious shoulder wound—an injury from a large caliber musket ball that troubled him well into old age—during the Texans' attack that captured the strong Mexican fortified position, manned only by a token garrison of soldados, on the morning of October 10, 1835.

McCulloch was the only Texian hit during the attack on the old Spanish mission turned fortress situated on a slight rise on the San Antonio River, Presidio la Bahia. But, in many ways, McCulloch might have been the most symbolic casualty of the entire Texas Revolution, because issues of slavery and race were primary determinants leading to open warfare between Mexico and its Anglo-Celtic settlers, which included free blacks who have been mostly forgotten. For instance, Kentucky-born Benjamin Rush Milam, a forty-three-year-old War of 1812 veteran who was later killed in leading the attack on the Alamo against Cos' forces on December 5, 1835, has been long seen as the "First Hero of the Texas Revolution," while McCulloch's earlier revolutionary role has been long overlooked, primarily because of his color and the darkest secret of the Texas Revolution, slavery.[19]

During the same month that Emily was destined to arrive in Texas for the first time in her life, the Texians, thanks in part to Milam's leadership role and Texian courage, scored their greatest victory of the 1835 Texas campaign by capturing San Antonio de Béxar, forcing the surrender of Cos' forces trapped in the Alamo on December 9. A principal guide of one of the two Texian assault columns, commanded by Francis White Johnson, was a free black, Hendrick Arnold. Described as "one of the oldest and boldest pioneers of the West," Arnold returned from a hunting trip just in time to lead Milam and his 300 volunteers in the final assault on San Antonio.

Texian leaders, including Milam, "valued Arnold's expertise so highly that they delayed the attack for a day so that he could participate." Most significant, this free African American soldier—an authentic black Texian of distinction—was highly respected by white Texians, and they clearly needed his services to reap their greatest success in 1835. The Texas Revolution's demands and the mutual defense of the Texian homeland created a greater bond of some free blacks to their white neighbors, because they believed they were fighting for common interests and a mutual goal: to hurl the Mexican troops out of Texas and win independence.

Arnold was a close companion and good friend of the best Texian scout of the Texas Revolutionary Army, Erastus "Deaf" Smith. He hailed from the Tejano town of San Antonio de Béxar, where both Arnold and Smith lived as neighbors and among the few Americans from the United States. While Smith—born in Duchess County, New York, north of New York City and the author of a 1836 poem that honored the memory of the fallen Milam, whom he described as "a high, heroic soul"—has gained widespread recognition as the Texians' best scout, Arnold has been forgotten in part because of his color. Working as a highly-effective white-black scouting team, they provided invaluable and timely intelligence to the Texas revolutionary army from beginning to end.

Arnold was a frontiersman and a legendary hunter who had pursued the herds of migrating buffalo across the central plains and other big game. He had wed the stepdaughter of Smith's first wife, who was Tejano. The two were both married to Tejano women, indicating their successful assimilation into Tejano culture and society. Both men spoke Spanish and knew the manners and customs of not only the Tejanos, but more importantly, their opponents from Mexico. After arriving in San Antonio in 1821 from Natchez, Mississippi, where he was raised, Smith married the wealthy, attractive Tejano widow Guadalupe Ruiz Duran, a descendent of the first Canary Islanders who settled in San Antonio de Béxar and were among the town's elite. They had four daughters, three of whom survived to adulthood.

Providing reliable service from the beginning to end of the Texas Revolution, Arnold continued to serve in his father-in-law's spy company during the San Jacinto campaign, after Houston had made Smith his chief of scouts. Smith won recognition as "the far famed Spy [Scout] of Texas," unlike Arnold. Arnold's contributions and sacrifices to the winning of Texas independence were valuable and came at no small price. In January 1836, he petitioned for aid from the Texas government to assist his hard-pressed family, because his family members "are in a state of destitution [and] they have been reduced thereto by the present struggle for liberty" that brought poverty to so many settlers in Texas.

Greenbury Logan was another little-known daring and resourceful free black who served with distinction in the "Army of the People" of Texas. He was a strong-armed blacksmith who lived in Missouri before migrating to Texas in 1831. Logan had been born a slave in Kentucky in 1799, before journeying west across the Mississippi River to Missouri. Most significant, and like Emily, he came to Texas with the luxury of free status and pride in that status that was respected in the lands of Mexico. Logan had already made his Texas dream come true in Brazoria County after receiving a league of land on Chocolate Bayou, which emptied into a western extension of Galveston Bay.

Here, he made his living primarily as a blacksmith, becoming a respected member of the local white community. And he once again found love in 1833, evidently after the death of first wife, Judah. Logan purchased a slave named Caroline Williamson, and then set her free. He married the young woman on December 30, 1833. Thereafter, the two lived in this pristine land that he defended with his life during the struggle for Texas' independence. Caroline's liberation was perhaps the way by which Emily's own mother had gained her freedom from a man named West in the northeast.

Despite the full rights that he had enjoyed as a Mexican citizen, Logan first fought Mexicans in the battle of Concepción on October 28, 1835. He then served in the struggle for San Antonio de Béxar's possession in December. While charging in the ranks beside his white Texian comrades upon the besieged Mexican garrison, Logan was wounded in the assault. The fighting included vicious house-to-house combat that swirled through the Tejano town of mostly one-story adobe buildings of San Antonio, which was situated amid the sprawling prairie and sea of grass that seemed to have no end. Logan was so seriously injured in risking his life for Texas' independence that his days as a skilled blacksmith were over.

Eventually these two free blacks, McCulloch and Arnold, received donation land grants of either 640 acres or bounty land grants of 320 acres from a thankful Texas republic for their valuable services in San Antonio's capture and during the war. Another black soldier, Private Thomas Stephens, a slave, also served Texas in the victory that resulted in the expulsion of all Mexican troops under Cos from Texas soil by the end of 1835.[20] Other free blacks served as soldiers and with distinction in the cause of Texas besides McCulloch, Stephens, and Arnold, but their stories have been lost. These three African American revolutionaries were merely the most notable representative examples of the many achievements and contributions of free blacks in Texas' quest for independence.

Emily probably never heard of these inspiring roles of the hard-fighting free black soldiers in the Texas Revolution. With the exception of Morgan, she was destined to gain not a positive but an overall initial negative impression of Texas in regard to people of color. Coming from a state without slavery and familiar with humanitarian and abolitionist leaders, especially Jocelyn, and having enjoyed a much-coveted free status for her entire life, Emily was about to receive a severe shock from her association with an Anglo-Celtic culture, society, and economy in Texas that solidly rested upon slavery.

Most Texas settlers had migrated from the South, bringing thousands of slaves and their own Southern-based ideas about race with them across the Sabine. These Anglo-Celtic settlers had transformed Texas into a southwestern frontier that was firmly based upon the institution of slavery. By 1835, Texas was part of a vast slave empire, where cotton culture dominated, becoming merely an extension, the westernmost, of the Deep South.[21]

Emily would suddenly find herself in the heart of black Texas, where most of the 5,000 slaves worked the cotton fields in the east. Here, along the fertile river valleys of the Brazos and Colorado Rivers, African American women, children and men toiled endlessly on small farms in corn and wheat fields. But the vast majority labored on the large cotton plantations, and even some sugar cane plantations, of wealthy planters.[22]

In 1825, the constituent congress of the newly created state of Coahuila and Texas had threatened to enact laws in the new constitution to abolish slavery. Such a measure which would have destroyed the Anglo-Celtic economic progress and ambitions for an even more prosperous Texas that would rival Louisiana.

But the enterprising colonists from the United States had developed a clever legal means to circumvent Mexico's lawful restrictions on importing thousands of slaves to Texas and the Mexican government mandate that no one born in the state was to be a slave. The Texians, therefore, relied on the legal loop-hole of indentured servitude. Slaves from the United States were now carried into Texas as indentured servants, after signing ninety-nine-year contracts, or lifetime servitude. Of course, few, if any slaves, lived long enough to embrace freedom, after the passing of nearly a full century. Therefore, the thousands of blacks laboring on Mexico's fertile lands of Texas were doomed to a lifetime of slavery, as if they had never departed the United States.[23]

Emily certainly would have been horrified to learn of the sad fate that befell unfortunate Texas slaves, such as a young "girl of color" named Clarissa. Marmaduke D. Sandifer signed a lifetime indentured servant contract with her at San Felipe de Austin, Texas, on Christmas Day 1833. Illiterate and not knowing the awful details of the legal document that she was forced to sign to guarantee in writing her own lifetime servitude, Clarissa made a binding, legal agreement for the complete "renouncing and disclaiming all her right and claim to personal liberty for & during a term of ninety-nine years."[24]

Clarissa had been originally the property of Judge Robert McAlpin Williamson. He was a respected leading citizen of San Felipe de Austin, the capital of the Austin Colony located on the Brazos River, and the editor of the frontier newspaper called *The Cotton Plant*. Williamson might have sold Clarissa perhaps as a result of his 1831 divorce or later for economic reasons.[25]

If Clarissa was an attractive young woman, then almost certainly the worst was yet to come for her at the hands of her new owner, if a bachelor or one who was unfaithful to his wife. Former slave Harriet Jacobs described how the prettiest black women often became targets of the white owner's lust, which ensured not only a hasty initial purchase but eventually a quick sale with the arrival of the mulatto children, so as not to upset the wife and result in domestic turmoil.[26]

For the Anglo-Celtic settlers, such legal safeguards and circumvention of the Mexican legal system by this effective indentured servitude strategy was absolutely necessary, because President Vicente Guerrero, himself of African heritage, had abolished slavery in Mexico on September 15, 1829, and now the Mexican republic was more intent on fulfilling its humanitarian and egalitarian legacies. Emily could have readily identified with this great Mexican national liberator from Spanish rule, as opposed to the current popular leader of the American people, President Andrew Jackson, a former slave trader. Jackson, of Irish descent and from South Carolina, was a large slave-owner, like the republic's first president, George Washington, and the most distinguished of founding fathers, Thomas Jefferson. Jefferson's longtime mulatto mistress on the picturesque hilltop at Monticello, just outside Charlottesville, Virginia, was Sally Hemings, an attractive slave of white and black parentage and the half sister of his own wife.[27] At a time when Emily was closely connected to the work of the leading northern abolitionists, especially Jocelyn, the president (Jackson) of the American nation in which she resided actually led the fight against abolitionists and their humanitarian activities in the North.[28]

But indentured servitude of blacks was only a temporary and impotent measure for the white Texas settlers if Mexico City decided to suddenly dispatch a large liberating army north of the Rio Grande into Texas to enforce the enlightenment sentiment behind President Guerrero's 1829 decree. One of the key factors in causing Texians to revolt was the threat to their robust institution of slavery posed by an abolitionist Mexico. In the words of William H. Wharton, who feared Mexico's omnipresent threat to Texas' vibrant, lucrative brand of slavery that supported a highly-profitable economic model: "With a sickly philanthropy worthy of the abolitionists of these United States, they have, contrary to justice, and to law, intermeddled with our slave population, and have even impotently threatened ... to emancipate them, and induce them to turn their arms against their masters."[29]

Wharton's words represented no degree of unfounded paranoia among the Texians from an early date. Mexico City officials had dispatched United States–educated Juan Nepomuceno Almonte, a mixed-race officer of promise and whose fate would be closely intertwined with Emily in April 1836, to Texas in 1834 on a secret fact-finding mission. Here, among the thriving Anglo-Celtic settlements, the intelligent, gifted Almonte, a noble spirit who would served as Santa Anna's chief of staff during the 1836 Texas Campaign, personally enlightened slaves who had been smuggled illegally into Texas about their personal liberty as guaranteed by the Guerrero 1829 decree. Such activities certainly raised the ire of white Texans, helping to sow the seeds for eventual open conflict with Mexico. White Texans most of all feared that an invading Mexican army on Texas soil would liberate the slaves and "let them loose upon their [owners'] families" in a war of vengeance and racial hatred unleashed as never before.[30]

Almonte was specifically instructed by enlightened leaders in Mexico City "to make it known to the slaves who had been brought into the Republic in circumvention of the law, that [law] gives them freedom by the mere act of stepping on territory of the Republic, and that the Supreme Government and the authorities will declare them free at the moment they seek refuge in the republic."[31] For his 1834 mission, Colonel Almonte was also directed in writing from Mexico City to "assure the free people of color on behalf of the government that their property, their fields of industry, and everything that might contribute to their welfare and prosperity will be guaranteed them—if they settle in the place given to them—with the understanding that the government does not rate men by their color, by their origin, or by their nationality, but rather by their works, [so] they can aspire equally to the top posts and assignments."[32] Therefore, the Mexican Republic directed Almonte to emphasize to all free blacks in Texas "that the territory of the Republic offers them an inviolable asylum and the total enjoyment of the political and civil rights if they settle according to established laws and swear to obey" Mexico's laws.[33]

Of course, these were unimaginable concepts and sentiments for a large percentage of Texas settlers from the Deep South, which Almonte declared in no uncertain terms were "the most backward in the course of civilization."[34] The Texians went to war in 1835 against Mexico in the name of "liberty," so as not to become "slaves" of Mexico, while protecting slavery to ensure the future prosperity of Texas. Agreeing with the moral positions of abolitionist Mexico and its anti-slavery leaders, angry anti-slave northerners viewed the Texas Revolution as little more than a conspiratorial bid of greedy slave-owners of both Texas and the South to steal the vast expanse of Mexico's northern province away merely in order to secure "bigger pens to cram slaves in" and reap greater profits from the labor of an unfortunate people in lifetime bondage.[35]

While the Texian settlers were worried about the slaves, they badly underestimated the resolve of Mexico's leaders to regain Texas and its soldiers (mostly mixed race and Indians). Therefore, confidence reigned supreme among the Texian and United States volunteers for not only a successful outcome but also an easy victory from the beginning.

General Manuel de Mier y Terán discovered the leading role that race played in the thinking of Anglo-Celtic settlers during his 1828 inspection tour of Texas. In a June 24, 1828, letter to the governor of Coahuila and Texas, Teran described the high level of "disdain that most of the colonists have developed toward Mexicans, judging that our republic consists only of ignorant mulattoes and Indians."[36]

Though perhaps unknown to her at this time, Emily was about to enter a land of plenty, blessed by nature and seemingly God himself but cursed by man because of his greed to reap profits at the expense of his fellow man. This fertile, picturesque land was now not only ripped apart by the ethnic, racial, and religious conflict between Anglo-Celts and Mexicans within the context of a larger Mexican civil war that divided Mexican and Tejanos in a states' rights versus centralized government clash, but also was threatened by racial war between black and white, if the slaves of Texas rose up in revolt, whenever Mexican forces invaded to avenge Cos' humiliating surrender of San Antonio de Béxar.

From her abolitionist friends, especially Jocelyn, who hated the South's powerful slave regime and all that it represented, Emily probably learned that some risk would be involved in her living and working for a year in Texas, because slavery was so firmly entrenched in this new land of so much promise. By this time, Emily D. West wanted nothing more than the opportunity to make a major change in her daily existence in an effort to get ahead in life, especially now that she was in her mid–thirties. For the first time in her life, she was about to view something that she had never seen before: hundreds of African Americans in bondage and a system of servitude that she had only heard horror stories about, perhaps from own mother.

Most of all, and as likely warned to her by Jocelyn in the North, Emily had to worry about what might happen to her in Texas if she ever became separated from her employer, Morgan, and her duties at the hotel in New Washington. If that ever happened, she could be kidnapped and then sold as a slave to any opportunistic Texian, who only had to take a large amount of cash out of his wallet to purchase her or offer a bale or two of cotton in exchange for Emily D. West. Therefore, in preparing to leave New York City for the journey to Texas aboard one of the New Washington Association's company ships, Emily made sure that she took her "free papers" with her to verify her coveted free status, just in case she found herself in such danger.

Of course, a white kidnapper could easily tear up her free papers in order to reap a hefty profit from the sale of a woman far from home and who was in the prime of life, healthy, and strong, qualities that were sure to bring a high price for Emily in Texas. And if Emily was attractive, then she would fetch an even higher price on the open market. Emily, therefore, evidently kept her papers that verified her free status in a secure place on her person for safe-keeping, and perhaps even under lock and key. After all, if she ever lost her "free" papers while in the midst of a robust slave regime, then it would only be her word against the word of a profit-seeking white person that she was in fact a free person from the Northeast. And Emily, despite a New England accent that revealed her roots, would be in serious trouble, if that person might be a respected member of the community, and whose word was beyond dispute. And in a slavery-dominated Texas and even before a white judge and jury in San Felipe de Austin, Emily's word and pleas for release would count for nothing, because she was black and without rights among slave-owners.[37]

If unlucky once on Texas soil and if she suffered the fate of kidnapping by whites who only desired to reap a massive profit, Emily might well find herself soon working in the cotton fields of the sprawling cotton plantation of Virginia-born Jared Ellison Groce, the wealthiest, largest slave-owner, and most successful cotton planter in Texas. In early 1822, Groce migrated from Alabama with more than ninety slaves and a burning desire to resurrect the Deep South planter's dream west of the Sabine. On the bluffs overlooking the swirling Brazos River in the Austin Colony, he established the first cotton plantation, known as Bernardo, in Texas.[38]

During his 1828 tour to gather information about the situation in Texas for the leadership in Mexico City, Manuel de Mier y Terán and his party rested at the Groce Plantation situated on the finest cotton lands along the Brazos River in the "Upper Country," in a settler's words, some distance from the Gulf Coast and above San Felipe de Austin. In his most revealing diary, Teran described how Groce "is the richest property owner in the Austin colony. He has 105 slaves of all ages and both sexes [and] his main crop is cotton.... He lives with a young man, his son, and another white man among the huts of the negroes.... On this evening [January 31, 1828] the black men and women gathered at the master's house and held a dance, which I am told is customary every Saturday night."[39] But, of course, these dances among the slaves under the moonlight along the Brazos were certainly not ones that Emily ever wanted to take part, after she reached Texas soil.

However, the risks to Emily went far beyond a kidnapping and forced entry into slavery. By this time across the United States, white women who desired to embark upon a journey to Texas were discouraged and cautioned to do otherwise, because too many risks were involved. Quite simply, any lengthy sojourn to Texas was generally considered to be far "too adventurous [and dangerous] for a female."[40] But Emily D. West was not only about to make the journey to the distant western frontier, but also planned to live in Texas for an entire year.[41]

She might have read the inspiring words of another free black woman, Maria Stewart, who challenged black women to become more active in shaping not only their own destinies and futures but also those of all free blacks. She wrote in her 1831 pamphlet, *Religion and the Pure Principles of Morality, the Sure Foundation On Which We Must Build*, "Shall it any longer be said of the daughters of Africa, they have no ambition, they have no force?"[42] Emily D. West had accepted Maria Stewart's challenge, and sought to answer that question in her own way, and with actions rather than words.

CHAPTER IV

Texas Bound

In bustling New York City amid the gathering cool of autumn, Emily was not dwelling on negatives or worst case scenarios, when she was finally on the brink of her departure and the beginning of her own Texas adventure. In November 1835 when the cold winds and rains had already descended upon the northeastern seaboard to remind her that another harsh winter was on the way, Emily perhaps knew that it was time to go south like the lengthy, V-shaped flocks of migratory Canadian geese, which had already departed and now fed undisturbed in seemingly countless numbers in the fields and picturesque meadows of Texas.

The first challenge was simply getting to this remote section of Mexico's northeastern frontier. Most African Americans had been brought by their owners as slaves across the shallow waters—especially in summertime—of the Sabine River to Texas from the Deep South, after journeying hundreds of miles west by wagon or on foot with their masters. She would come south by water in a schooner.

With high hopes for the future and after having made all necessary preparations, Emily boarded the *Flash* in New York harbor in early November. This was the first time in Emily's life that she, a lifelong landlubber who very likely knew not how to swim like most people of the day, was about to embark upon a trip by sea. Purchased by the New York City investors, the *Flash* was owned by the New Washington Association. Formerly a prized possession of the Galveston Bay and Texas Land Company, the *Flash* had its home port at Anahuac, Texas.

When part of the Galveston Bay and Texas Land Company venture and before his close involvement with the New Washington Association, Morgan had only recently operated a general store at Anahauc with partner James Reed before it went bankrupt in 1834. The store was near where the Trinity River entered the northeast edge of Galveston Bay northeast of and across the bay from New Washington, where Emily was destined to shortly work. With Emily and with more than a dozen newly-hired artisans and laborers of the New Washington Association aboard, the crowded *Flash* sailed out of New York Harbor and into the Atlantic amid the chill of autumn and high expectations.

The 1,700-mile journey to east Texas by sea was not without considerable risk. As a typical sailing ship of the 1830s, the *Flash* was subject to the ever-capricious whims of the wind, tides, and an angry sea from a tempest or hurricane, as if for the amusement of Poseidon. A good many ships sailing out of New York City were lost at sea, with all crewmen and passengers going down with the ship.

Now a New Washington Association employee and looking forward to a fresh start in life in a far-away land, Emily was not the only African American onboard the vessel. Emily was in company with other free blacks, including Diana Leonard and teenage George Cooper, who also hailed from New Haven. No doubt, these individuals, especially Leonard, gave her a certain measure of personal comfort and fond memories of her hometown during the long journey. Equally as ambitious as Emily, these two free blacks had also signed up with Morgan to work for one year at New Washington, and embraced the Texas challenge. Amid balmy fall weather and the promise of a new day, Emily traveled south in the *Flash*, which eased its way not far from the timbered shoreline of the eastern seaboard with her new employer, Morgan, on board.[1]

Emily might well have felt much like another adventuresome northern woman, New York–born Teresa Griffin-Viele, of Irish descent. Griffin-Viele likewise journeyed to Texas in a sailing vessel that was likewise tossed by the waves. She had a most unpleasant trip about the crowded vessel, which included "a family of (two or three dozen, I should think) small infants, under the charge of an old black 'aunty,' who was kept in a continual state of excitement, all being sea-sick at the same time."[2] On her first voyage and especially if rough weather was encountered along the way, Emily very likely experienced seasickness at some point during the long journey.

After pushing slightly southwest down the east coast for around three hundred miles, the *Flash* made good time and entered the Chesapeake Bay. The vessel then pushed north up the bay's wide waters to reach the major eastern port of Baltimore, Maryland, just before the arrival of mid–November. Here, at the city's magnificent inner harbor of placid waters surrounded by hills, additional passengers were picked up and taken aboard the schooner. Foremost among these new passengers was Miranda West Zavala, the young wife of Lorenzo de Zavala, a primary founder and investor of the New Washington Association and opponent of Santa Anna. She brought aboard along her three children, two boys and a girl. They were all under the age of five.

Departing before winter's arrival, the Zavala family were on their way to rejoin Lorenzo in the fair, sunny, and summer-like weather of Texas that was so unlike the northeast this time of year. Sophisticated, highly-educated, and refined, Lorenzo was a leading revolutionary and political leader of Mexico and now a zealous, diehard friend of the Texas revolutionaries. He was destined to become the vice president of the future Texas Republic. A diehard republican, an admirer of the political system and constitution of the United States, and proud creole from the Yucatan, Zavala had resigned as the prestigious Mexican ambassador post in Paris in protest Santa Anna's rise to dictator, after he scraped the liberal 1824 constitution.

At Lorenzo's personal request, the trustworthy Morgan, a level-headed, responsible man who could be depended upon, served as the personal escort and trusty guardian for Zavala's wife and children. Emily served as housekeeper, or nanny, for the three children for the trip's remainder. She evidently had a special fondness for children. If Emily loved children in part because she perhaps had none of her own either by choice or fate, she might well have volunteered for this duty. Emily's responsibilities began early as the primary caretaker for the Zavala children, which also revealed that she was responsible, nurturing, and mature, aboard the *Flash*.

For whatever reason, the forty-two-year-old husband had his wife's first name changed from Miranda to Emilia on their marriage license in November 1831, or almost exactly five years previous. By the time Emily met Mrs. Zavala for the first time aboard the *Flash*, the native New Yorker was in her mid–twenties. Mrs. Zavala was a cultured, world-traveled aristocrat of upper class status: the antithesis of the homespun, thirty-five-year-old Emily of relatively little means and lower class status. Doubtless the two women talked at some length about the kids. And, of course, they got to know one another quite well in the schooner's cramped quarters for an extended period, while Emily cared for the children.

Besides looking out for the children's welfare on the tossing vessel, Emily also might have served Mrs. Zavala as a domestic servant.[3]

Almost certainly unknown to her at the time, Emily now cared for the beloved children of one of the top revolutionary leaders of Texas and a key player in the story of the Texas Revolution. Zavala became a distinguished signer of the Texas Declaration of Independence, which was penned to paper by members of the Texas constitutional convention on March 2, 1836, at Washington-on-the-Brazos. A Virginian at the historic signing at Washington-on-the-Brazos that created the new Texas Republic paid a glowing tribute to Zavala. William Fairfax Gray described this dynamic Mexican revolutionary, who had turned his back on his native country to cast his fate with the revolutionary cause of Texas, as "the celebrated Lorenzo de Zavalla [sic], favorably known to the political and literary world, by the high offices he has filled [including now as the interim vice president], his Republican integrity, and the beautiful productions of his pen."[4]

Gray was a highly-educated, cultured land speculator from Fredericksburg, Virginia, who represented two wealthy Washington, D.C., investors in Texas land. He penned this tribute in his diary: "Lorenzo de Zavala, the most interesting man in Texas. He is a native of Yucatan [which had long resisted the central government]; was Governor of the State of Mexico five years, minister of the fiscal department and Ambassador to France from the Republic of Mexico, which post he renounced [in protest against Santa Anna's dictatorship] then resided for some time in the United States.... He now lives on his estate on Buffalo Bayou, near Galveston Bay. He is a fine writer and a Republican; a fine statesman.... Has published a volume of travels in the United States, printed in Paris in the Spanish language."[5]

Emily was now in close contact with a most distinguished political family in revolutionary Texas. On her first journey by sea this November that took her farther from home than ever before, Emily must have marveled at the seemingly endless expanse of the Atlantic. She very likely worried about the possibility of shipwrecking, while the *Flash* headed on a steady course south with sails open and full of sea breeze. Day after day, the *Flash* knifed through the Atlantic's rough waters, moving parallel to the South's major port cities, Wilmington, North Carolina, Savannah, Georgia, and Charleston, South Carolina, respectively.

Emily was unable to fully realize that these were the South's longtime major eastern ports of entry for the thousands of slave ships that carried their "black gold" across the hellish Middle Passage from West Africa for generations. If the *Flash* was damaged in a raging storm and forced to reach port for repairs, as a free black woman Emily would have to risk whatever might come in these Deep South ports. Fortunately, the worst of the hurricane season had passed by this time, minimizing such risks of sailing the Atlantic and the Gulf of Mexico.

Cutting south through the Atlantic's waters and with white sails billowing in the wind, the *Flash* then passed along the primeval wilderness of the east Florida coast and the old Spanish town of St. Augustine. In facing invasions dispatched south from pro-slavery Georgia politicians and slave-owners who lusted for the rich cotton lands of Florida, hard-fighting black and mulatto militias of the Spanish had long played leading roles in saving St. Augustine and keeping it for Spain since the late 1700s.

Emily likely knew nothing about the bitter conflict with the Seminole, which was very much about race, that was about to erupt in this wild land during this very month, December 1835, the Second Seminole War. American cotton planters and slave-owners, especially those in Georgia, coveted the new fertile lands of Florida, and the United States government was determined to acquire Florida, which meant eliminating the native people.

However, the young Seminole leader Osceola, who had been raised in the Creek country of Alabama, decided to oppose the United States government's harsh policy of the forced removal of the Seminole to the West. His people, the Creek and including himself and his own mother, already had been pushed out of Alabama by Andy Jackson's hard-hitting ways. Osceola was determined to fight to the bitter end before he relinquished the untamed, picturesque land he loved. Osceola, who was married to a free black woman who was evidently a former slave, laid plans to strike back with a pent-up fury directed at the white interlopers.

Ill-fated Major Francis L. Dade and his small column of more than 100 United States regulars in bright blue uniforms were shot down by hidden Seminole warriors in a clever ambush that was sprung northeast of Tampa, Florida, on the chilly morning of December 28, 1835, during the infamous Dade Massacre. Arriving on the field by horseback to exact revenge from years of servitude and abuse under slavery after the last United States soldiers were cut down in a hail of Seminole bullets, escaped slaves from Florida plantations then slaughtered the few remaining white soldiers, wounded, helpless, and lying amid the thick clumps of sawgrass and palmettos, with knives, axes, and tomahawks. The news of the systematic destruction of Dade's command sent shock waves rippling across the South, especially among slave owners, because in truth this was "a Negro, not an Indian war," concluded General Thomas Sidney Jesup. A capable Virginian, Jesup, faced his greatest challenge in commanding ill-prepared United States forces in Florida.

The Second Seminole War was destined to rage in Florida's semi-tropical wilderness until 1842 in what became America's most lengthy guerrilla conflict until Vietnam. Former slaves, Seminoles, and Black Seminoles, who were Africans who had merged with the Indians to form a new race who opposed the invaders of their sacred Florida homeland, resisted to the bitter end against the United States Army's might. Year after year, the ex-slaves and Black Seminole were among the most fierce fighters, because they knew that capture meant a quick return to a miserable life in slavery on the Deep South's cotton plantations in Florida and nearby Georgia.[6]

Emily was about to enter a western frontier land that was yet often at risk of Indian attack, especially if strong Mexican forces marched north from Mexico City in an effort to reclaim Texas. By this time, east Texas settlers were nervous and anxiety-ridden about the worst case scenario: "We [are] here as if we were on a powder magazine: and if the spark once takes, there is no retreat. Let the Indian war whoop be here once sounded, and a worse tale would be related than the last massacre by the Seminole Indians in Florida."[7]

As Emily had learned as a free black woman, not only had New Haven and New York City been the center of racial unrest in the mid–1830s, but also race played a key role simultaneously in two wars at opposite ends of the South, the Second Seminole War and the Texas Revolution. But race was also resulting in conflict in the North. Therefore, complex issues of race and conflicts between races were now being fought out in dramatic fashion from northern urban ghettos, such as the Five Points, to the humid swamps of Florida and to the east Texas frontier. As a strange destiny would have it amid the twisting, unpredictable contours of American history, Emily suddenly found herself in the center of two of the three major racial clashes in America during the mid–1830s.

After a lengthy journey of around 1,700 miles by sea from November to late December and after almost certainly ascending the Mississippi for around 65 miles to reach the bustling port of New Orleans before continuing on to Texas, the New Washington Association schooner named the *Flash* then continued its journey to the nascent settlement and business enterprise known as New Washington. After leaving the Mississippi's brown waters, the journey continued southwest across the Gulf of Mexico and through its rougher waters for another several days. Finally easing out of the gulf and into more placid waters near the shore of the Texas mainland, the *Flash* neared its final destination. If standing on the open deck at this time, Emily must have felt relief upon first sight of the Texas shoreline, while the now swift-sailing schooner headed straight toward the thin chain of flat, sandy barrier islands, covered in greasegrass and brush timber, that separated the gulf's blue waters from the Texas mainland.

The *Flash* then pushed past the northeast end of the lengthy barrier island, Galveston Island, to enter the placid waters of the lower bays (East and West Bay) that led north to the upper bays, Galveston Bay on the left on the western shore, and Trinity Bay on the right on the eastern shore. Finally the lengthy trip from New York City to Texas was nearing its end toward December's conclusion, but it was not without continued risk for Emily. Hidden sand bars in the dark, murky waters yet posed serious hazards to the *Flash*. Indeed, the *Flash* was destined to sink because of pilot error during a similar attempt to enter Galveston Bay in May 1837. If Emily was seasick from the trip across the Gulf of Mexico, then she would have been especially eager to finally reach land to escape the misery and cramped quarters. And caring for the three small Zavala children might have proved especially challenging during the lengthy journey aboard the crowded vessel.

After passing safely through the narrow opening between the windswept peninsula of Point Bolivar (also known as Bolivar Point of the so-called Bolivar Peninsula) on the northeast and Galveston Island to the southwest, the *Flash* then sailed a short distance north across the calm waters of the bay's wide expanse, which had been created millions of years ago by the relentless entry of the San Jacinto and Trinity Rivers into the sea. At long last with the turbid waters becoming gradually more shallow upon approaching the western side of Upper Bay (Galveston Bay proper), the schooner arrived at Clopper's Point under the late December sunshine of east Texas. The *Flash* was tied up to Morgan's lengthy, wooden dock. Emily had arrived in Texas, and with no fanfare whatsoever. No doubt, Emily felt a sigh of relief with a successful docking at Morgan's wharf and upon stepping onto Texas soil for the first time in her life.

What Emily now saw around her was a most diverse and picturesque region that was geographically unique. A new world of wilderness surrounded her like a dense, green shroud that no longer existed in her native New England. Covered in dense timber, Clopper's Point was a small peninsula that jutted northeastward at the northwest head (San Jacinto Bay) of Galveston Bay, the largest estuary in all Texas, where the San Jacinto River and the bay met. Here, the freshwater inflows from an array of rivers, creeks, and bayous mixed with the saltwater from the gulf to create a nutrient-rich environment for all manner of marine and aquatic life.

Situated on relatively high ground and generally safe from flooding, except during a hurricane surge, near the mouth of the southeast-flowing San Jacinto River, where it entered Galveston Bay's northwest corner, this fertile, low-lying land was ideal for cotton cultivation. The most promising, unspoiled area was now part of the sprawling James Morgan plantation. Here, on the wooded peninsula sandwiched between the mouth of the San Jacinto River and Upper Galveston Bay, Morgan's plantation now served as the nucleus of the New Washington Association's vast land-holdings and the tiny, upstart community of New Washington. The new town held considerable promise and potential.

An Anglo-Celtic presence had been evident on this picturesque peninsula of fertile land since 1822. Clopper's Point had been first known as Rightor's Point, named by its first white settler, Nicholas Rightor. In true pioneer fashion, he built a small log cabin at the point's end to overlook the natural beauty of the expansive bay, taking advantage of the refreshing winds sweeping in from the gulf to ease the suffocating summer heat and humidity. Rightor then sold this slightly improved property to Johnson Calhoun Hunter. With pride, he promptly named it Hunter's Point in the custom of the day. Therefore, by 1824, much of the land in and around Morgan's Point was originally part of the Johnson Calhoun Hunter and Enoch Grinson land grants of 1824.

Then, four years later and with an eye for acquiring the best land with the most potential, Joseph Chambers Clopper, a brash young newcomer and Cincinnati trader from the bustling city on the Ohio River, bought the property. Back in the summer of 1828, the color-conscious young man had visited San Antonio, where his father operated a general store. Young Clopper became instantly enchanted with Tejano culture and people, especially the pretty senoritas of the lightest hue in the prevalent cultural tradition of most Anglo males in Texas.

Then, on December 22, 1834, about a year before Emily's arrival, Clopper sold his choice section of 1,600 acres, nestled between the San Jacinto River and Galveston Bay, to James Morgan. Because of its strategic location and ideal site for future trade and commercial development, the peninsula had always reaped profits for people, who speculated wisely and then sold it quickly. As the chief Texas agent and manager for the New Washington Association, Morgan had purchased these prime acres on December 22, 1834, for the cost of only $3,200, which represented the vast bulk of the money advanced by the company's opportunistic New York City investors, in promissory notes for the old Clopper homestead. Morgan officially held the title for the property in trust for the New Washington Association.

Like a silent sentinel overlooking a golden promise with seemingly boundless potential, Clopper's Point—before it became known Morgan's Point as to this day—stood at the northwestern head of Upper Galveston Bay. Trinity Bay, an adjoining sub-bay, was situated opposite Morgan's Point and northeast of Upper Galveston Bay. Like San Jacinto Bay to the west, Trinity Bay was another arm of Galveston Bay, with the north-south flowing Trinity River entering Trinity Bay's head. This adjacent bay was well within easy sight of Emily when she stood at the end of the point and looked northeast across both bays that had been named after the rivers (San Jacinto and Trinity) that entered them. Expansive Trinity Bay consisted of a brackish combination of brownish fresh water from inland Texas and salt water from the gulf: the unspoiled and yet untamed natural environment of a wildlife-rich estuary of considerable beauty. Located immediately northwest of Clopper's Point was tiny Lower San Jacinto Bay, an inlet off, and south, of the San Jacinto River, just before it entered the northwestern edge of Upper Galveston Bay.

Offering a spectacle of natural beauty, what Emily now saw around her for the first time along the spit of land known as Clopper's Point was a marshy, heavily-wooded, flat coastal plain intersected with brownish-colored streams, creeks, bayous, and small rivers. For the first time in her life, she also saw groves of orange and lemon trees under the bright, summer-like sunshine of December. These trees had been planted by old man Clopper and his three sons, and, of course, their slaves, who worked from sunup to sundown. The slaves were the forgotten Texian pioneers whose sweat and muscle played such a large role in transforming a wilderness known as Tejas into a prosperous civilization.

According to Morgan's estimation, the finest orange grove in all Texas was now situated in picturesque fashion along the bay's waters. Therefore, Morgan had christened his sprawling plantation on Clopper's Point with the appropriately enticing name of Orange Grove.

In a letter, this enterprising man raised in North Carolina bragged how his fine, luxurious orange grove was "the only bearing grove in all Texas." Herds of lean Spanish cattle, the forerunner of the legendary Texas longhorn, with expansive horns roamed the pasture lands of the point and the surrounding area to feed off the high, lush prairie grasses of the Gulf Coastal Plain. These cattle represented not only a reliable food source but also a potential future export.

Having just come from a congested urban environment, Emily must have marveled at the dazzling new natural environment and the pristine beauty in this most scenic of areas. This young black woman from the northeast, who had always lived in urban areas, now viewed a pristine wilderness area for the first time in her life. Her new semi-tropical surroundings included a wide expanse of life-rich salt marshes, filled with high cord grass and enriched by the timeless tidal flux, along the northwest corner of Upper Galveston Bay, and the mysterious-looking bald cypress swamps and groves of giant magnolias and oaks that lined the dark-hued rivers and the wind-swept bay like an impregnable green wall. Long strands of Spanish moss hung down not only from giant cypress but also ancient oaks that presented a primeval appearance.

Emily also saw the vast, flowing seagrass meadows and pristine coastal prairies filled with exotic-looking wildlife of what was a natural paradise. Here, inland rivers and streams eased lazily southeast to enter the Gulf of Mexico as from time immemorial. At this time of year, Canadian geese from the north country had flown down to winter along the sun-baked Texas coast, where food was plentiful, people were few, and temperatures were warm. For the first time, Emily also saw strange looking vegetation that she had never seen before, such as occasional stubby mesquite trees and towering cypress that kissed the blues skies along the plain.

White egrets, majestic fishing eagles, sandpiper-like avocets, roseate spoonbills of bright pink colors, the omnipresent gulls, military-like formations of brown pelicans gliding majestically only inches above the water in a dignified silence before suddenly swooping straight down in a swift plunge to snatch an unlucky mullet, and all types of seabirds were seen by Emily for the first time. And all manner of waterfowl passed over the sky in numbers too great to count. They all drew rich nourishment from the coastal plain blessed by the heavy doses of sunshine, warm rains, and nutrients carried from the upcountry.

Fresh water alligators lay amid the tangled underbrush or were hidden in underwater holes in creeks, marshes, and bayous, including the appropriately named Chocolate Bayou, because of its deep brownish color, in west Galveston Bay. Emily certainly saw alligators, either males in the water or females protecting nests, and perhaps even black bears, which roamed the low-lying bottoms of hardwood timber and lingered near Clopper's Point in search of food.[8]

Lurking silently below muddy, brown waters and only revealing the top of flat heads, eyes, and nostrils, the presence of large alligators were indeed a threat in his primeval gulf coastal wilderness, along with poisonous snakes, especially the cottonmouth water moccasin. North Carolina–born Noah Smithwick, who had migrated to the Sterling C. Robertson Colony from the Upper South (Tennessee) in 1827 at the age of nineteen, described how the east Texas coastal lands that lined dark-hued, "sluggish river[s], which crept along between low banks thickly set with tall trees, from the branches of which depended upon long streamers of Spanish moss swarming with mosquitoes and pregnant of malaria [and] Alligators, gaunt and grim ... lay in wait among the moss and drift for any unwary creature that might come down to drink."[9] In June of 1836 when Emily was yet in Texas, a settler named Gray B. King was attacked by a giant alligator on Double Bay located just below Anahauc, northwest of New Washington on the other side of Trinity Bay.

Before the eyes of his horrified wife and three children, the unfortunate King "was taken under water by the alligator after a short struggle, and never seen afterwards!"[10] And newly-arrived settlers, encamped at the mouth of the Brazos before pushing upriver to the capital of the Austin Colony (San Felipe de Austin) the next morning, were suddenly awakened by

> piercing screams, and rushing to the place from whence they proceeded found a huge alligator making for the river, dragging a 14-year-old negro girl [a slave] by the arm. He had crawled into a tent, where a number of persons were sleeping, and, whether from accident or choice I cannot say, seized the darky and struck a bee-line for the river, which he would have reached on time with his prey but for his inveterate foes, [dogs,] who rushed upon him and, through finding no vulnerable point to attack, swarmed around, harassing and delaying his retreat till the men pulled themselves together and came to the rescue, when, seeing the odds decidedly against him, his alligatorship relinquished his prize and sought his own safety in the river.[11]

From such well-publicized incidents that involved unfortunate slaves, one of the racial stereotypes (as if a sufficient number were already not in existence) that developed among some whites of frontier Texas was that the alligator actually preferred and possessed a "decided preference for human flesh, particularly negroes."[12]

But unknown to Emily was a most unsettling fact that mocked the serenity of this pristine natural world that she saw around her as far as the eye could see, a far uglier reality and greater horror than even the hungriest alligators. Along the waters of Clear Creek near where it emptied into Galveston Bay after its 41-mile journey east through virgin lands and not far from New Washington, groups of Cuban slaves, up to fifty in number and including children, were smuggled from Cuba to Texas soil. Here, they were treated "like cattle" before sent to the auction block for sale to eager Texas bidders.[13] The smuggling of slaves to Texas from Cuba was now big business by the time of Emily's arrival at New Washington. In fact, the running of slaves into Texas from Cuba had only increased with the Texas Revolution's outbreak. Throughout the early to mid-1830s, eager Texian buyers purchased Cuban slaves cheaper by way of this illegal traffic than at the New Orleans slave markets.[14]

So many slaves were smuggled into Texas that they were also then driven east for sale in Louisiana. William A. Fletcher described how his father "had been a slave driver or overseer in Texas at an early date, later on in Louisiana, he was up on the goods and abuses of the system as practised [sic], for he had the advantage while in Texas of having charge of fifteen 'lively bucks,' as he called them, who were just from their nativity, and who he ran to Louisiana from the Brazos River."[15]

In one of his intelligence-filled reports made during his 1834, a horrified Colonel Almonte emphasized, "Another one of the most notable abuses in Texas is the scandalous importation, no longer of slaves born in the United States of the North, but of Africans brought from the island of Cuba, who still speak not a word of Spanish or English."[16]

However, the vast majority of slaves in Texas had been brought by land from the Deep South. Adeline Marshall, who labored on a plantation in the Brazos River country, was one of these slaves. In her own words: "Don't know nothin' 'bout myself 'cept [that while living and working on an Oyster Creek, Texas, plantation below Galveston Bay, her master] says I's a South Car'lina nigger [who] he bought back dere and brung to Texas when I [was] jes' a baby."[17]

And a slave woman named Eda Rains never forgot how, "we lef' Little Rock [Arkansas and] we came through in a [covered] wagon to Texas."[18]

But obscuring and hiding the ugly realities of slavery, the pristine beauty of the virgin lands around Galveston Bay was what most of all impressed Emily, who saw so many exotic and exciting sights that she had never seen before. Later in 1836, one amazed American volunteer, stationed in a military encampment on Galveston Island, described Galveston Island (the town of Galveston would not be established until 1837) and Bay in glowing terms because the region "abounds in game. You can need not go four miles from our camp to shoot as many deer as you want; and you can stand in the tent door and shoot as many land or water fowls as you wish; and the bay is literally alive with fish of an excellent kind."[19] But wealthy developers and opportunists in the northeast already envisioned establishing a great port city on Galveston Island.[20]

Indeed, during his 1828 inspection of Texas for the enlightenment of leaders, including the president, in Mexico City, Manuel de Mier y Terán, a polished officer who possessed a sense of compassion for enslaved Africans on Texas soil, penned in his diary how among the Texas settlers, "Another issue of great interest is that the Galveston Bay be opened to them, and that all Texas trade pass through there."[21] Likewise, during his inspection tour of Texas in 1834, Colonel Juan Nepomuceno Almonte was impressed because as a future thriving port, "The best one with the best location is, without any doubt, Galveston. Its bay is spacious and secure."[22]

And even before he reached Texas soil, of which he had heard so much, land speculator William Fairfax Gray early learned "that Galveston Bay will become the principal commercial depot of Texas. A company of New York capitalists have purchased a league of land on the island, including [Jean] Lafitte's [sic] old fort, on which they design building the city of Galveston."[23]

Unknown to Emily in December 1835 when she sailed past Galveston Island on the *Flash*, the remains of another old fort stood in decay and silence at nearby Bolivar Point. Here, southern Maryland-born Mrs. James Herbert Wilkinson Long, "the Mother of Texas," and her black servant and slave named Kiamata had earlier made quite a name for themselves. During the early summer of 1819 before Mexico broke away from Spain, Kiamata was first brought at age twelve by Jane Long to Texas from Natchez, Mississippi, where she evidently had been born.

Long joined her revolutionary-minded husband, Dr. James Long, and his filibuster expedition. Masked by the rhetoric of spreading republicanism, these revolutionaries from Louisiana had been lured primarily by the lust for rich Texas lands. Here, they established the "Republic of Texas" in defiance of Spanish authority. Kiamata was also known as Kian and Ki by members of the Long family and friends. After the expedition and republic collapsed in the wake of the resurgent Spanish Royalist backlash and Dr. Long became a prisoner in Mexico, the two women, one black, one white, at Bolivar Point were left on their own. During the winter of 1821–1822, Jane and Kian defended the fort, known simply as Las Casas, with spirit. These women worked together as an effective fighting team. They manned a cannon and a raised a defiant makeshift banner of silk—perhaps the first Lone Star flag that might have been designed by both—to repel a Karankawa attack.[24]

From the beginning, Morgan, an opportunistic man of vision, viewed this yet wild region around Galveston Bay as the promised land. In representing the New Washington Association as its leading agent in Texas and a decade after the Karankawa people had been pushed aside by Austin and his early settlers, including around thirty of Jared Ellison Groce's armed slaves, Morgan had chosen an excellent site to create a new town around which a colony of industrious, hard-working settlers could develop the land and prosper for generations to come, or so it seemed.

By the time that Emily arrived at New Washington, Morgan and the company had built a general store and a large warehouse. These two structures and only a few private wooden houses made up the tiny frontier community, the nascent foundation for what everyone, especially the New York City investors, hoped would rapidly mushroom into a thriving town and commercial enterprise. The company's two double-masted schooners hauled merchandise and passengers across the Gulf of Mexico from New Orleans to New Washington.

The New Washington Association's strategic plan was based upon the birthing of a great city on Galveston Bay that would eventually rival New Orleans. This intoxicated vision of unlimited growth and future greatness at an obscure location was not unlike that of Alexander the Great in 331 BC, when he chose the site of Alexandria, Egypt, at the head of the Nile River, where it entered the Mediterranean Sea, because "the place was most beautiful for founding a city" of limitless potential on the Mediterranean's southeast coast: the future "crossroads of the entire world." In establishing the first of thirty cities named after himself and one that the Macedonian envisioned would become "the El Dorado of the Hellenistic Age," Alexander the Great made his most long-lasting contributions to civilization across the known ancient world. Therefore, the highest hopes of the New Washington Association's investors and entrepreneurial members became focused on this relatively remote site at the northwestern corner of Upper Galveston Bay: the golden dream of New Washington.

Thanks to the outbreak of the Texas Revolution, this grand vision, indicated by the upstart community having been named for Washington, D.C., had grown even larger. Morgan and his associates now hoped that this well-positioned town might serve as a future seat of Texas government comparable to Washington, D.C., if independence was eventually won from Mexico and if a new independent republic was founded. Consequently, these visionary optimists, especially Morgan, already called this place "Washington-on-the-Bay."

As could be expected, Morgan and his little town on the wide bay actively supported the Texas Revolution. Morgan was an active revolutionary, knowing that severing ties with Mexico by the winning of Texas independence would guarantee New Washington's promising future. Therefore, a large amount of supplies and munitions bound for the Texians in arms were steadily funneled into New Washington from New Orleans, including by the company's schooners. Entirely unknown to her, Emily was about to go to work at a place and location that supplied Texian revolutionaries in rebellion against Mexico. Therefore, if a Mexican Army marched into Texas in 1836 to restore the republic's authority, then New Washington would certainly be at the center of the storm, because it was a legitimate and lucrative war target.

Clopper's Point was destined to never flower into a great metropolis but it became instead today's tiny, but proud, community of La Porte. The war would wreak havoc upon New Washington, and it was overshadowed by Galveston (founded in 1837), on nearby Galveston Island at the bay's lower end, a thriving city after the Texas Revolution as envisioned by land speculators across the United States. In addition, America's fourth largest city in the Twentieth Century was destined to prosper only a short distance from New Washington and just to the northwest, Houston, Texas. Therefore, in future decades, New Washington, sandwiched between the future towns of Houston and Galveston, languished in obscurity, becoming a lonely, isolated backwater compared to these two towns which grew into magnificent American cities after the winning of Texas independence.

In many ways, the idealistic vision of Morgan and other investors, who placed hefty bets for the successful development of Clopper's Point, was not unlike John Winthrop, who established his own shining "city upon a Hill" (the Massachusetts Bay Colony), although more in economic rather than religious terms. But in the future, the unpredictable course of the Texas Revolution—wars always have the uncanny tendency to lead to unforeseen consequences—was destined to thwart the ambitious plans for New Washington's future growth. As fate would have it, New Washington would survive neither the eventful year of 1836 or the war that was destined to change Texas forever.[25]

In a glowing letter, Swartwout described his idealistic vision for New Washington. He concluded with limitless faith in the ultimate realization of his great dream in regard to the potential of the relative high ground of Clopper's Point and its seemingly endless promise: "In a word, that must be the site for the Seaboard City" of future centuries.[26] An ambitious big time wheeler-and-dealer of New York City, Swartwout's grandiose entrepreneurial vision coincided with that of Stephen Fuller Austin. An intellectual, stoic leader, Austin had declared that "Texas is my mistress." He emphasized, "My object and ambition was to succeed with the enterprise and lay a foundation for the fortune of thousands. I have never lost sight of that main and great object, and for that reason and that along I have succeeded."[27] Therefore, as Austin maintained, "Years ago, I enlisted myself as the slave of this Colony."[28]

As a respected and proper gentleman of New York City high society, Swartwout viewed limitless potential in the fledgling Texas enterprise—despite yet only a dream and existing almost solely on paper—and envisioned the emergence of a great city second to none in the South, not even New Orleans. He wrote in a letter how he expected New Washington to "become as large and as imposing as N. York herself! I think seriously that N. W. [New Washington] is more likely to become the seat of Govt." With boundless hope for the future, he penned to his friend Morgan, "I wish we had called our place Now York!"[29]

But the New Washington Association was much more than simply a city development and commercial enterprise. All in all, the association owned more than four thousand acres, purchased by Morgan, beyond Clopper's Point, among the fertile lands situated along the San Jacinto, Sabine, Neches, and Trinity Rivers. Quite simply, this vast domain was "among the best-body of lands ever selected in any Country," wrote the ever-optimistic Morgan.[30]

Emily started to work for Morgan at the little settlement of New Washington one week after her arrival in Texas, which included "any kind of house work" required as defined by the terms of her employment contract. She faced a host of challenges as a naive newcomer to the western frontier of east Texas. She had entered a cultural, natural, and climatic environment that was utterly dissimilar, almost alien, to her, especially when compared to the familiar land, accents, cultural norms, and faces of her native New England.

Most of all, Texas was a raw frontier region of relatively few women, even at the capital of the Austin Colony, San Felipe de Austin. Emily was now living in an utterly strange, almost forbidding, place that was as unpredictable as the Texas weather in December: intense heat and high humidity in summertime; prone of hurricanes sweeping in with terrific force from the Gulf of Mexico during summer months and in early fall; clouds of swarming insects, especially mosquitoes, and exotic wildlife of every variety, even the poisonous kind; torrential rainstorms; a sparsely settled region that was culturally, historically, and legally a Tejano land; and the possibility of Indian attack, especially from savage Comanche warriors, as long feared by east Texas settlers. These wide-ranging Comanche, long known for their lethal surprise attacks, were even a nagging concern for the men of the Alamo by early 1836.

Compared to life in the more genteel, refined world of New Haven where she had been born, Emily was now suddenly vulnerable simply because life on the western frontier was not only more precarious but also far more unpredictable. As a housekeeper who worked at the New Washington Hotel and perhaps occasionally at the Morgan Plantation, at some point, she also saw fellow African Americans working in the fields.

Emily might have worried that Morgan, if unscrupulous enough to violate the contract's terms, would also put her to work in the cotton fields of his plantation, making preparations for next year's crop. If this was the case, then Emily possessed yet another incentive, if one was needed, to do an extremely good job in working at the New Washington Hotel. Here, she served primarily as a housekeeper. In this capacity, she had to do "any kind of house work," as specified in the contract, required by Morgan. But in fact, that position entailed a host of other responsibilities beyond that of a domestic.

After all, Emily was bright, fairly well educated, and literate. In addition, Emily hailed from a bustling urban environment, and she knew the ways of the world and all about human nature, both the good and the bad. As a free black for her entire life, she was long used to making her own decisions. Therefore, Emily might well have served as a clerk at the one-story wooden New Washington Hotel. At this time and especially on the Texas frontier, operating and even working in a hotel, or "innkeeping," was a prestigious occupation, and one of the few respectable jobs open to women and considered acceptable by all levels of society. In the community of Brazoria near the mouth of the Brazos River, Jane Long, along with her faithful black servant Kian, operated the Brazoria Inn, which was popular with travelers far and wide.

In late December, Emily began housekeeping duties at the New Washington Hotel. Here, she witnessed the flow of visitors who traveled back and forth from the United States to the Texas interior, or those travelers who stayed at the hotel during the winter weather that was relatively mild compared to Emily's native northeast. It is easy to envision the transplanted New Englander eagerly embracing her new responsibilities and challenges on Texas soil. She was determined to live up to the obligations of her contract, and Emily was motivated by a strong desire to succeed. She must have initially basked in the drastic change and new Gulf Coast environment that promised her a brighter future. For the first time in her life, she experienced no severe winter weather as in her native New England. Along the picturesque Galveston Bay's shores where gentle waves washed upon the western shore and squawking sea gulls circled above New Washington, Emily's first days were filled with a seemingly endless amount of fresh air, bright sunshine, and warm weather. Emily no longer missed the biting cold and the bitter sting of the harsh northeastern winters, especially the howling winds, ice and snow storms.

Emily no doubt felt some curiosity about the surrounding subtropical, exotic environment that seemed so novel and foreign to her. However, at least to a certain extent, what she viewed around her must have also reinvigorated Emily, who had now become part of the western frontier experience. In many ways, she had embodied the very essence of the pioneering spirit, eager for a new start in life.

The predominate first impression of Texas from migrants who had journeyed from the United States and western Europe was one of awe and wonder. Wide-eyed immigrants of all classes, races, colors, and cultures viewed Texas as an almost unbelievable natural paradise yet largely untouched and scarred by man. An enterprising Irish immigrant and entrepreneur, recently from New York, who had established a store, wharf, and warehouse on Lavaca Bay, about 70 miles down the Gulf Coast from Morgan's Point, John Joseph Linn, was impressed beyond all expectations: "Texas was then a terrestrial paradise. Health, Plenty and Good-Will teemed throughout the land."[31]

And William Fairfax Gray, a Southern gentlemen traveling in east Texas, penned in his diary on February 4, 1836, how Texas was seen by one and all as the "Garden Spot of the World."[32] Like so many Sons of Erin, Ireland-born Father Michael, or Miguel, Muldoon described "Tejas [as] a country as lovely in its appearance as a park in England [and] in its fertility it is as rich as the [Nile] Delta of Egypt."[33] Likewise enchanted by what he saw in the seemingly endless bounty and beauty of Texas and with considerable understatement in 1834, Colonel Almonte reported to his superiors with some of his usual diplomatic flair how Texas consisted "lands of considerable worth of which [Mexico City] is perhaps unaware."[34]

But it was the prospects for development and an economic boom that caused most people in the United States, including the New York City investors of the New Washington Association, to look upon Texas as the land of opportunity: "Nature has evidently given to Texas commercial advantages, which she has denied to almost every other part of Mexico; indeed, few countries, if any one, are more favorably situated for carrying on an extensive and lucrative foreign and domestic traffic."[35] But first, the land itself had to be tamed, and that required hard, industrious settlers from across the United States. And Stephen Fuller Austin was just the man to have embarked upon the arduous task of colonizing Texas. From the beginning and inspired by a civilizing mission, he had been motivated by a burning "ambition to try and redeem [Texas] from the wilderness."[36]

Like so many other settlers, an eager immigrant from Scotland, David Edward, was likewise enraptured by the bounty, promise, and beauty that Texas had to offer. As he wrote in 1836: "The province of Texas in general, for native beauty, and the lower division in particular for exuberant fecundity, is excelled by no other country I have ever known [and] its spontaneous productions meet the astonished traveler at every step, in such abundance, as can scarcely be believed by one who has not had an opportunity of seeing and judging for himself."[37]

Disgruntled by the fickle nature of United States politics, greedy and self-serving politicians, and his resounding defeat by the power of the Jackson political machine that resulted in the Tennessean losing his Congressional seat and his disillusionment about the American nation's republicanism and future that was dominated by slave interests, David Crockett departed the United States with a mixture of contempt and disgust. He crossed the Red River to enter the pristine wilderness of Texas in the same month, December, that Emily arrived. In Crockett's final letter home before meeting his death at the Alamo on March 6, 1836, he described the fertile and bountiful Red River country as "the richest country in the world."[38] And during his 1828 inspection tour of Texas, one of the first words that Teran wrote in his diary was that the "beauty of this country surpasses all description."[39]

Emily's own personal opinions of Texas were very likely comparable to those of Linn, Crockett, Teran, Edward, and a host of others who marveled at what they saw. Indeed, some people considered the lush area along Galveston Bay, including Clopper's Point and nascent New Washington, to be one of the most picturesque in all Texas. Swartwout, the president of the New Washington Association, described the vast lands of east Texas owned by the New Washington Association as "the prettiest & finest place any where in the whole of Texas."[40]

Wearing sunbonnets, straw hats, and handkerchiefs on heads and carrying family Bibles and babies in their arms in some cases, courageous women played important roles in helping to transform a wild frontier region into a civilization. Besides those women like Emily who were employed by Morgan at the budding New Washington settlement, other black women, single and married, had migrated to Texas as domestics, such as laundresses and housekeepers.

However, historians have generally excluded the contributions of these determined black and white pioneer women, even though they consisted of around half of the migrants who journeyed west almost always with families (unlike Emily), and played key roles in the story of the Texas frontier experience.

Unfortunately for the historical record, no women, although deserving of recognition and acknowledgment, have been more forgotten than the pioneer daughters, black and white, of Texas. Among Austin's original "Three Hundred" settlers, at least nine women were independent, self-sufficient heads of households. And by 1826, a census revealed that at least eleven households of the 290 individuals in the Austin Colony were headed by hard-working pioneer women, most likely widows. Unfortunately, almost all of these early pioneer women and their contributions have been lost in the history books, except in the case of the ever-resilient, remarkable Jane Long. In April 1827, she finally gained a league of land of her own along the Brazos just below San Felipe de Austin by way of Austin's personal efforts to reward a woman who was already considered a Texas heroine second to none.

If Emily felt some discouragement or missed friends and family, especially during the Christmas season of 1835, which was certainly the warmest that she ever experienced in her life, then she simply bore in stoic fashion and in the pioneering tradition. After all, she had signed a one-year contact. Emily was determined to uphold her good name and reputation by honoring the terms of the contract, while fulfilling Jocelyn's faith in her. Besides her race and free status, Emily also might have felt pride in that fact that she hailed from New Haven and Connecticut. For Emily and unlike other pioneering women who easily became disheartened and shortly returned back East, there was now no turning or going back. She was determined to make the most of the opportunity that she had decided to exploit to the fullest in Texas, when she had made her initial decision back in New York City.

She had escaped the poverty and squalor of an increasingly hostile, anti–free black urban environment of a major American city to literally be reborn as a different individual in a new land by this fresh start in life. Emily most likely maintained her high spirits and enthusiasm about what was an exciting new beginning for her. If nothing else, Emily's new life in Texas was a novelty, a thrilling new experience, and an exhilarating adventure that she embraced to the fullest, without regrets or looking back.

One woman who had been brought to Texas as a slave was Fanny. She was owned by William McFarland, who freed her in 1835. Fanny McFarland remained in Harris County, where Clopper's Point was located, and made a pioneering life on her own. At some point, she might have even made an acquaintance of Emily, if she traveled to New Washington for whatever reason.

Because she had journeyed west on her new adventure without husband or family, Emily was unique because she was in fact one of the very few free black women who migrated on her own free will to the Texas frontier, where slavery dominated the society and economy, which had been transferred mostly from the Deep South. In this sense, Emily was part of a rare breed of adventurous pioneering women regardless of race. Most white pioneer women, the so-called "Emigrant Brides," who traveled to Texas, hailed from either rural areas or small town environments of the South or Midwest, unlike Emily, who journeyed from a major northeastern urban area.[41]

And Emily was also the very antithesis of most single white women who had migrated to Texas from large urban areas, where they had been hustlers, prostitutes, crass opportunists on the make, or whores, without husbands. Another exception to this rule, even though she hailed from the sin-filled port of New Orleans, was attractive Harriet Moore Page, born in 1810. She had only recently migrated to the untamed Texas frontier with her husband, Solomon

Opposite: A female servant of African heritage. Emily very likely might well have looked more like this woman than the stereotypical and mythical light-skinned "Yellow Rose of Texas" (author's collection).

An African American woman working in a Southern cotton field (author's collection).

C. Page, who was an irresponsible gambler, and two children, just before the beginning of the Texas Revolution. Because of her husband's debts, she had provided for the family by opening her own notions store in New Orleans, saving a good sum of money.

Both Harriet and her unreliable husband then caught a serious case of Texas fever, and prepared to depart New Orleans. Her father and brother had already journeyed to Texas, settling in the Brazoria area to the southwest of New Washington. The enterprising Harriet

African American youngster picking cotton in the South (author's collection).

hoped to open a new store in Brazoria above the mouth of the Brazos, where a lively business was guaranteed to supply the settlers of the Austin Colony and the capital upriver.[42]

Although not typical pioneers, Harriet and her husband were nevertheless just part of the overall larger historical migration of an entire generation of enterprising Anglo-Celtic people, or the Texians on Texas soil, who were remarkable "Americans from the North [and] who were born to colonize," in Colonel Juan Nepomuceno Almonte's complimentary words in 1834, when he inspected Texas to report on developments for the unknowing leaders in Mexico City.[43]

Cultured easterner, William Fairfax Gray described Brazoria as "a small place, some twenty or thirty houses, looking decayed, dirty, uncomfortable."[44] During his 1834 inspection tour of Texas and in regard to the capital of the Austin Colony, San Felipe de Austin, the astute and erudite Colonel Almonte noted a longtime characteristic of the Anglo-Celtic pioneers not shared by so many people of Mexico, because of so vastly different cultures, histories, and legacies less rooted in what had been bestowed by ancient Rome, which left its deep imprint upon Spain, which was then transferred by the Spanish to the New World: "This *villa* was founded in 1824, and its population has not grown much since then because the Anglo Americans do not like to create big towns when there are lands [readily available] to cultivate."[45]

Emily also encountered the ancient homeland of a new people, the Tejanos, whom she had never seen before. The Tejano were citizens of Mexico born and raised in Texas, and proud of it. They possessed a distinctive, rich culture that was as vibrant as Anglo-Celtic or African American culture and flourished despite the adversity and hardship. By the time Emily arrived with high hopes in east Texas to make a new start, more than 4,000 Tejanos called Tejas their home. Most Tejanos were concentrated in east Texas at Nacogdoches, while the vast majority lived around Goliad, San Antonio de Béxar, and Victoria, which was located on the Gulf Coastal Plain southeast of San Antonio de Béxar.

The people, who proudly claimed Mexican heritage but yet loved the native homeland of Tejas with a passion and were in fact the original Texans after the Indians, the Karankawa on the Gulf Coastal Plain of east Texas, possessed deep roots there. One American described these content and happy Tejanos as "a quiet, orderly, and cheerful" people. Like the common people caught in the horrors of all wars, the Tejanos found themselves trapped in the middle of the raging civil war in Texas during the dramatic showdown between the Anglo-Celtic settlers and Mexico by 1835.

Therefore, Tejanos fought on both sides in the 1835–1836 conflict, including in the early March 1836 struggle at the Alamo. More than half a dozen Tejano defenders served in the Alamo's heroic defense against the odds, and Captain Juan Nepomuceno Seguín's hard-riding Tejanos rose to the fore and performed wonders against Santa Anna's forces at the battle of San Jacinto on April 21, 1836. Interestingly, most Tejano volunteers were Béxarenos, who hailed from San Antonio de Béxar to contradict the stereotype of a purely ethnic conflict between Anglo-Celts and Mexicans.

Indeed, Tejanos served in the ranks of Santa Anna's attackers on the Alamo in the early morning blackness. Many upper class Tejanos were engaged as rancheros in a pastoral lifestyle that was part of a distinctive and rich Mexican and Tejano culture on the remote northern frontier. These Tejanos focused on cattle raising (a regional characteristic of southern Spain) on the arid grasslands of their sprawling rancherias, a cultural legacy that stemmed from a deep-seated cultural tradition inherited from the Spanish, who had in turn learned that skill from the Islamic Moors of the central plains of Andalus (today's Andalusia) centuries ago in southern Spain. Most significant, the Tejanos were not slave-owners like their Anglo-Celtic neighbors, who concentrated heavily on raising cotton which required slave labor, from mostly the South. Some of the foremost Americans like James Bowie thrived in the vibrant Tejano environment of San Antonio. Thanks in part to his lower Louisiana upbringing in a multi-cultural Cajun country, Bowie acclimated smoothly to Tejano life and culture, especially after marrying into the Tejano aristocracy.

Transplanted Americans in San Antonio married Tejanas, which bestowed not only a faithful, Catholic religion–motivated wife, but also immediate Mexican citizenship upon them and then a 25 percent land bonus by 1825. One of these men who easily acclimated into Tejano ways was Missouri-born John William Smith, an expert Texan scout fluent in Spanish during the Texas Revolutionary period, when in his mid–forties. He married the enchanting María de Jesús Curbelo, "a young Spanish lady of much wealth and beauty." A future signer of the Texas Declaration of Independence, Smith had married up into one of the most prominent and respected San Antonio families, which traced its roots back 300 years to the Canary Islands, located just off the African coast. By this time, Smith was proud of "his Mexican family," in the words of an American, who might have been envious of the happiness that Smith had found so far from the United States and with a pretty woman of a different race.

And Juana Navarro, who cared for a sick James Bowie during the siege of the Alamo and survived the slaughter of the mostly Anglo-Celtic garrison with her son Alejo Pérez, married Dr. Horatio Alexander Alsbury in January 1836. Fated to die in the vicious fighting at the Alamo, Eliel Melton was married to a Tejano woman named Juana. These men from the United States began new lives in Texas and found personal happiness, after marrying attractive, family-oriented Tejano wives, or tejanas, who closely embraced the Catholic faith, family, and a traditional, conservative lifestyle. Tejano society in Texas was the fulfillment of the concept of a multi-racial society and community. Most of all, these transplanted Americans were open-minded, and mingled easily and well with Tejano society, which they respected and enjoyed, because it provided an easy-going grace and dignity often not found in American society. Ireland-born John Joseph Linn, who spoke fluent Spanish and hailed from a historically more humanistic society and culture than found in the United States, was highly respected among the Tejanos, who affectionately called him Juan Linn.[46]

For good reason but only in time, young, inexperienced Noah Smithwick seriously regretted (wisdom came with age) not marrying a Tejano lady, whom he considered no beauty at the time because she was not blonde and blue-eyed, for the rest of his life. Ever color and race conscious, he recalled many years later how at San Antonio "Old Gasper Flores was land commissioner and had almost unlimited power in the way of land grants. He offered me any quantity of land, accompanied by the hand of his daughter, a little squatty girl, dark, almost, as an Indian. I was young then and disposed to be rather fastidious in such matters, and so declined the honor of the alliance, thus throwing away the chance of a lifetime."[47]

Having migrated to Texas from the Upper South in 1827, Smithwick thought not too highly of the thoroughly acclimated Kentucky-born Philip Dimmit, who had settled in San Antonio before establishing trading posts along the Guadalupe River. He was popular with the Tejano people for his fair dealings and prejudice-free views, in part because he "had a Mexican wife [María Luisa Lazo], and was, for all practical purposes, a Mexican."[48]

Besides matters of love and the natural beauty of dark-eyed Latino (or Tejano in this case) women of kind hearts and mild dispositions, these transplanted American males were likewise motivated to marry by the lure of the Mexican law that granted an additional one-fourth league of land, more than 1,000 acres, for marrying a Mexican citizen.[49]

Consequently, Noah Smithwick's lament about not marrying the Tejano girl and from a respected family of San Antonio was as sincere as it was long-lasting.[50] However, as expressed during his first visit to Texas, encountering a different people and culture (besides slaves) for the first time was not a pleasant experience for some aristocratic Southerners, especially traditional, conservative types like middle-aged William Fairfax Gray. Hailing from the old colonial town of Fredericksburg, Virginia, on the waters of the Rappahannock River and a devotee of his culture and its values based on race, Gray saw now no beauty in the Tejano people. A true product and son of the South, he had been blinded by the racial prejudice, xenophobia, and cultural ignorance of his native land. In his diary on February 1, 1836, he described the Tejanos as "a swarthy, dirty looking people, much resembling our mulattoes, some of them nearly black, but having straight hair."[51]

Racist views of the settlers and visitors from the United States was keenly noticed by the racially-conscious Colonel Almonte in 1834. Almonte, of mixed race, lamented the artificial divisions that existed like a brick wall between the two peoples largely because of race, concluding how the norteamericano newcomers "can never live in harmony with Mexicans [and] I am a man who admires the foreigners for their industry, activity, etc. I have friendly relations with several of them, and I am frequently in their company. Yet, I know very few of them who in good faith wish to unite with the Mexicans."[52]

Later demonstrating more open-mindedness than upon his initial arrival in Texas, Gray soon overcame some of his initial racial and cultural prejudices that had first stemmed from only outward appearances. After observing Tejano life more closely in the largely Tejano community of Nacogdoches, Gray displayed a growing admiration when he penned in his diary two days later how "there are among them some intelligent and respectable people, and their character generally is that of a quiet, orderly, cheerful people, fond of dancing and gambling" at night.[53] On February 4, Gray demonstrated great curiosity about the richness and novel (to him) features of Tejano culture and life, describing how "last night there was a Mexican [Tejano] ball, or fandango, at the other end of town" distant from the Anglo section of Nacogdoches. He also noted how the "Mexicans hold their fandangos at the *Monte*, or gambling house, of Miguel Cortenoz."[54]

But while Nacogdoches was an old, established community and the largest town in east Texas near the United States border, New Washington was far more remote and yet more of a dream than a reality. In his fledgling business Morgan also might have employed some Tejanos, even though he had signed up mostly free blacks from the North. In associating with Tejanos, then Emily would have been surprised to learn of a revered icon of Tejano religious worship that she had never seen or heard about before—a dark-skinned Madonna. Unlike the traditional white images of the Virgin Mary that she had known back in New Haven and everywhere else in the United States, Emily might have heard about the most revered feature of Tejano worship, the Virgin of Guadalupe. She was the Tejanos,' Mexicans,' and Indians' Virgin Mary. Most startling to this free black woman from New Haven, this Madonna's skin was nearly as dark as Emily's own, and she was never depicted with the Christ child as in Anglo religious imagery and iconography.[55]

If some Tejanos worked for the New Washington Association, then Emily very likely picked up a few words of Spanish, learning about a frontier people in Mexico's northern province and their distinctive culture. At some point, therefore, Emily might well have made friends with Tejanas. She might have eaten Tejano food, like corn tortillas instead of bread as back in the northeast, for the first time. On the Texas frontier, Noah Smithwick noted how one female slave was "down on her knees before a little bed of glowing coals on which lay a piece of sheet iron on which a couple of tortillas were baking, while by a series of pats she was preparing a third one for the griddle."[56]

Like this female slave in Noah Smithwick's account of life in early Texas, Emily was almost certainly introduced to various features and aspects of Tejano culture, which was entirely new to her. For example, if she had not packed a sufficient amount of warm clothing without accounting for the cold winter nights even in a semi-tropical environment, despite warm temperatures in daytime, especially with the sudden arrival of a frigid "blue norther," Emily could have compensated by utilizing articles of Tejano clothing. On cold evenings and nights, Emily might have worn a wide, fringed cotton or wool shawl known as a rebozo. Ideal for cold Texas nights, this warm garment had been long worn by Mexican and Tejano women of all classes. Or the native New Englander also might have donned a heavier cotton or wool serape, which was essentially a colorful blanket garment. For the first time at New Washington, Emily also might have taken sips from a cup of the ancient Aztec drink that was so popular among the Mexican and Tejano people, chocolate. Chocolate was so popular that Teran toured Texas in 1828 with a supply of chocolate. The hasty expenditure of chocolate upset the cultured Mexican officer, who noted the setback with regret in his diary.

Meanwhile, Emily's initial housekeeping duties at the hotel at New Washington included that of laundress, washing clothes, sheets, and bedspreads. In addition, she might have served as a seamstress, using a large wooden spinning wheel, and sewing to repair sheets, pillow cases, and clothing. Here, Emily also utilized her culinary skills, preparing and cooking dinners for the hotel's boarders. She no doubt utilized new ingredients, perhaps like white

"Mexican" corn that was larger than United States corn. But because Emily had been educated in the North and was literate, she worked not only as a clerk but also as a bookkeeper on some of the hotel's paperwork to assist in the daily operations. After all, at such rustic hotels, large and plain wooden structures in frontier Texas, female slaves were known to sometimes serve as hotel clerks, signing in guests and doing paperwork.[57]

Fortunately for Emily after her recent experiences in New Haven and New York City, the environment at New Washington was relatively prejudice-free. She might have received more favorable treatment or even flattering attention from men because women were scarce in a remote frontier setting. In addition, Emily was fortunate to have formed a binding contract with a relatively liberal, fair-minded man, or so it initially seemed. Morgan later wrote in a letter: "I ... hope to see Texas free'd of slavery."[58]

At this time, Emily was not the only American with the last name of West in Texas. One of the political leaders of the Texian revolutionaries was Tennessee-born Claiborne West. Now living in Liberty, he had migrated to Texas from Louisiana in 1824. West was destined to be one of the signers of the Texas Declaration of Independence at Washington-on-the-Brazos on March 2, 1836, when Texas "assumed a stand among the nations of the earth," in one Texian's words.[59] To his homespun neighbors, the ambitious West was yet known as "Sawyer West," because of his occupation before embarking upon an ambitious political career.[60]

What Emily could not have possibly known was that she had entered a southwestern frontier land that already possessed a lengthy heritage of African American people. In fact, this legacy of the black experience in Texas was much older than in her native Connecticut. Indeed, blacks had lived, loved, and survived in Texas longer than any other region of the United States, and hundreds of years before the arrival of the first white colonists to Texas from the United States. The history of both slavery and free blacks in New Spain, later Mexico, extended back centuries.

This distinguished legacy first began with black Spanish Conquistadors who helped to conquer the mighty Aztec with an unbeatable blend of courage and superior weaponry, gaining their own personal freedom in the process. By 1640, New Spain possessed the second largest number of Africans in bondage in the world, after the conquered Aztec and Mayan Indians failed to provide a durable enslaved work force, thanks to the ravages of European diseases and Spanish brutality. New Spain also had long contained the largest number of free blacks, mostly mulattos, in the Americas.

While slavery in New Spain declined with the end of the Portuguese slave trade, the free black population in this new land skyrocketed. By 1810, or only twenty-five years before Emily arrived in Texas with high hopes, New Spain possessed a thriving free black population of nearly 625,000, or ten percent of the overall population. Unlike in the United States where most blacks remained enslaved, the Spanish government and the Catholic Church, in the business of saving souls, had early bestowed equality upon free people of African descent as royal subjects with souls, recognizing their basic humanity.

Some major Mexican cities like Vera Cruz, a busy port on the Gulf of Mexico east of Mexico City, contained a population of which 60 percent were of African heritage by the end of the sixteenth century. Mexico City likewise possessed a large population of slaves and free blacks, containing more than 11,600 people of African descent as early as 1571. West African culture, traditions, and folkways not only survived but also thrived sufficiently in the very heart of Mexico City to cause considerable alarm among government and church officials.

By the second half of the sixteenth century, the creole class, including those of African heritage born in New Spain, constituted the largest freed and free population in the Western Hemisphere. Thanks largely to the influences of the Church and the Catholic faith that deemed blacks as equal to everyone else, this unique demographic continued well into the nineteenth century. Most significant, the creole population consisted mostly of mulattos, who were children of black slaves from primarily Congo and Angola, fathered by whites, either Spaniards or those of Spanish descent. Therefore, the mulatto population grew far larger than the actual number of slaves. Africans also mixed with the descendants of the pre-Columbians, or Indians, passing as mestizos in Mexican society. Mulatto children were spawned both from marriage and unions outside slavery. For instance, one Spaniard, Juan de Llanes, was married to an attractive free mulatto woman named Juana Diaz in 1564. Another free mulatto woman of Mexico City and of African descent during this formative colonial period was a thirty-year-old born in Castile. She had lived in a port city in southern Spain before migrating to New Spain. Her name was Ana Caballero. Ana's father was a Spaniard. Her mother was a black woman named Brianda Rodriquez. She was a proud descendant of the Islamic Moors who had first invaded Spain from north Africa in a jihad and occupied most of Spain for seven centuries, before the Reconquista by a resurgent Castile, which blended religion and nationalism into a crusading zeal that spilled over to the New World to descend upon the Aztec.

Mirroring the history of Mexico proper, the black presence in Texas extended back long before the first European settlement in the New World. When the Islamic Moors, including African warriors, from north Africa conquered most of the Iberian Peninsula in the Seventh Century, AD, the native people of Spain mixed with the Africans during seven centuries of occupation to create an entirely new people, the Spaniard. Indeed, the Spaniard was the product of centuries of miscegenation, including by way of the Visigoths, who had reigned supreme in Spain before the arrival of the crusading Moors. However, quite unlike the English, the Spaniards' penchant for miscegenation reached its zenith in the New World.

An adventurous black explorer named Esteban accompanied the first Spanish expedition into Texas. Meanwhile, other blacks were early discovered living among the Indians at the mouth of the Rio Grande River by Spanish explorers. In addition, Spanish soldiers of African descent, or free blacks who campaigned beside white Spanish troops from the Iberian Peninsula, served for extended periods among the isolated east Texas garrisons since the late 1600s. Generations of free blacks, born in both Mexico and Texas, had called Tejas home—hence they were essentially not only black creoles but also black Tejanos—by the time Emily arrived in Texas in December 1835.

After 1803 when the Louisiana Territory became part of the United States following Napoleon's bargain sale to Jefferson, who envisioned an expanding republic based upon the yeoman farmer, free blacks began to migrate west to Texas from Louisiana and other portions of the South. For good reason, they feared the prospect of possible future enslavement with the United States purchase of the Louisiana Territory. Thanks to Jefferson's purchase from France in what was the largest land transaction in American history, Texas served as an early haven for free blacks, mostly mulattos, who migrated across the Sabine and into Texas from the east.

Once on Mexican soil, escaped slaves from the United States gained legal and political rights under Mexican law, benefiting from a more liberal and fluid social system less based upon skin color than east of the Sabine; whereas one drop of black blood equated to slave status in the United States, a single drop of white blood bestowed greater equality in Mexico. Therefore, unlike in the United States, abundant economic opportunities existed for free blacks in Texas, as they were accepted as equal citizens by both the government and the Church. In addition, they could purchase land west of the Sabine to become farmers or ranchers. Here, they could raise families and crops in peace and prosperity while living as free men and women of the Republic of Mexico. A sizeable black presence in Texas predated the Nineteenth Century. As revealed by the Spanish census in 1793, more mulatto females lived in Texas than black women by a sizeable percentage—167 "mulattas" to only 19 black women, both free and slave.

Far from Mexico City, the northern frontier was a place where different races had long met and mingled as one. Three free black families were even part of Stephen Austin's Colony, the first Anglo-Celtic settlement in Texas, centered around the lower reaches of Brazos and Colorado Rivers. From the beginning under Spain and then Mexico, interracial couples found Texas as much of a haven as free blacks. Only a year before Emily migrated to Texas, Harriet Newell Sands journeyed southwest to Texas from Michigan with her white common law husband. And in Harris County and near where Emily worked at New Washington, Merrit M. Coates lived with his slave Violet Hamlet, whom he loved, respected, and treated in affectionate terms and dignity as his wife: an impossibility in the United States. He fathered children, such as Martha, and died in 1827.

Most significant, mulatto children were accepted and embraced by Spanish and Mexican culture, society, and the Church as not only free but also as equal citizens, unlike in the United States. Leaving the United States, therefore, free blacks moved to Texas to ensure that their children remained free, with some passing as whites and assimilating into society at large, along with future generations of their children. After all, Mexico, including Texas, had been a place where races—Spanish, Indian, black—had long lived together and mingled to become one, intermarrying freely and without hostile opposition or social ostracization as in the United States, where legal restrictions forbade such interracial unions and society severely punished such racial indiscretions seen as against man's moral and God's law.[61]

Another successful free black of mixed blood who found the good life in Texas was Hendrick Arnold. He served as a faithful soldier and daring scout of the Texas Revolution. His father, Daniel Arnold, had migrated from Mississippi, a land devoted to cotton production and slavery, and came to Texas in 1826 with his wife, Rachel. Among the first migrants to Texas from the United States, this interracial family settled in the Austin Colony. In total, three free black families established firm roots in the Austin Colony. Hendrick continued the cross-racial pattern by marrying a pretty Tejano, Maria. She was the stepdaughter of Erastus, or "Deaf," Smith, who was the best scout in Texas. Along with their daughter, Juanita, they lived peacefully beside their San Antonio neighbors, who were almost exclusively Tejano.[62]

A lengthy relationship between a white settler and black woman, named Puss, took place on the Texas frontier. John F. Webber, who was respected in the Bastrop community and known for his homespun skills as a physician, fell in love a slave of another planter. He had a child by her to further cement the bond. But because his beloved "was yet the property of another, without whose consent he could not provide for nor protect [his child], he faced the consequences like a man," in Noah Smithwick's words.[63]

Fortunately for the child and mother, Webber was far too "conscientious to abandon his 'yellow,' or mulatto, offspring and its sable mother to a life of slavery," penned Smithwick, who found a sense of nobility in this story of interracial love on the Texas frontier and admiration for a man who followed his heart and convictions. Webber "purchased them from their owner, who, cognizant of the situation, took advantage of it to drive a sharp bargain."[64]

He then created his own world, a log house and a sturdy log fort, on Webber's prairie southeast of the future site of Austin. Here, he "took his family and acknowledged them before the world [but] there were others I wot of that were not so brave," critiqued Smithwick.[65] In the end, "the Webber family of course could not mingle with the white people, and, owing to the strong prejudice against free negroes, they were not allowed to mix with the slaves, even had they so desired; so they were constrained to keep to themselves. Still there wasn't a white woman in the vicinity but knew and liked Puss, as Webber's dusky helpmeet was called, and in truth they had cause to like her, if there was need of help, Puss was ever ready to render assistance, without money and without price. Webber's house was always open to any one who chose to avail himself of its hospitality, and no human being ever went away from its doors hungry."[66]

During his 1828 inspection tour of Texas, Teran discovered in the Red River country what was more common in Texas than in the United States: "We saw another [small log cabin], where we were told a German lived with a black woman."[67] In the Austin Colony, Columbus R. Patton migrated to the Brazos River country in early 1834, with lofty ambitions and with future riches in mind. On April 4, 1834, and as the eldest son acting on behalf of his father, he purchased the extensive property of one of Austin's original 300 settlers, Martin Varner, for $13,000. Here, along the picturesque waters of Varner Creek in the Brazos River country, Patton envisioned a great sugar plantation that would produce a large fortune. A future soldier of the Texas Revolution along with this two brothers, William and St. Clair Patton, Columbus operated the new sugar plantation with the labor of more than fifty slaves owned by the Patton family. One of these slaves was named Rachel. She not only became Patton's lover but also his mistress and common-law wife. Patton moved Rachel, who evidently was attractive, from the miserable slave quarters and into the Pattons' newly-built two-story Greek Revival mansion in true Deep South style.[68]

Outraged by the obvious breach in the social and racial order and Deep South cultural values seamlessly transferred west of the Sabine, Texian neighbors complained that Rachel, who was as bold as she was enchanting to Patton, "acted as the plantation mistress, issuing directions to the overseer, including overseer to whip other slaves, and donned ladies' finery to sit in the white section of the church."[69]

The fortunate Rachel might well have enjoyed the most privileges of any young slave woman in all Texas. For almost everyone else in slavery, daily life offered relatively few advantages or opportunities of any kind. To overcome adversity in slavery, the slave family, in which women served as matriarchs that held the family together, endured and survived in Texas. The values of a matriarchical society had been transferred from West Africa. A strong religious faith, the power of prayer, and a lively music tradition helped to keep spirits and hope alive. Here, on the western frontier west of the Sabine, "the 'Juda' dance [was popular] among the negroes" of east Texas.[70] And talented black slave fiddlers—like Mose, who was owned by Arkansas-born Jesse G. Thompson, who was destined to die a heroic death in the slaughter at the Alamo, in the lower Bernard River country near the gulf and southwest of Emily's New Washington—entertained black and white across Texas by their splendid playing.[71]

At one festive dance near the small settlement of Columbia, on the Brazos River near the head of navigation, which had been established by Josiah Hugh Bell in 1823, "an old darky" of Zeno Philips, one of Austin's "Old Three Hundred" colonists and who owned twenty-two slaves in 1826, fiddled the night away, while "another negro scraped on a cotton hoe with a case knife" to provide rhythm.[72] When Emily was working at New Washington, Phillips owned a number of slaves, including women like Lucy, who was valued at $700, and Lila, who was valued at one hundred dollars less than Lucy. He also was the master of a young girl, Adeline, worth only $120 on the open market because of her young age and limitations as a productive worker.[73]

The name of Emily was a popular among free blacks and slaves in Harris County, Texas. Among the few free blacks in this single county that bordered Galveston Bay on the northwest, during the period that Emily was present in the area, were young Emily Routh and later Emily Mimms, along with her children. Emily Husk, the daughter of a free black mother, Richmond County, Georgia–born Zilpha Husk, called Harris County home in the 1830s. Emily D. West might have briefly seen or met one of these free blacks in Harris County were they ever near Morgan's Point or had they visited New Washington. Zilpha arrived in Texas in the same year as Emily.

According to the dictates of his January 1837 will, which had been drawn up when Emily West was yet present at New Washington, the gulf plain estate of plantation owner James Routh, a wealthy citizen who lived on Galveston Bay, freed Sylvia and her daughter, Emily, and four other daughters and a son. He also bestowed upon Sylvia and her family more than 300 acres, and made ample legal provisions for the children's education. However, according to the will, two children—Mary Jane and Sally Ann—were to remain domestic servants in the home of the wife, Ophelia, of James Morgan, who served as one of the will's executors at Clopper's Point, until they became twenty-one.[74]

And Emily was also a popular name among white female pioneers in Texas. John Fuller Austin's favorite sister was Emily Austin-Perry, and she was an early settler of Texas. Emily was married to Dr. James Aeneas E. Perry. Austin designed her fine two-story log-cabin on the Lower Brazos River plantation known as Orozimbo Plantation, which lay along the fertile river bottoms about ten miles below San Felipe de Austin. In true paternalistic style that had been transferred from the Deep South, Perry family members referred in writing to the slaves as "the black ones." Here, during the early 1830s, Emily Austin-Perry supervised lunches and dinners at her stately, but rustic, mansion, with attentive black servants waiting on tables and serving the best venison, or white-tailed deer, steaks and a tasty "rabbit soup."[75]

One of the most successful free blacks in Texas was North Carolina–born William Goyens. Born in the fertile Piedmont of Moore County in south central North Carolina in 1794, he possessed a mixture of black, Cherokee, and white blood. Married to a white woman, his father, William Goyens, a free mulatto American Revolutionary war veteran, gained his freedom by way of his faithful North Carolina military service. The light-skinned Goyens migrated to Texas at an early date (1820) not long before the establishment of the Austin Colony. Utilizing strong arms and skills that had evolved from a respected avocation in North Carolina, he initially became a blacksmith in Nacogdoches.

But Goyens demonstrated entrepreneurial skill and vision far beyond that of just a common blacksmith. With a businessman's savvy and opportunistic instincts, Goyens speculated heavily in land, traded with Indians, lent out money at high interest, hauled freight to market, built and repaired wagons, and engaged in sawmill and gristmill operations, carpentry work, and gunsmithing. He eventually became a man of wealth and prestige. But now, like Emily at New Washington, he was yet vulnerable as a free man, because slavery thrived in Texas among the Anglo-Celtic settlers. This omnipresent threat of enslavement became only too real and horrifying for Goyens, when a group of Louisiana whites overpowered him. They attempted to sell Goyens as a slave in 1826, after he had ventured too far from Mexican territory in crossing the Sabine. He made the mistake of having entered Louisiana, where sugar cane and cotton were profitable cash crops and slave trading a thriving business. But Goyens eventually escaped his captors.

Just west of the old Tejano community of Nacogdoches, Goyens thrived at his home and center of operations that he had appropriately christened Goyens Hill, which was located at the edge of Indian country. Here, he managed his boarding house (not unlike the New Washington Hotel) on the main road—the El Camino Real (the King's Highway) or the Old San Antonio Road—that led from the pine forests of east Texas to San Antonio. Following in his father's footsteps, Goyens married a white wife, Mary Lindsey from Georgia, in 1832, in a ceremony officiated by a Catholic priest, whose parishioners were mostly mixed-race. As in Goyens's case, Texas continued to provide a safe and inviting haven for interracial couples, unlike in the United States. Goyens's amazing success was partly attributed to the fact that he so early and thoroughly acclimated—unlike the vast majority of Anglo-Celts in Texas—deeply into Tejano culture and society at all levels, mixing with the Tejano elite and the lower class with equal grace and understanding.

By the time of the Texas Revolution and Emily's arrival, Goyens possessed thousands of acres, some of his own slaves, and a fine herd of cattle on the open prairie of what was ideal grazing country. He was well-known to some of the leading men of Texas, including Sam Houston, a friend who relied on Goyens's considerable influence with the Indians. Speaking the Cherokee language with fluency and respected for a rare frontier integrity and honesty by Texians, Indians, and Tejanos alike, Goyens also served as a patriot during the Texas Revolution.

Most importantly in overall strategic terms, this free black man helped to ensure that the Indians would not ally with Santa Anna's Mexicans in early 1836 and then after the decisive victory at San Jacinto, when the young Texas republic continued to be vulnerable to reconquest, because Mexico requested to recognize the loss of Texas. Eventually, Goyens acquired more than 12,000 acres, earning the esteem of the leading men of Texas. Goyens's amazing success also caused considerable disbelief and envy among a good many fellow Texians because of his color.[76]

The outbreak of the Texas Revolution, if the pro-slavery Texians emerged victorious, threatened these carefully-nurtured dynamics based upon racial tolerance and equality. Arnold prospered as a rancher and operated a gristmill in the hill country north of San Antonio. On January 5, 1836, and shortly after Emily arrived in Texas to begin anew, the provincial Texas government officially and legally barred free blacks from entering Texas. Clearly, the Texians did not want free blacks (always seen as a threat by slave-owners) in their midst and as part of a new Anglo-Celtic Texas based largely upon an entrenched institution of slavery.

Emily also would have been shocked to have learned what happened in east Texas not long before her December arrival at New Washington. After the Texas Revolution erupted at Gonzales and the stunning news of the fighting between Mexican soldiers and colonists spread, a number of armed slaves rose up in revolt along the Brazos River. With an instinctive sense of good timing, they wisely sought to take advantage of the opportunity, believing that liberating Mexican troops were fast approaching. However, in their eagerness to gain their long-sought freedom, these ebony rebels, who hated slavery, were mistakenly premature in rising up in the balmy weather of mid–October.

Because the Brazos River, which flowed southeast through fertile lands before entering the gulf, was the heart of cotton country and the most heavily slave populated region of

Texas and part of the Austin Colony, the settlers feared that the contagion of black rebellion would spread far and wide, while white settler rebellion against Mexico was underway that might well result in a two-front war. After all, such a two-front war could not be won by the badly-outnumbered Texians in a slightly surreal case of black revolutionaries simultaneously battling against white revolutionaries and with the same objective in mind: liberty. This slave uprising was put down quickly before damage was inflicted, with the usual grim reprisals of whipping and hanging for captured rebels. More than a hundred slaves were severely punished to serve as a stern lesson to other blacks, who dared to contemplate revolting against their masters. As desperate as it was ambitious, the rebellious slaves of east Texas allegedly planned to take over the cotton plantations, turn the whites into slaves, and ship the Austin Colony's ever-increasing number of cotton bales straight "to New Orleans" to reap their fortunes in a new economic and social world order in which blacks now ruled. The slaves had learned well of the benefits of capitalism and exploitation from their oppressors.[77]

While working at New Washington Emily also saw other women of color who were not free but slaves. Morgan, a Southerner, himself owned slaves, who worked either in or around the settlement. At least initially, this sad sight of blacks in bondage almost certainly tore at her heart and soul. Emily might have talked to female slaves, perhaps for the first time, learning of their brutalizing experiences in slavery. If so, then Emily acquired a greater awareness about slavery's horrors and an advanced appreciation for her own lot in life. More than anyone else, Emily knew that her own life could have been so different, if not for some many random twists and turns of fate. At this time and in the manner of Emily D. West, some female slaves in Texas carried with pride their own last names instead of the names of their masters, such as Emily Graves.[78]

What black women, both slave and free, faithfully continued amid adversity in Texas, and elsewhere across the slave-owning South, was successfully maintaining her elevated maternal place at the center of black family life and serving as extended family's leaders and role models, while creating their own unique definition of what it meant to be a woman. A heavy burden of responsibilities was embraced by these women to ensure survival for themselves and family members in a harsh, unforgiving environment that was slavery.

Although unexplored by traditional historians, the crucial role played by black women, both slave and free, on the Texas frontier was vital in perpetuating the survival of a long-suffering people in bondage and maintaining a woman's traditional matriarchal role as in West Africa. Covering an immense unspoiled area, the wild Texas frontier contained relatively few people, and most of these inhabitants were males. Relatively few white women faced the rigors of harsh and often cruel life in frontier Texas. Most of the white males who migrated to Texas during the 1820s and 1830s were unmarried, or left argumentative, unloved wives, like William Barret Travis, behind in the United States. The lack of white women in a typical western frontier environment in turn elevated the importance of black women, because they filled a good many roles formerly dominated by white females. Slave women across east Texas cooked, cleaned, sowed seeds, harvested crops, sewed clothes, and served as laundresses and domestics, when not working in the fields of corn or cotton.[79]

Noah Smithwick described the predominant Southern demographics of the hardy, industrious settlers of the Austin Colony: "Comparatively few families resided in town[s of the colony, including the capital of San Felipe de Austin], most of them going out on farms. On the farms [or plantations in this case], too, were to be found the wealthier portion of the colonists, who, having brought out slaves, were opening up cotton plantations."[80]

Emily may have never seen the capital on the Brazos, San Felipe de Austin, which fairly teemed with slaves. Smithwick wrote of San Felipe de Austin in 1827: "Twenty-five or perhaps thirty log cabins strung along the west bank of the Brazos was all there was of it, while the whole human population of all ages and colors could not have exceeded 200," including slaves.[81] But the rustic village along the Brazos turned lively, whenever music, especially fiddle playing, filled the air and brought residents to life during well-attended community dances. Typical of a frontier setting, white women were scarce. Smithwick wrote, "So great was the dearth of female society in San Felipe that during my whole residence there—'28 to '31— there was not a ball or party of any kind in which ladies participated."[82]

Nevertheless, these community dances were quite lively affairs. Judge Robert McAlpin Williamson, the future "Patrick Henry of Texas," an early leading War Party member and a longtime voice for Texas independence, not only played the fiddle, along with black musicians, but also sang. He sang what was considered one of "his best choruses," from an old slave tune: "Rose, Rose, coal black Rose, I nebber see a nigger dat I lub like Rose."[83] Williamson's popular, jaunty song, actually an African American tune that had been incorporated into white western culture, was in fact an early antecedent of the song "The Yellow Rose of Texas." Even more, this popular song provided an early foundation of the legend of black feminine beauty of a kind that allegedly brought about Santa Anna's downfall at San Jacinto by a light-colored, or "yellow," slave woman named Emily.

When living as a free black woman in both the northeast United States and in this strange land of slavery (Texas), Emily gained a distinct measure of equality to males in the matriarchal tradition. In the words of historian Deborah Gray White, who explained the importance of the maternal tradition brought across the Atlantic from West Africa: "Most slave girls grew up believing that boys and girls were equal. Had they been white and free, they would have learned the contemporary wisdom of nineteenth-century America, that women were the maidservants of men, that women were feeble and delicate, intellectually unfit for all but the most rudimentary education."[84]

Unprotected by the law, lacking male protection from father, husbands, or brothers under slavery's oppression where the master's will reigned supreme, and occupying the lowest rung of the social order, what was created out of the sheer will to survive were self-reliant, independent, and resilient black women, both in slavery and outside slavery, who continued the historic West African legacy and tradition of a matriarchal society. This sense of equality, independent spirit, and self-sufficiency were among factors that explained why Emily D. West decided to take the risk of coming to Texas in the first place.[85]

And quite likely, the liberating experiences for women of all ages and races on the western frontier, including Emily, assisted in the lengthy maturation and seasoning process of eventually creating a "new democratic woman." This woman underwent the character-molding forge of adversity and unprecedented challenges to become something new, unique, and novel, as explained by Frederick Jackson Turner in his much-acclaimed Turner Thesis.[86]

Like other women who sought to make the best of it on the western frontier and by her daily experiences in facing a host of new challenges in Texas, Emily would have felt a sense of accomplishment and pride in her role in New Washington, which was so unlike New Haven and New York City. She was an adventurous female pioneer in a vanguard role at Morgan's Point, a rare free black woman who was making a life for herself as best she could in a new land. Therefore, in a feeling shared by many white men and women across the western frontier, Emily quite likely felt a healthy measure of satisfaction in the fact that she was helping "to make the settlement a success."[87]

But life was almost certainly not easy or rosy for Emily at New Washington during a natural adjustment to new surroundings, a new boss, and an entirely new environment far from home. Inevitability, she missed certain aspects of her native Connecticut homeland and perhaps even New York City to some degree, especially if she yet had family members or a husband or lover at either place. But all of these things had to be left behind in her bid for a new start and to get ahead in life. Most of all, Emily had to make a quick adjustment from a fast-paced life in a large northeastern urban area to the most rustic, slow-moving pace of a very small community. Without knowing anyone, except Morgan, among these roughhewn Texians, including slave-owners, or having family in New Washington or anywhere else in Texas, she no doubt missed those things that she was loved: familiar faces and places of her past.

And, if a religious person, as most evidence has indicated because of her close association with Jocelyn and the religious black community of New Haven, Emily might would have missed New England's Congregationalist faith—nonexistent on the Texas frontier—and Jocelyn's lively African American church, full of spirited gospel music, singing and shouting, and loud praise to God, situated on the cobblestone thoroughfare known as Temple Street. While the majority of blacks in New Haven claimed this denomination that was so prevalent in New England, other African Africans were Methodists, Episcopalians, and Baptists. But now Emily was part of a much different environment, where Catholicism dominated, as Mexico was a Catholic nation and Texas was yet a Tejano land. As Emily learned, Texas was a world apart from the urbanized northeast of which she was familiar, with different peoples, races, foods, religion, climate, flora and fauna, languages, habits, and culture.[88]

She never learned of a prime source of inspiration in regard to a good many dynamic women of Mexico, who were yet proud of their distinctive Castilian heritage, especially in regard to the legendary, iconic Queen Isabella of Spain. Along with husband King Ferdinand of Aragon, the remarkable, beautiful, and fair-haired queen, thanks to her Visigoth ancestors from Germany, was a leading spirit and inspirational force behind Spain's great religious mission and national saga known as the Reconquesta. With cross and sword, the Spaniards hurled the Islamic Moors off the Iberian Peninsula in the greatest victory for Catholic Spain. Then, after the Moors were driven back to north Africa, Queen Isabella also played a key role in sending forth the adventuresome Italian sailor named Christopher Columbus on his expedition to discover the riches of the New World in 1492.[89]

But, of course, Emily's local influences were hardly so grandiose, stemming from a small, localized environment along the remote gulf coast of east Texas. Emily's initial impressions and experiences in Texas were not unlike that of a remarkable black woman of a powerful religious faith, who endured some of life's greatest trials because of her color. Clara Brown journeyed west for many of the same reasons that propelled Emily to Texas.

In 1835, the same year Emily traveled to Texas, Brown watched in horror as her youngest daughter, Eliza Jane, was sold on the auction block in Russellville, Kentucky. The rest of her family disappeared forever when her husband, Richard, and the two remaining children, Richard, Jr., and Margaret, were sold to different owners. But despite such searing experiences that left deep scars that never healed, Clara persevered by relying on her religious faith. She remained strong, refusing to lose her dignity or Christian values in a cruel environment where Christ seemed not to exist. As if trying to escape the ghosts and nightmares of the past, she eventually headed west for a new start, leaving everything behind except her religious faith. After journeying toward the setting sun, Clara became the first black settler in Colorado and eventually a successful entrepreneur.[90]

But what was entirely different about Clara Brown's experiences in the western frontier and Emily's life on the southwest frontier was that the native New Englander now quite suddenly found herself in a land that was about to once again be swept by the ever-unpredictable winds of war. As fate would have it, Emily was now in a region that would soon become a dangerous war zone in part because Morgan was actively supplying the rustic Texas revolutionaries by way of his extensive commercial links with New Orleans.

New Washington would shortly become a prime target of invading Mexican troops, if they ever advanced as far east as the Gulf of Mexico. A manmade storm, swirling from deep inside Mexico's depths and organized by Santa Anna, was about descend upon Texas. Giddy by their past successes, the Texians, who now basked in a dangerous hubris and overconfidence by what they had accomplished so easily during the 1835 Texas Campaign by driving the last Mexican troops out of Texas with the capture of San Antonio, were never more vulnerable by early 1836.

The illusion that the war between Mexico and the Texians and their allies, United States volunteers, had actually ended in December 1835—the month Emily landed with high hopes in Texas—and that Mexico City would never dare attempt to reassert its authority over Texas, was soon proved utterly false, when Santa Anna and his strong Army of Operations marched north from deep in Mexico in early 1836. Santa Anna was determined to crush resistance in the rebellious northern province to keep the Mexican Republic intact. As early as October 1835 and before driving the last Mexican soldados out of Texas after the dramatic victory at San Antonio, the Texians were especially worried that if ever a "merciless soldiery" from Mexico City pushed into Texas in overwhelming numbers, then they would "give liberty to our slaves, and to make slaves of ourselves."[91]

The initial slave unrest at the revolution's beginning was swiftly crushed and because Cos' outnumbered forces had been early placed on the defensive, the ebony threat had steadily diminished during the winter of 1835–1836. However, old fears among the colonists were once again rekindled when rumors of the impending march of Santa Anna's army reached the Anglo-Celtic communities of east Texas, where a heavy concentration of slaves were located. Indeed, in early 1836, the Texians anticipated that Santa Anna's strategy was to "send in troops by sea to excite the negroes" to revolt. But the greatest fear—which was destined to reach new heights after the Alamo's fall in early March 1836—was that Santa Anna's army, upholding the nation's hatred and abolition of slavery, would surge deep into Texas' interior and sweep into east Texas in a holy war of liberation to free the slaves that would spark slave insurrections and a bloody racial war on the Saint-Domingue model.[92]

Even Santa Anna—long depicted by generations of Texans and Americans as the most inhuman of monsters (essentially America's 19th Century version of Adolf Hitler)—was anti-slavery, unlike the Anglo-Celts, who had cast their fate, destiny, and future with slavery. He demonstrated considerable sympathy to "those wretches [who] moan in chains [and] in a country whose kind laws protect the liberty of man without distinction of cast or color" in a slave-free Mexico.[93]

Santa Anna's words were no exaggeration, and not meant for propaganda purposes. As he had seen in 1828 in Texas, a saddened and sickened Teran, who now more appreciated the enlightenment of Mexico in regard to slavery and free blacks, described the horror of slavery in Texas in his June 30, 1828, report to the president of Mexico, because the slave masters "commit the barbarities on their slaves that are so common where men live in a relationship so contradictory to their nature; they pull the teeth, they set dogs upon them to tear them apart, and the mildest of them will whip the slaves until they are flayed."[94]

Santa Anna planned to sweep across Texas with the force of the blustery cold front from the north known as a "blue norther," with a determination "that all blacks be freed" in Texas.⁹⁵ Of course, Emily knew nothing about these remarkable developments far to the south or Father José María Morelos' 1813 declaration that "slavery is forbidden forever" in their land which was won by Mexico's revolutionaries from the rule of Spain.⁹⁶

Perhaps Santa Anna had read the sound written strategic advice given to Mexico's leaders by Teran in late 1829 not long after his most enlightening tour of Texas: "If war should break out [in Texas], it would be expedient to suppress it in a single campaign."⁹⁷ Indeed, Santa Anna's bold strategic plan was now to march swiftly into Texas in a late winter campaign. Most importantly, this strike was planned for a time when very few in Texas anticipated such an unorthodox timetable to launch a strike deep into the heart of Texas: the recipe to catch the overconfident Texians and their United States volunteer allies by surprise.

The acting Texas governor of the revolutionary government, James W. Robinson, issued a fiery appeal on January 19, 1836. He warned the people, both Anglo-Celts and Tejanos, of Santa Anna's advance, and "that an immediate attack was expected.... March, then, with the blessings of your household Gods, to the western frontier [and] give him [Santa Anna] 'war to the knife, and the knife to the hilt.' Let him know how freemen can die, and how freemen will *live*."⁹⁸

Ignored by generations of traditional historians who have minimized the importance of slavery in fueling the bitter conflict between Texas and Mexico, Santa Anna and his mixed-race soldados embarked upon the 1836 Texas Campaign in part to defend the "natural rights" of African Americans in bondage by upholding President Guerrero's abolition decree of 1829. In this way, the Republic of Mexico—and quite unlike the United States—was determined and destined to nobly live up to its most lofty egalitarian principles, upon which the republic had been founded, and the enlightened humanitarian "philanthropy of the Mexican nation."⁹⁹ Besides the inspirational influence of revolutionary (including from the American Revolution) and Age of Enlightenment legacies that emphasized the bestowing of freedom to slaves, one American explained in a letter the often overlooked factor of race: "Few persons are aware that the Mexican Army is composed of a population at least half Indian; they seem, indeed, at first view to be all Indian."¹⁰⁰

The dark-hued son of an Indian mother, Colonel Juan Nepomuceno Almonte was one such man who proudly wore a resplendent officer's uniform of Mexico and embraced the most enlightened humanitarian principles of his republic. During the long march from deep inside Mexico to Texas, he served on Santa Anna's staff as his chief advisor. In an early 1835 letter, Almonte revealed the sense of outrage and the common attitude of the majority of Mexicans by this time: "The audacity of those [Texian] colonists is now intolerable, as it the protection given them by the authorities in New Orleans."¹⁰¹

Meanwhile, revolutionary officials and leaders were busily crafting laws and a constitution for the yet to be declared new republic of Texas that would solidly entrench and safeguard slavery in Texas for generations to come. Every last vestige of the liberal, progressive, and humanitarian anti-slavery legal legacies of Mexico was eliminated in the new Texas Constitution that was more in tune to the antiquated values of the 18th Century than the 19th Century. Harsh and discriminatory legal provisions would strike especially hard at free blacks, who were widely viewed by Texians as not only entirely unsuitable examples for slaves but also direct threats to the future safety of the institution of slavery. Therefore, while Emily busily performed her duties at New Washington, unmindful of the dramatic revolutionary events taking place in Texas, "the initial drafts of the March [1836] constitution in a straightforward manner forbid admission [to Texas] of all free blacks" in the future.¹⁰²

These future legal actions directed specifically at people of color, both slave and free, confirmed the worst fears of Mexican officials and leaders. José María Tornel, Mexico's infuriated secretary of war who was influenced by the Enlightenment's liberal values and legacies, described how the "land speculators of Texas have tried to convert it into a mart of human flesh where the slaves of the south might be sold and others from Africa might be introduced, since it is not possible to do it directly through the United States."[103]

Following on Emily's heels to Texas but carrying a rifle instead of the optimism for a bright, shining future in a new land, young Charles Ferris from Buffalo, New York, rushed off to serve in the Texas Army. He was so eager to serve that he quit his boring, if not dead-end, job as a clerk at the Buffalo Post Office and left a newly married and pregnant wife, the unfortunate, if not confused, Hester Ann Bivins, behind with his mother just to serve as a proud soldier volunteering in the cause of Texas.[104]

During the 1836 campaign, as during the previous year, courageous Texian women performed their patriotic duties in supporting the war effort and people's rebellion against a more powerful Mexico. When two indignant editors of *The Telegraph and Texas Register* condemned "some" male colonists from the east Texas settlements for skulking from duty and failing to serve in the Texas Army, they spoke glowingly of the many selfless sacrifices of so many young girls and women. In early March 1836, Thomas Gay and John R. Jones paid a fine tribute to the heroic, but too often forgotten, women of Texas, who had embraced the struggle for independence as their own:

> It is with pleasure and satisfaction, that not only the men, but even the women are nobly contributing all the service in their power in defense of our country. A few days since, when despatches were to be sent to every part of the country, an elderly lady, well known to many in this colony, on hearing of the present alarming invasion [of Santa Anna's army], carried, with the least possible delay, the intelligence into a settlement on the Brazos below. Many other ladies are doing every thing in their power in providing clothing, and articles of equipment for those going to the field.[105]

The women of Texas played a key, although unsung, role in the winning of Texas independence and from an early date. These courageous women in the east Texas settlements became diehard Texian revolutionaries, risking their lives for what they believed was right. Most importantly, they warmly embraced the people's struggle like a holy war, encouraging their sons and husbands to fight for the great dream of an independent Texas.

Chapter V

Slaughter at the Alamo

While talking to the people of Texas of all ranks during early 1836 and now far from his Rappahannock River hometown, William Fairfax Gray was struck by the boundless optimism of the Texians and their much-boasted ability to easily vanquish Santa Anna and any Mexican army, regardless of size, sent forth into Texas. In his diary on February 16, 1836, even while Santa Anna's powerful army marched ever-closer to its first strategic objective of San Antonio and the old Franciscan mission known as the Alamo, Gray wrote after speaking to a confident member of the Texas revolutionary government: "Like most of the Texans that I have met with he has a *Munchausen-like* idea of Texan prowess and of Mexican imbecility and insignificance."[1]

Texians saw their struggle as comparable to that of their revolutionary forefathers, assuming that same glorious conclusion in the founding of a new nation. Therefore, a dangerous hubris was all pervasive by early 1836. Prophetically and with sage insight that was virtually non-existent among the cocky Texians, whose overconfidence was without foundation, after their string of 1835 successes, the astute Virginian also wrote, "I fear it will prove a fatal error."[2]

Taking a chapter out of the book of Napoleon Bonaparte's campaigns and his brilliant battlefield successes that had made him the master of Europe, Santa Anna descended upon the hapless band of mostly Anglo-Celtic defenders of San Antonio like a whirlwind. At the head of around 6,000 hard-marching troops who had been toughened by the long trek north, he completely surprised the garrison by quickly capturing San Antonio without a shot fired in anger. Santa Anna then bottled them up in the Alamo on February 23, sealing their fate without losing a man.

Rumors of Santa Anna's advance had existed for months but were ignored. This savvy Creole, master politician, and *veracruzano* (from the province of Vera Cruz), who had long lionized Napoleon, had caught the San Antonio garrison so unprepared that fewer than 200 men were fortunate to escape to the Alamo east of the town.[3]

Here, on the wide, open prairie along the San Antonio River, the dramatic showdown at the Alamo was now firmly set in place. Symbolically and appropriately, yet another bloody clash of arms was destined to be fought at a place that long had been the graveyard of overconfident revolutionaries of multiple colors and races. With ample justification not long after the Alamo's fall, journalist George W. Kendall simply concluded: "This place has been the scene of more and harder fought battles than any other city in America."[4] But another American was more accurate by describing how, and for ample good reason, San Antonio "is here called a slaughter pen, many battles having been fought in it, and a vast number of lives lost."[5]

As early as January 14, the first and most forgotten commander of the Alamo, North Carolina–born Colonel James Clinton Neill, a slave-owner who had departed the Alamo just before Santa Anna's arrival to return to his Texas home in time to save himself, prophetically described, "I have not now more than seventy-five men fit for duty. Unless we are reinforced and victualed, we must become an easy prey to the enemy, in case of an attack."[6] But the garrison at San Antonio and the Alamo had not been reinforced by the time that Santa Anna arrived so suddenly like a "blue norther." No one was more responsible for the ill-fated decision to make a stand to defend the Alamo to the bitter end than Neill, an old Indian fighter with militia experience under Andy Jackson during the 1814 Creek War that had badly betrayed him in regard to sound judgment.[7]

A defiant, over-confident Neill had previously demonstrated a cunning skill in the grisly frontier art of "sending destruction upon the Indians," in one settler's words, which included injecting an unlucky captured Indian with the smallpox virus and then sending him back to his tribe to spread the deadly disease, when Neill was serving as an adjutant of a ranger company. He wrote on January 19 that "if drawn within the walls [of the Alamo, then we] will defend the garrison to the last."[8]

Not only the Alamo garrison, but also the Texas government was caught off guard by Santa Anna's arrival, despite the many warnings, largely because of its own folly. William Fairfax Gray, an ever-observant Virginian whose personal views were not tainted by local Texian pride and prejudices, described in his diary—in which he noted that the name "Alamo" meant "Cottonwood"—how at San Felipe de Austin (the colony's capital), an "express was received last night [February 19] which brings intelligence of the approach of the Mexican army; 1,000 men have passed the Rio Grande. It is not known where Santa Anna is, but this is supposed to be the advance of the grand invading army. He has sworn to win Texas or lose Mexico. The Texians say if he crosses the Rio Grande he will never return alive."[9]

Paving the way to disaster, including at the Alamo, this widespread overconfidence at the highest levels of the Texas government was badly misplaced and most ill-timed. By this time, Santa Anna's soldiers were highly motivated, having embarked upon a crusade to maintain the territorial integrity of the Mexican nation. At the Neches River crossing, the boundary between Texas and Coahuila, Santa Anna had recently proclaimed to his assembled troops: "Our most sacred duties have brought us to these uninhabited lands and demand our engaging in combat against a rabble of wretched adventurers [who are only] pretenders to our acres of Texas."[10]

Neither Emily, especially as a free black, nor the most vocal abolitionists in America and England would have been enamored with the backgrounds of the Alamo's three most famous leaders, William Barret Travis, James Bowie, and David Crockett. Both Travis and Bowie had slaves with them when they found themselves suddenly trapped inside the crumbling Alamo on February 23. Here, caught in a certain death-trap from which there was no escape, Bowie's slave girl, who cooked for him, was named Bettie. She was described as "an old negro woman," but she was probably closer to middle age. Reflecting his background as a southern Louisiana planter and a longtime slave-trader, who had reaped a fortune in selling "black gold," Bowie also had a male slave with him at the Alamo, Sam.

And although a well-known frontiersman from west Tennessee who had opposed the powerful slave interests that dominated politics in Washington, D.C., Crockett had sold a slave girl named Adeline for $300 to pay off political campaign debts in the early 1830s. The Alamo's young, inexperienced commander by the time Santa Anna launched his attack on March 6, Travis had sold a five-year-old boy for only $225 on Christmas Day 1834. As a cruel fate would have it, this sale on the auction block was certainly the saddest Christmas Day for the hapless youngster of African heritage.[11]

But bonds between master and slave often went quite deep, and even more than could be expected. Bowie had a trusty comrade whom he rode beside on a wide-ranging expedition against the Indians of north Texas in November 1831—his "little Charles, the mulatto servant." Charles rapidly loaded firearms for Bowie during the fighting against some of the most fierce warriors of the southern Great Plains, and at a time when a quickly loaded rifle often meant the difference between life and death.[12]

Knowing that the small garrison had no escape, Santa Anna laid siege to the Alamo, moving up artillery pieces to batter the undermanned limestone and adobe walls with impunity. Colonel Juan Nepomuceno Almonte described in his diary on Wednesday, February 24, of the bombardment's effectiveness: "A brisk fire was kept up from [an advanced battery 350 yards distant from the Alamo] until the 18 pounder and another piece was dismounted.... At evening the music [of the Mexican brass band] struck up, and went to entertain the enemy with it and some grenades."[13]

On this same day and knowing that reinforcements were now the only hope, Travis penned his stirring appeal to "All AMERICANS IN THE WORLD" for assistance: "I am besieged by a thousand Mexicans, with Santa Anna at their head.... Fellow-citizens, assist me now, for the good of all, for if they are flushed with one victory, they will be much harder to conquer. I shall defend myself to the last extremity, and die as becomes a soldier. I never intend to retreat or surrender. Victory or death."[14]

Travis's desperate request for assistance brought no response. When Travis's appeal reached the center of government at Washington-on-the-Brazos on February 28, William Fairfax Gray, who rode into the town on February 23, recorded with disgust in his diary on that day: "Another express is received from Travis, dated the 24th, stating that Santa Anna, with his army, were in Béxar. He is determined to defend the place to the last, and called earnestly for assistance. Some are going, but the *vile rabble* here cannot be moved."[15]

Meanwhile, the siege of the Alamo continued unabated, with doomed defenders standing firm, hoping, praying, and waiting for assistance from the east Texas settlements that would never come. In his diary, Colonel Almonte described on the bitter cold of Saturday, February 27, "The northern wind was strong at day break, and continued all the night .... It was determined to cut off the water from the enemy on the side next to the old mill. There was little firing from either side during the day [while] the enemy worked hard to repair some entrenchments" weakened by the bombardment.[16]

A smug Santa Anna, knowing that he had his quarry within his grasp, took time during the relative lull on February 27 to pen a report for a courier to take back to Mexico City: "To date, the [Alamo's defenders] have manifested their stubbornness while availing themselves of the strong position which they hold awaiting large assistance from their colonies and the United States of the North, but they will soon receive their final reproach. After taking the Fort of the Alamo, I will continue my operations on Goliad, Brazonia and other fortified points so that the campaign to the Sabine River which forms the boundary between this republic and that of the North may be terminated before the rainy season."[17]

Travis took full command of the Alamo when his co-commander Bowie fell sick, in both body and soul, on March 2. The native Louisianan was taken to a private room in the low barracks that formed part of the Alamo's southern wall. As an inspirational natural leader, Bowie's loss sapped some of the spirit out of the already badly-depleted garrison. In much the same way, a series of tragic personal losses had already taken some of the fighting spirit out of Bowie by this time. He had lost his pretty Tejano wife Ursula, father-in-law, and mother-in-law, and a child in the fatal September 1833 cholera epidemic which so cruelly struck them down.[18]

Commenting on a young woman from one of the leading aristocratic families of San Antonio, Noah Smithwick described how Ursula Bowie "was of a pure Castilian type and very handsome. I know that she had a deep hold on Bowie's affections. Strong man that he was, I have seen the tears course down his cheeks while lamenting her untimely death" in Saltillo.[19] In contrast to his popular image of a wild, frontier knife-fighter who enjoyed cutting his victims to pieces for little more than amusement, Bowie was a more complex individual. Bowie "had a tender heart and benevolent heart for the weak, distressed and poor," but not toward blacks.[20]

On March 3, Travis wrote of the increasingly gloomy situation inside the besieged fortress, which had been taking a severe pounding: "At least two hundred shells have fallen inside of our works without having injured a single man. A blood-red banner waves from the [San Fernando] church of Bejar, and in the camp above us, in token that the war is one of vengeance against rebels; they have declared us as such, and demanded that we should surrender at discretion, or that this garrison should be put to the sword. Their threats have no influence on me, or my men, but to make all fight with desperation."[21]

Travis's appeals for assistance that reached the revolutionary government at Washington-on-the Brazos continued to go unheeded. On Wednesday, March 2, when Dr. James Grant's small force was annihilated by the capable General Juan José Urrea and his forces at Agua Dulce Creek and the day that Texas independence was declared, William Fairfax Gray recorded the hubris in his diary: "Col. [James Walker] Fannin was on the march from Goliad with 350 men [almost all United States volunteers] for the aid of Travis [and therefore] it is believed the Alamo is safe."[22]

Eager to reap a quick victory, Santa Anna developed a master plan to overpower the isolated, diminutive garrison. After nearly two weeks of siege and a steady bombardment that frayed the nerves and eroded the defenders' stamina, he suddenly ordered artillery firing to cease earlier than usual on the late afternoon of March 5. Naturally, the worn garrison eventually fell into a deep sleep, leaving the Alamo more vulnerable than ever before. Santa Anna had already ordered assault columns from four directions to strike each wall simultaneously in the predawn darkness of March 6. All the while, Santa Anna's red flag of no quarter flew in the cold prairie breeze from the steeple of the tower of San Fernando Church, which faced the central plaza in the heart of San Antonio de Béxar west of the Alamo. More than 1,000 chosen Mexican infantrymen lay poised on the grassy prairie with sharpened bayonets, while the late winter winds blew from the northwest, awaiting Santa Anna's signal to attack.

As planned in exacting detail, the infantry assault surged across the open ground and fallow fields shrouded in blackness upon Santa Anna's signal, catching the garrison by surprise to ensure that resistance would be overcome in relatively short order. Quite simply, Travis and his tiny garrison never had a chance, because the sprawling mission complex was all but indefensible. The compound of the old Franciscan mission was immense, consisting of an extensive perimeter of 440 yards—much too large to defend by fewer than 200 sleepy and surprised men who were not professional soldiers or even adequately trained—that included a great enclosed space of nearly three acres. Engineer Green B. Jameson's words summed up the garrison's fatal situation, "The Alamo never was built by a military people for a fortress."[23]

And contrary to the prevalent xenophobic and racial stereotype that any number of Texians and Americans could whip an entire Mexican Army, and that Santa Anna's Mexicans were terribly "afraid to move against our riflemen," as asserted in an overly-optimistic newspaper editorial and commonly believed in Texas, such was hardly the case.[24] As if knowing as much, a more realistic-thinking officer with the command under Georgia-born Colonel James Walker Fannin, Jr., at Goliad, southeast of San Antonio, feared the worst for the small band of Texians and United States defenders at the Alamo. In a most prophetic letter, this knowledgeable soldier from Tallahassee, Florida, wrote quite correctly how by "a courier yesterday [March 9 and three days after the Alamo's fall], from San Antonio, we learned that our little band of 200, still maintained their situation at the Alamo [but] I fear [that the Alamo] has fallen before this. From its situation and construction, I cannot believe it possible so small a band could maintain it, against such fearful odds. David Crockett is one of the number in the fort."[25]

Indeed, the men of the Alamo were fighting not only against the odds but also against a cruel fate. The *National Intelligencer* in Washington, D.C., published a letter from an insightful Virginian, who understood some harsh realities of this revolt against Mexico: "The Mexicans have now some veteran soldiers in the field, and good officers; French, English, and AMERICAN. It is a war of extermination. I am afraid, until Uncle Sam gives them a helping hand, the Texians will be in a bad situation."[26]

The hand-picked assault troops of Santa Anna's army were about to demonstrate the truth of this evaluation of the military situation at the Alamo. What has been most often overlooked about the struggle for the Alamo's possession was the role of its black defenders, both slave and free. One of these forgotten black soldiers of the Alamo was known simply as John. He had been a clerk in the San Antonio store of Francis L. DeSauque, who hailed from Philadelphia. The scanty existing evidence about him has indicated that John was probably a free man. Most importantly, he "fought to the death as a rifleman" on the cold morning of March 6, 1836, forfeiting his life for what he believed was right.[27]

And Travis's slave, Joe, also fought as a rifleman. When the attack suddenly erupted in the haunting winter darkness that shrouded the lonely prairie outside the Alamo's walls, he followed his master, Travis, to the brewing defense of the north wall, where the Mexican attackers concentrated their greatest effort. Evidently Joe was not aware that Santa Anna was on a campaign to free the slaves, including Joe himself. Amid the swirling chaos of battle, Joe was wounded, but survived the hellish struggle, unlike his white comrades and South Carolina–born master, who had migrated to Texas from Alabama.

In his early twenties and described as "very black," Joe had been born in Alabama, which was now a rich land of cotton like east Texas. In May 1833, he had been a resident of Harrisburg (founded in 1825 and now part of today's Houston), Texas, on the eastern stretches of Buffalo Bayou and about twenty-fives miles northwest of Emily now working at New Washington, before he was purchased by Travis in February 1834.

Despite Joe's faithful service to his master, Travis wrote in 1835, "I have had Joe for the year; I cannot say, whether I will sell him or not." Nevertheless, Joe was faithfully at his master's side in helping to defend the Alamo's north wall amid the confused fighting in the predawn darkness, while the Mexicans began to pour into the compound. Joe nearly died for his loyalty to the master who had contemplated selling him off not long before the final showdown at the Alamo.[28]

In an 1837 newspaper runaway notice that offered a nice reward for his capture after he had escaped a new master and the horrors of slavery after Travis' death, Joe was described as "about twenty-five years of age, five feet ten or eleven inches high, very black and good countenance."[29]

Susanna Dickinson was set free by the Alamo's victors after losing her husband when the Alamo was overwhelmed. Captain Almeron Dickinson was a Gonzales blacksmith, Indian fighter, and veteran of the "Lexington of the Texas Revolution," who commanded the battery of guns on the elevated platform in the church's rear with courage and distinction. But in fact it was a close call for Susanna in a way that had nothing to do with combat. She almost became an Anglo mistress of Santa Anna, who saw an opportunity to possess the young, dark-haired widow. As he boldly proposed, no doubt expecting immediate compliance, Santa Anna wanted to take Susanna and her daughter back to Mexico City.

However, the chivalric, ever-humane Colonel Juan Nepomuceno Almonte, despite his recently hardened stance toward the Anglo-Celts in Texas and his hatred of slavery, convinced Santa Anna to set the grieving widow free. The west Tennessee-born Susanna, a pretty country girl of relatively little sophistication, was allowed by Santa Anna to depart the Alamo with her fifteen-month-old child, Angelina, who was thereafter known as "the Babe of the Alamo," and "a colored manservant." Fleeing the scene of slaughter, the weary band of survivors proceeded first to Gonzales, where the Texas Revolution had begun with so much optimism in October, and then eventually to San Felipe de Austin.[30]

However, this "colored manservant" who ventured forth from the Alamo with Susanna Dickinson was not Joe as long assumed by historians. Tejano Enrique Esparza mistakenly assumed that, "Señor Travis had a negro slave named Joe.... Santa Anna sent Mrs. Dickerson [sic] on a horse to Gonzales with Joe to help her long."[31]

But in fact Joe was not released by Mexican forces at this time but later. Joe then joined the small party of Alamo survivors, including the black manservant, on the road that stretched across the grassy prairie to the western frontier town of Gonzales.[32] As reported in the *Telegraph and Texas Register*, Joe was most fortunate on the morning of March 6, having been "the only man from the colonies who was not put to death" at the Alamo.[33]

Colonel Almonte, debonair, color-blind, and blessed with a kind heart, assigned his body servant and cook, a free man, Benjamin Harris, to accompany Mrs. Dickinson's small party for added protection, before reaching Gonzales on March 13. Clearly, the gallant Almonte was Susanna Dickinson's guardian angel on the untamed Texas frontier. Well-dressed in comfortable Mexican garb of cotton and described as "quite a dapper little colored gentleman," Harris also carried copies of printed proclamations, written by the bilingual Almonte on Santa Anna's orders, promising mercy to the Texas colonists if they submitted, but threatening harsh treatment for the volunteers, who represented no nation, from the United States, which was not at war with Mexico.[34]

Another African American survivor of the Alamo massacre was a black woman of unknown name. She was the servant of a white defender, almost certainly from the South, who was killed at the Alamo. She became part of the Navarro family, whose sisters, Gertrudis and Juana, likewise survived the thirteen day siege of the Alamo, and stayed with them at their father's home in San Antonio, after the slaughter in the old Franciscan mission.[35]

Evidently, she was the anonymous black woman who was mentioned in a rare summer 1836 letter back to Missouri from a soldier in Texas, or she might have been Bowie's slave Betty: "every soul with the exception of one old negro woman, massacred [and] they were most cruelly massacred."[36]

After the slaughter when nothing was left in the smoke-wreathed Alamo in regard to the band of defenders, but piles of bodies, a young Tejano girl of San Antonio de Béxar ventured into the nightmarish plaza in the hope of finding her American lover alive. But, of course, she was cruelly disappointed. Upon finding his blood-stained body inside the Alamo, she tearfully "folded his hands across his breast, wiped the grime from his pallid face, placed a small cross on his breast, and when ordered away [by Mexican soldiers], she dipped her handkerchief in his blood and carried it away in her bosom."[37]

But at least the pain and suffering was over for this particular beloved Alamo defender, who met his maker in the early morning chill. Such was not the case for the slaves who had been found alive by the victorious Mexicans, who were liberators of black men and women at the Alamo.

Of course, the slaves who had been trapped inside the Alamo during the thirteen days of siege had no idea that their fates and futures were already permanently decided by the Texians themselves. Slavery was destined to become the permanent law of the land, thanks to the early March decisions of the delegates at Washington-on-the-Brazos, but only if decisive victory was secured by the Texas revolutionaries and their allies from the United States. Despite having served his master (Travis) faithfully, including in the Alamo's defense, Joe was destined to remain a slave in Texas, after decisive victory was won by Houston at San Jacinto. After he finally escaped his new Texas slave-owner in the following spring and at a time when he was yet haunted and traumatized by what he had witnessed during the nightmarish slaughter at the Alamo, the native black Alabamian was hunted down like a wild animal and captured. He was then returned to slavery on Texas soil.

Unknown to Emily at New Washington, the Constitutional Committee at Washington-on-the-Brazos, a name that took some of the popular appeal away from the carefully crafted name of New Washington, had drafted its first provisions for a declaration of independence on March 1, and then issued the declaration the following day on March 2. Then, a new constitution for the infant Republic of Texas was adopted on March 16. One of these new provisions focused exclusively on the subject of the fate of the now unwanted free blacks on Texas soil in a new slave republic: "No free person of African descent shall be permitted to emigrate and reside in this republic, unless by special act of Congress, which must specify the person by name."[38]

Because the majority of the Alamo defenders hailed from the South and either owned slaves or were pro-slavery and because such legalistic provisions that codified slavery would become permanent if Santa Anna was defeated, Emily certainly would not have viewed the men of the Alamo as freedom fighters by any stretch of the imagination, given not only her color but her abolitionist connections and sentiments.[39] Distinguished historian Frederick Merk wrote in regard to even non-slaving Texians and United States volunteers of the Alamo and the Texas Revolution: "They did have, however, visions of cotton plantations in the future" on their minds.[40]

Because of the massive amount of aid, especially fighting men from the United States, Santa Anna's rage had been fueled by the fact that he was waging a war not as much against Texian colonists as against hundreds of well-armed, highly-motivated volunteer soldiers. This demographic was no exaggeration or aberration, because the vast majority of Texians remained safely in their east Texas settlements.

Even the Alamo garrison consisted of relatively few Texians. Therefore, after wiping out the Alamo defenders and capturing a blue battle-flag of the volunteer company from the United States known as the New Orleans Greys, which had been formed in New Orleans in October 1835, an angry Santa Anna denounced the "treacherous colonists, and ... their abettors, who came from parts of the United States of the North."[41]

In his March 6, 1836, report to Mexico City, Santa Anna was determined to expose the true composition of the Texas revolutionaries to the eyes of the world, exposing illegal United

Fall of the Alamo and the attempted escape of a large number of defenders, March 6, 1836. Sketch by Gary Zaboly (author's collection).

States intervention in a conflict on Mexico soil, where Santa Anna was only attempting to keep the increasingly fragile young republic from fragmenting: "The courier is carrying one of the flags of the enemy's battalions [companies] captured this day, for by looking at it yourselves you will know better the true intentions of the traitorous colonists, and their cooperators of the ports of the United States of the North."[42]

Santa Anna was actually more correct in his estimation than he realized. Indeed, the disciplined soldiers of the New Orleans Greys, finely-uniformed and well-armed on United States soil, had played the leading role in capturing San Antonio in December 1835, and in serving as some of the best fighters of the Texas Revolution in 1835 and 1836.[43]

Despite the determined attempts of a number of Texas governors, including future president George W. Bush, to secure its return to Texas, the fine, silk flag of the New Orleans Greys, marked "First Company Texan Volunteers! From New Orleans," has remained in Mexico's possession in the archives at Mexico City's revered Chapultepec Castle. Symbolically, Chapultepec Castle was captured in an improbable infantry assault by mostly United States regulars, including a young West Point–trained officer named George Edward Pickett of "Pickett's Charge" fame, up the 400-foot hill, that rose up like a mountain from the level plain filled with flowing, ripe cornfields, on September 13, 1847, during the Mexican-American War.

Here, at the museum atop Chapultepec that offers a dazzling view of Mexico City, the blue battle-flag of a volunteer company from the United States has been occasionally on display, not unlike the decorative Islamic Moorish battle-flags captured by Christian Spaniards during the Reconquesta. These are now on display in Spain as trophies of heroic Catholic warriors who won all Spain from the tight fundamentalist grip of Islam. Not unlike the Texas Revolution, the lengthy struggle in Spain had been just another bitter religious war that was marred by no quarter warfare of both sides.

Provoking Santa Anna's rage, the New Orleans Greys' flag was decorated with a large American Eagle and the words "God and Liberty," fusing republican philosophies with religious fervor that motivated the young men and boys of the most famous volunteer company of the Texas Revolution.[44]

In Santa Anna's and the Mexican Army's Cross Hairs

Emily was now in the midst of not only an especially vicious Mexican civil war—liberals (republicans) versus conservatives—but also an increasingly ugly conflict over the possession of Texas and one in which her own native country was heavily involved. This brutal war, seemingly dictated by a harsh will of its own, was about to blow like a "blue norther" ever-closer and directly toward Emily D. West and the little settlement on the quiet, tranquil bay, New Washington, in the days ahead.

Emily very likely had no idea that war was headed her way, or that Morgan and the association were active players in the revolt against Mexico. Indeed, the new Texas government had chartered the New Washington Association's two schooners, the *Flash* and the *Kosciuszko*, appropriately named after the gifted Polish engineer and hero, Thaddeus Kosciuszko, of the American Revolution, to transport United States volunteers, arms, supplies, and munitions from New Orleans to the Texas revolutionaries, just as the *Flash* had transported Emily to Texas in late 1835.[45]

But the steady flow of eager volunteers and assistance from the United States had been much too late to save the tiny Alamo garrison, which had been trapped beyond the limits of the western frontier of Anglo-Celtic settlement. One of the first shocking reports of what happened at the Alamo on the morning of March 6 came from a letter written by Mississippi-born Andrew Briscoe. He had served as the respected captain of the Liberty Volunteers, who hailed from a community (Liberty, founded in 1831 and located on the Trinity River, and where Travis had once practiced law) just northeast of Emily at New Washington, during the 1835 siege of Béxar.

After leaving the battlefield to serve on the political field, Briscoe was now a delegate at the Convention at Washington-on-the-Brazos. Providing rare details of the final struggle at the Alamo, Briscoe's letter was published in *The Louisiana Advertiser* in New Orleans: "The whole garrison was put to the sword [and] all fought desperately, until entirely cut down; the rest were murdered. The brave and gallant Travis, to prevent himself from falling into the hands of the enemy, shot himself. Not an individual escaped .... Colonel's James Bowie and David Crockett are among the slain—the first was murdered in his bed, to which he had been confined by illness—the latter fell fighting like a tiger."[46]

Shocked by the news, the people of Nashville, the capital of Tennessee, read about the tragedy at the Alamo in the pages of the *National Banner and Nashville Whig*:

> Poor Davy Crockett—we lament the fate of the sick Bowie—we [also] feel sad and angry by turns when we think of the butchery of the gallant Travis; but there is something in the untimely end of the poor Tennessean, that almost wrings a tear from us. It is too bad—by all that is good, it is too bad. The quaint, the laughter moving, but the fearless and upright Crockett, to be butchered by such a wretch as Santa Anna—it is not to be borne! .... Alas poor Davy! Thou art gone forever from the earth, but thy blood cries aloud from it for vengeance. It will be repaid, terribly, awfully, or we know not the nature of his countrymen.[47]

The stunning news of the Alamo's fall and the garrison's annihilation sent shock waves not only across Texas but also the United States. However, the destruction of the tiny Alamo garrison with such brutal swiftness motivated and inspired hundreds of United States volunteers to come to the aid of Texas, setting the stage for the final showdown at San Jacinto on April 21.

Likewise, the people of Texas were aroused to action, taking to the field in larger numbers than anytime since the 1835 campaign. Thirteen-year-old John Holland Jenkins, whose family had migrated from the Demopolis, Alabama, area, to settle in the remote upper reaches of the Colorado River in the Bastrop area of the western frontier, was one of the Texians who came forth to cast his fate with the struggle for liberty. As he wrote: "I began to use every effort to gain my mother's consent for me to enter the army. It was all in vain ... until the siege of the Alamo, when a new call came for men [and] I thought there had never been such fun as serving as a Texas soldier marching against Mexico." Like hundreds of young volunteers who were consumed and intoxicated with dreams of participating in a glorious martial adventure, Private Jenkins, barely age thirteen and a proud member of the Mina Volunteers, had much to learn about life and the brutal ways of war.[48]

For quite a few days after the Alamo's fall, not even the Texian politicians at Washington-on-the-Brazos knew what had happened to the men there. They blissfully remained oblivious to the wiping out of Travis and his diminutive command of roughhewn revolutionaries, who had been so confident of success. No one was sure of the Alamo garrison's fate, because no more messages were forthcoming to the rustic village along the Brazos.

Meanwhile, at Washington-on-the-Brazos, William Fairfax Gray continued to be impressed in many ways by the highly-respected Mexican revolutionary who had been elected interim vice president, Lorenzo de Zavala, "whose character and attainments interest me. He has kindly offered to give me lessons in Spanish .... He is obliging, kind and very polite."[49]

The following day, March 10, Gray recorded the lingering mystery that haunted the atmosphere of the convention at Washington-on-the-Brazos: "No news yet from the Alamo, and much anxiety is felt for the fate of the brave men there. It is obvious that they must be surrounded and all communication with them cut off."[50] Three days later and a week after the Alamo's fall, Gray scribbled in his diary on this cheerless Sunday of the heightened tension in the air along the Brazos: "No intelligence yet from the Alamo. The anxiety begins to be intense. Mr. [North Carolina-born Jesse B.] Badgett and Dr. [Virginia-born Benjamin Briggs] Goodrich, members of the Convention, have brothers there, and Mr. [Judge Jesse] Grimes, another member, has a son there."[51]

Virginia-born John Calvin Goodrich, who had migrated with his brother to Texas in 1834, Albert Calvin Grimes, born in Georgia and who served as orderly sergeant of Captain William R. Carey's artillery company, were both killed at the Alamo.[52] Benjamin Briggs Goodrich wrote a sad March 15 letter to his brother Edmund "to inform my relations in Tennessee of the massacre of my poor brother John [who] was murdered" at the Alamo.[53] Most importantly, he warned his brother to be very gentle and careful in regard to relaying the tragic news about the annihilation of the Alamo garrison: "Approach poor old mother cautiously with the awful news, for I fear her much worn out constitution will not survive the shock."[54]

On Tuesday, March 15, 1836, and nearly 10 days after the Alamo's fall, the often bickering and self-serving officials of the government at Washington-on-the-Brazos finally received reliable intelligence "of the fall of the Alamo beyond a doubt," as a gloomy Gray wrote in his diary.[55] The Alamo's demise was only the beginning of the a long list of tragedies and disasters that distinguished the Texas Campaign of 1836 and sent the infant Texas Republic reeling, until it lay perilously close to the edge of extinction.

CHAPTER VI

Muddy Roads Leading to San Jacinto

At San Antonio, Santa Anna envisioned the conquest of all of Texas with a sense of renewed clarity, after the slaughter in the old mission on March 6. With renewed confidence for more victories to come, he now embarked upon well-laid, sound plans to conclude the 1836 Texas Campaign with an advance deeper into Texas and all the way to the Gulf Coast. "I planned to advance swiftly against the rebellious colonists, as I felt that the campaign should be finished before the spring floods,"[1] he wrote.

However, relishing his success at San Antonio and falling victim to hubris, the over-confident Santa Anna remained for days, which had grown cold and with the wind blustery from the northwest, at the Tejano town. Here, at San Antonio, Santa Anna's troops rested and recuperated not only from the battle but also from the long march north over rough terrain, including northern Mexico's arid mountains and bitterly cold winter weather. While awaiting the arrival of additional units to reach San Antonio from the south, along with his treasury and long line of commissary trains which arrived finally on March 10, Santa Anna knew little of the geography and natural obstacles that lay beyond San Antonio, however.

He especially lacked knowledge about the area around Galveston Bay, where Emily worked at New Washington. After all, the self-styled "Napoleon of the West" had never seen the Gulf Coastal Plain around Upper Galveston Bay or New Washington. As a former wide-eyed "gentleman cadet" and then a young cavalry officer yet to shave for the first time but overflowing with ambition, Santa Anna had early learned how to deal ruthlessly with Texas rebels, while serving under his battle-hardened mentor General Joaquín de Arredondo. Arredondo himself had given final approval for the establishment of the Austin Colony, as if never suspecting that Mexico would have to go to war against these industrious, but decidedly temperamental, norteamerico settlers.

But the farthest north that Santa Anna ever had been in Texas was San Antonio. At that time so long ago in the foggy past when Texas had been inhabited by an earlier generation of fiery revolutionaries who opposed the central government, he had been part of the New Spanish Royal expeditionary force that had marched north to smash a people's rebellion. Young Santa Anna and his comrades under Arredondo had ruthlessly crushed hundreds of Tejano, Indian and Anglo-Celtic rebels of the so-called Republican Army of Texas from the United States at the battle of Medina on bloody August 16, 1813.

But after wiping out the Alamo garrison, the remainder of the Texas 1836 Campaign was not going to be quite as easy as the immensely confident generalísimo thought. Santa Anna had failed to take into account that the prairie grasses had not yet risen sufficiently to sustain his army's horses of his cavalry and logistical supply line for an advance farther east, before the spring rains brought new growth and bright green color of the lush grasslands that extended toward the sunrise.

In the days ahead, this fundamental miscalculation was destined to slow the Mexican advance, and then the pursuit of Houston's band of men. By this time on the western frontier, a nascent force had initially organized at Gonzales as an Alamo relief force before the Texas commander-in-chief, Houston, arrived from Washington-on-the-Brazos on March 11. Houston then took charge of several hundred Texian and United States volunteers who had been under former Alamo commander James Clinton Neill.[2]

After abandoning Gonzales, which was torched by the Texians to deny its possession to Santa Anna, Houston's small force retired east and toward the dark waters of the Colorado River, that flowed southeast through the fertile prairie lands into the Gulf of Mexico, on March 13, after Susanna Dickinson arrived to tell of the slaughter at the Alamo. Houston embarked upon his lengthy retreat only two days after Santa Anna's advance, or center, column, under General Ramírez y Sesma, an experienced cavalryman with considerable leadership and tactical ability, moved out from San Antonio to initiate the 1836 Texas Campaign's final phase. Sesma started from Béxar on March 11 and pushed east with his vanguard division toward the vulnerable population and political center of Texas, the Austin Colony and its capital of San Felipe de Austin. Hard-hitting General Urrea, a young, dark-haired natural leader born in Tuscon, Sonora (now Arizona), but with family roots back in Durango, Mexico, led the right wing column north up the Gulf Coast to the southeast.

General Antonio López de Santa Anna (author's collection).

Like almost everyone else in the Mexican Army, Urrea had nothing but contempt for the Texian revolutionaries, whom he described as "ragtag rabble." The Alamo's relatively weak defense only fueled greater contempt for their untrained, ill-equipped opponent: an all but inevitable development under the circumstances that even transcended cultural and racial biases. Meanwhile, General Antonio Gaona, who had also advanced from San Antonio up the El Camino Real, led the northern column above the center column under Sesma, whose objective was to reach Nacogdoches near the Louisiana border and the Sabine River, heading eastward into an unfamiliar region of dense pine forests.

Embracing the ruthless concept of ethnic cleansing to sweep Texas clean of Anglo-

Celts, Santa Anna now targeted the east Texas settlements for systematic destruction to exploit his Alamo victory and end the roughhewn civilization as constructed so laboriously by the settlers from the United States and their slaves. In part to appease the Catholic Church, which had funded his invasion of Texas, Santa Anna wanted a Catholic Texas filled with Mexican immigrants instead of troublesome norteamericanos. And this requirement meant that "all their dwellings need to disappear lest they entertain the hope of ever returning to them" and Texas.

Under bright sunshine, Santa Anna himself departed San Antonio on March's last day. His belated departure from San Antonio indicated Santa Anna's conviction that the war was all but over by this time. After all, only Houston's small group of untrained citizen soldiers—the last organized force of homespun revolutionaries remaining in Texas—had to be swept aside and crushed by his victorious legions.

But placing sound wisdom before rashness, Houston steadily withdrew east, declining to make a stand for the chance to fight another day. He and his band of Texas rebels disappeared into the expanse of broad prairie lands that seemed to stretch forever, heading toward the dark forests of stately pines farther east. All in all, this was an omin-ously strange, almost eerie land that remained a mystery to the fighting men from Mexico. Consequently, Santa Anna knew neither Houston's location nor his intentions; he was groping for an elusive opponent in unfamiliar territory while far from logistical support and Mexico City.

Southeast of San Antonio, the right, or southern, wing of Santa Anna's invasion force, led by the capable General Urrea, captured the Goliad garrison. This especially ill-fated force consisted of inexperienced volunteers who only recently had been determined never to retreat or surrender, revealing their misplaced bravado. Fannin's sizeable command, consisting entirely of United States volunteers, had moved out from its secure stone and adobe presidio, La Bahia, at Goliad on the San Antonio River in an ill-advised attempt to march thirty miles northeast to Victoria, on the east bank of the Guadalupe River, as ordered by Houston. Long hampered by indecision and ego-driven and political in-fighting within the unruly force of volunteers, Fannin had been forced to surrender. He allowed his command to get caught on the open prairie by crack Mexican cavalry—the worst fate for Anglo-Celtic riflemen—and trapped at the battle of Coleto Creek on March 19. None of Fannin's men, almost all novices to the ways of war, could possibly imagine the cruel fate that awaited them. Meanwhile, Emily D. West continued to work at New Washington, about 175 miles to the northeast, oblivious to the tragic events unfolding at Goliad, directly south of Gonzales, and the overall course of the Texas Revolution.

More than 300 prisoners, not knowing what Santa Anna had in store for them, were marched out of Presidio La Bahia, now called Fort Defiance, on the guise that they would be returned to the United States. Instead, they were taken out into the prairies outside Goliad and executed on Palm Sunday, March 27. As reported by one newspaperman who described the massacre that made the slaughter of the Alamo garrison pale in comparison: "All [were] put to the sword, but five who escaped, and only two of them Georgians." These surviving Georgians were members of the doomed Georgia Battalion of Permanent Volunteers, which had been organized by William Ward in Macon in mid–November 1835. The weapons that they laid down at Coleto Creek to seal their fate were from the Georgia State Arsenal. Scores of young men and boys of the Georgia Battalion never saw their homes in Macon, Columbus, and Milledgeville again.

One of those unfortunate men who was killed in the infamous Goliad Massacre on that horrible Palm Sunday on the open prairie just southwest of Emily and New Washington was

Peter Allen, a proud and free African American. He was the son of the founder of the African Methodist Episcopal Church, Richard Allen, who had purchased his freedom in late 1783. This defiant free black man executed at Goliad was Philadelphia, Pennsylvania—born Peter Allen. Around the year 1805, Peter had been born of Richard, who became the revered bishop of the African Methodist Episcopal Church, and a free black woman named Sarah Bass. From Isle of Wight County in the Chesapeake country of eastern Virginia, she had first come to Philadelphia at age eight as a slave. Sarah married her husband in March 1801 as a free woman. Peter's parents were active in reform movements, including promoting the sacred cause of abolition.

Peter Allen had migrated from the Philadelphia area to Huntsville, Alabama, in 1835, just in time to get caught up in the excitement over the outbreak of the Texas Revolution. Peter shortly married a slave woman named Mary, but dramatic events in far-away Texas were destined to take him far from home. He was only one of a number of African Americans who had enthusiastically joined volunteer companies in the United States to assist the Texas revolutionaries and to make Texas free of Mexican rule. He enlisted as a musician, or "flutist," in Captain Peyton S. Wyatt's company of Huntsville volunteers on October 31, 1835.

Just before the slaughter at Goliad in a selfless decision that ensured his own execution, making him the first black "Texian" to die for Texas independence, Allen refused the offer of freedom from the Mexicans, who liberated the slaves on Texas soil, because of his color. Sealing his own fate and destruction to Mexican bullets and bayonets, Peter Allen merely stated to his captors, "I'll just go along with the rest of the boys."[3]

Like the men of the Alamo whose bodies were consumed in the raging fires of the large funeral pyres that were situated on both sides of the majestic rows of cottonwood trees along the Alameda that led to San Antonio de Béxar from the east, the bodies of hundreds of Fannin's slain men, including Peter Allen, whose skin color no longer made any difference, were burned, as if to cover up the evidence of what was a hideous crime against humanity.[4]

While Santa Anna brought an everlasting shame to his republic and Mexican arms for what happened at Goliad, a remarkable Latino woman of courage and compassion rose to the fore during the massacre, Francita Alavéz. She played the leading role in saving nearly 100 captives of the Nashville, Tennessee, battalion of volunteers at the port of Copano on Copano Bay. She convinced Mexico officers that Santa Anna's no quarter policy was immoral and should be reversed, an argument that paid dividends for the hapless, unarmed Tennessee volunteers in custody.

No lackey like so many other officers who wanted only to please the generalísimo and were yes men, the gallant Urrea, a man of honor with great pride in his vocation, not only agreed with Alavéz, but also convinced Santa Anna to spare the volunteers of the Ireland-born William Parsons Miller's Nashville Battalion on a legal technicality, because they had been captured without arms since weapons had been shipped aboard another vessel. As a hard-working nurse who faithfully attended the wounded Americans, who had been carried to the presidio at Goliad from the Coleta battlefield on the open prairie, she saw them as fellow human beings instead of devils from the north. To Alavéz, these young men and boys were not the hated enemy, overcoming a host of Mexican prejudices about a different race, culture, and religion.

For humanity's sake, she simply overlooked the fact that these men were her country's enemies, who had come to Texas not as settlers, but as soldiers to assist the Texians in wresting Texas away from Mexico. A determined woman on her own personal mission amid the insanity and brutality of war, Alavéz then saved more captive United States volunteers by hiding them on the eve of fatal Palm Sunday, the day of the Goliad slaughter. Unlike the prisoners, who were unaware of their tragic fates, she knew of the execution orders, which only fueled her frantic efforts to save as many young men and boys as possible. For her heroism, especially in the face of Santa Anna's execution orders, Alavéz earned well-deserved recognition as the "Angel of Goliad."

An orphan who had early learned of adversity in life, Francita was raised by a wealthy family in the sprawling city of San Luis Potosí, located on the sun-baked, north central plains of the Mexican Plateau. Here, she worked as a lowly domestic servant. When Santa Anna's army organized at San Luis Potosí before the long trek north into Texas and to a rendezvous with destiny at the Alamo, this attractive young Latino woman fell in love with one of Urrea's dashing young cavalry officers, Captain Telesforo Alavéz. Therefore, she had enthusiastically accompanied him, Urrea's handsome paymaster, on the march north and throughout the 1836 Texas Campaign, sharing the same dangers and deprivations as the men in the ranks.

But the resourceful Alavéz was not finished in saving a good many American lives at Goliad and at considerable risk to herself. After the Goliad Massacre on that awful Palm Sunday that mocked the strict religious observances in the Mexican encampment, Captain Alavéz was assigned to Victoria, Texas, which had been named in honor of Mexico's first president, General Guadalupe Victoria. Francita then accompanied him to the town on the coastal plain and near the Gulf Coast about 140 miles southwest of Emily at New Washington. Here, about forty miles from the Gulf Coast, she saved the lives of other captive Americans, more United States volunteers, about to be executed by the Mexicans. For her tireless, determined efforts to save men of a different race and faith, this pious young woman of the Catholic faith, Francita Alavéz, deserved not only the title of the Angel of Goliad, but also renown as the angel of Copano and Victoria.[5]

The slaughter of hundreds of young men and boys from the United States at Goliad had been all but inevitable because of the failings of both the political and military leadership of Texas. Henry Ripley had penned a prophetic letter on March 11, 1836, from Goliad to his father, War of 1812 General Eleazar W. Ripley, that strongly denounced the folly of Texas leaders. And because of this self-destruction of Fannin's command, young Henry Ripley concluded correctly with fatal resignation, "In all probability the men now in the field will die at their posts. For myself, I have that opinion [but] it would be dishonorable for me to leave Texas now."[6] Santa Anna's men, meanwhile, were equally resolute and determined in this conflict, "burn[ing] to distinguish themselves in defence of the sacred rights of the nation."[7]

Meanwhile, northeast of Goliad, Houston pushed farther east, reaching the Colorado River, now swollen with the first spring rains, on March 17. Most of all, he knew that he needed a good natural barrier between him and his relentless pursuers. Houston and his ragtag force crossed the river on March 19. Once on the river's east side, these soldiers felt safer, especially after burning the ferry. Here, Houston planned to organize his forces, consisting of only around 600 men, and to increase their numbers east of the Colorado, where almost all of the Texians lived.[8]

Meanwhile, in pursuit of the wily Houston, the lengthy column of Sesma's troops reached the west bank of the Colorado on March 20. Naturally desiring to avenge the Alamo as soon as possible, Houston's untrained citizen-soldiers were over-eager, wanting nothing more than an opportunity to launch an attack. But Houston wisely knew that more time was needed to create an army, before risking a climactic showdown for the possession of Texas.[9]

After learning on March 23 of the defeat and surrender of Fannin and several hundred of his volunteers from hard-riding scouts, Houston ordered his diminutive army, now the only remaining Texian force in the field after the swift elimination of Fannin's command, to retire farther east from the Colorado River line and toward San Felipe de Austin, situated on the Brazos River, on March 26. He reached the capital of the Austin Colony two days later and while Fannin's men were executed on March 27, with his disgruntled men complaining along the way. By this time, the members of the convention had already fled for their lives, knowing that Santa Anna would have them shot out-of-hand, if taken.

Houston had already withdrawn 120 miles east since departing from Gonzales, situated on the open prairie just east of San Antonio de Béxar, and on the western frontier. Then, on March 29, Houston marched his unruly band of volunteers north from San Felipe de Austin to Jared Ellison Groce's Plantation, a prettily situated place known as Bernardo on the west bank of the Brazos. Here, some of the leading members of government, now refugees like Zavala, the Yucatan revolutionary, had stayed for several days before continuing east toward the Gulf Coast.

Having created his own cotton kingdom after relocating from the Deep South, Groce was the largest slave owner and wealthiest planter in the Austin Colony. Groce's sprawling plantation was about twenty miles north of San Felipe and south of Washington-on-the-Brazos. Houston's weary band of soldiers, disgusted about having steadily retired before Santa Anna's advance, encamped in a placid setting amid protective oak thickets along the calm, dark waters of the Brazos River on March 30. Here, on the river's west bank, the foot-sore Texians gained some much needed rest, while basking in the recently arrived warm weather of spring. Best of all, everyone knew that spring rains were about to unleash a deluge upon the land: a guarantee that Santa Anna's advance would be slowed.

Having taken "a very strong position" along the Brazos had caused Houston to abandon the seat of government at San Felipe de Austin to the south. But in a war to the death that was the 1836 Texas Campaign, the loss of a town was preferable to losing an army. During this emergency situation, military considerations superseded political priorities; this was a wise decision by the astute Houston under the circumstances. As Houston explained his overall campaign strategy, which was one of simple survival by this time, lest all Texas be lost and reclaimed by Mexico: "I [was] determined to retreat and get as near to Andrew Jackson and the old flag as I could."[10]

Houston's tactical and strategic reasoning was sound. What lay just beyond the Sabine River, or the Texas border with Louisiana, was ample United States forces under the command of General Edmund Gaines, who was in contact with Houston, and, of course, Andy Jackson in the White House. Most of all, Houston hoped that by literally taking the war to the distant border of the United States, he could perhaps spark much-needed armed intervention by an eager President Jackson, who had long coveted Texas, to save the people of Texas, the ad hoc volunteer army, and the young republic.

The independent republic of Texas now faced a premature death hardly before it had been born, while the lingering remains of a fast-crumbling Anglo-Celtic civilization west of the Sabine were also at stake. Houston's plan was essentially a gigantic ambush designed to lure Santa Anna ever-eastward and all the way to the Gulf Coast, because Gaines was more than ready and willing to cross the Sabine to assist Houston and his fellow countrymen now in dire straits. Houston was relying upon a wise Fabian policy of withdrawal eastward like the Russians in facing Napoleon in 1812.[11]

This most tantalizing bait of smashing Houston's army and reaching the Sabine was irresistible to Santa Anna, because of his well-known imperial impatience, his eagerness to end the amateurish, homespun rebellion of Anglo-Celtic rebels, and due to so many past easy successes reaped by these tough fighting men from Mexico over the Texians. Taking advantage of the opportunity presented to him, Santa Anna also wanted to reach the Sabine to fortify Mexico's long-existing claim that this watercourse was the international border, not the Neches River: an opportunistic concept that a land-hungry, Manifest Destiny–inspired President Jackson warmly embraced. For good reason, an increasingly complacent Santa Anna, who was originally concerned about the distinct possibility of meeting United States troops on Texas soil west of the Sabine, felt great relief in encountering no United States regulars and no serious Texian opposition during the push east: "Our military campaign was a military parade" toward east Texas. The campaign also eased ever-closer to Emily D. West at New Washington.[12]

Santa Anna's army continued to advance in three large columns, with two sweeping east and Urrea's column north up the coast. Each of these Mexican columns headed toward the Sabine River and the Louisiana border, while hunting for Houston's ghost command hidden amid the thick hardwood forests and dense canebrakes and to sweep the Anglo-Celtic colonists off Texas soil once and for all. Santa Anna was determined to reclaim all of Texas. And this grand strategic objective to regain national sovereignty meant driving away the interlopers, who had prematurely concluded that Texas was their own land and not part of the Republic of Mexico.

After crossing the Colorado, Sesma's center column continued to push toward San Felipe de Austin, hoping to keep Houston's volunteer army from gathering additional strength. However, Houston benefited from the precious two week period—from March 30 to April 12—to train his raw citizen-soldiers with monotonous regularity across the level cotton fields, nestled between a placid lake and the Brazos, amid the river bottoms on the plantation at Groce's Landing. Wisely, Houston was diligent about training his rookies in arms for the fateful, inevitable meeting with Santa Anna in the near future to decide the fate of Texas.[13]

But the overall momentum of Santa Anna's pursuit subsided after Fannin and his sizeable command were eliminated at Goliad on Palm Sunday, March 27, in the brutal killing machine he had fashioned for norteamericano rebels. Wiping out Fannin's force fueled conviction among Santa Anna and his troops that the war was all but over.

Confidence among the victors increased to new highs as one victory followed another on Texas soil, while spirits plummeted in Houston's command. Hundreds of Houston's volunteers deserted and took furloughs to assist families in escaping Santa Anna's wrath and harsh judgment that bordered on the sadistic. By this time, Santa Anna had destroyed the two largest organized armed opposition forces in Texas, the San Antonio and Goliad garrisons. Only Houston remained in the field along the Brazos, more of a token force than a serious threat of any kind. Like a poker player in a high stakes game, which indeed the Texas Campaign of 1836 was, Houston kept his plans to himself, and his tiny army of inexperienced volunteers was yet a work in progress.

The ever-growing over-confidence and contempt for his opponent that now consumed the generalísimo, who had never been defeated by any soldiers from the United States, was well-founded. Since leaving San Antonio, Santa Anna encountered no opposition. Needing to return to Mexico City to resume his presidential responsibilities and to reap of laurels of a successful campaign in Texas which seemingly had been now restored to the republic, Santa Anna made plans to return to Mexico by sea, after mopping up any remaining scattered pockets of resistance. Indicating his firm belief that decisive victory already had been won despite a sage warning from his more realistic-thinking top lieutenants, who urged caution in undertaking a swift advance so far from Mexico, Santa Anna even dispatched his cavalry brigade back to Mexico.[14]

As if an ill omen for Mexico's future fortunes in Texas, a dense bank of dark clouds, bringing a drop in temperatures, rolled in from the west. Then, the torrential rains of spring drenched the lands east of the Colorado River like a tropical monsoon. Yet mostly an untamed wilderness, this region was heavily-wooded compared to northern Mexico and also the arid, central plains of Texas, where the San Antonio River trickled through. Reminding them that they were far from home, this was an alien environment for the young soldados, especially those from the tropics, who had marched north from deep inside Mexico and across the northern desert regions of few trees and little water.

About to be crossed by Santa Anna's forces yet on the west side of the rain-swollen Colorado River, this seemingly endless expanse of land known as Tejas became more low-lying east of the Brazos River as the gently rolling terrain began to descend to the gulf. Combined with the spring rains, such a landscape would prove more difficult, slowing the Mexican Army's advance.

Sesma's center column, which targeted San Felipe de Austin for capture and the vulnerable heart of the Austin Colony, was moving directly toward Emily and New Washington. Situated perpendicular to the Brazos River that flowed southeast and into the Gulf of Mexico at Velasco, south of Galveston Bay, lay the slow-moving Buffalo Bayou that eased through the Gulf Coastal Plain. Running straight west-east from Harrisburg, Buffalo Bayou entered the southeast flowing San Jacinto River at Lynch's Ferry, or Lynchburg, before these dark waters, heavy with sediment by the spring rain's runoff from the rich farmlands and sprawling cotton plantations, entered the brown expanse of Upper Galveston Bay.

And New Washington, where Emily remained at work at the hotel day after day, stood just below Buffalo Bayou and southeast of Lynch's Ferry. At this time, no one on either side yet fully realized how important these obscure, remote points on the ill-defined maps of east Texas would soon become in determining the war's final outcome and the destiny of Texas. The crossfire of war was coming straight to Emily, who had never before seen the horrors of war, and the little settlement known as New Washington.

Beginning in mid–March, rain poured down from black skies and turned the narrow dirt roads, winding through the gently rolling Texas countryside and dank forests like snakes, into quagmires. Both fate and nature seemed now to be working hand-in-hand against the advance of Santa Anna and his pursuers. Houston and his men, of course, saw these spring rains as a godsend, because they knew that Santa Anna was determined to purge this promised land of Anglo-Celtics.

On Santa Anna's orders, the Mexicans were executing those revolutionaries whom they found under arms, which only increased the terror and fueled the exodus of civilians, men, women, and children, eastward and then across the Sabine. As Lieutenant Colonel José Enrique de la Peña, of the crack Zapadores, or Sapper, Battalion, described the deluge in his diary on March 30: "The day began with abundant rain but our march continued; by three o'clock in the afternoon we had several violent storms, which made the road impassable, and the march cumbersome."[15]

Like the Texians and United States volunteers before the beginning of the 1836 Texas Campaign, Santa Anna had violated one of the basic axioms of war continuing to seriously underestimate his task of subjugating and reclaiming such a broad expanse of Texas. Santa Anna had to divide his army into four parts to accomplish these goals, including leaving a sizeable force in the occupation of San Antonio. In the tactical manner of Caesar in advancing his Roman legions through hostile territory with the purpose of catching an opponent by surprise, Santa Anna's eastward advance was divided into three parts or three parallel columns, casually overlooking the peril of the time-honored concept of "divide and conquer" in regard to his own army. Caesar was a military genius who knew how to brilliantly maneuver separated columns to eliminate an adversary far from Rome, and Santa Anna was not, especially when far from Mexico City. All the while, Sesma's vanguard division, the center column, was about to push farther east and straight toward New Washington and Emily, after crossing the Colorado once the brown waters receded from the deluge.

Quite simply, Santa Anna had become a victim of his own considerable success in Texas, wiping out rebel resistance with ease whenever he found it. Because he had no idea where Houston was located or the exact nature of his plans, Santa Anna pushed forward "with no prearranged plan and no firm base of operations," while deep in enemy and unfamiliar territory and far from support. Despite reaping success at every point, this was yet a risky undertaking, even against undisciplined, rowdy Texians, who took democratic excesses to new heights and fought among themselves more than they fought Mexican invaders.

Therefore, some experienced Mexican officers and even common soldiers continued to experience a sense of growing, if not prophetic, unease, while pushing ever-deeper into Texas and closer to the Gulf Coast. After all, the soldados realized that they were in an alien environment and too far from home, which became more apparent upon seeing buffalo herds and flocks of wild turkeys feeding in the meadows and roosting in trees at night, for the first time. Some of the wiser men in the Mexican Army's ranks even began to sense that some sort of a disaster awaited them and even their revered "El Presidente" amid the somber woodlands of east Texas in the days ahead. Increasing with each passing day, this nagging concern was well-founded.

Houston spent March 30 to April 12 at Groce's cotton plantation. A former officer of the United States Army, Houston's heroics at the battle of Horseshoe Bend under Andy Jackson during the Creek War had played a part in his appointment to overall leadership of Texas arms. This timely respite was most beneficial. Here, Houston trained and drilled his volunteers for the final showdown to determine the fate of Texas, making them more formidable than ever before. And, most importantly, Houston's ad hoc force had grown to over 1,000 men, with Texians flocking to the ranks now that most of the United States volunteers in Texas had been slaughtered at the Alamo and Goliad. De la Pena's words explained the clash of dual convictions in the Mexican Army's ranks: "Some, among them the commander in chief, believed the campaign to be at an end, with little left to be done; others expressed contrary opinions saying that it was just beginning, and even went as far as to predict an ill-fated end."[16]

In a letter written on the last day of March, a Pennsylvania merchant, who had migrated with his family to Texas only to get caught amid the swirl of the Texas Revolution and the chaos of the flight toward the border, described the panic that gripped the Texian civilians and the role played by the women of Texas in attempting to save themselves, their families, and belongings: "Almost the entire settlers west of the Brazos moved over ... women driving the teams and stock [toward the Sabine]. Before my family left the place [Nacogdoches] the two preceding days, and in three days hence we shall have no female in the place [as] all the female part of the families are seeking safety beyond the Sabine."[17] Another settler near the end of March revealed in a letter the extent of the flight along the Gulf Coastal Plain: "The women and children have all left the town [of Matagorda, farther down the Gulf Coast around 110 miles southwest of New Washington], as they are also leaving all parts of Texas.—Every thing appears to be quite deserted."[18]

By the end of March, Emily remained busy with her daily chores and responsibilities at New Washington, very likely without knowing details of what was happening elsewhere that caused most white women of east Texas to take flight.[19] Most ominous of all, rumors swirled through the Texian settlements that terrified the wives and daughters of Texas that "Santa Anna is now in Texas, with 8000 cavalry, with which he is scouring the country, committing the most horrid cruelties, putting to death every one he meets, without regard to age, sex, or condition [and the] females are usually given up to the brutal passions of the soldiers and afterwards butchered."[20]

On March 21, William Fairfax Gray penned in his diary how the panic consumed the political leaders of the new Texas Republic, because the "cabinet this morning left Groce's for Harrisburg."[21] Along the way in riding across an expanse of prairie that glowed to the horizon in every direction, Gray was awed by the beauty of the land so passionately coveted by both sides in this war. He scribbled in his diary on March 22 how the "beautiful woods of the San Jacinto [River] lay eastward to our left, and near enough to distinguish the deep green of the cedar and pine which abounds there [and] Zavala pointed out to me some of his possessions. He has five leagues [more than 22,000 acres] on the San Jacinto."[22]

The following day, Zavala, the interim vice president of the world's newest republic, invited William Fairfax Gray to stay at his home. In his diary, Gray described now the mounted party "arrived at Zavala's before 2 o'clock" on March 23.[23] Gray continued: "Zavala only owns one labor of land here .... It is beautifully situated on a point at the junction of Buffalo Bayou and *Old San Jacinto*, the present San Jacinto running some distance off. The house is small, one large room, three small bed closets..... Mrs. Zavala is a fine, beautiful women, of tall dignified persona and ladylike manners, black eyes, twenty-seven years old, a native of the State of New York; maiden name West. She is the second wife of the Vice-President; the first was a lady of Yucatan, and the mother of young Lorenzo," Jr.[24]

Gray continued to reveal his fascination with the captivating Mrs. Zavala, whose beauty, sophistication, and charm were renowned far and wide, especially on the unruly frontier: "Mrs. Zavala spent one year in the City of Mexico after her marriage, and speaks the Spanish language fluently. She and her husband always converse in Spanish when alone. She was also in Paris with her husband when he was minister of the Mexican Republic at that court. She has but one house servant, an Irish girl, the same that accompanied her to Paris, who is chambermaid and nurse, one black woman in the kitchen, who is cook, etc."[25]

Clearly, interim vice president Zavala and his pretty wife, who yet dressed as if back in her native New York, had found a measure of personal happiness and peace on an obscure place along the tranquil waters of Buffalo Bayou, which was lined with virgin oaks draped in Spanish moss. However, this peace enjoyed by the Zavala family along Buffalo Bayou was about to be shattered by the arrival of Santa Anna's forces.

Decisive April in Texas

By early April, Emily began to see the first refugees streaming into New Washington, fleeing Santa Anna's advance in the great panic that had gripped the Texians, especially the women and children, whose husbands now served under Houston. Hundreds of panicked civilians were headed for Lynch's Ferry to cross the San Jacinto River, an imposing natural obstacle, now rain-swollen, before reaching safety, which lay just across the border in Louisiana. Emily also saw slaves who yet faithfully remained with white families, who needed their assistance during the crisis.[26] She might have been perplexed by the sense of loyalty displayed by these blacks, who would have been immediately freed if they encountered Mexican soldiers on Texas soil.

On the night of April 4, the day that Santa Anna himself reached Beason's Crossing on the Colorado River, William Fairfax Gray, the opportunistic Virginia land speculator, and other greedy land speculators reached New Washington, after their flight from Lynchburg and approaching Mexican troops, in a small open boat. Another vessel, the *Cayuga*, also reached Morgan's Point from Harrisburg at about the same time. Gray and his four friends stayed at the New Washington Hotel, where Emily worked since late December. Here, they "got a bowl of milk and bread at Morgan's, and slept there."[27] Emily possibly prepared this scanty fare for Gray and his associates, or was nearby.

On the morning of April 5, Emily saw that the sidewheeler steamboat *Cayuga*, bound for Galveston Island, was crowded with refugees who were desperate and determined to leave the Texas mainland before it was too late. However, Emily was bound by contract and her own personal sense of honor not to leave New Washington, despite the increased chaos and indications that the Mexican Army was headed her way. She no doubt feared joining the crowd of refugees bound for the United States, because she saw so many black faces—slaves, not free blacks—in the crowds of civilians.

One of the refugees aboard the *Cayuga*, which stayed at New Washington on Tuesday, April 5, to take on fuel (cut wood), who came ashore at New Washington was the hard-luck New Orleans beauty Harriet Moore Page, who was yet well-dressed compared to the other rustic Texian women around her. Emily certainly saw Page during her stay at New Washington. Harriett's gambler husband, Solomon Page, had abandoned her and her children to fend for themselves in the wilderness along Austin Bayou, located just north of the Brazos River and near the Gulf Coast, in the Brazoria area. "I only trusted that God would help," Harriett said in this turbulent time. But she had finally decided it was the right time to leave Texas to escape the certainty of even harder times with war clouds closing in over Harriet, who seemingly always had trouble coming her way.[28]

Meanwhile on this warm Tuesday, Gray and his friends toured Morgan's extensive properties that were part of the New Washington Association, with the owner-agent. Gray was not impressed by the upstart, pretentious settlement known as New Washington and wrote in his diary: "Walked with Morgan to see his orange grove [perhaps where Emily tasted her first fresh orange], and the new town of Crockett that he means to lay out. He lives at a place called Clopper's Point, now by the tasteless name of *New Washington*. He apologizes for the name by ascribing it to the will of some gentlemen in New York, who have become interested in the new city."[29]

On Wednesday, April 6, Emily once again saw a vessel that she recognized and knew quite well, the *Flash*, which arrived at New Washington. But the swift schooner had changed dramatically in appearance since when she had been brought to Texas for the first time aboard the *Flash* from New York City. Now heavily armed and a war vessel of the nascent Texas Navy, the *Flash* was soon to embark on an important mission up the brown waters of the Brazos: transporting two cannon, known as the "Twin Sisters," to Houston's army that possessed not a single artillery piece up to this time. The final showdown, where the winner would take all, was fast-approaching.

Now situated on Galveston Island from their transport across the Gulf of Mexico, the two cannon arrived at Groce's Plantation and eventually reached Houston's army on April 11, after their lengthy journey down the Ohio from Cincinnati and then down the Mississippi.[30] In his diary, Gray described the morning of April 6: "We were called up this morning by Morgan, but the boat [the *Cayuga*] did not get off until near 8 o'clock. In about an hour we met the schooner *Flash*, belonging to Morgan…. She had the Secretary of the Navy [Robert Potter] on board, and a number of ladies from the Brazos, whose husbands were in the army, seeking safety in flight."[31]

Basking in his string of successes that caused celebrations in Mexico City, a thoroughly smug Santa Anna had originally planned to return to Mexico on April 1. At that time, he planned to allow the capable General Vincente Filísola to finish the job of mopping up what little resistance remained in Texas to complete the subjugation of Anglo-Celtic settlement and civilization west of the Sabine. But Santa Anna's optimistic plans vanished, when it was learned that the strength of Houston's army was more sizeable than expected.[32]

Even while marching along muddy roads in the pelting Texas rain and thinking of Latino homes and families so far away in the beloved fatherland, Mexican soldados were amazed by what they saw in Texas. What they viewed around them was a virgin land rich in natural resources and blessed with an unsurpassed natural beauty that mocked the relative sterility of the deserts of northern Mexico. Bright blankets of wild flowers in seemingly endless colors, especially scarlet and blue, covered the pastures and prairies like a carpet after the refreshing spring rains that brought new life to a land seemingly blessed by God.

Texas was one of the most bountiful and promising regions in the entire Mexican republic: a fertile, precious region worth fighting and dying for, to keep to the thinking of both the Texians and Mexicans during this campaign that would decide who would possess this rich land. Many of Santa Anna's troops, never so far north before, literally fell in love with the sheer natural beauty of this pristine land, as did the Texians when they first migrated west of the Sabine. An enchanted Lieutenant Colonel de la Pena, romantic-minded and a poet at heart, marveled on April 7, "We passed through some prairies so beautiful that I lack words to describe them. It was all a field of lilies and poppies of an exquisite and unique variety, not only in their varied colors but also because of the forms nature had given them. The soul expanded, and it is difficult to explain the joy that I felt in its enchantment."[33]

Even more than wiping out Houston's band, which he considered almost inconsequential at this time, Santa Anna desired to capture the rebel political leaders of the Texas government, interim President David Gouverneur Burnet and interim Vice President Lorenzo de Zavala. While Houston, the Tennessee governor before his own poor judgment in the form of a misplaced love ended his promising political future, had reverted from thinking like a politician to a general in terms of a wise overall strategy, Santa Anna simultaneously went the other direction in no longer thinking like a general, but more like a politician. No small part of the formula calculated to ending the people's revolution in Texas now meant eliminating the revolutionary governing body of the troublesome breakaway province: the other part of Santa Anna's strategy, after his soldados had already wiped out hundreds of United States volunteers at the Alamo and Goliad.

In the early morning hours of April 7 and after having crossed the Colorado River the previous day, Santa Anna decided to strike at the head of the snake. He now led a task force of 200 hand-picked infantrymen and 80 horse soldiers northward, after crossing the spring-fed San Bernard River that flowed southeast into the gulf. In a calculated dash and bold attempt to surprise and capture the Texas government thought to be at San Felipe de Austin,

Santa Anna and his carefully-selected advance troops pushed rapidly forward to deliver a crushing political and psychological blow in a bid to end the conflict once and for all.

But the crude frontier town of mostly log cabins on the brown Brazos River had been evacuated and burned down by Houston, after the newly-elected government had opted to flee for Harrisburg, on the turbid waters of Buffalo Bayou, in present-day Houston, Texas. As he discovered on a warm April 7, a frustrated Santa Anna had missed his flushed quarry, after pushing far ahead of Sesma's column. He also discovered that San Felipe de Austin had been reduced to ashes. Such a mounted strike revealed Santa Anna's instincts as a cavalryman had dominated his thinking more than an army commander focused on sound strategy and less spectacular tactics. He had taken his eye off Houston's army, stationary at Groce's Plantation on the Brazos, which should have been his primary target.

Santa Anna decided to concentrate his divergent columns below San Felipe de Austin on the Brazos to bring his army together once more. In a contemptuous dismissal of the last remaining large Anglo-Celtic force in the field, Santa Anna now marched away, or south, from Houston's army that had remained stationary for two weeks at Groce's Plantation until April 12. Santa Anna now pushed south along the river to concentrate his forces at Thompson's Crossing on the lower Brazos River. On the march south, Mexican troops reached the cabin of a mulatto man named Wilson, who lived with his white wife. The mulatto was dispatched south to reconnoiter the Thompson's Ferry area by the advance guard, but Wilson never returned. He was a loyal Texian, having already warned his white comrades of Santa Anna's approach.

Near Thompson's Ferry, Santa Anna learned that Houston's Army, after departing Groce's Plantation on April 12 and crossing the Brazos on the same day by way of the steamboat *Yellowstone*, was headed southeast toward Harrisburg, on the eastern headwaters of Buffalo Bayou. Eager to finish this rebellion with one decisive stroke, Santa Anna would not wait for his army's concentration of force, which would have ensured certain victory over Houston's diminutive command. After seizing Thompson's Ferry and a very startled ferryman, Santa Anna and his vanguard crossed to the east side on April 12.

With Harrisburg only thirty miles distant, he now led his advance task force onward and even farther away from his main army in pursuit of the Texas government, now fleeing east toward the United States, the Sabine, and safety. Moving east to the south of Houston's Army, Santa Anna's fast-moving task force consisted of only around 500 hand-picked troops whom he proudly considered the best available men, all veterans. Eager to end the rebellion with one bold stroke, Santa Anna and this advance guard pushed far ahead of the main army and deeper into the virtual wilderness east of the Brazos: another violation of sound military axioms by the generalísimo, whose personal philosophy and risk-taking personality combined to lead him ever-onward.

Caught up in the excitement of the chase because the fleeing Texas cabinet and president were rumored to be at Harrisburg, the army's commander had seemingly reverted to this old days as a young Royal cavalry officer of the Vera Cruz Lancers instead of the nation's leader and the army's commander. Riding across the springtime prairies and a rain-soaked country like a sporting Virginia gentleman on a fox hunt and sensing victory that he felt lay just before him over the eastern horizon, Santa Anna and his advance unit pushed onward.[34]

Santa Anna's actions were in keeping with not only his personality, but also his past in the fine art of counterinsurgency. In fact, Santa Anna's rise to fame derived from such reckless but successful missions as a young man when he rode at the head of his men from the tierra caliente (hot lowlands) when hunting down Mexican guerrillas in Vera Cruz Province, where he had been born. Santa Anna's successful counterinsurgency efforts made him well-known to officials in Mexico City. Therefore, by April 1836, Santa Anna possessed ample experience in the fine art of vanquishing rebels, Mexican, Tejano, Indian, or Anglo-Celt, and was fully capable of stamping out rebellion in Texas.[35]

Throughout this period, Emily was yet at New Washington, while war clouds drew ever-closer. She would have certainly rejoiced if she knew that people of color were being liberated across east Texas. With their masters fleeing for their lives before Santa Anna's advance, many blacks simply slipped away and quietly left, never to return. In an April 7, 1836, letter, one American, who had just escaped the turmoil of Texas and wrote from a steamboat taking him to safety and beyond Santa Anna's reach, described how "many negroes have runaway—in some instances whole plantations of them had gone off in a body."[36]

And Virginian William Fairfax Gray also felt consternation in regard to the panic and chaos that had gripped Texas. Like Anglo-Celtic civilization, the old social order of Texas was not only collapsing, but also dying, thanks to Santa Anna's relentless advance. Gray described how, when approaching Galveston Bay on April 22, 1836, "we start[l]ed three runaway negroes, who fled and plunged through a bayou at our approach [and] one of them had a gun."[37]

After General Sesma's column of the vanguard division had joined him for a joint crossing of the Brazos, and benefiting from timely intelligence gained from both free blacks and slaves who talked freely about Texian movements, Santa Anna had detailed his campaign objectives to Italian-born General Filísola, second in command and a former freedom fighter in the lengthy guerrilla war against Napoleon's invading French in Spain, which became the "Spanish Ulcer," at this point: "Since the operations of the Army should not be paralyzed, I have decided to depart with a section to Harrisburg, where the principal [political] leaders of the rebellion are located and to which entitled General Houston is marching with the band he has united and calls by the name of the Army of Texas."[38]

Santa Anna's fateful decision was destined to "alter the fate of three nations."[39] By this time, Santa Anna knew that Houston was pushing in the same direction—eastward—as himself, or toward Harrisburg. However, he was unaware that Houston now knew exactly what he was up to in regard to his latest strategy made on the move. During Santa Anna's late April 10 council of war on the banks of the San Bernard River—the last river before the Brazos to the east—at Elizabeth Powell's Inn, south of the San Felipe de Austin and "on a stream called Guajolote," in Colonel Almonte's words, vital intelligence for Houston's ears had been gained.

Here, at "Widow" Powell's inn that was not unlike the New Washington Hotel where Emily worked, Elizabeth's son, who understood Spanish well, had heard Santa Anna outline the breadth of his ambitious campaign plans, including leading the vanguard task force on his own and all the way to Harrisburg: timely intelligence that had been relayed to Houston, convincing him to depart the vicinity of San Felipe de Austin, which he had burned to the ground to deny the Mexicans their prestigious trophy of the Austin Colony's capital, on April 12 and to cross the Brazos and then head southeast toward Harrisburg.

But most importantly, on April 7, Houston had also learned a vital piece of intelligence thanks to a report from the free black named Wilson, who had been scooped up by Houston's scouts: that Santa Anna himself was leading a small advance vanguard and hence was vulnerable in the foremost ranks, separated from the main army.

Santa Anna pushed northeast in an attempt to capture the refugee Texas government at Harrisburg. Meanwhile an inexperienced Houston, who had never commanded so many men before, dared not confront Santa Anna with his ill-equipped and poorly trained army. Instead, he planned to continue a steady withdrawal ever-eastward to gain the road to Nacogdoches, Texas, an escape route that led to greater safety near the United States border.[40]

As an insightful editorial in the *Richmond Enquirer* summed up the situation, "The Texans are few in numbers, and the troops of Santa Anna are well trained and disciplined. It is, therefore, the more necessary to await a favorable moment, when the Texians are well prepared to meet and conquer their enemy. Such was the policy of Washington, and it may be prudent to follow it in this instance."[41] But Santa Anna had already promised that the colonist "reinforcements from New Orleans, Mobile, Boston, New York and other ports ... are insignificant" to save Texas.[42]

At this time, the people of New Washington, including Emily, had even more than just the approach of Santa Anna's Army to worry about, especially since Morgan had been engaged in running war munitions and supplies, secured in New Orleans, from his wharf and warehouse to the Texian rebels. Like most American women, especially those from the East, nothing was more feared than possible capture by Indians, especially the fearsome Comanche, who were thought at this time to be allied with Santa Anna along with other tribes. Emily was almost certainly concerned because the people across Texas had long feared Santa Anna's forces uniting with Indian tribes to wage a war of vengeance upon the colonists now largely defenseless in their flight. As reported in the April 28, 1836, edition of *The Herald*, New York City, the Mexican Army's advance toward Louisiana caused "new and extraordinary sensation over the whole south [because] Santa Anna has proclaimed the emancipation of the slaves in Texas, and called the Indians to his aid."[43]

In the alarmed words of one Texian: "It is reported that the Mexican cavalry had come through the above [east Texas] settlements and joined the Indians in our immediate neighborhood, and were bringing them down upon us [and] Mexican soldiers [are] a more inhuman and savage enemy than even the North American Indian, as the dread tale of the massacre of the Alamo must inform you."[44]

If such reports swirling through the east Texas communities were true, then Emily now risked the possibility of falling victim to a massacre along with the small number of whites at New Washington, if the fierce Comanche struck, especially revenge-seeking warriors who had once called the Galveston area home, before the white interlopers had pushed them deep into the interior. Therefore, not only revenge, but also securing their ancient homelands were motivators among the Indians by the spring of 1836. Helping to fuel the panic, newspaper editors warned whites how "Santa Anna had engaged the Camache [sic] Indians against the Texians, and that they would bring 10,000 warriors into the field, of whom 5000 were mounted cavalry."[45]

As one Texian explained the escalating fears of the women of Texas, no doubt including Emily and others at New Washington, at this time: "The idea was horrible, that when they laid down at night, they might be waked by the Indian whoop only to feel their tomahawks" striking out of the blackness of isolated cabins, rural communities, and small towns like New Washington.[46]

But Santa Anna was not concerned about securing Indian allies, because they were not needed since he was not encountering opposition of any kind and considered the conquest of Texas nearly complete. A swift campaign would finish off the pesky Texians, who would rise no more after suffering one more punishing blow, believed Santa Anna. He now believed, in de la Pena's words, "the campaign to be at an end, with little left to be done," except to capture the fleeing political leaders of the renegade Texas government.[47]

Combined with Santa Anna's relentless push east, the threats of Indian reprisals and possible slave revolts spread even wilder panic among the colonists, who fled for the Louisiana border during the "Runaway Scrape." This mass hysteria that consumed the people of Texas first began after the massacre of the Alamo and Goliad garrisons, and only became worse with each passing day. The Texians now feared the Mexican soldado as much as the Comanche warrior and black slave in rebellion, and for ample good reason. Some of Santa Anna's soldados, such as his trusty scout from San Antonio de Béxar, Rafael Morales, were part Comanche. A New Orleans newspaper recorded an untruth that only fueled the panic across Texas: "So far as the Mexican army had advanced, they had made an indiscriminate slaughter of women and children. The orders given to the soldiery being to spare the life of no individual over ten years of age."[48] In order to generate support for the Texian cause, this is a classic case of the Texan and United States propaganda that sullied even the reputation of the chivalric, noble Colonel Almonte.[49]

But African Americans across Texas felt no fear of reprisal or danger for that matter, but viewed the Mexican Army's arrival as the long-awaited day of jubilee. For the first time in their lives, men, women, and children of African descent were liberated from the shackles of slavery whenever Mexican troops appeared to set them free. As in comparable situations when liberty was bestowed, almost certainly some blacks cried tears of joy. As if to destroy any visage of the institution of slavery and the cotton-based economy of the Anglo-Celts, Santa Anna's soldados burned down cotton gins that made cotton culture in Texas so productive and profitable.[50]

By this time, Colonel James Morgan, now no longer serving as an active agent of the New Washington Association because of the hectic wartime situation but yet in a position to protect its interests, had been placed by Houston in charge of fortifying Galveston Island, which was to serve as a final toehold and defensive position of the homespun revolutionaries on Texas soil. By April 8, Morgan had rounded up and utilized nearly 150 slaves, both men and women, to labor in the construction of earthen fortifications on the island's eastern end at Compeachy Point.

Evidently concerned about the large planter backlash even in an emergency and crisis situation such as the throes of revolution that had going badly for the rebels, interim president Burnet had authorized another officer "to *hire* hands" for the job. However, barely a week later, Secretary of War Thomas Jefferson Rusk gave Morgan permission to impress only the slaves of certain owners and plantations of Galveston Island.[51] Morgan's efforts paid dividends, and he demonstrated the same industriousness that had garnered him the position as the Texas agent of the New Washington Association. Impressed by Morgan's efforts, William Fairfax Gray noted in his diary on April 7, "The government is now making efforts to fortify the place, so as to be able to repel them. Colonel Morgan, who is a merchant, and the founder of New Washington, where he lives, has been appointed Commandant of the Post, and is entering on his duties with great zeal and activity."[52]

Meanwhile, on April 14, Santa Anna continued to lead his relatively small advance force, only 700 troops, in a desperate effort to catch up to the renegade Texas government leaders, especially interim president David Gouverneur Burnet, at Harrisburg. He had left Sesma's vanguard division at Thompson's Crossing, or Old Fort (Fort Bend)—southwest of Harrisburg and around twenty miles down-river from San Felipe de Austin—on the Brazos River, where the main body of the Mexican Army had been ordered to concentrate under General Filísola. However, and unrealized by him, Santa Anna's reckless effort to put a quick end to this troublesome rebellion in one stroke by capturing Harrisburg and the Texas government was taken at considerable risk, "unwittingly exposing himself and endangering the campaign" and jeopardizing its significant gains to date.[53]

However, for the audacious Santa Anna, who had learned his lessons well from reading about his idol Napoleon, it was all well worth the risk, because, in his own words, "A single blow would have been mortal to their cause" at this time.[54] On April 13 from his headquarters at Thompson's Ferry before departing with his vanguard in the dash to capture Harrisburg, Santa Anna had ordered Filísola, who commanded the main force at Old Fort, to dispatch General Martín Perfecto de Cos and 500 men and three cannon to join him. But besides his own folly of personally attempting to intercept the fleeing Texas government at Harrisburg, Santa Anna made a gross mistake in not specifically requesting the best trained and most experienced troops in orders to either Filísola or Cos.

Therefore, he missed his chance to secure the army's most reliable troops in case of a final showdown west of the Sabine, if Houston decided to turn and stake everything in one last battle: a glaring oversight and crucial error for which he would pay dearly in the days ahead. Now in the uncharted territory that he had never seen before after having crossed the Brazos, Santa Anna and his relatively small vanguard became increasingly more vulnerable in pushing so far east ahead of the main column. Only an hour before midnight of April 15, Santa Anna finally neared a burning Harrisburg that had been partially torched to deny it to the invader. In fact, the refugee Texas government had fled to New Washington, ensuring that Santa Anna followed. The war was coming ever closer to Emily D. West.

After having thrown caution to the wind in his all-out effort to capture the Texas political leaders and cabinet, Santa Anna, his trusty adjutant, and only fifteen hand-picked dragoons galloped into Harrisburg on Buffalo Bayou. But the Texas revolutionary officials of the infant Texas were long gone. Here, while the burning timbers of houses yet crackled, he was informed by printers of the *Telegraph and Texas Register* that the exiled band of Texas political leaders, including President Burnet, the vice president, and cabinet members had fled in the nick of time southeast to New Washington and Upper Galveston Bay. The flight of the cabinet had been a wise decision, because almost certain execution awaited them if captured by Santa Anna.

Santa Anna was naturally angry over having again just missed achieving his goal of capturing his own fellow countryman Zavala (an ideal target for setting a grim example of the high cost of defying his authority to other republican-minded Mexicans), and one of the leading land speculators in Burnet, who had sold his massive land grant to New York investors for a nice profit. In disgust and an outburst to temper against the newspaper that had condemned him for so long, Santa Anna ordered his men to hurl the printing press of the *Telegraph and Texas Register* into Buffalo Bayou's deep waters. With some relish, he then completed burning down what little remained of the rustic village of Harrisburg, situated on Buffalo Bayou's south bank.

Sensing he was near his elusive goal and probably lusting at the mere thought of executing interim President Burnet and Vice President Zavala, Santa Anna ordered Colonel Juan Nepomuceno Almonte and his select cavalrymen to dash forward in an attempt to surprise the refugee Texas government at New Washington, where Emily continued to work. As fate would have it, the winds of war and an uncertain future were headed directly toward Emily.

Meanwhile, on the same day after pushing through the broad prairie lands only recently turned bright green from the spring rains, the advance elements of Houston's Army reached a vital crossroads and the most "fateful fork in the road" in the storied history of Texas.

Here, near the modest home of Abraham Roberts in a small Texian community known as New Kentucky that revealed its antecedents in the state, the narrow road, now little more than a ribbon of mud, split in two. One road led southeast through the pine forests and cotton fields to Harrisburg—scouts had informed Houston that Santa Anna and around 750 men had reached the town—and the other road led northeast across the San Jacinto River to Nacogdoches and the United States border along the Sabine.

Here, at this obscure, muddy crossroads amid the seemingly haunted, semi-tropical hardwood forests on April 16, was not only a major turning point of the San Jacinto Campaign, but also of the history of Texas. Houston was not even part of this most momentous decision in choosing the road and army's future direction and role in the most important campaign in the story of Texas.

Making their own decision in true frontier fashion while their commander was in the column's rear, the foremost of Houston's young men and boys simply acted on their own in taking the Harrisburg Road, the right fork, and marching southeast through the dark forests draped in early springtime splendor. Unknown to Houston at the time, they made the most important decision of the campaign and in Texas history, marching southeast toward Harrisburg and beyond it New Washington, where Emily remained oblivious to the most dramatic developments of the Texas Revolution.

By this time after having turned to the right down the Harrisburg Road, General Houston's men were in high spirits with expectations of finally coming to grips with Santa Anna to settle old scores and decide the fate of Texas once and for all.[55]

Ensuring a final showdown for the possession of Texas, Houston's Army and Santa Anna's advancing troops headed in the same direction—east—and toward a rendezvous with destiny and the inevitable decisive clash of arms. At a brisk pace, the war continued to evolve, change, and move steadily closer to New Washington and Emily, who had no idea what fate and the war's fortunes had in store for her in the near future. Thousands of fleeing colonists took their slaves with them east toward the Sabine, while other more opportunistic blacks escaped from masters by slipping away and disappearing into the dark forests and swamps.

All the while, Mexicans troops continued to liberate the slaves that they encountered along the way. As a free black woman standing in the path of a fast-approaching storm, fueled by Santa Anna's will and determination that had first risen deep in Mexico, Emily's future was about to take a new, radical course.[56]

War Comes to New Washington

The conflict in Texas had taken on the ugliest characteristics of a brutal war between two distinct cultures, nationalities, and races, with blacks caught in the middle. After the Alamo's fall, Santa Anna burned the bodies of the estimated 187 Alamo defenders in three great funeral pyres, situated around the stately cottonwood trees of the Alameda, to wipe away all traces of the young men and boys who had defended the old Franciscan mission along the San Antonio River.

Never able to forget the sight, Pablo Diaz, born in Monclova, Mexico, around 1818, described the horror that illuminated the prairie surrounding the Alamo: "An immense pillar of flame shot up a short distance to the south and east of the Alamo and the dense smoke from it rose high into the clouds. I saw it burn for two days and nights around the Alameda."[57]

And now in much the same way as he had ordered the final destruction of the remains of the Alamo defenders, Santa Anna was determined to sweep the Anglo-Celtic presence entirely out of Texas. He, therefore, had emphasized to his soldados that Texas "should be razed to the ground, so that this immense desert [in the future] might serve as a wall between Mexico and the United States."[58] Houston and his men were in fact helping Santa Anna accomplish his destructive mission, after having employed a scorched earth policy. Houston had learned his tactical lessons well from reading about the tenacity of Russian resistance against a powerful invader in 1812. Houston's men not only "burned San Felippe [*sic*] de Austin [but also] destroyed all the country in their retreat," according to one account that appeared in the *New Orleans Bee*, in Louisiana.[59]

All the while, the march of Santa Anna's army continued to cause a wild exodus of Anglo-Celtic settlers, whole families, with their slaves in tow. The "Runaway Scrape" was doing more permanent damage to the foundation of Anglo-Celtic settlement than the fiery torches of Santa Anna's soldados. At the New Washington Hotel where she worked along the main road leading inland from the nascent port and northwest to Harrisburg, Emily no doubt viewed with growing alarm the sight of throngs of panicked refugees streaming into New Washington, before continuing on to Lynchburg, where they could cross the Sabine to gain Louisiana's safety.

Was Emily not panic-stricken or even afraid, after what she had experienced during the racial strife in New York City? She decided not to join the flood of civilians departing Texas as fast as they could, embarking upon a flight for safety. Despite knowing that the war was coming ever-closer by the day, she remained faithfully with her employer and assignment at New Washington. Regardless of what the war might bring her way, Emily was determined to fulfill her one-year contractual obligation, revealing a measure of character (which corresponded with her past) and commitment in a precarious situation that was growing more dangerous. After all, she possessed her free status papers, which would have ensured her safety in Louisiana, if she had decided to leave Texas like so many others.

With each mile he penetrated into the unfamiliar surroundings of the Gulf Coastal Plain, Santa Anna grew more eager to catch up to and eliminate the refugee Texas government, especially Zavala, which was yet his primary target rather than Houston's army. Described by one American historian as "an explosive little mestizo from Yucatan," Zavala had been exiled for his liberal ways, including opposition to the Catholic Church's almost unlimited power. Santa Anna, the conservative whose campaign in Texas was financed by the Church, needed to get his hands on Zavala, who was rightfully seen as the most dangerous of republican exiles, to garner more political support and popularity across Mexico.

After arriving at New Washington in the nick of time, the leaders of the Texas government took quarters in New Washington Association's hotel, where Emily had worked for months, finding a good place to eat and rest, before continuing on to escape Santa Anna's greedy clutches. Emily now saw the leading statesmen, including the interim president—Burnet—and interim vice president—Zavala—of the infant Republic of Texas. Distinguished by a thick, shaggy head of hair, the articulate New Jersey–born Burnet lived in a "simple four-room home called Oakland," with his wife, "a good looking woman," in William Fairfax Gray's opinion, on the appropriately named Burnet Bay, located just north of New Washington and farther up the ever-shrinking width of the body of water at the head of Galveston Bay.

Here, at the New Washington Hotel, Emily very likely heard their war-related conversations with increasing concerns about the fate of what now seemed like a dying fledgling republic, and their fears if captured by Santa Anna, which was surely an automatic death sentence. She might have even washed the clothes or cooked the meals of these leading statesmen, who had led the Texas experiment in nationhood and the birth of a new republic. Fortunately, no imaginative writer has yet suggested that Emily, since she had been so often portrayed as so alluring and irresistible to men in the tradition of "The Yellow Rose of Texas" mythology, was involved in a tryst with either Burnet or Zavala, given the seemingly-endless myth-making process about Emily D. West and her life. New Washington had prematurely and quite unexpectedly now fulfilled Morgan's and Swartwout's most ambitious visions by now becoming the nation's temporary capital, after the arrival of the refugee government.

Hoping to capture the fleeing members of the renegade Texas government as ordered by Santa Anna, Colonel Almonte and his cavalrymen, well-equipped, and heavily-armed, had been dispatched to New Washington. With the energetic Almonte, recently appointed as a major general in Sesma's vanguard division, the finely-uniformed dragoons, looking decidedly Napoleonic, now rode eastward toward New Washington without a let-up, despite the blazing sun and rising dust along the narrow road hewn through the dark pine forests that smelled fresh after the spring rains and the advent of warmer weather.

Upholding the tradition of the elite qualities of the Mexican cavalry, which was Mexico's most revered and best military arm, Almonte and his hard-riding dragoons galloped into New Washington in a swirl of dust. Of a "mulatto complexion," as his mother Brígida Almonte was pure Indian, Colonel Almonte, who had first gone to war at an early age in battling beside his warrior-priest father against Spain for the dream of Mexican independence and also to end slavery, almost succeeded in his vital mission in capturing the leading members of the Texas revolutionary government on the morning of April 16.

Emily witnessed and was part of the stirring drama that had suddenly descended upon New Washington like a whirlwind, with the arrival of Almonte and his cavalrymen. In fact, she might even have been one of the workers, mostly men, who had been assigned to help load one of Morgan's flatboats at the wharf and warehouse with war munitions for the Texas revolutionaries, when the Mexican cavalrymen thundered into New Washington with pistols and carbines at the ready.

After having been warned just in time by a worn, dust-covered teenage courier of Almonte's rapid approach, interim President Burnet and other revolutionary government officials had moved quickly to escape. With their panicked families placed safely onboard at almost the last minute, the political heads of the Texas Republic hurriedly pushed off in a large wooden skiff from Clopper's Point and a New Washington now swarming with Almonte's dragoons. The desperate escapees slipped into the warm waters of Upper Galveston Bay just before the Mexican cavalrymen reached the shore.

The interim president and his party, including Mrs. Zavala and her children, who had reached Texas in December 1835 aboard the *Flash* with Emily, were perhaps assisted by Emily at some point to facilitate their narrow escape. The Zavala family had been forced to abandon their beloved home, which already had been visited by a Mexican cavalry patrol dispatched by Santa Anna to nab the interim vice president and an old enemy on the picturesque shores of Buffalo Bayou. Emily most likely assisted the Zavala family and their belongings onto the skiff when time was rapidly running out, only minutes before Mexican cavalry arrived to capture New Washington. Emily's timely actions, along with the assistance of others, indicated that a certain bond had been forged with the Zavala family during the long trip to Texas, when she had helped to care for the three children.

A flatboat, now loaded with Morgan's personal property and munitions, that been hauling war supplies to the *Flash* from Morgan's warehouse at the wharf, was filled with a jumble of very nervous cabinet members. Emily was evidently present when the cavalrymen arrived at the shore of the bay, not long after the two boats—the skiff with the president and vice president's family and flatboat with cabinet members—slipped into the brackish waters of Galveston Bay. Afterwards around fifty Mexican horse soldiers, including the suave Colonel Almonte, suddenly reined up at the shore before Emily's eyes with weapons drawn. Fluent in English from having been sent as a young man to New Orleans to receive a fine education in a leading Catholic school operated by Jesuits, Almonte almost certainly spoke to Emily at some point. He perhaps mentioned that no harm would come to her, if he ascertained some fear in Emily's eyes or heard her concerns about her safety among soldiers since she was an American. And she had been working at a place that helped to fuel the rebellion against Mexico.

However, since Santa Anna's men had been freeing the slaves across Texas, she had no reason for concern. Therefore, the Mexicans almost certainly initially assumed that Emily was also a slave, until she indicated otherwise at some point, and almost certainly to Colonel Almonte, who commanded the cavalry detail. Emily, in consequence, was not freed by Almonte and his troopers, except in regard to her contract with the New Washington Association, which the fortunes of war had severed.

After aligning along the muddy bank overlooking the wide expanse of Upper Galveston Bay which glimmered from the bright sunlight, the foremost Mexican dragoons were about to unleash a volley on the exposed interim President Burnet, wife Hannah Este Burnet, who had been born in Morristown, New Jersey, in December 1800, and children in the wooden skiff only around forty yards away. Fortunately for the Burnet family and belying his role as one of Santa Anna's most trusted advisors and top lieutenants, the ever-compassionate and chivalric Colonel Almonte rose to the fore. Proud of a most distinguished family and legacy that he desired to remain stainless in this war against rebels, Almonte was the illegitimate son of one of Mexico's most cherished revolutionaries of the struggle for independence against Spain, Father José María Morelos. A revered leader of his people who was yet looked upon like a George Washington-figure, Morelos was executed by the Spanish. As a royalist, Santa Anna had fought against Almonte's priest-revolutionary father.

In keeping with the family tradition of doing what was morally right regardless of the circumstances, Almonte ordered for no cavalrymen, whose carbines were at the ready, to open fire on the helpless refugees. A true humanitarian of high moral character, he feared that his men, more horsemen than marksmen, might hit Mrs. Burnet and other women and children who were exposed in the open skiff. At the last second, Almonte even pushed aside the weapon of one eager cavalryman about to open fire.

Ever the astute politician and eager to curry favor at election time, Houston later claimed that Burnet had been nearly captured at New Washington, because he had delayed his departure in retrieving a demijohn of fine brandy of which he was most fond: a most odd accusation coming from a man whom the Cherokee knew intimately as "Big Drunk." But Houston had good reason to disparage Burnet, because the interim vice president had long angrily denounced Houston for failing to turn and face Santa Anna instead of withdrawing across much of Texas. He had ordered Houston to "fight [as] you must retreat no further," so that Texas would be saved and not left to Santa Anna's army.

After escaping by the narrowest of margins across the expansive bay of salty water, Texas government leaders hoped to find refuge on Galveston Island. They knew that Santa Anna was not acting in concert with the Mexican Navy, fearing no united effort to capture the narrow barrier island, which allowed agile vessels like the *Flash* to sail from the island to the mainland unimpeded. By this time, Emily might have lost contact with her two friends and fellow free blacks, who were likewise in Morgan's employment and possibly from New Haven like herself. Evidently these free African Americans, and no doubt some of Morgan's slaves, had been working at Morgan's large, wooden warehouse on the bay when they were ordered aboard the flatboat to work the oars. These two men of African heritage, including George Cooper, now frantically rowed the flatboat's oars across Upper Galveston Bay, taking government cabinet members who believed that all Texas should be saved as a land of slavery.

Thankful that her black friends had escaped, Emily watched the sight of the last Texas government officials successfully vacating the Texan mainland. She also felt comfort that Mrs. Zavala and her children had escaped. Meanwhile, located just below a New Washington which was now captured by Mexican cavalrymen, the *Flash* lay in calm waters and in anchor awaiting the anticipated arrival of the beleaguered Texas president and other refugees to transfer them to the safety of Galveston Island.[60]

Colonel Almonte was a noble spirit in part because of an affinity and grudging respect for Americans and what they had accomplished in Texas by their industriousness (and slaves) transforming a wilderness into a civilization. When living in the United States, Almonte had seen much to admire, especially in republican theory, reminding him of what his own father had fought and died to achieve by creating a land of equality for all people and races. Later in this decisive spring of 1836, one American described Almonte "as the reputed natural son of a Spanish [mestizo] priest, by a full-blooded Mexican woman. He has a good countenance—was educated in Europe [New Orleans], and speaks English well, and is regarded as a man of superior talents."[61] In his hatred of slavery, Almonte continued the equality spirit and enlightened tradition of his father, Father Morelos, who was "the most extraordinary man produced by the war of independence," in part because he proudly declared in 1813 that "slavery is forever forbidden" in Mexico.[62]

Almonte was the antithesis of the stereotypical image, reinforced by Santa Anna, of the unethical and brutal, if not sadistic, Mexican military leader. Perhaps the most indispensable officer in the Army of Operations because of his intelligence and knowledge of Texas and Americans, Almonte now served capably as Santa Anna's chief advisor, aide-de-camp, and leading expert on Texas during the most ambitious campaign in the tortured history of Mexico. During the final stages of the battle of the Alamo, Almonte had personally intervened to save Susannah Dickinson, who had married Almeron at age sixteen, during the confused fighting in the early morning half-light when some soldados were consumed with bloodlust in slaughtering Americans. Almonte was exceptional in many ways, contradicting stereotypes about people of mixed race and earning the respect of the highest placed leaders of Mexico. He was blessed with a host of talents, competency in almost everything he embarked upon, a sharp sense of humor, fine, polished manners that were almost European, a strict sense of morality, and a lively personality with a zest for life.

In this year of decision that was to determine the fate of Texas, an observant American described the sophisticated Almonte, who was almost as comfortable among Americans as Mexicans, as one who loved

> cracking his jokes, as well as conversing freely and laughing heartily with all who are intimate with him .... He is said to be 33 years of age—although a few would take him to be not over 25. He is of a copper or Indian complexion, with a thick head of straight, black glossy hair.

Although he speaks the English language well, yet a glance at him [will] convince you that he is a Mexican or Spaniard. He is a short, thick-set, square built young man, with a large head and broad, open mouth and features—very muscular, active and lively. His countenance as well as conversation is very intelligent. There is a noble sincerity and frankness depicted in his countenance and manner.[63]

Emily could not have been more fortunate than in having been swept up by Mexican troops under the benevolent Almonte. This gifted intellectual had a soft spot for people of color, both slave and free. Almonte was concerned about the welfare of all people, like his warrior-priest father, regardless of color or race. After all, Mexico was a multi-cultural and mixed-race republic quite unlike the United States, and Almonte now fought for this young nation.

As earlier revealed in his kind treatment of Susanna Dickinson, including having successfully convinced Santa Anna, who rarely changed his mind especially in regard to women or sexual matters, not to transport the newly-made widow to Mexico after the Alamo's fall, he was perhaps the best qualified officer in Santa Anna's Army to now serve as Emily's protector and guardian. Almonte acted as Emily's proverbial knight in shining armor, especially in the presence of foreign troops far from home and who had little affinity for Americans.

Almonte placed no blame or responsibility on Emily because of her role in working at a place that helped to fuel revolution against Mexico. As with all women and in the manner of a proper Nineteenth Century gentleman of his class and elevated station, he treated her well. Emily was probably not aware that Almonte had only recently convinced Santa Anna to allow Susanna Dickinson (he had become enamored with the young Tennessean) and her daughter to be set free, instead of taking them to Mexico City. Here, Dickinson would have certainly become Santa Anna's concubine. Almonte had also made sure that the Dickinson family traveled safely on the open road and in Indian country, directing his black servant, Benjamin Harris, who spoke English, to escort them east to Gonzales.

After ignoring Santa Anna's desire to eliminate the rebel government officials as quickly as possible, Colonel Almonte immediately sent word to Santa Anna, who was now at Harrisburg, to hurry forward to join him at New Washington. In a fast-paced campaign, Almonte and his handful of worn Mexican dragoons rested, watered horses and secured fodder at New Washington. Unknown to Emily at this time as she watched the soldados around her, New Washington was destined to soon suffer Harrisburg's combustible fate, about twenty miles to the west.

This picturesque place of so many soaring ambitions and high hopes, including those of Emily and of the New Washington Association, had yet to become a real town—rather than a remote frontier outpost and infant settlement along Upper Galveston Bay—by mid–April 1836. All that New Washington consisted of at this time was the New Washington Hotel, where Emily worked and evidently lived; the New Washington Association's fine warehouse now filled with supplies, mostly foodstuffs but also war munitions for the Texas rebels; and a few small wooden residences of workers and settlers. The large warehouse, located at the wharf, had been originally built primarily for the storage of bales of cotton of "white gold" harvested by Morgan's slaves on his sprawling plantation.

This point of land where Jacinto Bay met and jutted into the northwest corner of Upper Galveston Bay was strategically important. Galveston Bay was a primary point of entry for zealous young volunteers, supplies, and munitions from the United States, especially New Orleans, fueling the infant Texas Revolution from the beginning. With such a huge stake in

Texas independence, Morgan and the New Washington Association had played an early key role in supporting the rebellion against Mexico, including before Emily's arrival.

After passing a bill for the purchase of four schooners for the new Texas Navy on November 25, 1835, the General Council had chartered the association's two schooners, the *Flash* and the *Kosciuszko*, to transport United States munitions, guns, volunteers, and supplies from New Orleans to Texas. On April 9, 1836, the *Kosciuszko* was on yet another mission to New Orleans to gather men, supplies, and munitions for the war effort. But making the most timely and invaluable contribution of all, the *Flash* carried the two cannons, the "Twin Sisters," to Houston's Army, which arrived on April 16. The wealthy chairman of the board of the New Washington Association and its largest investor, Samuel Swartwout had not only funneled sizeable funds to the war effort, but also helped to secure loans to support the Texas revolutionaries in their struggle against the odds. He had shipped war supplies to Texas at his own expense and generated widespread support for the Texas rebellion in New York City, where he resided, and the North.

Seeing himself as a savior to the people of Texas during their darkest hour, Swartwout described to Morgan in a letter how he had "sent them [the Texas revolutionaries] money & Bread when they were heartbroken & dispirited, starving and flying from that Brute Santa Anna [and] saved them from [being] perished." Evidently, these supplies included foodstuffs which were now stored in Morgan's sprawling warehouse. Morgan, who became a Texas Army colonel in late March 1836 after the Alamo's fall, had been dispatched by President David Burnet in September 1835 to New Orleans, where Colonel Almonte had been educated in the Jesuit Catholic tradition, to obtain war munitions and supplies for the Texas revolutionaries. Since the Texas revolutionary government possessed relatively little money or resources but seemingly endless amounts of land (actually Mexico's land), if the revolt succeeded, Morgan had used land scrips totaling 100,000 acres for payment.[64]

After receiving Almonte's message to join him at New Washington, Santa Anna and 700 troops departed Harrisburg, which was only around twenty miles northwest of Emily at New Washington, after they burned Harrisburg to the ground. Harrisburg was reduced to ashes in keeping with Santa Anna's plans to cleanse Texas of the Anglo-Celtic presence. On April 18, Santa Anna and his vanguard reached New Washington, joining with Colonel Almonte and his advanced group of dragoons. After two days of resting, rounding up Morgan's more than 100 cattle for slaughter to ensure a supply of rations of freshly-cooked beefsteak, and consuming the ample amount of supplies (meant for the Texas revolutionaries) that had been captured at New Washington, Santa Anna ordered everything burned down on April 20. The torch was applied to New Washington, and the dreams of Morgan and the New Washington Association went up in flames.

Santa Anna vented his frustration on the upstart town on the bay not only because interim President Burnet had so narrowly escaped Almonte's clutches, but also because a large amount of war munitions for the Texian rebels had been found in Morgan's warehouse. The nascent settlement was a legitimate military target in this rebellion so heavily supported by New Orleans.

Viewing the destructiveness of war for the first time, Emily watched as the red and yellow flames roared and leaped higher into the clear Texas sky, consuming the bright promise of New Washington in short order. Years of planning and hard work vanished in only minutes. The New Washington Hotel, where Emily had worked since December, likewise burned to the ground. Emily had now lost the only place where since had lived and worked since coming to Texas four months before. She now had no place to go.

The promising, upstart town of New Washington, the grandiose plan that had been mocked by William Fairfax Gray because of its presumptuous name, was reduced to ashes before Emily's eyes. In a letter to Swartwout, an embittered Morgan, who incorrectly blamed Almonte for the infant town's destruction rather than Santa Anna because he was now away in command of Galveston Island, angrily denounced "the destroyer of N[ew] W[ashington] the fiend Almonte—who destroyed our property there out of revenge for what our Co. [had] done for Texas."[65] However, in his letter and as if to disguise the clandestine revolutionary activities that would have implicated the New Washington Association in violating United States neutrality laws, Morgan of course only hinted that New Washington had served as a key supply depot of supplies and munitions sent from New Orleans.[66]

By the time that Santa Anna torched New Washington, Morgan had been away for some time. After the Alamo had been overwhelmed on the bloody morning of March 6, Colonel Morgan had been assigned the task of establishing a much-needed refugee camp. This was Camp Travis, which was named for the Alamo's fallen commander and yet another martyr to the cause of Texas. Camp Travis was established to care for the flood of civilians fleeing the Mexican Army's relentless eastward advance. Playing a key emergency role in saving a good many Texian families, the New Washington Association's two schooners, including the *Flash*, transported refugees from New Washington to nearby Galveston Island just to the south. Therefore, by the time the Mexicans took possession of New Washington, Morgan was busily preparing Galveston Island for defense, securing supplies, and setting up housing for the throngs of homeless men, women and children in a sad refugee camp that eventually swelled to more than 1,000 people.

Because it was a narrow barrier island located just off, and parallel to, the Texas mainland, Galveston Island was now one of the safest pieces of real estate in Texas without a Mexican naval threat in this almost exclusively land-based campaign for Texas' possession. Located directly south of Clopper's Point and New Washington where Emily remained with the occupying Mexican troops, the northern tip of this narrow strip of land, where the city of Galveston eventually rose, provided the entry point into Galveston Bay for ships from the Gulf of Mexico. Morgan eventually employed a good deal of impressed slave labor to build up the island's defenses. South Carolina–born Colonel Thomas Jefferson Rusk, who served as the fledgling Republic of Texas' secretary of war of the renegade Texas government in exile and not long after he had won distinction at San Jacinto, gave Morgan official permission to impress slaves (a most sensitive issue to slave-owners, especially with liberating Mexican troops on the move) for duty on April 16.[67]

Meanwhile, the *Flash*, captained by a seasoned, reliable seafarer named Luke Favel, had sailed away from Mexican-held New Washington, with now nothing remaining on the location but smoking ruins, to reach Galveston Island on April 19. Here, the next day, the schooner "*Flash* [dis]embarked all the members of the Texan cabinet who were at the Point, their wives and children." Then, with great relief, interim president Burnet and the refugees joined Colonel Morgan and his command on the sandy, almost treeless barrier island. By the narrowest of margins, Galveston Island now became the new home of the exiled Texas government that existed in name only, after escaping New Washington in the nick of time. The once boundless and tantalizing Anglo-Celtic dream of a magnificent Texas Republic of endless prosperity had been now reduced to little more than a bleak, sandy, and wind-swept barrier island in the middle of nowhere.[68]

When she had watched the narrow escape of President Burnet and his family members down Galveston Bay, Emily no doubt felt a sense of relief. However, she would have felt less sympathy had she known of Burnet's contemptuous opinions about people of color. Burnet possessed strong pro-slavery views and was the leader of a slave republic based largely upon cotton cultivation. Like most Texians, he considered Tejanos and Mexicans as members of "a mongrel race of degenerate Spaniards and Indians more depraved than they."[69]

But despite New Washington having been burned to the ground and having his greatest dream cruelly dashed by flaming Mexican torches, Morgan hereafter demonstrated considerable compassion toward the Mexican prisoners-of-war after the battle of San Jacinto. He attended to their welfare like a true Christian gentleman. Morgan's efforts, including improving sanitation, would save a good many lives of Santa Anna's suffering men when they were in bad shape on unhealthy Galveston Island.[70]

No longer the speculator or businessman hoping to strike it rich, Morgan was now a proud Texian and revolutionary, after gaining a colonel's rank near the end of March. Indeed, if Santa Anna was not defeated and hurled back from Texas soil, then it hardly mattered that New Washington had been destroyed, because Texas would be lost forever. Therefore, he no longer thought or acted as the manager and agent of the New Washington Association, only taking orders from his military superiors, especially Houston. Indeed, while supervising Mexican prisoners on Galveston Island in the near future, Morgan would be fully prepared, if ordered by Houston to do so, to kill hundreds of Mexican prisoners in grisly Goliad fashion rather than taking the risk of having these fighting men freed to turn on the Texans, if Mexican forces renewed the offensive and achieved significant gains.[71]

Meanwhile, the campaign to determine the fate of Texas continued to be played out on the Gulf Coastal Plain. Despite the exhaustive efforts and hard marching of his worn soldados so far from their homeland, Santa Anna pushed north toward the mouth of Buffalo Bayou, after departing New Washington on April 20 and leaving it in flames. Thinking of an effective checkmate, Santa Anna planned to reach Lynchburg Ferry to block Houston's path of withdrawal east across the Sabine to Louisiana, and then deliver a crushing defeat on Houston's rabble of undisciplined volunteers. But the Creole general, whose home was his vast estate Manga de Clavo in Vera Cruz Province, had no idea that Houston's forces were now advancing behind him: the pursuer had suddenly become the pursued and quite unexpectedly.[72]

To Santa Anna and his soldados, this fight on Texas soil was very much a righteous, holy war, including liberating the slaves, resulting in and partly justifying the gross brutalities and ugly excesses, including the burning down of Harrisburg and New Washington and even the massacre of the Alamo and Goliad garrisons. After all, rebellious Texas colonists and then a massive influx of volunteers only recently from the United States had attempted to wrest the province of Texas from Mexico and claim it as their own out of righteous indignation that Mexico City had refused to relinquish this fertile land without a fight. As his nation's president and in obedience of the Congress in Mexico City, Santa Anna was required to thwart this determined bid by any means possible, and to win Texas back for the fragile, mixed-race republic.

In his own words that were not false or hollow to the young American men and boys who had died at the Alamo and Goliad: "I, as chief executive of the government, zealous in the fulfillment of my duties to my country, declared that I would maintain the territorial integrity whatever the cost [and] I took pride in being the first to strike in defense of the independence, honor, and rights of my nation."[73]

But even more, this escalating conflict continued to be a war of liberation for slaves of Texas. In a February 16, 1836, letter, Santa Anna wrote with a sense of indignation how "there exists in Texas a considerable number of slaves, introduced here by their owners under certain legal pretexts [indentured servitude]; but who, according to our laws, should be free." And in another letter, Santa Anna emphasized how he and the republic were morally bound to liberate the slaves, staying true to the republic's founding principles, especially the mid–September 1829 abolition of slavery: "Given that the laws of the Republic prohibit slavery it is our duty to ensure they are everywhere respected," especially in Texas.[74]

Because of her color, Colonel Almonte's cavalrymen had "freed" Emily upon taking possession of New Washington, evidently assuming that she was a slave. Having nowhere else to go in a pro-slavery Texas where she was a stranger and no white person could be entirely trusted, Emily stayed at New Washington, because of her contract and since Almonte's exhausted soldados remained encamped along the bay, living off the corn and beef from Morgan's herds of cattle that were gathered by Mexican cavalrymen.

Contrary to myth, Emily was not captured by Santa Anna's advancing troops on the New Washington Road, which led north to Lynch's Ferry, Lynchburg, and San Jacinto, in a desperate attempt to flee Santa Anna's approach and reach the relative safety of the Louisiana border, like so many white settlers. Therefore, along with other free blacks from New Haven, Emily remained with Mexican forces, who sympathized with the plight of blacks in Texas, immediately before the battle of San Jacinto and just southeast of the future battlefield of the plain of Hyacinth along Buffalo Bayou.

The soldados, now smoking tobacco from Morgan's warehouse that also yielded sacks of flour, were unaware that Emily was a free woman who had signed a one-year contract to work at Morgan's Point. And, without knowing how to speak Spanish, Emily was unable to communicate with the soldados, even if anyone had wanted to listen, except with Colonel Almonte. Most likely, another free black woman, Diana Leonard, also remained at New Washington at this time. Along with other free blacks, Diana also had worked for Morgan on a one-year contract at New Washington since December 1835.

Other black indentured servants under Morgan's employment, besides George Cooper from New Haven, were either taken by the Mexicans for domestic work or they willingly joined Santa Anna's men if entirely given freedom of movement, which was most likely the case. One of these blacks was a young "yellow boy" named Turner. Morgan hired Turner as an apprentice in New York City when he contracted with other black apprentices and free blacks like Emily.

Turner, consequently, belonged to Morgan as an employee. Turner's intelligence and skilled position as a printer's apprentice indicated some degree of education or training in the North, or perhaps as a former slave whom the master, possibly his own father, which was often the case, had early designated for an artisan position. Turner journeyed to Texas from either New Haven or New York City like Emily. A free man of ability and mixed race, Turner was a hard-working printer's apprentice for the *Telegraph and Texas Register,* which was the first successful and only the second permanent newspaper in Texas.

The popular revolutionary newspaper served as the official organ of the Texas Republic, after having been established as a faithful register of passing events by three enterprising journalists, including New Yorkers Gail and Thomas H. Borden, even though none possessed newspaper experience. Intelligent, hard-working Thomas H. Borden, whose facial features included high cheekbones and a distinct look of determination, later grew extremely wealthy, after founding the Borden Milk Company. From the colony's capital of San Felipe de Austin, the newspaper's first issue appeared on October 10, 1835, not long after the open clash of arms at Gonzales.

In a final gesture of contempt for all of the harsh words printed about him after capturing Harrisburg, where the press had been removed for safety's sake, Santa Anna ended the anti–Mexican vehemence by sinking the printing press into Buffalo Bayou's muddy bottom. Until the very end, the conscientious editors had been preparing one final April 14 edition and risking all in the process in order to print the latest revolutionary news. The *Telegraph and Texas Register* had been named as the official voice and newspaper of the infant Texas Republic on April 13.

Evidently, all of Morgan's African Americans—free blacks under employment contracts and slaves—were swept up by the advance elements of the Mexican Army and became part of it, either willingly or by friendly persuasion. Emily made sure that she would not leave New Washington without what was always most important, her coveted "free" papers, especially if the Mexican forces were defeated by the Texians in a final showdown on the coastal plain.[75]

Now safely on Galveston Island where Colonel Morgan commanded, interim President Burnet later ordered Morgan to round up "all the colored persons on the island" over the age of fourteen to work on strengthening the fortifications, just in case Mexican forces attempted to land.[76] Had Emily escaped with the Texas political leaders to Galveston Island, she might well have been put to work like a slave and treated like one for the first time in her life, because her job at New Washington was no more. After all, Morgan himself was a slave owner. Emily benefited by remaining in the hands of Mexican forces.[77]

There is no evidence that Emily was forced against her will to accompany Santa Anna's Army for the dozen or so miles north from New Washington to the field of San Jacinto. But with New Washington burned down on Santa Anna's orders, she had to go somewhere. As part of the seemingly endless sexualization of Emily by popular writers who have been determined to create the most sensational of stories, the myth has been generally accepted that she was already a rape victim at New Washington. And, therefore, she had supposedly been taken by the Mexican troops for sexual purposes, as if to obscure the fact that Santa Anna's men were liberators, not abusers, of blacks in Texas. The roots of this old racial stereotype of the widespread rape of Texian women by Santa Anna's soldados stemmed from Texian wartime propaganda based upon white America's obsession and paranoia about race mixing. Utilizing masterful propaganda that was sure to strike a nerve among Americans, the alleged threat of Mexican males in army uniforms as rapists and vile abusers of white womanhood had been spread by the Texians in the hope of garnering United States support when Santa Anna marched through Texas unchecked.

These sensational, but entirely unfounded, stories of raping Mexican soldiers were also perpetuated by volunteer officers from the United States, who wanted to fill up the ranks of their companies to enhance their own military careers. Therefore, they created fictional tales of "our virgins defiled," which was not the case. United States newspapers even printed outlandish sensational stories of the alleged sexual abuse of Susanna Dickinson by Mexican officers, after she was taken into custody after the Alamo's fall. Perhaps the most morally conscious man in Santa Anna's Army, Colonel Almonte, was even falsely accused of crimes against defenseless citizens of New Washington, including ordering the execution of women. This propaganda was most likely churned out by eastern journalists in the pay of Samuel Swartwout, who was Morgan's good friend and the leading investor of the New Washington Association.

No documentation or evidence has been found of Mexican rapes of Anglo or Texian (or white) women during the 1836 Texas Campaign, including after San Antonio was captured and occupied by Santa Anna's troops for a considerable length of time. Such stereotypes linger to this day that blacks and Mexicans are sensual beings more obsessed with sex than whites and therefore driven by desires beyond their control or reason. Of course, the alleged lust of black males for white women has been one of the longest existing racist stereotypes that has served as a moral justification for harsh treatment and discrimination at all levels (an American caste system and apartheid) in order to keep people of color in their subordinate places in American society well into the Twenty-first Century.

But soldados in Texas did not rape or abuse African American women, though the same could not be said for Texian slave-owners: a classic case of white projection and distorting the truth. In the longtime tradition of the Mexican military, especially when on campaign, females were utilized by Mexican soldiers primarily as washerwomen, cooks, or domestic servants. After all, the Mexican troops were on a lengthy campaign far from support systems and Mexico during rainy weather and muddy country in a strange land. The soldados, both officers and enlisted men, needed uniforms washed, wood collected for campfires, and meals cooked, along with a good many other typical camp chores. Emily most likely assisted in those chores.

During this grueling campaign across such a wide area of Texas, Mexican troops primarily utilized black women, if not releasing them outright to go their own way, as laundresses. Emily West and Diana Leonard were very likely no exception in this regard. The seemingly endless sexualization of Emily by so many popular authors, both men and women, has been applied to her even before San Jacinto, where the mythology and sensationalization of Emily as sensual vamp and unthinking carnal creature reached its zenith.

For instance, one recent author has even suggested that Morgan might have originally signed up Emily for the express purpose of making her his own mulatto concubine, because of his penchant for "a number of young and attractive mulatto slaves to keep him company while away from his wife." Adding another layer of sexualization and sensationalism, such an unverifiable claim has provided more fuel for the fictionalization that has obscured the real Emily D. West. Of course, this alleged Morgan-Emily concubinage is just idle speculation that ignores the fact that Morgan, known for his stability and mature qualities that explained why so many large New York investors, who knew how to judge their man, had chosen Morgan as their Texas agent for the New Washington Association, loved his wife. He and Celia Gordon Morgan enjoyed a happy marriage. Fortunately at this time, no writer has continued the fictionalizing tradition of excessive sexualization of this free black woman from the northeast to foster the added tale that Emily was sexually involved with Colonel Almonte at New Washington, before Santa Anna's arrival.

Because of the mythical power of the Emily legend and its seemingly endless romantic embellishments, what has been most forgotten about the Emily D. West story is that she almost certainly was anything but a fiery, self-sacrificing Texas patriot willing to give her all to save Texas from Santa Anna's grasp, as the popular mythology portrays her. Without considering the complexities of race and the issue of slavery, historians have simply assumed in convoluted logic that because she was living in Texas, she was no different from the average white Texians in regard to revolutionary sentiments. But this was simply not the case, because Emily's belief and value systems were the antithesis of those of white Texians, especially slave-owners.

As far as most slaves in Texas were concerned, Santa Anna's war was a glorious, ennobling crusade that bestowed freedom, in much the same way a generation later, thousands of slaves, men, women, and entire families, flocked to Abraham Lincoln's invading armies across the

South during the Civil War. In accompanying their liberators out of grateful desire to assist them in their holy and moral war against slavery, large numbers of black women served as cooks and laundresses for invading Union armies. Some of these newly-freed African American women worked in the headquarters of high ranking officers, like George Armstrong Custer, across the South. A newly-freed Virginia slave, Eliza Brown, joined Custer and served as his headquarters cook beginning during the summer of 1863, not long after the battle of Gettysburg, Pennsylvania. After forming a bond with the long-haired "Boy General," she stayed with Custer until 1869 on the Great Plains during the Indian Wars. Custer's wife, Elizabeth, or "Libbie," and like the general himself, admired and respected Eliza for her strength of character, spirit, and sense of determination. Likewise, and as indicated by all existing historical evidence, Emily D. West possessed such sterling qualities, and she was a person of the same mold.

In a desire to create an authentic Texas hero and folk heroine, writers have created an Emily who was fiercely pro–Texan and patriotic. This Emily was forced against her will to go with Santa Anna's advance force after the burning down of New Washington. However, this was almost certainly not the case. Like liberated slaves across the South, Emily was now without a home, daily sustenance, or even a roof over her head. Therefore, the Mexican Army, especially one that liberated slaves and was sympathetic to the plight of long-suffering blacks, became a safe and secure refuge for her in many basic ways. Emily was now among mostly mixed-race soldiers who were anti-slavery and pro-black, a situation unlike what she had known either in the North or at New Washington. She had never seen so many soldiers with dark eyes and brown faces. In fact, she might have felt more at home among these mixed-raced people of humanitarian inclinations and beside smiling, friendly brown faces than among any whites in the United States, including in her native New Haven.

What she now saw in the mostly dark-hued faces of Santa Anna's soldados might have taken her by surprise, pleasantly at that. These young men and boys in the Mexican Army's enlisted ranks, unlike the aristocratic officer corps consisting mostly of men of Spanish descent, were either mostly Indian or of mixed race heritage, mestizos and mulattos. The vast majority of Santa Anna's soldados were full-blood Indians, or of part Indian and part Spanish ancestry. Typical of many soldados, one teenager in Santa Anna's ranks was described as "a copper colored boy," who might have looked much like Emily herself in color, if she was of mixed race. One of Houston's men later described how some of the Mexican soldados under Santa Anna were "very dark, approximating the negro race." The coppery color of this Mexican boy was in sharp contrast to one of Santa Anna's officers named Santiago Rabia, born in Spain in 1804. Rabia was distinguished by a thick mop of blonde hair and blue eyes that revealed his ancient Visigothic heritage, from the days when the Visigoths, a Germanic people, had ruled Spain, before the Moorish conquest. But Rabia was a noticeable exception to the rule in Santa Anna's ranks dominated by fighting men of color. After all, even Almonte had a "mulatto complexion," in the words of one American, who could not help noting the colonel's mixed race heritage.

Emily now saw a good many hardened fighting men from Mexico's depths who were very likely darker than herself, if a mulatto. She certainly understood why the people of Mexico, Santa Anna, and his soldados had taken such a firm stand against slavery in Texas in respecting their republic's 1829 abolition of slavery decree and liberal traditions. Emily saw their burning desire to wipe slavery off the face of Texas because they (like northerners of the Civil War generation) considered it a dark curse and moral sin rather than a blessing like so many Texians, especially those from the Deep South, who saw slavery as benefiting the so-called "heathen" blacks because of the alleged bestowing of Christianity and much-touted civilizing influences. Emily's enlightened views, including that slavery was a sin and against God's will—that reflected her background, free status, and abolitionist connections so unlike those of the Texians—could not have been more different. In this regard, she almost certainly agreed with Frederick Douglass, the son of a slave woman and white slave-master, who declared that the "existence of slavery in this country [United States] brands your republicanism as a sham, your humanity as a base pretense, and your Christianity as a lie."

After the burning of New Washington, Emily also saw and related to the young women known as soldaderas in Santa Anna's army. Continuing a deep-seated cultural and military tradition since pre–Columbian times when Aztec warriors went to war and created one of the New World's greatest empires before the arrival of the Spanish Conquistadors, these resilient women "soldiers" of the Mexican Army filled roles comparable to the men who served in the quartermaster and commissary corps in supporting the army during active campaigning. Women who assisted the Mexican Army were proud of the tradition of the soldadera which extended back not only to the legacy of women warriors in Mesoamerican warrior societies but also to the popular mystical tales of a dark-hued war goddesses.

Even Mexico's most iconic and enduring inspirational religious symbol of Mexican unity, Our Lady of Guadalupe ("Mother of God, Mother of the Americas") was employed as a respected dark-skinned war goddess by the lower class revolutionaries of Indian, Afro-Mexicans, and blacks who rebelled against their Spanish masters in 1810, which marked the beginning of Mexico's struggle for independence. This most revered religious symbol and imagery of the Mexican people inspired generations of Mexican women to serve with revolutionary and national armies to assist the men in the ranks.

Continuing the tradition on Texas soil, large numbers of soldaderas served faithfully with and in support of Santa Anna's troops. On foot and demonstrating considerable stamina, they had marched into Texas for hundreds of miles with the Mexican nation's primary army just to be beside husbands, sons, and brothers. Along the way, they set up camp after each day's exhausting march, gathered firewood, washed clothes, and cared for the sick and wounded. However, medical care was the most vital role provided by these self-sacrificing soldaderas, because Santa Anna, in his desire to strike quickly and catch the Texians by surprise before the onset of spring, had decided not to bring a medical corps, and its accompanying wagons and ambulances, into Texas to care for the wounded.

In total, more than 1,500 women and children had initially trudged into Texas with Santa Anna's fast-moving army that had raced north to surprise the Alamo's defenders and seal their fate. However, after the lengthy march north over difficult mountainous terrain and even a winter blizzard that swept through northern Mexico, only around 300 soldaderas had reached San Antonio and the bloody showdown at the Alamo. Almost certainly after departing New Washington, Emily was surprised to see that some kind-hearted soldaderas, who were invaluable to the men in Santa Anna's ranks, were of mixed race, including those men entirely of African heritage or with a large measure of black blood.[78]

The vast majority of the soldaderas were of Aztec heritage, and they now continued a traditional supportive role of this ancient indigenous culture of the Mexican people, as they proudly called themselves. The most respected and famed fighting men of the ancient Mexican civilization held an exceptionally high status in a warrior-based society. These premier warriors, but only the unmarried ones who hailed from a strict traditional and conservative culture that even executed adulterers, were accompanied in war by their faithful female companions, who were known as the auianime. The status of Aztec women in society was elevated higher by the reverence paid to the many priestesses, or the ciuaquacuilli (woman-priest). Long before the arrival of Spanish Conquistadors and the brutal conquest of Mexico, one of the most sacred ceremonies of these ancient people was the feast to the great goddess Toei, or "our grandmother." During ritual ceremonies, especially religious celebrations, the auianime, with long dark hair flowing, danced beside her warrior. Therefore, the soldaderas of Santa Anna's army, wearing crucifixes like good Catholics and devout followers of the inspirational legacy of Our Lady of Guadalupe, continued a host of proud traditions from the misty ancestral homeland now so far away.[79]

The soldadera tradition was much misunderstood, if not entirely incomprehensible, to the Spanish Conquistadors in the 1500s as the Texians and United States volunteers in 1836. Mirroring the misconceptions about Emily's role at San Jacinto, so the soldaderas were viewed as little more than prostitutes by the Spanish, who possessed no comparable tradition in their military. Indeed, in the words of historian Jacques Soustelle, the "profession of the auianime, whom the Spanish chroniclers tend to treat as whores ... was not only recognised, but valued."[80]

As dark as these women, one of Santa Anna's top officers, twenty-eight-year-old Lieutenant Colonel José Nicolás de la Portilla, the commander of the Yucatan Infantry Permanente Regiment now serving under Urrea and a native of Jalapa, Province of Vera Cruz, where Santa Anna had been born, was so dark in color that his nickname was El Indio.[81] And another Texian, deeply imbued with the cultural concepts of the South, described some fighting men of Mexico with a measure of shock and surprise, because "their faces were nearly as black as negroes."[82]

But the vast majority of Santa Anna's men were of mostly Indian ancestry and members of the lower class, or peasantry, who had been impressed into military service. But these Indians of Aztec ancestry possessed a most distinguished heritage of a warrior race that had once conquered all other tribes for hundreds of miles around Mexico City. Despite "the epic defense of Mexico," the mighty Aztec Empire had been conquered by Cortéz and his band of Conquistadors—thanks to European diseases, Toledo swords of steel and other superior weapons—who had pushed the Moors off the Iberian Peninsula in an earlier dramatic clash of two advanced cultures and societies not unlike the showdown that was the Texas Revolution. Having no idea of the distinguished Aztec warrior cultural legacy that was yet alive and well in the ranks of Santa Anna's army, one American wrote, "They look like North American Indians, with respect to color."[83]

While overlooking the fact that some American volunteers had raped Tejano women during the course of the Texas Revolution, the erroneous assumption that Emily was raped by Mexican soldiers either at New Washington or on the way to San Jacinto has given more credence to the myth that her unbridled sexuality rose to the fore with Santa Anna on April 21. Such assumptions are devoid of understanding of the heritage and complexities of the Mexican people, Catholicism's omnipresent influence, the religious and cultural makeup of the average soldado, or the vital role played by the soldaderas, a moderating influence since they included wives, sisters, and other relatives, in bolstering morale, stability, and maternal support.

In truth, therefore, a far greater chance actually existed for Emily to have been raped by white Texans, who merely continued this dark legacy of plantation slavery across the Deep South in Texas, rather than by Mexican soldiery, including those of African heritage, who now liberated the slaves across Texas. No documentation has been found of any Mexican soldiers raping slave women, especially when so many Mexican "whores," in de la Pena's words that reflected the usual upper class outlook upon lower class women of Indian or mixed race heritage, followed the army. Evidence has revealed that Mexican troops treated liberated African Americans with a sincere measure of sympathy, compassion, and even pity.

Upon first sight of the generalísimo and his vanguard after he reached New Washington on April 18, Emily may have been struck by Santa Anna's autocratic bearing and command presence. Santa Anna was also a polished and experienced ladies' man, even though he had been married since March 1825. Although considerably embellished by endless gossip and rumor, "Tales of his ... excesses with both women and drugs" became well-known across Mexico and "His 'way with women' was legendary" throughout his life.[84]

For instance, on the third day of the Alamo siege, Santa Anna had been focused on a conquest that had nothing to do with the besieged garrison of Texian rebels, his burning desire to emulate his idol Napoleon, or the reaping of military laurels to impress Mexico City. On this Thursday just outside the Tejano community of San Antonio de Béxar, Santa Anna's soldados had advanced closer to the Alamo, tightening their grip on the doomed garrison. They searched through the little makeshift shacks—or jacales—of an adjacent community, Pueblo de Valero, south of the Alamo along the Gonzales Road that led eastward across the prairies and clumps of mesquite along the creek bottoms. Here, Mexican troops hunted for good, suitable timber to build a bridge across the clear waters of the spring-fed San Antonio River for the express purpose of moving forward cannon to the river's east side. Instead, in one of the huts, they discovered an aged mother and her pretty seventeen-year-old daughter, Melchora Barrera. Both Tejanas had remained hidden in their small house during the sharp exchanges of gun and cannon fire since February 23, when Santa Anna's army reached San Antonio to surprise the garrison.[85]

In a rare account, Sergeant Francisco Bercerra recalled the incident: "The General entered a house, and found a lady, and her daughter. The [Tejano] girl was beautiful.... General [Manuel Fernández] Castrillón related what happened to the President. Santa Anna was in a great fever to see the pretty girl. He told Gen. Castrillón he wanted her, and asked him to carry a message to her mother.... Gen. Santa Anna commanded the lady and her daughter to be taken to his quarters; and Gen. [José Vincente] Minon executed the order. He delivered Santa Anna's message to the mother. She replied that she was a respectable lady of good family ... and [he] could not get her daughter except by marriage."[86]

Therefore, as if eagerly exploiting an enemy's tactical weakness on the battlefield, Santa Anna, ignoring the fact that he was already married, found someone qualified to favorably impersonate a priest for marrying him to this attractive daughter of a Mexican officer, who died some time previous to the siege of the Alamo. The "obsequious pseudo-priest consented to solemnize the marriage in Gen. Santa Anna's quarters [and] the wedding took place late in February [on the 25th]. The honeymoon lasted until the army marched for the Guadalupe river. The deceived and trusting girl was sent to San Luis Potosí in the carriage of Gen. [José Vincente] Minon. In due course of time she became the mother of a son. I do not know when she ascertained that Gen. Santa Anna was already a married man, and the father of a family, and that she had been made a victim of a foul and rascally plot."[87] Indeed, not only the "beautiful, young bexarena," but also her mother, were sent back to Mexico in Santa Anna's exquisite carriage by the time that the rains of Texas fell harder and the roads became almost impassable in April.[88]

This teenage Tejano, brought up in a strict Catholic faith and in obedience to God, served as Santa Anna's female companion and wife during the siege of the Alamo. Of course, Santa Anna's fake marriage and the deflowering of the young girl was a slap in the face of the good Catholics in the ranks and the Catholic Church, which had funded his bold thrust into Texas.

For Santa Anna, as he had long demonstrated, the moral concept of faithfulness to his wife and living by Catholicism's dictates was of relatively little meaning to him, when it came to his own pleasure seeking and personal gratification. Therefore, Santa Anna was well known for a wide variety of excesses. The generalísimo was certainly an immoral cad in masterminding the mock marriage in San Antonio, but Santa Anna was no rapist. He had sufficient charm, good looks, and experience to make an easy conquest of Melchora, a rural peasant girl, with considerable finesse. After all, she had been tricked by the marriage ceremony and the quite forceful impression that she had been most fortunate to have been wed to Mexico's revered leader.

Perhaps he had grown tired of his marriage that was more than a decade ago, and perhaps his wife had lost her youthful looks, which he placed a high priority upon, by this time. Santa Anna's fascination with youthful beauty was not unlike the thirty-six-year-old Houston, who married twenty-year-old Eliza Allen of Tennessee in late January 1828, when he was Tennessee's governor. However, this was a short, doomed marriage that sent a disillusioned Houston on his way to Texas and a new destiny that seemed ordained by fate itself.

Santa Anna's real wife, Doña Inés García, "was a Spanish lady of property, a native of Alvarado," in Extremadura in southwest Spain. She became his wife at age fourteen and had initially embarked upon the Texas Campaign with her husband. But the rain-swollen waters of the Medina River, below San Antonio, had caused the stately carriage to turn back at the beginning of February's third week 1836. Clearly, for his ego and self-image as much as, if not more than, for his physical needs or carnal lusts, Santa Anna needed a youthful, attractive female companion.[89]

Tejano María de Jesús Delgado Buquor presented a rare account to the *San Antonio Express* in 1907 which alluded to Santa Anna's mock marriage to Melchora Barrera: "During the siege, Mrs. Buquor says she saw General Santa Anna many times and she bears testimony to his well known penchant for amours in that she related how he seized a young girl living near her home and held the maiden captive during his stay in the city."[90]

Reflecting in part the realities of the frontier experience where people of various races and cultures were in close contact and often mixed in intimate ways, Houston himself possessed a quite varied, if not exotic, appetite for women. In a controversial, unruly life without discipline—especially after his marriage's collapse—and often with a groggy mind befuddled and soaked with alcohol, especially corn whisky, and even opium, Houston had been intimate with all types of women from a broad spectrum of humanity and races: "patricians and white trash, whores and unfaithful wives, Creoles, Indians, mulattoes, and black slaves."[91] But Houston's preference long had been lying with "some Indian maiden" as in the days of his youth.[92]

Therefore, it was most ironic that Houston's marriage with Eliza Allen early dissolved. Houston's disastrous marriage resulted in his mid–April 1829 resignation as Tennessee's governor and departure from the state capital of Nashville. As revealed in a rare March 1829 published account, Houston left the marriage because "he accused her of infidelity, and of illicit intercourse with *negroes*!"[93]

Not even Santa Anna's legendary sexual appetite compared to the many different hues and backgrounds of Houston's lovers. After he resigned as Tennessee's governor, Houston enjoyed a long-term relationship with a young, attractive Cherokee woman named Tiana Rogers in the Arkansas Territory, taking her as his wife. Perhaps the odds might have been actually better that Houston—not Santa Anna—had a tryst with Emily D. West, if anyone slept with her, although neither case was likely. But if so, then would such a tryst have served as a possible motivation to partly explain why Houston wrote the alleged "Emily" letter about her alleged sexual role at San Jacinto?

At this time for the jaded Santa Anna, there was no motivation to experience an exotic novelty or a new sexual experience with this young black woman named Emily, even if she had been available or even willing and waiting, if that was the case. Santa Anna had grown up around plenty of people of African descent from his home port in low-lying, often yellow-fever ravished Vera Cruz, where he had been born in 1794. Here, the people of Vera Cruz were his greatest longtime supporters throughout his lengthy military and political career as Mexico's strongman. This old colonial city on the Gulf of Mexico, where Cortez and his conquistadors had first landed so long ago, contained a large percentage of blacks. Santa Anna, therefore, would have been familiar with black women, including their exploitation by the Spanish as paramours or concubines, since his early childhood. People of African descent had been brought in chains from both the Caribbean and Africa to work the gulf plain's sugar and cotton plantations operated by wealthy Spanish owners. It is not known but the middle-class creole household of the Santa Anna family, which considered itself "white" in regard to social status and physical appearances because the patriarch was an aristocratic Spaniard, very likely contained black servants at some point when he was a young man.[94]

By early 1836, Santa Anna was yet handsome, physically fit, and dashing, although of middle-age. Emily certainly noticed him at New Washington, after his arrival with much fanfare. As described by a Texan, Joseph Andrews, who would see him after his capture at San Jacinto and as published in the *New York Daily Advertiser*, Santa Anna "is about 45 years of age, of rather small statue, dark complexion, black hair, bright eyes, and altogether a good looking man."[95] Another American wrote how Santa Anna's "complexion is a little tawny; but he shows more of the Moorish [from Spain] than the Mexican tincture. He might pass for a white man; but would not pass for a native [American or Indian], in the United States."[96]

And in regard to women, especially the young, pretty ones, and waging war, Santa Anna was the embodiment of the old saying, "all is fair in love and war." A capable lieutenant colonel in the elite Sapper Battalion, Lieutenant Colonel José Enrique de la Peña complained with a measure of contempt of the seemingly endless complexities and contradictions of Santa Anna, "who himself does everything without rules."[97] Part of breaking these rules and traditions of a strict Mexican and Catholic society was having a fancy carriage accompany him with a mistress during this campaign across Texas, after he departed San Antonio. Evidently this carriage—and his mistress who was certainly not Emily—would be with him at San Jacinto.[98]

Therefore, in the end, Santa Anna was not delayed at New Washington because of engaging in sex with Emily—yet another myth that has developed from the larger myth of the alleged Santa Anna–Emily liaison at San Jacinto. In a popular work, author David Nevin described how Santa Anna "was so confident that he repaired to rest for two days at nearby Morgan's plantation, finding pleasure in opium and a handsome slave girl named Emily."[99] Already by this time, if Emily had in fact engaged in sex with all the males, Texian, Mexican, and black, that writers and historians have claimed, then she might not have possessed sufficient physical strength to make the trek from New Washington to San Jacinto.

Meanwhile, moving steadily onward by a mixture of fate, fortune, and a series of sharp reversals, including at the Alamo, Houston's troops wearily continued to push through the gloomy pine and oak forests of the humid coastal plain toward Harrisburg. On the night of

April 16–17, Houston had learned that Santa Anna, now around twenty-five miles distant, had entered Harrisburg. Consequently, the ragtag Texas Army continued to move southeast along muddy roads and through the dripping trees toward Harrisburg on the warm morning of April 17. Around noon on April 18, the Texians and United States volunteers reached the charred ruins of Harrisburg. What they saw around them raised indignation and longings for revenge. Men uttered in pent-up rage, "The Mexicans did that, too," along with slaughter the Alamo and Goliad commands. It was now obvious to one and all that Santa Anna was waging a campaign of what would be called ethnic cleansing today.[100]

Obscure amid a semi-tropical wilderness, Lynch's Ferry, situated across the San Jacinto River and located at the mouth of the river, suddenly became the most strategic point in all Texas. As Santa Anna ascertained, if the Mexicans gained the ferry—the only crossing point amid an uncharted, heavily-wooded area dominated by a maze of deep bayous, creeks, and the San Jacinto River of the swampy coastal plain—first as planned, then Houston and his band of undisciplined men, who had never fought together before, would be trapped and then destroyed with ease between two Mexican forces.[101]

But Santa Anna had expended too much time and effort at first Harrisburg and then New Washington, where two days were wasted by the most advanced Mexican forces, in first attempting to overtake the rebel government, especially the hated Zavala, and then destroying both places. Both failed efforts to overtake the fast-moving Texas government further divided Santa Anna's forces to make his overly-aggressive vanguard, which Santa Anna led in person, more vulnerable with each passing mile. This was destined to come back and haunt him at a little-known grassy plain situated amid the virgin forests and marshlands called San Jacinto. As fate would have it, Emily was witness to the swirl of dramatic events at New Washington that had a dramatic impact on the campaign's final outcome. And, more importantly, she would be at center-stage in the upcoming decisive showdown at San Jacinto, where the fate of Texas was decided once and for all.[102]

The precious time wasted by Santa Anna at New Washington, where Mexican troops had spent two days in resting, gathering more than 100 head of cattle by lancers who were anything but frontier cowboys, and gorging on freshly-slaughtered beef, proved most costly in the end. But a greater liability was Santa Anna's soaring confidence, which continued to be unbounded, as he neared the Gulf Coast. Indeed, week after week, all ragtag Texian opposition, ill-led, uncoordinated, and badly-timed, to the generalísimo's relentless march had been easily and systematically swept away wherever this feeble resistance had been met. And, since marching east from San Antonio more than 150 miles across mostly prairie lands from the arid western frontier, Santa Anna had nearly reached the semi-tropical, water-soaked shores of the Gulf of Mexico without encountering any serious resistance of any kind. For Santa Anna, the Texas Campaign had become little more than a picnic, with losses unbelievably low. By this time, therefore, the conquest of all Texas seemed complete.[103]

Now Santa Anna had committed not only the fundamental tactical error of having divided his army into segments over a wide area and beyond mutually supporting distance when advancing deep into unfamiliar enemy territory, but he had taken his usual laser-like focus off what should have been his main objective: the destruction of Houston's army. Thinking more like a politician than a strategist and invigorated in the excitement of the hunt as during his youth as a cavalry officer destroying guerrilla bands in Vera Cruz Province, Santa Anna had committed the folly of chasing after the members of a refugee government in a lengthy, wasted effort, while having ignored Houston and his growing army: the recipe for disaster.

Worst of all, Santa Anna had moved swiftly and ever-farther away from his logistical support system and the bulk of his army, while pushing deeper into the humid, flat and jungle-like lowlands of the Gulf Coast, where visibility was low and open ground was rare. As Napoleon would have instantly recognized, this was not the ground upon which to fight a decisive battle for the possession of Texas. But Santa Anna, in keeping with his reckless nature and daring personality, was bound to violate even the most basic Napoleonic axioms in the pursuit of glory, laurels, and, most of all, decisive victory.[104]

In the end, Santa Anna's demise was largely of his own making, because of his impatience, over-confidence, and excessive focus on political rather than pressing military priorities. He was literally a victim of his own successes, which fueled a heady over-confidence that was fully warranted under the circumstances. Not only had Santa Anna been overly-intent on capturing the refugee Texas government in wild flight, but he also wanted to end his troublesome Texas Campaign as soon as possible, because Mexico's acting president in Mexico City, in his absence, had died.

This new development in the nation's capital left his political base and future potentially uncertain in a country rife with political intrigue, torn by civil war, and having a lengthy history of military coups. Largely because of political developments in Mexico City around 750 miles away and as a young lieutenant of the Vera Cruz Lancers, Santa Anna had led the frantic race toward the coast, originally to have been led by a top lieutenant, first to Harrisburg, and then to Lynch's Ferry in a last-ditch gamble to capture the Texas government and swiftly end the conflict.[105]

By this time, few Americans, especially Texians who had been pushed aside by Santa Anna's seemingly unstoppable advance, believed that Houston and his ad hoc army of unruly volunteers possessed even the remotest chance of prevailing in the upcoming climactic confrontation to decide the fate of Texas. Voicing a decidedly minority position, Swartwout, the chairman of the board of the New Washington Association, wrote to Morgan from New York City with a surprising optimism based upon the hope of not losing his massive investment: "We know if Santa Anna succeeds, we lose all. We look for news daily, and, I, being a madman in favour of the cause [of Texas Independence], predict that Sam Houston will whip Santa Anna to death & then hang the d____d scoundrel in the bargain."[106] Most people across America would have considered Swartwout a "madman" for naively believing that Houston had any chance of winning a great victory amid the tangled oak and cypress thickets of the humid coastal lowlands.

Emily D. West had journeyed to Texas in the hope for a better life and a more stable, peaceful existence. But she had been closely connected to the wife and children of the foremost political revolutionary, whom Santa Anna desperately wanted to capture and execute to settle old scores, the Yucatan-born Lorenzo de Zavala. Santa Anna wanted Zavala's death because it would be most symbolic, while also sending a strong signal to the Mexican lovers of America's republicanism and democracy, which they viewed as a cure for Mexico's seemingly endless woes. Zavala was a republican hero to the Mexican people and liberals all across the land. He was now the foremost and leading Mexican revolutionary against Santa Anna and his centralized rule. Back when they had been friends, which seemed like a lifetime ago, the dynamic Zavala had been appointed by Santa Anna as the diplomatic minister to France at Paris.

But he had angrily resigned in disgust because of the generalísimo's greedy power grab and rise to dictator. Quite unintentionally, therefore, Zavala had indirectly played a large role in making his old friend Santa Anna now more vulnerable than ever before to Houston.

The lure of capturing and executing Zavala had drawn Santa Anna farther away from the main army. Santa Anna was most eager to get his hands on the interim vice president of the Texas Republic, riding ever-onward toward the Gulf Coast at the head of his men.

Houston himself was now in Texas only because of an unpredictable and sudden change in the course of his life, because he believed that his young wife had slept with blacks. All of these strange circumstances had now united to set the stage for the final showdown at San Jacinto and to place Santa Anna ever-closer to where the Zavala clan lived at Buffalo Bayou, because of the generalísimo's desire to capture his former friend.[107]

As reported across the United States, "Gen. Houston has adopted the excellent plan of gradually evacuating the country, and falling back to ... the Sabine, till he has Santa Anna's army completely in his power."[108] Now a lowly, free black woman from the northeast suddenly found herself in the ranks of a fast-moving unit of soldados under Santa Anna's immediate command that was destined for the plain of San Jacinto. Emily D. West was more vulnerable than she had been in her life, after having been literally swept up by the struggle over the heart and soul of Texas. The climactic battle for Texas was about to erupt in full fury.

CHAPTER VII

Climactic Showdown at San Jacinto

After the fiascos at the Alamo and Goliad, most people across Texas and the United States expected Houston and his small band of ill-trained volunteers to likewise meet with disasters. A cynical "gentleman" in New Orleans described the military situation in Texas: "The Texas business is making some noise here [the Crescent City] at this moment. Santa Anna is driving General Houston before him. The garrisons at La Bahia, or Goliad, as well as that of San Antonio, have been cut off almost to a man. Houston, with a small force, much exaggerated I imagine, is falling back behind the Colorado. My opinion is, they will be nearly exterminated! It has become a war of fanaticism, and they will fight HASTA EL CUCHILLO!"[1]

However, fortune began to smile upon the cause of Texas in its darkest hour. On a timely April 18 reconnaissance while the rustic soldiers of the revolutionary army rested near Harrisburg, Houston's most trusty scouts—capable Erastus "Deaf" Smith, who rode a swift mustang and wore some Mexican garb, including large-sized Mexican spurs, and Captain Henry Karnes, who commanded the mounted patrol—had captured three Mexicans riding along the narrow dirt road that led west to the Brazos in the afternoon heat. One dismayed prisoner was a courier, wearing a uniform with a captain's rank and a large sombrero, from Mexico City. The officer's rank indicated that he was no ordinary courier, and carried information of some importance. What these opportunistic Texas scouts gained was an intelligence coup second to none. Smith and Karnes now possessed letters for Santa Anna and Filísola. Translated without an error in meaning by Major Lorenzo de Zavala, Jr., "a fine, sprightly youth" who was the son of the interim vice president and a diehard Mexican revolutionary who had fallen in love with the concept of republicanism like his father, a General Filísola dispatch to Santa Anna revealed how wide his divisions were scattered over a vast area, and well beyond mutual supporting distance.

Upon intense questions and the necessary threats to elicit honest answers, the pressured Mexican courier, Captain Miguel Bachiller, told of Santa Anna's movements and general location: that the generalísimo had ridden toward the coast, then turned, and was now headed northwest from New Washington toward Lynchburg along the New Washington Road. Most importantly, he also revealed the fact that Santa Anna himself was in command of only a relatively small vanguard, now far ahead of his widely-separated army, of only around 600 men.

Knowing nothing of this strange, low-lying countryside near the gulf or Houston's movements or plans, Santa Anna was now in an exposed position and more vulnerable than ever before. While Houston now possessed Santa Anna's plans, Santa Anna incorrectly believed that Houston's forces were yet headed farther east toward Nacogdoches, which meant that they would have to cross the wide San Jacinto River at Lynch's Ferry. Here, Santa Anna planned to ambush the arriving band of Texians; all in all, a very good plan that was calculated to annihilate yet another band of bungling revolutionaries.

This vital intelligence gained by Karnes and Smith fueled Houston's effort to reach the ferry at Lynchburg first before Santa Anna in an intense race, after he crossed to the south side of Buffalo Bayou in a rickety ferry boat and a log raft on the following day, April 19. In addition, the fighting spirit and desire for revenge among the Texians and United States volunteers was heightened, because one of the Mexican couriers carried the deerskin saddle bag, initialed "W.B.T.," of the Alamo's South Carolina–born commander, Travis. Many Texians, therefore, had already made up their minds that once they met the Mexican troops on the battlefield, they would take few, if any, prisoners. Houston's rustics in rebellion early planned to return the no-quarter policy that Santa Anna had unleashed upon the men of the Alamo and Goliad.

Never knowing of Houston's intelligence coup, Santa Anna possessed complete confidence in the wisdom of his strategy. He planned to gain Lynch's Ferry and Lynchburg to block the Texians' retreat and nab his quarry in one swoop. He also hoped to prevent Houston's forces from joining the exiled Texas government on Galveston Island to reunite the military and political arms of the resistance effort. Santa Anna assumed that the last Texian force in the field would continue to avoid a direct confrontation as throughout the six-week withdrawal eastward and toward the Gulf Coast.[2] Therefore, on the morning of April 19, Santa Anna dispatched a cavalry patrol of hard-riding dragoons north to reconnoiter toward Lynchburg to ascertain the whereabouts of Houston's motley group of "land thieves" and homespun revolutionaries.[3]

In the words of William Fairfax Gray, Lynchburg "was laid out for a town some years ago, but it will never be a town, one or two houses and a saw mill, built by President Burnet, but which was not profitable, and is not now worked …. It is just below the junction of the San Jacinto and Buffalo Bayou, on the road" that led to the Sabine River and the Louisiana border.[4]

The long-running chess game between two career military men and politicians now boiled down to a simple race between Houston and Santa Anna to reach the now most important strategic objective in Texas, Lynch's Ferry. This campaign to determine the fate of Texas was about to be decided by an inevitable clash of arms at some point amid the lowlands of the plain of San Jacinto, which was bounded on three sides by water and marshland.

After all, on April 19, Santa Anna had learned that Houston's Army, after having departed the smoking ruins of Harrisburg, now marched straight east along Buffalo Bayou toward Lynchburg, just east of Harrisburg, and farther down Buffalo Bayou. By pushing about a dozen miles northwest along the New Washington Road, Santa Anna and his 600-man advance task force pushed onward in an attempt to reach Lynch's Ferry, before Houston gained it and before the Texian revolutionaries could slip off the mainland and reach the safety of Galveston Island.

Meanwhile, Houston also was enlightened about Mexican movements by one of Morgan's African Americans, Turner. He was the apprentice printer of the *Telegraph and Texas Register* and signed at New York City by Morgan, like Emily. After having been taken at New Washington along with Emily and at least one additional free black from New Haven, George Cooper, Turner had just slipped from Mexican forces before presenting Houston's scout on the morning of April 20 with additional intelligence. This "yellow boy" stated that the Mexicans were only eight miles away at New Washington and "on the way back to Harrisburg."[5]

Angered by the sight of dark clouds of smoke indicating New Washington's destruction and the ruin of Morgan's and the New Washington Association's grandiose dreams of a great city on Upper Galveston Bay and the burning down of Harrisburg, Houston's soldiers finally prepared for a showdown with Santa Anna. Reaching the level plain of San Jacinto, which spread across the northern tip of the peninsula, with no Mexican troops in sight in the early morning hours of April 20, after a grueling all-night march, Houston won the race to Lynch's Ferry by only three hours. This obscure ferry was a vital and now strategic crossing of the San Jacinto River near its junction with Buffalo Bayou. In quieter days, Lynch's Ferry had hauled people, herds of cattle, and covered wagons, the "light Dearborn or Jersey wagons," across the wide San Jacinto River, a murky, tidal watercourse, to the tiny, rustic community of Lynchburg on the east bank. Large numbers of civilian refugees, with their black slaves and worldly possessions in tow, from across Texas had already poured across the ferry to escape Santa Anna's relentless advance.

Knowing that this was his last opportunity to make a stand, Houston carefully choose the ground—a grassy prairie stretching between waterways and woodlands on the coastal plain—to make a fight about half a mile west of Lynch's Ferry. By mid–morning on April 20, Houston had taken a position on relatively high ground that stood along the south bank of Buffalo Bayou and beside the east-west running Harrisburg Road and parallel to Buffalo Bayou's south bank, just above where the chocolate-colored bayou joined the San Jacinto River. Orders were issued from Houston's headquarters for the men to rest and eat a breakfast.

Hidden in the dense stand of virgin timber, including towering, ancient cypress trees, festooned by lengthy strands of Spanish moss, like those that covered the Gulf Coast from Louisiana to Mississippi, Houston and his troops faced south toward an expanse of open ground, which was a natural coastal prairie. More importantly, he faced toward the New Washington Road from where he knew Santa Anna was now marching north as fast as possible with the desire to end the Texas rebellion with one last master stroke. This expanse of level prairie, a luxuriant grassland known as the plain of Hyacinth, stood before Houston's concealed position in the thick stands of timber lining the south bank of Buffalo Bayou, offering an open field of fire, if Santa Anna decided to attack.

Therefore, Santa Anna discovered that an unknown number of Houston's soldiers were in a key position astride the strategic crossroads of the Harrisburg and New Washington Road and before Lynch's Ferry just to the east along the Harrisburg Road. But he had no way of knowing how many Texans and United States volunteers were hidden in the dark woodlands, virgin timber and thick underbrush along Buffalo Bayou's south bank. Was this only a straggling rear-guard force of just a handful of desperate men, or Houston's entire army recently reinforced by an unknown number of United States volunteers, who had just arrived from east of the Sabine? Santa Anna simply had no way of knowing.

As hoped and planned, Houston faced Santa Anna, now with only 600 men. He confronted Santa Anna before the generalísimo could link up with the bulk of his troops under his second in command, Filísola. Most importantly, Houston's force stood squarely between Santa Anna's vanguard and the bulk of his army. Nevertheless, the ever-aggressive instincts of Santa Anna called for the unleashing of an attack immediately with his seasoned veterans, including victors of the Alamo.

However, he was deterred from launching a large-scale strike because he was unable to ascertain the strength, location, or disposition of Houston's force hidden in the dense thickets along Buffalo Bayou. Knowledgeable about the winning ways and tactics of his idol Napoleon, therefore, Santa Anna was forced to send a lengthy line of skirmishers forward in a probe to ascertain what exactly lay before him in the mysterious thickets along the bayou. Hot skirmishing between Mexicans, including the much-feared Lancers, and Texians erupted over the grassy plain of San Jacinto, echoing and rising higher like the day's summer-like heat along the Gulf Coastal Plain.

Frustrated at having lost the high stakes race to Lynch's Ferry by a mere three hours, Santa Anna's 600-man force occupied an advance position on solid ground amid an island of timber just west of the New Washington Road. Then, after deciding that the Texians posed no serious threat for offensive operations on the assumption that relatively few men opposed him, Santa Anna encamped on slightly high ground at the northern edge of the open plain of Hyacinth that was surrounded by water on three sides, a virtual island amid the summer-like forests of bright green, in the swampy coastal lowlands. Here, on solid ground, he set up his encampment in a wedge between the San Jacinto River and Peggy's Lake. Ominously, Santa Anna possessed so few troopers that he could not afford the luxury of a reserve.

Santa Anna only now realized that he had wasted far too much time at the place Emily had called home in Texas since December 1835, New Washington. Clearly, Houston had benefited from Santa Anna's systematic and vengeful destruction of the property of the New Washington Association and Morgan, who was also an investor of the Galveston Bay and Texas Land Company, which had once sought to enlist Houston in promoting the project.

However, in setting up his tented encampment only a quarter of a mile from Houston's army and on the open, grassy plain of San Jacinto in part because he could not see his opponent's numbers along Buffalo Bayou, Santa Anna had placed himself in a very vulnerable position, a thin peninsula of open ground, the San Jacinto plain, surrounded by water on three sides. Here in the swamp, he could be trapped by an attacker, with 300-foot wide Buffalo Bayou and with the dark-colored bayou less than a mile to the north; the San Jacinto River, which flowed southeast, to the right, or east; and a small bay, known as Peggy's Lake just west of the river, some 500 yards to his rear, or south. And beyond Peggy's Lake was an expanse of marshland.

If anything at all suddenly went wrong or unexpectedly happened (especially a surprise attack) along Buffalo Bayou, Santa Anna would not be able to retreat or escape either to the north, south, or east. Here, nevertheless, the yet supremely-overconfident Santa Anna decided to await the arrival of General Cos and his 500 men and three pieces of artillery, which he had requested on April 13 to join his small vanguard. These much-needed reinforcements had been ordered by Santa Anna from the main body of the Mexican Army, under General Filísola, at Thompson's Crossing on the Brazos directly to the west.[6]

To the Mexican troops so far from home, this strange, low-lying land and unmapped terrain along the Gulf Coast around this patch of open ground known as the plain of Hyacinth, or San Jacinto, had a mysterious, if not sinister, quality to it and its unfordable watercourses. William Bollaert described the field of San Jacinto and its vicinity, including "Buffalo Bayou—like to a canal; the bottom wooded principally with Pine—owing to sandy soil—fine magnolias in flower [but] This is not the land for plantations—too poor."[7]

One of Houston's men provided a better overall description of the field of San Jacinto in an April 1836 letter to his brother: "This place [is] situated at the junction of the San Jacinto river and the Bayou Buffalo. The two streams form what is called the San Jacinto Bay, on the east side of which [is situated] Lynchburg, or rather Lynch's ferry, for in reality there is no town or village to be seen; and, on the west there is a most beautiful prairie, handsomely variegated, with small groves of timber."[8]

Evidently, by her own choice because she had nowhere else to go after New Washington was burned to the ground, Emily accompanied the vanguard of Santa Anna's army from Morgan's Point to San Jacinto, about 12 miles northwest of where she had worked for the last four months. Emily could probably see the rising smoke from a burning New Washington and Morgan's hotel. She most likely was part of the soldaderas who followed the army, mixing in with the other women, including liberated African Americans, who had gained their freedom from the soldados in Napoleonic Era uniforms or traditional white cotton peasant garb.

Most importantly, Houston's well-concealed position in the belt of dense thickets of ancient oaks, pines, and cypress along Buffalo Bayou's south bank was a good one. Situated on relatively high ground, this screening wall of greenery blinded and baffled Santa Anna, deterring any serious thought of a large-scale attack across the open, grass-covered prairie. Houston's force was out of sight of Mexican forces, concealing both his recently-augmented strength and even offensive intentions, if the Tennessean was so inclined. Therefore, Santa Anna was shocked and surprised when the Texians had suddenly opened fire with not one but two cannons during the hot skirmishing that extended well into the afternoon of April 20.

Houston's force had taken possession of these two small-caliber guns on April 12 at Harrisburg. These "Twin Sisters" had been dispatched to Texas by the citizens of Cincinnati, Ohio. In a patriotic fever to support their fellow Americans in Texas, they had contributed their own money to have the cannon cast in the bustling Ohio River port city, after learning the terrible news of the Alamo and Goliad disasters. Incredibly, Santa Anna had brought only one cannon with his diminutive advance task force. Santa Anna was outnumbered in regard to artillery by the "Twin Sisters," which were named for the twin daughters of Dr. C. C. Rice.

The "Twin Sisters" proved to be a godsend that bolstered the strength and morale of Houston's Army. The firing of these two little iron cannon by uniformed Texian gunners fortified the resolve and confidence among this small force of citizen-soldiers from Texas and the United States. Indeed, these Buckeye State guns were a most timely and badly-needed addition to an ill-trained volunteer army facing its greatest crisis to date.

After a lengthy journey by steamboat first southwest down the Ohio, then south down the Mississippi to New Orleans, and then across Gulf of Mexico, these two matching 6-pounders had been transported west up Buffalo Bayou to Harrisburg by the *Flash*. Here, Houston had taken possession of the "Twin Sisters," thanks to the *Flash*, which had also brought the hopeful Emily to Texas in December 1835.[9]

Light skirmishing continued to erupt across the San Jacinto plain throughout the hot afternoon on April 20. Houston's small contingent of cavalry and Mexican Lancers clashed on the grassy plain under the bright sunshine. But nothing was achieved by either side except getting a few unlucky men killed, before the decisive battle was fought. Meanwhile, General Cos and his reinforcements continued to push at the double-quick and ever-farther east in a desperate bid to reinforce Santa Anna's task force. If Cos arrived in time, then Santa Anna would have a total strength of barely 1,000 men. With just 900 volunteer troops at his disposal,

Houston would be slightly outnumbered once Cos arrived. Therefore, as his critics later charged, perhaps Houston would have been wise to have unleashed an attack on April 20, before Cos' reinforcements reached Santa Anna, as urged by his over-eager men, who could hardly wait.[10]

Houston had no idea how many more Mexican reinforcements were on the way. It was becoming more obvious for almost everyone, except Houston, in the ranks that an attack almost certainly would have to be made the following day, April 21, before Santa Anna's task force, now vulnerable so far ahead of the main body of the Mexican Army under Filísola to the west, was reinforced.[11]

The core of the Emily Morgan myth, based upon the obscure Bollaert reference, was that Emily now performed her patriotic duty to save Texas by allegedly giving her body up for amusement and sexual comfort. She allegedly allowed Santa Anna his sexual pleasure and fulfilled his carnal desires, so that Houston's forces would be presented with a golden opportunity to catch the enemy by surprise by attacking on the afternoon of April 21.

Among arguments against this popular fable is that Emily, at age thirty-six, was already too old for the youth-obsessed Santa Anna, whose eye for Latino women (Mexican or Tejano) seldom wandered to anyone over the age of twenty. He had married Doña Inés García when she was fourteen and Malchora Barrera at seventeen. And Santa Anna's history with women clearly indicated his decided preference was for Latino women. No record has been found that Santa Anna ever went outside his race for sex.[12]

If in fact Emily, almost certainly like other so-called Mexican or Tejano camp followers who served his headquarters, might have been around or even in Santa Anna's large silken tent, or "closeted in the tent" as described in the Bollaert reference, then her role was almost certainly that of a servant instead of a sexual partner. If anything, she might have attended Santa Anna or a member of his headquarters staff perhaps serving food and drink or washing clothes.

Emily had been hired as a cook and housekeeper by Morgan, and she was skilled in this work. Another free black woman who had been with Emily at New Washington was very likely also with her at San Jacinto. Diana Leonard had signed up to work one year at New Washington for Morgan in New York City, like Emily. Could the "Yellow Rose of Texas" story have been Diana? Almost certainly not, as the incident likely never occurred at all.

But now situated in the Mexican encampment at San Jacinto and perhaps with Diana, who was a friend from New Haven, Emily merely fulfilled the typical role of a soldadera and any number of women who served at Santa Anna's large headquarters in an army noted for its top-heaviness in regard to a officer corps. By this time, the vast majority of soldaderas had been left far behind by the vanguard's rapid advance, and, therefore, the Mexican soldiers needed the typical domestic chores. But most likely Emily was not used as a personal servant of Santa Anna, because the "El Presidente" had his own faithful and prized servants who attended him at San Jacinto. Emily was surely with Santa Anna's advance task force not as a sexual object or Santa Anna's concubine, but as a competent domestic worker, as she had been at the New Washington Hotel. In keeping with the Southern-based customs of the day, even Houston was attended by his own black servant, Willis, who spoke fluent Spanish, at San Jacinto.

Despite evidence to the contrary, the central foundation of the "Yellow Rose of Texas" myth was that the Mexican "president ordered her assigned as a servant in his marquee, or presidential tent" expressly for sexual gratification.[13] But this highly imagined and much celebrated tryst scenario makes little sense for many reasons. Emily spoke only English and Santa Anna only Spanish. They shared no commonalities in culture, proclivities or language that would have made the alleged liaison more probable. Santa Anna knew next to nothing about either black or United States culture. Santa Anna already relied upon a master chef to satisfy his lavish aristocratic tastes in Colonel Almonte's servant Benjamin Harris, who cooked for both Santa Anna and Almonte. Therefore, Emily's culinary skills were not needed at Santa Anna's headquarters, and, therefore, not sought.

Besides Emily, other liberated black men, women and children who had either escaped slavery or had been liberated by Santa Anna's march through Texas had linked up with the Mexican Army by this time. These former slaves might have been attached to traditional servant or soldadera duties at Santa Anna's headquarters on the field of San Jacinto. As Lieutenant Colonel de la Pena, whose men now lacked soldaderas, recorded in his memoir, based upon his diary, on April 11, during the march on San Felipe de Austin: "We met several natives, a mulatto woman, two Negro women, and several Negro men, who were very useful in making the [river] crossing and who washed our clothes."[14]

Emily was with Santa Anna's vanguard in part because these were so few soldaderas with this advanced, fast-moving task force. Mexican women, wives, lovers, and relatives of the young men and boys in the ranks had been left far behind, and others helped to fill the void. The myth that Emily was taken with the army for sex, because of her alleged promiscuousness combined with her alleged breathtaking beauty and the alleged savagery of lustful Mexican soldiers—from the most humble private to the army's commander—simply does not bear up to the facts.

Emily's duties were probably similar to those of Bettie, a woman of African descent who was liberated when the Alamo fell. Bettie had been the cook of James Bowie. After liberation with Bowie's death on March 6, Bettie had accompanied the Mexican Army, including later when it withdrew back to Mexico after Santa Anna's defeat at San Jacinto. Her situations, duties, and personal odyssey had nothing whatsoever to do with either Bettie's physical appearance or sexuality. Former slaves like Bettie possessed ample good reason to devote her services to the Mexican Army. These ex-slaves were aware that if Santa Anna and his army were defeated, then this reversal would ensure the permanent entrenchment of slavery in Texas. Consequently, when Santa Anna was defeated at San Jacinto, Bettie would seek the abolitionist haven of Mexico, accompanying the withdrawing Mexican Army to the safe haven of Matamoros, the longtime promised land for Texas slaves, around 350 miles south of the Brazos River country.

Near the mouth of the Rio Grande River at the tiny town of Bagdad, just east of Matamoros and beside the relentless pounding gulf surf, she eventually found steady employment as a cook for William Neale, of Scotch-Irish ancestry, for a number of years. However, her ever-present fear of being kidnapped by Texians and returned to slavery's horrors in the sweltering cotton-fields of Texas later caused Bettie to flee deeper into Mexico's interior. She finally settled in Monterrey in the cool, picturesque mountains of northern Mexico.[15]

Much like Canada for slaves fleeing north, Matamoros had long served as a safe haven for slaves in Texas seeking freedom during the 1820s and 1830s. Escaped Texas slaves were drawn to the freedom that was symbolized by this picturesque city, with its majestic twin-towered cathedral, the city's pride and joy, on the central plaza. The Texas Revolution's opening guns in early October 1835 only accelerated the freedom flight of escaped African Americans to this Mexican city nestled on the twisting north bank of the Rio Grande just before it reached the gulf. Later in 1836 and for good reason, Texas slave-owners dispatched official representatives to Matamoros in an unsuccessful attempt to reclaim their escaped slaves, who had fled to the city in droves.[16]

Meanwhile, Santa Anna had upped the ante at San Jacinto, while Houston remained inactive early on April 21. At about 9:00 o'clock on the warm morning of April 21, General Cos and four hundred troops of his hard-marching division finally reached the field of San Jacinto, after an exhausting sprint that had consumed all of the previous night. A chorus of wild cheering suddenly erupted in the Mexican encampment with the reinforcements' timely arrival, offering bad news and heralding trouble ahead for Houston and his men. The long push east all the way from the Brazos to nearly the gulf to link with Santa Anna, now near the coast, was so grueling that around 100 soldados of Cos' division never reached San Jacinto.

Large numbers of exhausted men remained far to the rear, assisting supply and baggage wagons forward along muddy roads as rapidly as possible. Cos' much-anticipated reinforcements consisted of soldados from the battalions of Guerrero, Toluca, and Aldama, along with two companies of the Guadalajara Battalion. Only the troops of the Toluca Battalion and Aladama, under General Cos, had seen action during the assault on the Alamo, when they struck first the west and then the north wall like the majority of Santa Anna's attackers in the early morning darkness of March 6.

Unfortunately for Santa Anna, most of Cos' soldados were raw recruits who had been conscripted and impressed into service against their will. In the customary manner of acquiring additional troops before a campaign, they had been systematically picked up, including by force by impressment officers and gangs, in northern Mexico's towns during the army's march north to a rendezvous with a bloody destiny at the Alamo. Hailing mostly from the towns of Saltillo and San Luis Potosí, they had served in Santa Anna's army for only several months. These soldados had yet to receive their baptismal fire, and they were anything but reliable troops, especially in a key battlefield situation. The entire 300-man Guadalajaro Battalion consisted of non-veterans. These soldados were not the kind of fighting men that Santa Anna now needed. Because of their state of exhaustion, sore feet, and worn-out condition, Santa Anna ordered Cos' men to stack arms and to sleep in a nearby grove of timber that offered concealment from Houston's men.[17]

Boding ill for Mexican fortunes, Cos was a nervous, if not anxious, commander. He was in fact taking a great risk by even appearing on the field of San Jacinto at this time, having violated his "parole of honor" from his surrender of the Alamo in December 1835. During this period, Cos was described by one American as having "large, long black whiskers, sun-burnt at the ends, and red, sandy moustaches. His complexion is sun-burnt, and he wears little gold rings in his ears. He is a cousin to Santa Anna."[18]

Santa Anna grew to seriously lament how the 100 men, dependable veterans instead of untrained "raw recruits," who had been left far behind Cos' column, "never joined us" on the field of San Jacinto in time for the final clash of arms.[19] Because this rapid push toward the Gulf Coast had been the last phase of a lengthy, grueling campaign, and because they were in a strange country so far from home, a good many Mexican troops, especially those unhappy peasants who had been impressed into the army, were not adequately prepared psychologically, physically, or emotionally for a decisive battle on April 21. In addition, these men from Mexico, including Santa Anna, had long considered the campaign all but over, expecting no serious fighting.

Even worse, a certain unease, a sense of foreboding, and an ominous feeling hung over the tented Mexican encampment on the plain of San Jacinto like a dark cloud. For some of these Catholic warriors, including Santa Anna himself, who wore silver and gold crucifixes and who revered the iconography of Our Lady of Guadalupe, consciences were troubled about having been ordered to slaughter so many Americans and Texians at the Alamo and Goliad. These mental torments among the most humanitarian soldados wreaked havoc on troubled minds. Devout Mexican soldiers knew that the killing of unarmed men violated the core values of Christianity. One of Santa Anna's adjutants, Colonel de la Portilla, was only recently reminded of the distinct possibility of a divine wrath about to be unleashed upon the men from Mexico, when Lieutenant Colonel de la Pena, of the elite Sapper Battalion, prayed with solemness, "Let us hope that we shall not have to pay for this."[20]

And another soldado, Rafael Morales, who was now in the encampment at San Jacinto, was haunted and tormented by the murderous executions after having obeyed orders to take part in firing upon a group of Texian prisoners. Among these unfortunate captives was a former childhood friend of Morales. Despite their former friendship, the hapless prisoner was executed along with his comrades.[21]

Santa Anna's men had good cause for concern. By this time, Houston's soldiers, without having been given specific orders to embrace a no quarter policy, had already come to their own grisly decision: the Mexican troops and their leaders would have a high price for having slaughtered hundreds of young men and boys. And almost as if God was a Texian, this frightfully high price that was to be exacted for the past sins of Santa Anna now guaranteed the most brutal of no quarter policies at San Jacinto.[22]

Quite independently of their commanding general and former Tennessee governor, these free-thinking, ever-independent frontier types from Texas had already come to their own grim conclusions. They also came to their own common sense conclusion that Santa Anna was not going to attack this late afternoon on April 21, and that now was the exactly right time to launch an attack, before additional Mexican reinforcements arrived on the field.[23]

The final dramatic showdown that would alter the fate of three nations was about to take place in the most unlikely and remote of places: an isolated, obscure section of swampy, humid lowlands of the Gulf Coastal Plain that was well-watered by Buffalo Bayou and the San Jacinto River. This was an unspoiled land where alligators, snakes, and mosquitoes thrived more than man—white, Indian, Tejano, or Mexican. Especially after the arrival of Cos' reinforcements and despite the skirmishing of the previous day, Santa Anna could not have been more confident at this time. De la Pena recorded the extent of the deeply-seated hubris, writing how Santa Anna now "greatly deprecated an enemy whom heretofore he had vanquished in every encounter when he had dared to show his face. He was over-confident, and he communicated this feeling to those under him, giving the enemy an advantage that he could not have had otherwise."[24]

Nevertheless, Santa Anna demonstrated some prudence. In the words of an increasingly concerned Colonel Pedro Delgado, of Santa Anna's staff and an artillery expert who believed that Santa Anna had chosen a bad position, "His Excellency ordered a breastwork to be erected for the cannon [and] it was constructed with pack-saddles, sacks of hard bread, baggage, etc. A trifling barricade of branches [an abatis] ran along this front and right."[25]

By the late afternoon on April 21, Santa Anna concluded that Houston was too weak to attack. After all, it was late in the day and the native Tennessean was only a disgraced norteamericano politician and amateur commander, who was now outnumbered after the arrival of reinforcements, who were commanded by his young brother-in-law (Cos). In fact, with timeless Napoleonic lessons in mind, the generalísimo had expected Houston to strike either the previous night or earlier this morning in an attempt to catch him by surprise.

Along with the hasty creation of the thin, makeshift line of breastworks across the grassy plain which was now colorful in its springtime splendor, Santa Anna felt added confidence for another reason. He knew that the Texans had spied the arrival of Cos' reinforcements and heard the loud reception for the new arrivals: seemingly a guaranteed powerful deterrent for any thought that Houston might possess of unleashing the tactical offensive on the hot afternoon of April 21.

Holding a strong defensive position on solid, relatively high ground in an island of timber along Buffalo Bayou, Houston had decided against an assault across wide stretch of open ground this morning, which made good sense under the circumstances. In the annals of military history, no greater folly could be found than an army's commander ordering a frontal attack across open ground in broad daylight against a fortified position.

However, itching for a fight and a chance to finally come to grips with a hated opponent, Houston's men in the ranks thought differently. Without military training or experience, they possessed their own ideas about the art of waging war not found in military textbooks or taught at military academies on both sides of the Atlantic. These rustics in rebellion began to advocate for Houston to take the tactical offensive. In what was in essence a mutiny on land rather than on sea, leading Texas officers and their disgruntled men, who yet felt humiliated by having been forced to withdraw and abandon so much territory before the advancing Mexicans, demanded that Houston unleash them, or they would attack on their own this afternoon, when the sun was yet high in the sky.[26]

Meanwhile, on the other side of the San Jacinto plain, Santa Anna felt that he had Houston and his revolutionary army of amateurs boxed in and at his mercy. In his own words: "I shut the enemy up in the low marshy angle of the country where its retreat was cut off by Buffalo Bayou and the San Jacinto [while] I myself occupied the highest part of the terrain."[27]

Therefore, Santa Anna allowed his forces, especially Cos' weary soldiers, to rest for the day's remainder: a prudent, necessary, and logical decision before the climactic battle, if it came the following day as he confidently envisioned. Then, he planned to crush Houston's pesky force once and for all, ending the campaign and this people's revolution in one final stroke on April 22. Santa Anna knew that Houston's army was weak, undisciplined, and seemingly only capable of retreat ever-eastward, before the relentless onslaught of Mexican troops. In fact, Santa Anna must have laughed knowing that the former Tennessee politician, known to drink, gasconade, and fornicate to excess as if solely dictated by his desires (the two commanders were much alike in many ways), had seemingly committed the ultimate folly of encamping with a formidable stream to his rear, Buffalo Bayou.

Houston's forces would have no escape rearward when the Mexicans attacked on April 22 to destroy the Texian rabble, just as the Alamo garrison had been wiped out to a man when trapped inside the old Franciscan mission. With the wide bayou of deep water to the Texians' rear and a rain-swollen river to their left, it indeed seemed that Santa Anna now held Houston securely in a trap of the Tennessean's own making. To Santa Anna, this situation appeared to be just another example of incompetent Texian leadership as seen at the Alamo, Goliad and throughout this disastrous campaign for the revolutionaries, who had risen up against Mexico with great expectations.

Santa Anna was confident of reaping an easy and decisive victory on April 22, and one that would be celebrated by everyone in Mexico City. More than ever before, he now "felt certain that he could cut them off and could enjoy the leisurely execution of the stragglers as they fled on foot. In a satisfied mood, he retired to his tent, secure in the knowledge that all was in order. Perhaps he indulged in his habit of taking opium [and] he relaxed, and so, apparently, did his troops. It was the siesta hour, and there appeared no threat from the Texans. [Santa Anna] posted no guards" around his encampment.[28]

Indeed, by around 3:00 p.m. on April 21, Houston's soldiers sensed the golden opportunity because of the silence and inactivity in Santa Anna's comatose encampment, which had grown sedate under the gulf plain's bright sunshine and heat of day. Therefore, Colonel Thomas Jefferson Rusk, the Texas Republic's secretary of war who had a close call with Mexican Lancers in the previous day's skirmishing, asked Captain Juan Seguin, the ever-reliable commander of a mounted Tejano company who hailed from his cattle ranch of Casa Blanca, a key question of vital importance: "if the Mexicans were not in the habit of taking a siesta at that hour." Upon receiving an affirmative reply from the Tejano captain, Rusk, the feisty, promising son of an Irish immigrant, had a revelation. He concluded how "the moment seemed favorable to attack the enemy."[29]

This is where the mythical story of "The Yellow Rose of Texas" adds another element with even larger role in setting the stage for Santa Anna's downfall. Thanks to the irresistible appeal of a promiscuous black seductress, according to the popular fiction instead of the realities of the tactical situation, Santa Anna had ordered his force to rest on the afternoon of April 21 primarily because of an overwhelming desire for Emily. In the words of one author, Santa Anna's lust was so inflamed that he neglected everything else because he "was in a hurry to get into the sack with Emily" inside his headquarters tent.[30]

Santa Anna was now well within sight of winning the crucial campaign not only to reclaim Texas but also to solidify his power base in Mexico City and to end the revolt in Texas in one stroke. And now with Houston's army only a short distance away in the humid, dense thickets along Buffalo Bayou and across a wide open stretch of coastal prairie, Santa Anna's mind and focus were certainly not directed to reckless sexual escapades, while in the midst of his troops, commanders, and personal staff during the most defining moment of the 1836 Texas Campaign.

Quite simply, no evidence exists that Santa Anna had become negligent because he desired to take Emily to bed, despite modern American historians' and writers' insistence. No Mexican historians have maintained that Santa Anna was involved in a liaison with Emily or anyone else on April 21. And if he had wanted Emily in a sexual way and was overwhelmed with lust upon first sight of her alleged ravishing beauty, then Santa Anna could have been with her during the respite of his two-day stay at New Washington, when he had ample leisure time and was not on a battlefield.[31]

In fact, instead of a mind focused on Emily's body, Santa Anna had been thinking about home, wife, and family. He was eager to end this campaign and return home as soon as possible. Once Houston was vanquished by his legions on April 22, Santa Anna planned to immediately leave Texas by sea. He had already ordered a ship to the port of Copano, located on Copano Bay, which was the northwest extension of Aransas Bay, to await his arrival, once Houston was vanquished.[32]

On this hot, humid afternoon on the Gulf Coastal Plain—so unlike the cool highlands of his Jalapa home that loomed above Vera Cruz's sweltering coastal lowlands—Santa Anna sought the shady comfort of his headquarters tent. Situated among the orderly array of white tents of his staff, the Napoleon of the West's large silk headquarters tent offered a source of relative comfort to him. In this sense, Santa Anna's home in the field while campaigning in Texas was not unlike "the royal tent" of Islamic rulers of Spain from ancient times, when they accompanied their armies against the Christians of the Catholic faith.

But in fact, this large field tent offered much more to Santa Anna than simply a place of comfort and luxury; it served as a busy command post. Here, Santa Anna studied his map of Texas, called in officers and received reports, and discussed strategy for the attack on Houston planned for the following morning. He also issued new orders to staff officers and commanders in the field both at San Jacinto and to the rear, where most of his army yet remained. And, of course, Santa Anna discussed military, tactical, and strategic matters with his top lieutenants in a council of war.

Santa Anna was not only the army's commander but also the leader of his country. He, therefore, had much official business to conduct, especially during active campaigning.

Santa Anna's utilization of a large tented headquarters in the field was in keeping with the penchant of his idol, Napoleon, when he had campaigned like a lightning bolt across Europe. Where he had crafted and dictated some of the most brilliant strategies in Nineteenth Century warfare, Napoleon's large headquarters tent was divided into two rooms—one for sleep and the other for work. Napoleon spent far more time working than sleeping. A table and folding chairs dominated Napoleon's work and study area. Santa Anna's headquarters tent was described as a large brown-and-white striped tent of a comparable size and sufficiently large for two rooms like that of his Corsican idol.[33]

Lieutenant Colonel de la Pena believed that Santa Anna had not brought a campaign tent with him from Mexico, which was highly unlikely, especially during a winter and spring campaign far north of the Rio Grande River. De la Pena surmised that Santa Anna's campaign tent might have been an American tent captured when the Alamo garrison was chased into the old mission of February 23 to seal their doom, and the Mexicans occupied San Antonio. They also took possession of the mercantile enterprises and stores, including those owned by a few Americans, in the almost exclusively Tejano town.

As de la Pena recorded in his memoir: "From among the goods and the tents found which the enemy had abandoned when they took hurried refuge in the Alamo, one of the tents erected was called the president's tent because it was placed in the premises occupied by his Excellency."[34] This was possibly the same tent Santa Ana now occupied at San Jacinto. In late 1835, the officials of the Texas General Council ordered "1 Grand Marquee and General's Marquee, equipage and fly."[35]

If this was the same tent ordered by the Texas General Council, it may have been acquired by the Mexicans in one of their victories on Texas soil. With the hot sun beating down and with many of his men resting by the early afternoon of April 21, Santa Anna's tented quarters on the field of San Jacinto was simply known as "His Excellency's tent" by the soldados in the ranks.[36]

After completing his official business, both military and political, Santa Anna, worn out from his frantic chase of the Texas government over such a wide area for more than a month, decided to rest in the afternoon heat. After unbuckling his fancy sword valued at $7,000 and no longer taking snuff from his decorative snuff box of gold, the generalísimo laid down in his bed in the spacious headquarters tent. He then took a catnap, reposing in a deep sleep of the weary. Most significant, Santa Anna himself revealed that he was sleeping at the time of Houston's surprise attack that afternoon. As he wrote in his autobiography, which was dominated by a good deal of embellishment and even outright fiction to make himself look much better in the historical record, not unlike Napoleon, who effectively fashioned his own story to create the "Napoleonic legend" as we know it today: "At two o'clock of a hot afternoon, April 21, 1836, I lay sleeping in the shade of an oak tree, hoping for cooler weather to begin my countermarch."[37]

Santa Anna was evidently attempting to create the image of a bold commander who campaigned out in the open like the men in the ranks. A good deal of far more accurate evidence has indicated that Santa Anna was in fact sleeping peacefully in his tent and not under the oak tree nor having sex at this time. For Santa Anna, the image was calculated to present a commander who was close to his men, sharing their trials and suffering. After all, sleeping under a tree like a lowly, mixed-race common soldier of mostly Indian heritage was a most unpresidential and most uncharacteristic repose for an aristocratic Creole and the nation's president with a well-known penchant for enjoying luxury and comfort to an extreme degree.

In his autobiography—written in Nassau, Bahamas, in 1874, nearly forty years after the battle of San Jacinto—Santa Anna was entirely wrong in regard to how he depicted the setting and situation at San Jacinto. Houston's attack was launched just after 4:00—not 2:00, as Santa Anna emphasized—in the afternoon, not striking Santa Anna's encampment until two more hours after the time stated by the army's commander in this much-distorted account.

And second, Santa Anna was certainly not sleeping outside in the open under a full-leafed tree at a time when he possessed his large, exquisite silk headquarters tent set up nearby so that he could be sheltered from biting insects, the encampment's noise, and the afternoon heat and humidity. Santa Anna's campaign tent was located toward the rear, among his staff members' tents, and not far behind the makeshift barricade that had been established to defend the Mexican encampment and the seasoned front-line troops, who were regulars of the Matamoros Permanent Battalion, guarding the foremost position. As a Creole member of the privileged ruling class and the nation's president, Santa Anna enjoyed the best of everything, including silken bed sheets and as much comfort as possible when campaigning in the field. Therefore, the large headquarters tent was where Santa Anna found rest and some peace.[38]

With Santa Anna sleeping soundly in his headquarters tent, most of his troops continued to similarly relax in the afternoon heat and humidity, resting up for the climactic battle that was now inevitable, when they would open the attack on Houston's hidden position in the thick belt of timber along Buffalo Bayou on April 22. By this time, the calm serenity that had descended upon the field was almost total. Never forgetting the moment, Colonel Pedro Delgado, a respected member of Santa Anna's staff, wrote, "No important incidence took place until 4:40 p.m. At this fatal moment, the bugler on our right signaled the advance of the enemy upon that wing. His Excellency and Staff were asleep; the greater number of the men were also sleeping; of the rest, some were eating, others were scattered in the woods in search of boughs brought to prepare shelter. Our line was composed of musket stacks. Our cavalry were riding, bareback to and from water."[39]

Nothing was ever written in contemporary accounts from a Texian, United States volunteer, Mexican, black, or Tejano about Santa Anna having supposedly engaged in a liaison with a black woman named Emily. The only mention was the single Bollaert reference, which was written near the beginning of the Mexican-American War of 1846–1848. In truth, the embellishment of a drug-induced tryst between an African American woman and Santa Anna that changed the course of history came much later, with the writings of modern historians who have gone to great lengths to popularize the story.

Giving undeserved credence to the ever-growing popular myth, for instance, Houston biographer Marshall De Bruhl, without mentioning Emily's name, simply wrote: "The [Mexican] arms were stacked and the troops were either enjoying a siesta or going about their routine chores of an army in the field—carrying water, washing clothes, or gathering firewood. Santa Anna himself was supposedly passing the siesta with his mulatto mistress."[40]

However, all reliable accounts and the best existing evidence, including contemporary, have indicated that Santa Anna was asleep in his headquarters tent and not in bed with anyone. Some historians have simply passed along the speculation. Albert A. Nofi wrote how "Santa Anna himself was taking siesta in his tent, some say with the aid of opium and a young woman named Emily Morgan."[41]

Besides the alleged sexual tryst with Emily, Santa Anna has been widely ridiculed by generations of armchair historians for not placing pickets to guard the encampment. This assumption was only yet another popular myth about the battle of San Jacinto. In fact, Santa Anna actually went to considerable trouble to place a lengthy line of pickets and in readying the makeshift defenses to protect his encampment from attack. He had placed three dependable companies on guard on the right and the trusty Matamoros Permanent Battalion in position to protect the encampment's center along the front.

In fact, Santa Anna was so worn out from his tireless efforts in maximizing his encampment's safety throughout the morning of April 21, combined with having been up the entire previous night, he had been forced to retire to his headquarters tent to sleep. Santa Anna had been in a state of utter exhaustion over an extended period during the lengthy, time-consuming race to San Jacinto, after having ridden at the head of his troops nearly all the way to the gulf.

Therefore, in truth, he remained in his tent in a deep sleep rather than engaged in a lengthy, energetic marathon sexual tryst with Emily because of his insatiable carnal appetite and uncontrollable lust: the traditional portrayal of Santa Anna that represented not only a stereotype but also a caricature. Badly in need of rest after the most grueling campaign of his career, a weary Santa Anna had simply gone to sleep in his headquarters tent.[42] The capable General Manuel Fernández Castrillón, who was fated to be killed in Houston's attack on the Mexican encampment, was then left in charge of camp security before Santa Anna retired to his tent in the belief that his encampment was secure.[43]

By any measure, Santa Anna was a highly complex and contradictory individual, defying the simplistic stereotypes, especially the common view that he was endlessly obsessed with debauchery more than military matters, as so often portrayed by American historians and the most popular writers, both then and today. Despite his political intrigues, including the switching of sides to his advantage and many well-known actions directed at personal gain in the tradition of a long line of caudillos who led the Mexican nation, he was a devout Catholic and a true friend to blacks, especially those unfortunate men and women shackled by the bonds of slavery.

Like a true veteran and like so many soldiers on both sides, Santa Anna placed his faith in God, especially during the perils of wartime. At San Jacinto in his headquarters tent, he possessed a cherished "old fashioned black box, ornamented in front with a silver crucifix." Evidently, this was a religious relic given to him by his mother or wife. The combination of Santa Anna's religious faith and his personal sympathy for the plight of blacks may have also diminished any possibility of a tryst with Emily. With a revered priest officiating the wedding ceremony, he had married Doña Inés García, an attractive young lady of modest means, primarily for love and not money or lust in 1825. Santa Anna then fathered at least four children with her. When she died in 1844, he then married another young woman only forty-one days later rather than living in sin at a time when he was a highly eligible and yet a dashing, single man, who was blessed with good looks, a bright future, and considerable political influence.[44]

Rather than a lengthy, wild sexual interlude with Emily in his elaborate headquarters tent, as so often assumed because of long-existing stereotypes about both blacks and Mexicans, other authors have speculated on another cause of Santa Anna's seemingly incomprehensible behavior in allegedly not placing pickets to guard the encampment: the intoxicating effect of powerful drugs. Santa Anna certainly used opium to some degree when it was available, but usually for recreation and not in such a critical situation as he faced at San Jacinto. However, when the alleged Houston letter to Bollaert later described how Santa Anna was made vulnerable by the "influence" of Emily, then did that possibly mean that, as his headquarters servant, she brought him his supply of opium, if he possessed any (evidence indicates that he had none), rather than a sexual liaison?[45] Of course, the answer to this far-fetched scenario is mere speculation, and the proposition unlikely on multiple levels.

However, a good many authors have ignored all of the extant evidence, preferring to additionally embellish the alleged tryst between Santa Anna and Emily. James A. Michener, one of America's greatest story tellers, made a most lucrative career in churning out one best seller after another in production line fashion, becoming world famous in the process. Michener, who masterfully blended fiction with fact and occasional lofty flights of imagination, likewise set the San Jacinto stage for mindless debauchery by describing how Santa Anna, "convinced that the Texians would not dare to attack at that late hour when they were so badly outnumbered, had retired to his tent for the traditional siesta, perhaps made somnolent by the warm weather, a heavy meal, and a soupcon of opium."[46]

Michener simply could not resist mixing the tantalizing blend of interracial sex and drug abuse in his colorful story of the alleged Santa Anna–Emily liaison to a scandal-obsessed American audience. He lifted the mythical liaison story to new heights in his best selling 1985 work *Texas*. Embracing a host of stereotypes, Michener added credence to the popularity of the myth of the "Yellow Rose of Texas."

One of America's most popular writers helped to solidify the tale by describing the mythical scenario: "Santa Anna did not sleep. Taking a small dose of his favorite narcotic, opium, he called [to an aide] 'See if she's out there' and [then the aide] went to a nearby farmhouse where a beautiful young mulatto slave girl named Emily from the Morgan plantation was being kept, and she was delighted at the prospect of spending yet another siesta with the general."[47]

In this single passage, Michener achieved a great deal in regard to myth making, and certainly more than he could imagine. He not only gave new life to the popular story of the Santa Anna–Emily liaison and the most colorful and sexually-charged myth in Texas history, but also resurrected the oldest racist stereotype of the black woman as a hyper-sexual and brazen creative without control of her desires. Michener succeeded in transforming Emily into the stereotypical unthinking sexual creature, who was little more than a crass, sexually-charged whore without a hint of morality or decency.

However, Michener was only a product of his time, when the dominant image (the same as during slavery) of the black woman was extremely simplistic and most negative: emotion-driven, mindless, and unrestrained sexual beasts, and hence deserving of sexual exploitation and abuse by the alleged superior race. Conversely, the stereotype of black male hyper-sexuality has long served as a justification for the lynching of black males across the South to maintain the established caste order and system.[48]

Therefore, as creatively embellished by a good many imaginative writers and even modern historians who have conveniently ignored the facts, three distinct enduring myths have gradually developed and have been woven deeply into the very fabric of the story of San Jacinto to explain why Santa Anna was caught by surprise by Houston's attack: (1) not placing pickets to guard the camp and making other necessary defense arrangements to protect his encampment, and (2) the effect of opium addiction and overuse, which muddled and negated common sense, military judgment, and logic; and (3) of course, the tryst in Santa Anna's headquarters tent with Emily that blinded the generalísimo to all reality that existed around him.

None of these popular explanations of Santa Anna's ultimate downfall have supportive primary evidence to be taken seriously, however. When a prisoner not long after the battle of San Jacinto, Santa Anna would ask Houston for opium, which clearly indicated that the Creole had none of his own. An obliging Houston gave him some of his personal supply of opium. Then, on the field of San Jacinto, the two commanders of their respective armies "shar[ed] a pipe of opium." No wonder Santa Anna later described how "Samuel Houston treated us in a way that could hardly have been hoped for [and] his humane and generous conduct" was never forgotten. But after losing the battle of San Jacinto and Texas, Santa Anna possessed plenty of good reason to drown his sorrows in a euphoric drug stupor.[49]

Santa Anna's alleged addiction to opium has been almost as much embellished as the alleged Santa Anna–Emily tryst in the caudillo's headquarters tent. Santa Anna's "excesses with … drugs are tantamount to legends throughout Mexico and Texas. The tales of his addiction to opium [have] only added to the swaggering charms of the Hero of Tampico."[50] And so, the Emily–Santa Anna liaison story has likewise added to the enduring mystique, vilification, and roguish charms of the "Napoleon of the West."

Houston in fact shared a penchant for opium with Santa Anna. Houston's use, if not abuse, of opium caused one of his own officers, New York–born James Hazard Perry, to become highly critical of Houston and his questionable conduct during the 1836 Texas Campaign, before the final showdown at San Jacinto. Trained in the ministry and educated for three years at West Point from which he had journeyed to Texas in January 1836, Perry had long deplored the military incompetence that he saw all around him.

Perry blamed Houston's erratic behavior and shaky decision-making directly on "the effect of opium [because he] is in a condition between sleeping and walking, which amounts nearly to a state of insanity." Houston in fact gave Santa Anna opium from his personal supply, from which he had derived a drug-induced solace during the dismal six-week withdrawal east across so much of Texas.[51]

Opium more likely affected Houston's thinking and judgment during the campaign than Santa Anna's on the field of San Jacinto, even though Houston's widespread use of the opium poppy that ancients called the "joy plant" has been downplayed by American historians. Instead, they have incessantly insisted upon and emphasized Santa Anna's abuse of opium not only in leading to his downfall at San Jacinto but also to support the myth of the Emily–Santa Anna tryst. If political pressure was a factor, Houston was under much more criticism, including from an angry interim president Burnet and his own men in the ranks, for withdrawing across so much of Texas and almost to the Louisiana border and, hence, far more likely to partake in opium for relief, while Santa Anna, who continued to bask in a successful campaign, possessed much less reason than Houston to take opium during his victorious push across Texas.

Most significant, rumors about Houston's opium use were widely circulated throughout the ranks of his army long before the battle of San Jacinto, while Santa Anna's alleged use of opium came only after the battle. Even Santa Anna's actions in organizing both a defense and counterattack at San Jacinto before all Mexican resistance collapsed on the afternoon of April 21 also indicated that the generalísimo was in no opium-induced state.

By way of comparison, General Houston's well-known use of opium can perhaps explain some of the most glaring flaws in Houston's strategic and tactical thinking, as many of his officers and his enlisted men fully realized. Less than three weeks before the final showdown at San Jacinto, he wrote to Colonel Thomas Jefferson Rusk, the first secretary of war of the Texas Republic, and advised the government incorrectly based upon a dangerous delusion: "You may rest easy at Harrisburg, the enemy will never cross the Brazos" River.[52]

And Houston's faulty cognitive skills and reasoning were another reason why so many of his top subordinates and lieutenants, entirely unknown to their commander-in-chief at the time, had decided to launch an attack without him on April 22, before Houston decided to strike the Mexican encampment on the afternoon of April 21.[53]

What was the real situation at Santa Anna's tented headquarters by the afternoon of April 21 without the romance and embellishment? If someone named Emily had been at Santa Anna's headquarters tent, as indicated by the single Bollaert postwar reference—the only such existing documentation that has hinted as much—this could have been only one of a good many servants who attended to Santa Anna and his large staff, if that was indeed the case. Emily was a common slave name at the time. The Bollaert letter mentioned no last name.

But if in fact Emily D. West was assigned to duties at Santa Anna's headquarters, then what were the responsibilities of this free black woman from the northeast? If she was even present on the afternoon of April 21 before the generalísimo went to sleep she might have served food or handed Santa Anna a cut glass of fine wine from an exquisite wine decanter with a solid gold stopper, or from an expensive bottle taken from baskets of champagne that were later captured by the victorious Texans. Or she might have served him tea from a solid silver tea urn and perhaps added cream from a silver cream pot. Or Emily could have given him snuff from a decorative gold snuff box. Or Emily might have served the generalísimo a late lunch or dinner that fateful afternoon on fine exquisite china, with his monogram, before he decided to go to sleep. Or she might have cooked his dinner. If Emily was in fact in Santa Anna's tent as alleged, then it would have been very likely for a good many reasons other than sex. However, the bulk of the documentary evidence indicates that Emily neither was in Santa Anna's tent nor engaged in sex with Santa Anna or anyone else.

If she was situated in or near Santa Anna's headquarters, then Emily was most likely attached to the army simply for the purpose of washing clothes for Mexican soldiers, perhaps even Santa Anna or his headquarters staff: the usual menial role given to African American women when they were encountered by the Mexican Army in Texas. Around 4:00 in the afternoon, Santa Anna had fallen into "a deep sleep" in his headquarters tent, which contained fancy "furniture of silver, nicely arranged, such as a European prince might take with him into the field," according to one Texan, in order "to make the sultry Gulf Coast climate more comfortable for 'El Presidente.'"[54]

What the myth-makers have overlooked was the fact that Santa Anna possessed a distinct aversion to the intermingling of races. He lamented in regard to Mexico's fate as a failed nation state: "We have failed because of our deplorable racial mixture, and the responsibility for this sad state of affairs lies with the Spanish missionaries who saved the Indian from extinction."[55]

That Emily had no sexual relations with Santa Anna at San Jacinto on the afternoon of April 21 was obvious for other reasons, especially military. Would Santa Anna have been so negligent as to have actually engaged in sex, especially the rape of a reluctant Emily if necessary, in the enemy's presence, which was something that his idol Napoleon, who never took needless risks with his person, would have never committed—a cardinal sin—before a decisive battle? Was Santa Anna the out-of-control, sexually-obsessed psychopath, who enjoyed the act of forcing himself on defenseless women, including Emily, or was this common assumption only part of the myth to make the tale of sexual relations with Emily more plausible?

What did Santa Anna really think about black people and former slaves? Were women of African heritage in Texas, including Emily, actually targeted for crass victimization and exploitation by the most powerful man in Mexico for his own carnal pleasures and sexual amusement before the eyes of his own men and leading subordinates during the most important military campaign of his life?

Santa Anna's own words and actions revealed considerable empathy toward black people. He sincerely lamented the tragic plight of blacks in Texas as chattel exploited by hundreds of slave-owners in the sweltering cotton fields of east Texas. Santa Anna, consequently, sought to destroy the hated institution of slavery wherever he found it in the only province where it existed in the Republic of Mexico, which had officially abolished slavery in mid–September 1829.

In his sympathetic letters penned during the Texas Campaign, Santa Anna referred to African Americans as "these poor people" who were tragically fated to "suffer the pain of the[ir] chains." Santa Anna stated in no uncertain terms that they "should be free," and his liberating actions across Texas supported his seldom-quoted humanitarian words during the 1836 Texas Campaign. And symbolically on Texas soil, he now led a hardy mixed-raced soldiery, including blacks and Afro-Mexicans who were now the liberators of slaves, mirroring his own nation's demographics and abolitionism.[56]

At this time, the northern United States, especially the leading northern abolitionists like Garrison, looked at the 1836 role of Santa Anna quite differently, not only from Southerners and Texians, especially slave-owners, but also from today's traditional and conservative historians who have conveniently ignored the importance of slavery in the story of the Texas Revolution. After leading his army of liberation through Texas and even after his capture at San Jacinto, Santa Anna would be hailed as a hero in the North. He was welcomed as a genuine liberator by large numbers of Americans when he traveled to Washington, D.C., where slaves were yet sold on the auction block, to meet with President Jackson to legitimize signed treaties and confirm Texas independence. Santa Anna would be widely celebrated by many United States citizens as a true and authentic "hero of human liberty" for his anti-slavery war that he waged in Texas, until destiny turned so sharply and suddenly against him at San Jacinto.[57]

Besides the sincere humanitarian feeling and empathy that Santa Anna felt toward the plight of African Americans and the former slaves he liberated on the march through Texas, another long-overlooked factor also explained why there was no real possibility of Santa Anna's sexual exploitation of Emily. What has been forgotten about Santa Anna was that he was more religious but also more sympathetic to people of color than has been assumed by demonizing historians.

Ample evidence exists that Santa Anna certainly liked women, but only women of his own race, faith, and, most importantly, of a lighter skin color. This was a proclivity that reflected his own upper class standard of beauty. No evidence existed that he ever used physical force (but trickery was fine) on women to get his own way. His proclivities, therefore, did not include women of color primarily because of the racial difference. Instead Santa

Anna (who was light-skinned due to his Spanish blood/heritage) preferred light-skinned Latina women.

Santa Anna's Catholicism also played a role in this empathy toward slaves and people of color. Like his soldados in the ranks, Santa Anna was a devout Catholic and hater of slavery. What has been most often overlooked about the traditional story of the Texas Revolution was the fact that Santa Anna combined the dual concepts of religion and liberation on Texas soil. Most of all, he embraced the humanitarian faith of the Catholic Church and his republic's hatred of the institution of slavery to spread Catholicism and to destroy slavery by way of the sword in Texas like a Crusader of old. Therefore, as a student of history, especially Napoleon, Santa Anna viewed what he unleashed in Texas as a religious and anti-slavery war that was bringing a new day by the spreading of a liberation theology of sorts, fusing these diverse political, religious, and humanitarian concepts into one in what was a most potent mixture.

To be sure, the egotistical, cynical, and often utterly ruthless generalísimo was no saint, but he was also certainly not the stereotypical epitome of evil as so often portrayed not only by Texan and American writers but also by Mexican historians. That common portrayal, while embodying much merit, has been too simplistic. First and foremost, Santa Anna was a conservative who possessed the full backing and support of the Catholic Church. In Andrew Jackson's words, Santa Anna was "the favorite of the Priesthood," which favored the push into Texas to purge Mexican land of Protestants in the name of Catholicism.

For Santa Anna and the people of Mexico, the 1836 Texas Campaign was very much a holy crusade to purge the northern frontier of the stain of Protestantism that had become so deeply rooted in Texas soil. Despite the seemingly endless vilification of Santa Anna, Mexico's president, his people, and the Catholic Church saw the Protestant Texians as immoral, Catholicism-hating, and slave-owning heretics deserving of not only severe punishment but also annihilation in a modern Reconquista. Consequently, the Texians feared and were early convinced that Santa Anna was determined "to turn out the Protestants and establish the Roman Catholic Church" in Texas: a valid concern because Texas was Mexico's land, and Catholic Cathedrals dotted the land, especially in towns like San Antonio.

On the decisive field of San Jacinto and like so many soldados, Santa Anna wore a religious medal of Our Lady of Guadalupe, dated 1805, around his neck to provide physical protection, spiritual comfort to the soul, and inspiration. Our Lady of Guadalupe was the Indian Virgin Mary, the revered patron saint of the Mexican people, including Santa Anna and his soldados. The iconography and imaginary of Mexico's dark-hued Virgin Mary fortified and united the Mexican people more than any other single moral force.

Santa Anna hoped and prayed that the Our Lady of Guadalupe would look down favorably upon him and his army on April 21. Indeed, the Mexican Virgin Mary had long served as the only hope of liberty for the Mexican revolutionaries during their long battle for nationhood, won after more than a decade of bloody struggle in 1821, against the Spanish. Perhaps sex, especially rape, with Emily would have caused a religious-minded, superstitious Santa Anna to fall out of the good graces of Our Lady of Guadalupe just before the campaign's decisive battle.[58]

Santa Anna was of mixed heritage, having a Mexican mother and a Castilian or "a Spaniard from old Spain" father. Santa Anna almost always choose Latino women of a lighter hue than Emily. He also seemed to adhere to the adage that the lighter the woman, the better. For instance, Santa Anna had lusted after the blue-eyed, dark-haired Susanna Dickinson after the Alamo's fall. He offered to take her and her daughter back with him to

Mexico City. Susanna was perhaps "something of an exotic flower by Mexican standards" to a man long-accustomed to the dark-eyed, dark-haired Latino women of Mexico.

Santa Anna was probably in no shape to engage in any kind of sex by the afternoon of April 21. He almost certainly would have been too tired by this time to engage in a marathon sexual session with Emily or anyone else in his headquarters tent, even if that was in fact on his mind. He was facing a hidden enemy army only a short distance away and the fate of Texas was about to be determined. Santa Anna had been in the saddle for weeks, leading the vigorous pursuit of Houston's ragtag army almost to the Louisiana border, and had been up the previous night in perfecting dispositions of troops and defensive arrangements. A large meal and drink at his headquarters tent would have made him even more sedate, especially if he washed it down with a couple glasses of wine. All of these factors validate the first-person testimony that Santa Anna was asleep in his headquarters tent by 4:00 in the afternoon.

In Eighteenth Century and early Nineteenth Century European armies, it was not uncommon for aristocratic, worldly commanders, unburdened by religious or moral qualms, to make love to the wives of their subordinate commanders. These women then became mistresses. Far more knowledgeable and experienced about warfare than the ways of love, Napoleon himself engaged in this common practice, but only after his heart had been broken. He had discovered to his horror that wife Josephine was cheating on him back in Paris, France, while he was campaigning in far-away Egypt in 1798.

To console himself in his misery—as Josephine, an enchanting, love-wise Creole from the French West Indies, was the first love of his life—Napoleon then took a lieutenant's wife, blonde and buxom, as his mistress. She became known to the French soldiers of Napoleon's ill-fated Army of Egypt as "Cleopatra." Therefore, according to the military customs and traditions of the day, Santa Anna was in fact far more likely to make love to an officer's wife rather than a newly-freed slave or free black women. To transport a mistress in a covert manner, Santa Anna possessed a special carriage. This vehicle was described as a "magnificent coach," by which his mistress or mistresses traveled when campaigning. Not unlike those used by Napoleon's officers when on campaign, Santa Anna's special carriage—a love wagon of sorts—might have reached the field of San Jacinto by this time, if given a high priority.

If Santa Anna desired a women on the field of San Jacinto, then it logically would have been a well-dressed, charming companion—a Mexican's officer's wife–rather than Emily or a former slave. By comparison at this time, Emily was dressed in homespun and plain clothes, no doubt filthy by now, as a hotel worker of little means. And most likely, Emily had been employed in the Mexican encampment washing clothes like other black women, recently liberated and more than willing to assist their liberators and the soldaderas. Therefore, she was most likely not even near Santa Anna's headquarters tent by the afternoon of April 21.

A rather ordinary-looking, older Emily was certainly not the breathtaking beauty and sex goddess, of the "Yellow Rose of Texas" myth with the racial stereotypes of the hypersexual black woman, but in fact only "a jarringly homely washerwoman." If Santa Anna was engaged in any extra-circular carnal activities at San Jacinto, as implied by the long-hidden Bollaert reference, then it very likely would have been with an officer's wife or one of his favorite mistresses, perhaps one and the same by the time of the battle of San Jacinto. After all, any number of officers' wives were available as mistresses, after their soldier-husbands had been killed in the attack on the Alamo and other combat in Texas during this campaign.

Indeed, after the battle of San Jacinto, the Texian victors thoroughly searched the Mexican encampment. Not far from Santa Anna's headquarters tent, they found "the body of a very beautiful Mexican woman, and dressed 'very fine.'" She was just the type of woman who would have been brought by the generalísimo to San Jacinto in his special "coach." Unfortunately, she was killed accidentally by the hard-charging Texans. But the fact that this finely-dressed, beautiful woman was killed not far from Santa Anna's tent might well indicate that she was in fact Santa Anna's mistress.[59]

In truth, no evidence can be found that specifically states that a person named "Emily" was ever in Santa Anna's tent at San Jacinto, other than an "Emily" was "closeted in the tent" of Santa Anna from Bollaert's paragraph, which was allegedly written verbatim from the mysterious Houston letter that has never been found. All available evidence suggests that Emily was not even near Santa Anna's headquarters tent. Most likely, she was farther in the army's rear just north of Peggy's Lake. Here, other African Americans, both slave and free, who had joined up with Santa Anna's Army most likely could have been found on the afternoon of April 21. Among these African Americans in the Mexican encampment was the young free man George Cooper, also from New Haven, who was destined to watch the upcoming battle swirl around him.[60]

Santa Anna was fast asleep in his headquarters tent around 4:00 the sweltering afternoon of April 21, because of his own decision based primarily upon the premise that Houston would never attack. Santa Anna had informed the capable General Manuel Fernández Castrillón, born of a wealthy Criollo family in Havana, Cuba, that he was retiring to his tent for a quick "catnap rather than settle down for a siesta," leaving him in charge. Santa Anna had even handed Castrillón, the generalísimo's trusty aide-de-camp, his own fine Swiss watch, evidently to follow his specific instructions at certain designated times in the near future, after he retired into his headquarters tent.

Santa Anna took the precaution of having ordered Castrillón, who had been one of his top advisors since around 1822 and his most trustworthy chief lieutenant of his general staff, to make sure that the pickets remained on guard and in their assigned positions, where he had earlier ordered them. And, of course, Santa Anna advised his top lieutenant to wake him immediately at the first indication of any suspicious enemy activity or any new developments on the field. He requested to be soon awakened by Lieutenant Colonel Marcial Aguirre, a member of his general staff and an amiable, recently promoted former cavalry captain, who had survived the attack on the Alamo, as soon as Cos' troops had finished their lunch rations.[61]

Besides Mexican accounts that never mentioned anything about a woman named Emily, some of the best evidence that has verified that Santa Anna was fast asleep was later forthcoming from an American, evidently guarding Santa Anna's men, who acquired first-hand accounts from Mexican prisoners, including top leaders, who had been taken at San Jacinto. "As however the presence of Santa Anna and his officers here have placed me in possession of particulars not generally known. I dare say the details I am about to give you will be found worthy of attention," as he wrote to the editors of the *National Gazette*, Philadelphia, Pennsylvania, which published his account on June 11, 1836.[62] The author, one of Houston's soldiers at San Jacinto, wrote, "Santa Anna was quietly taking his siesta, when he was awoke by his aid with the news of our approach, which he swore was a damned lie."[63] The fact that Santa Anna was asleep at the critical moment was so well known that later even some "Mexican historians believe that he purposely took a nap and allowed himself to be taken prisoner."[64]

Most significant, none of these anti–Santa Anna Mexican historians have mentioned anything about the alleged Emily–Santa Anna liaison: the best way to have condemned Santa Anna for losing Texas by way of negligence and folly.[65]

Long overlooked by historians, the real forgotten and most important contribution to Houston's decisive victory at San Jacinto was indeed made by an African American. As recorded by de la Pena: "A slave appeared before Houston at three o'clock the afternoon of the 21st, informing him that General Santa Anna was sleeping and that his camp had delivered itself over to a feeling of confidence and great abandon. Houston hurried to take advantage of the beautiful opportunity that presented itself to him, to be freed of a critical and anxious situation. This explains why he decided to battle an enemy who had just received reinforcements of four hundred men."[66]

The key role of Santa Anna's repose in the fate of Texas was confirmed on May 7 to de la Pena by an eye-witness, Don Alejandro Alsbury. A member of Houston's army, Alsbury explained to de la Pena and other Mexican officers that Houston's surprise at San Jacinto had been largely because "Santa Anna was asleep."[67]

And an anonymous officer scribbled in his diary the same vital fact—Santa Anna was asleep—that confirmed Alsbury's report that Santa Anna was sleeping out of physical exhaustion at the time Houston attacked.[68] And Noah Smithwick, who arrived belatedly on the plain of San Jacinto, but learned of the battle's intimate details, described how "Santa Anna was snoozing away the time waiting for his scattered forces to rejoin him" at San Jacinto.[69]

Some modern historians, like James Donovan and Robert L. Scheina, have likewise concluded as much, sticking to the more credible evidence rather than succumbing to the temptation of embracing popular romantic myth. Indeed, after a lengthy campaign and in having been up all night on April 20 and after having been busy throughout the morning on horseback across the field in making defensive preparations and giving orders to protect the encampment against attack, Santa Anna was in a state of utter exhaustion.[70]

As verified by numerous accounts from both sides, the fact that Santa Anna was sleeping peacefully, rather than engaged in frantic love-making as if there were no tomorrow with Emily, at the time of the attack can be established beyond doubt, given the ample and primary documentation and his own words, which conformed with the views maintained by leading Mexican officers, such as Colonel Pedro Delgado of Santa Anna's staff, who were on the field that decisive afternoon.

That the army's commander was asleep was symbolic and in keeping with the fact that so many soldados of his advanced task force were likewise either asleep or in a state of sheer exhaustion by this time. In addition, by 4:00 in the afternoon, this was the traditional mid-afternoon siesta time deeply embedded in the traditions of Mexican culture and society. In his research, modern historian Gregg Dimmick verified the accounts of Colonel Pedro Delgado, Lieutenant Colonel de la Pena, and many other Mexican officers, that revealed how not only Santa Anna but also most of "the Mexicans were literally and figuratively caught sleeping."[71] Likewise Scheina concluded what was undeniable on the field of San Jacinto by writing how Houston's upcoming attack was successful in "literally catching Santa Anna asleep."[72]

Therefore, far more reliable contemporary accounts, documentation, and primary evidence have proved conclusively that Santa Anna was asleep by the time that Houston launched his attack, while only one account exists—Bollaert's obscure reference from the alleged Houston letter (and not a contemporary source at that) that was written nearly a decade after the battle of San Jacinto—that implied and hinted at a tryst between an "Emily" of no last name and Santa Anna. On the afternoon of April 21, Santa Anna had committed his most grievous error of the entire campaign and it was in regard to overall risky tactics and an unsound strategy, and this situation had nothing to do with Emily. Most of all, he was a victim of hubris and his own string of past successes—not Emily's alleged seductiveness, captivating beauty, or luscious body—that had long graced his military career, especially while campaigning in Texas.

Yet supremely overconfident after having pursued Houston's army more than 200 miles east for six weeks across most of Texas, winning every battle and quite correctly scornful of his ragtag norteamericano opponent, Santa Anna's encampment was enclosed by multiple bodies of water that could not be forded. Worst of all for Mexican forces thanks to his overriding hubris, he assumed that Houston's force would dare not attack on the afternoon of April 21, and that he retained all of the advantages. The entire Mexican encampment situated on the grassy prairie was exposed, despite the light breastwork that was more a weak facade and a dangerous, self-assuring illusion of defensive strength than a serious obstacle to attackers.

Because the soldados were without entrenching tools, no trenches had been dug or earthworks created for defensive protection at a time when Santa Anna's farthest advanced force, worn out and yet small, was positioned farther east and closer to the United States border than ever before, and from where Houston's reinforcements had come and more were now on the way. In his own mind, however, Santa Anna felt ample justification for his high level of over-confidence and boundless contempt for his untrained, bungling opponent, who had yet to win a battle in this campaign.

In fact, at no time during the course of the 1836 Texas Campaign had the Texians taken the offensive: a dismal performance marked by the height of folly and ineptitude of an unprecedented magnitude. And, now here on this remote, sun-baked plain of San Jacinto, the last thing that Santa Anna expected was an afternoon frontal attack from Houston's amateurs in rebellion. Continuing to perpetuate the myth of "The Yellow Rose of Texas" with an airy certitude, popular historian Marshall DeBruhl described how Santa Anna was now "passing the siesta with his mulatto mistress."[73]

And, of course in keeping with one of the most popular myths in the annals of Texas history, the name of this mulatto mistress was Emily. The truth was entirely different, however. Emily D. West was in Santa Anna's encampment, but not in the generalísimo's headquarters tent. The real Emily was not a victim of Santa Anna's unbridled lust and carnal desires in a large silk tent, but she was about to become caught amid the swirling chaos of a battle that altered the fate of three republics in short order.

Houston's Surprise Attack

Houston's instincts and timing could not have been better in this hot afternoon on the marshy gulf coastal plain. Just after reading Caesar's ancient classic *Gallic Wars*, and in order to placate his officers and men who had been long itching to attack, Houston gave the order to advance across the wide expanse of coastal prairie amid the early spring warmth at half past three o'clock.

After deploying from three columns and in a lengthy line that stretched across the prairie, Texians and United States volunteers moved forward without the detection of anyone in the Mexican encampment, despite marching across open ground covered in tall grass. A slight low rise in the middle of the plain helped to hide Houston's advance from Mexican eyes. Also assisting the attackers was the fact that the sun now lay low on the cloudless horizon on the bright, clear day, shining into and blinding the eyes of the Mexican sentinels if any peered south across the level ground.

Marsh area of the San Jacinto Battlefield (The San Jacinto Museum of History, Houston).

Fortunately for the slow-moving attackers with fixed bayonets, the slight rise and perhaps even a faint shimmering heat haze ensured minute after minute that any vigilant Mexican soldiers could not see the stealthy advance led by Houston. No doubt relieved after having taken so much criticism in not turning to attack Santa Anna in past weeks, the Tennessean, with sword in hand, was now mounted upon his light gray war charger, Saracen. As Houston had ordered, no soldier in the Texian ranks made the mistake of yelling or cheering to alert the quiet Mexican encampment. In perfect silence, they pushed relentlessly over the open ground of the plain of San Jacinto. They were full, not only from a recent meal, but also with confidence and the lust for revenge. By this time, motivation among Houston's men could not have been higher.

While Santa Anna's large silk tent, where the general now slept in peace and complete confidence, was located on the highest ground on the San Jacinto's plain's southern end, the makeshift breastwork earlier created by the soldados stood in a shallow defile behind a slight rise near the plain's grassy center. This overall situation and the blessings of geography guaranteed that the foremost Mexican troops, the experienced 240 men of the Matamoros Permanente Battalion, at the improvised defensive barrier stretching across the open ground, would not see Houston's advance, which was concealed behind the rise, until it was too late.

Thick, knee-high prairie grass also helped to mask Houston's advance rolling southward like a tidal wave in homespun cotton and buckskin instead of regular uniforms. Clearly, Santa Anna should have positioned his makeshift breastwork across the higher ground, where his headquarters tent was located, farther to the rear or south. But since arriving on the grassy plain of San Jacinto, neither he nor his high-ranking officers were overly concerned about the overall defensive situation. After so much success across Texas, they yet held a

Early 1900s postcard of San Jacinto Battlefield along Buffalo Bayou (author's collection).

great contempt for the "army of [land-grabbing] pirates" under Houston's command. However, one of Santa Anna's savvy Tejano scouts, whose instincts were correct about the encampment's vulnerability, had been worried, but his voiced concerns were ignored by one and all.

Perhaps, if washing clothes in the rear behind the makeshift breastwork at the northern end of the Mexican encampment with soldaderas who were engaged in the same work for the men in the ranks, Emily perhaps first heard a slight drumbeat in the distance to the north. If so, she could not have possibly realized that these drumbeats came from the hands of another free black who advanced across the sun-baked prairie in formation with his white peers in Houston's ranks. Before the surging line of hundreds of white soldiers from across the United States and Texas, this free African American hailed from New Orleans, perhaps the French Quarter on the Mississippi, before migrating to Texas to start a new life.[74]

This black musician, known simply as Dick, now marched in Houston's foremost ranks and played the jaunty tune "Will You Come to the Bower" with another drummer and four flutists, including one German, to inspire and fortify the resolve of Houston's advancing troops in pushing over such a wide stretch of open ground. A member of one of the Texas regular regiments, he now served on Houston's staff and was the only black drummer in Houston's Army during this dramatic showdown.

In fact, he had already awakened Houston's army at 4:00 a.m. on April 21. But Dick, a former slave from the Crescent City along the omnipresent "Father of Waters," was no stereotypical little drummer boy. Mature, knowledgeable, and with plenty of life experiences not unlike Emily D. West, Dick was a large man who dwarfed his smaller white comrades, especially the scrawny teenage farm boys who were now moving forward to engage in their first battle, with a head sprinkled with gray hair. As if to bring back the memories of the American Revolution when an earlier struggle had been won by rustic revolutionaries,

Houston's musicians, black and white, then broke into a spirited rendition of "Yankee Doodle."

Also surging onward in the Texian ranks was at least two more African Americans, but their names and stories have been lost to history. Other blacks served in non-combat roles. Now serving as a member of "Deaf" Smith's spies, or scouts, and one of Houston's best scouts of Smith's "Spy" Company, was Hendrick Arnold. He had guided a column in the attack on San Antonio that resulted in the Texians' and United States volunteers' greatest success before the clash of arms at San Jacinto. A free black fighting man, Arnold now advanced through the tall grass in the ranks of Houston's surging battle line of highly-motivated soldiers, who held muskets with bayonets, shotguns, and rifles at the ready. The other black soldier moving onward across the wide plain of San Jacinto was Kentucky-born Maxlin Smith, whose nickname was "Mack." He was the indentured servant, or slave, to Major Ben Fort Smith, who migrated to Texas with Smith, born around 1809, in 1832.

In addition, two slaves also marched forward in Houston's ranks, Mark Smith and James Robinson. Robinson had migrated from the South to Texas the previous month as a slave to Captain Robert Eden Handy, who now served as an aide-de-camp to Houston. Despite his lowly status or because of it, "Jim" Robinson was every inch an ebony fighter, refusing an offer to return home, evidently as a reward for loyal service, just for the chance to meet the Mexicans in battle.[75]

Houston's ranks surged onward under the bright afternoon sunshine, while the battle-flag, with a bare-breasted goddess of liberty in the center, waved over the line of the Second Texas Infantry Regiment. Houston's advance of the First and Second Texas Infantry Regiments continued unseen and unheard by the foremost Mexican troops. The Texians and United States volunteers demonstrated a surprising level of discipline by advancing in perfect silence so as not to betray their stealthy movement. Therefore, each yard that the Texians, who continued to hold their fire, surged across unseen by the soldados continued to spell the ultimate doom of Santa Anna's task force on this hot afternoon along the Gulf Coastal Plain.[76]

Slaughter at a Murky Tidal Lake

With sunlight reflecting off bayonets and the silk Lady Liberty battle-flag floating softly in the slight breeze sweeping off the gulf, the attackers stepped through the high clumps of green grass and the colorful prairie flowers, perhaps bluebonnets, at the height of the prairie's springtime beauty, after the recent deluge of heavy Texas rains. Most importantly, at this exact moment on this sun-splashed afternoon was the best of all times to launch an assault. Santa Anna and the Mexican troops had committed the cardinal sin of letting their guard down, and were too slow to respond to the threat. Worn down by a lengthy campaign in an alien land far from home, a large number of soldados continued to rest or sleep in the sweltering heat of mid–afternoon, while .753-caliber Brown Bess muskets, imported firearms from England and leftovers from the Napoleonic Wars, were stacked in neat rows according to army regulations. With Santa Anna in this tent and fast asleep, vigilance had slipped even further.

More of Santa Anna's initial directives to prevent surprise were ignored or overlooked by equally over-confident subordinates, while a lengthy line of Houston's attackers steadily approached to within one hundred yards of the quiet Mexican encampment without being seen. Not a single alarm from a bugler or drummer boy sounded the alert. In keeping with his handsome good looks, the tall, stately General Castrillón was shaving in his tent, as if back on a Sunday morning in his balmy, native Havana and about to go to dinner with a dark-haired Latina woman of his dreams. But at least, the refined and dignified Castrillón was wide awake, unlike Santa Anna and at least one of his top lieutenants, General Cos. In addition, Castrillón possessed a clear conscience and retained his moral bearings in this most brutal of campaigns, after having advocated mercy for Texian prisoners, including at the Alamo.

From this point and to the close of the fighting near sunset, almost nothing about what happened at San Jacinto resembled a traditional battle. Resistance among the surprised Mexican troops, especially General Cos' rookies in their first fight, would be not only far too late but also virtually non-existent. In a rare account written by one of Houston's men, the truth of the so-called "battle" of San Jacinto was revealed in full. He described how Houston's advancing line rolled ever-closer of the yet quiet Mexican encampment and then "gained a position within rifle distance of the enemy before they were aware of [the attacker's] presence. Two discharges of small arms, and cannon [the "Twin Sisters" in the line's center] loaded with musket balls, settled the affair; the Mexican soldiers then threw down their arms, most of them without firing, and begged for quarter," which was not given.[77]

Lieutenant Colonel de la Pena recounted how "a very few of the select companies were the only ones to give battle [because] the enemy advanced frontally with a body of infantry, two artillery pieces, and its cavalry to the left, in order to attract attention while the main body of the troops marched hidden behind tall grasses in order to flank our right, which they managed to do; that our troops were surrounded in a few moments."[78]

Indeed, Houston's steam-rolling attack when least expected was too much for Santa Anna's troops, because they had been caught completely by surprise, despite a Mexican bugler of the Matamoros Battalion who belatedly sounded the alarm. But by then, it was far too late to galvanize resistance. As with almost any commander-in-chief badly in need of rest and when within such close proximity of the enemy, Santa Anna had been asleep, most likely in his uniform: a catnap to restore his vitality and strength.

Santa Anna immediately raced out of his tent upon hearing the first blast and the sharp notes of a Mexican bugle slashing through the humid gulf air. Likewise top officers like Almonte and Castrillón attempted to rally their troops. The men of the Matamoros Battalion grabbed their muskets, while the homemade projectiles from the "Twin Sisters" roared overhead. The soldados of the Guerrero Permanente Battalion, under the command of thirty-eight-year-old Lieutenant Colonel Manuel Céspedes, who would be captured on this day in hell for the soldados so far from home, likewise formed to met the threat..

After having been awakened from his catnap, a nearly fully-dressed and now fully alerted Santa Anna, wearing a fine linen shirt but with no time to put on his lengthy leather boots as he now wore only slippers—sprang into action. He shouted orders amid the noise and confusion. Part of the popularized tryst myth was that Santa Anna emerged from his headquarters tent, where supposedly Emily was "closeted," only in his "white silk drawers," as he had been allegedly literally "caught with his pants down." The fact that Santa Anna was later captured not in his fancy general's uniform—obviously he removed it to disguise his identity to evade his pursuers and donned nondescript clothes of a slave—also led to the assumption that the generalísimo emerged from the headquarters tent without wearing a full uniform, because he had been dallying for too long with the allegedly ravishing Emily, whom no man could resist.

Indeed, the myth of the "Yellow Rose of Texas" has been the popular fiction that Emily's artful sensuality, hyper-sexuality, voluptuous figure, and irresistible beauty caused Santa Anna to emerge "in his silken drawers too late to rally his troops," a popular, iconic image that was in fact a misconception. Ample primary evidence and documentation shows that Santa Anna in fact took a vigorous role as a commander-in-chief to organize aggressive resistance. Having raced out of his headquarters tent and dashed a short distance to the north, Santa Anna reached the makeshift breastwork, where he attempted to organize a defense against the surprise attack. A capable officer who had initially stood atop an ammunition box to survey the field with considerable disbelief, Colonel Delgado recorded how Santa Anna and other officers were forced to drop to the ground when a hail of canister from the "Twin Sisters" whizzed close overhead. To minimize casualties, Santa Anna yelled, "Lie down! You will be hit." Delgado described the chaos swirling through the Mexican encampment: "I saw His Excellency running about in the utmost excitement, wringing his hands, and unable to give an order" in the smoke-laced noise and confusion.[79]

Contrary to the myth that he emerged far too late from his headquarters tent to organize any resistance, as emphasized in the Bollaert reference because Emily had detained him in bed for so long, and the unflattering portrait that a biased Colonel Delgado, who became one of the multitude of Santa Anna haters after San Jacinto, painted of the commander-in-chief, Santa Anna organized his troops. Instead of fleeing to save his own life, he even launched a desperate counterattack with two rapidly-rallied columns, including one under Lieutenant Colonel Céspedes. However, nothing could stop the momentum of the howling swarm of attackers by this time. These belated Mexican offensive counter thrusts were quickly overwhelmed by the raging tide of Houston's onrushing men, who would not be denied this afternoon. One shocked Mexican officer was convinced that Houston's soldiers were fearless because of an excessive use of good corn whiskey, but this was nothing more than raw courage and a burning desire to come to grips with their opponent.[80]

Storyteller Michener reached deeply into the drama-dominated recesses of his imagination to give vibrant life to one of the dramatic possible situations. With his usual masterful prose and soaring flights of fancy, America's famed author even blamed the Mexican Army's defeat on a number of hapless Mexican officers, who were unable to warn Santa Anna of Houston's attack in time, because his personal aides guarding his headquarters tent had refused to allow the commander-in-chief to be disturbed because "He's with the girl," and his sexual performance could not be interrupted. Michener continued: "Santa Anna, with Emily Morgan cowering naked behind him, looked [and saw Houston's charge across the prairie.] Grabbing his pants, Santa Anna took one terrified look at the carnage about to engulf his sleeping army, and fled."[81]

Despite Santa Anna's best efforts to not only organize a defense but also to mount a counterattack, a wave of panic swept the soldados, especially the inexperienced men, who never knew what hit them. After relatively feeble resistance, the rout of Mexican forces was now on and unstoppable. Born among the rolling and fertile green hills in Ireland's south in Cork County, Private Walter Payne Lane, who won an officer's rank for heroics displayed at San Jacinto and having migrated from Ohio, where his family had first settled in 1821 after departing the old sod of Ireland to Texas in early 1836, described how "they ran like turkeys" before the howling tide of Texians and United States volunteers, who gave no quarter for any soldado who came under their bayonets, pistols, shotguns, rifles, and musket-butts.[82]

Amid the swirling chaos that consumed the entirety of the Mexican encampment like a suddenly descending Texas blue norther—and with Mexicans, including officers, such as

Pedro Delago, who had attempted in vain to rally the troops, hurrying rearward—the servant of thirty-five-year-old Lieutenant Colonel Juan Bringas, one of Santa Anna's aide-de-camps who was soon captured, offered Santa Anna a horse. Santa Anna did not hesitate under the circumstances. In the nick of time and now realizing that he was much too far from the stately Spanish colonial mansions and wide boulevards of Mexico City, the generalísimo rode away from almost a certain death at the hands of revenge-seeking Anglo-Celts, who had plenty of old scores to settle after the massacres at Alamo and Goliad.[83]

What now occurred on the field of San Jacinto was in fact one of the great massacres of American and western history. Author Jeff Long said it best: "What followed was one of the great war atrocities in U.S. history that went on for hours, with rebel officers completely unable to corral their berserk troops."[84] A Texian captain said accurately but in less eloquent terms: "We followed the enemy, shooting and killing them, for more than a mile."[85]

Rather than a traditional battle in the conventional sense, what happened at San Jacinto was far from the mythical image of a glorious victory as reaped by Napoleon on the central plains of Europe, but in fact the ugliest of massacres, pure and simple. In the face of Houston's overpowering onslaught that had caught his opponent by surprise, Mexican resistance soon became non-existent, vanishing like the chances of Mexico's retention of Texas. Ignoring any officer's attempt to stop the slaughter, Houston's men went "berserk," thanks to the dark, bloody legacies of the Alamo and Goliad slaughters that now rose to the fore, taking their revenge on the defenseless men and boys, who had thrown down their weapons in their desire to escape and surrender.

A large percentage of Santa Anna's men at San Jacinto were recruits and not veterans who had slaughtered norteamericanos at either the Alamo or Goliad. Consequently, with the enraged attackers raising the battle-cries of "Alamo!" "Crockett!" "Travis!" and "Fannin!" (more common than the stereotypical "Remember the Alamo!") this unofficial declaration of no-quarter warfare was most ill-placed on San Jacinto's bloody plain.

Therefore, when so many inexperienced Mexican soldados, overwhelmed with fright and attempting in vain to surrender, cried, "Me no Alamo—me no la Bahia [or Goliad]," these young men and boys were not lying. They were in fact telling the truth, which of course was not believed by Houston's men. Nevertheless, the soldados, including men attempting to surrender and even wounded men lying helpless on the ground, were systematically slaughtered by Houston's men. The Texians and United States volunteers killed Santa Anna's men as if these peasants of mostly Indian heritage and impressed into service had been the authors of massacre instead of the Mexico City's cultured aristocrats and privileged, elitist politicians who were behind the Mexican Congress' no-quarter policy that had resulted in the deaths of so many Americans and Texians in March 1836.[86] Quite simply, these lower class individuals paid with their lives for the sins of the ruling class elite, especially Santa Anna.

Not long after all the bloodlust had been satisfied, one of Houston's men recalled sadly how the "poor Mexicans would hold up their hands, cross themselves, and sing out 'me no Alamo' but nothing would save them."[87] Unable to defend themselves and at the attackers' mercy, the terror was complete among the Mexican troops, especially among the hundreds of Cos' raw recruits who were already worn out from their sprint to reach San Jacinto. Unprepared for a bold frontal assault and without the benefit of trenches or earthworks, most solados never recovered from the shock of a surprise attack from an enemy that had seemingly appeared out of nowhere, rising up from out of the tall prairie grass to burst upon the thin breastwork that was literally pushed aside.

Besides calls for vengeance, the piercing war cries from the western frontier that resounded through the humid air of the San Jacinto plain were terrifying to young Mexican soldiers who were in their first, and last, battle. Twelve-year-old fifer Luis Espinosa of the Guerrero Permanente Battalion recalled how howling "Indians [were] among the enemy, judging by the yells that were heard during the battle."[88] This was no exaggeration. Even a Texian described how Houston's soldiers charged onward with what was a real "Indian war-whoop."[89]

One incredulous American never forgot the havoc wreaked upon Santa Anna's troops, "Of the whole right wing of the enemy, one man only escaped death. They were slaughtered" like cattle.[90]

Certainly one of the most tragic deaths on the Mexican side on gory April 21 was that of General Castrillón. This chivalric, noble native Cuban and a mature man of integrity from the Spanish Caribbean had attempted in vain to save surviving Texian prisoners, evidently even Crockett himself, at the end of the fighting at the Alamo, before Santa Anna ordered them killed. On this April afternoon in hell, General Castrillón immediately rushed to the barricade to take command of a chaotic situation, hoping to solidify resistance. Here, he valiantly attempted to rally his men to resist the surprise attack, but it was too little, too late.

Wearing a resplendent uniform and having just shaved as if about to have his portrait painted by a fine oil artist in Mexico City, Castrillón proudly refused to fly before an opponent, because he had never run in his lengthy career. He merely ignored the urgent pleas of his men to save himself. Castrillón made his own personal stand, not unlike the Alamo defenders. Rather than getting slaughtered at the breastwork, Castrillón's own troops had deserted him, fleeing south in panic toward Peggy's Lake in the encampment's rear. In desperation, he scrambled atop a wooden ammunition box to show his fleeing soldados that he was standing firm and refused to relinquish an inch of ground, beckoning his men not to run. Remaining dignified, heroic, and courageous to the very end on this awful afternoon of the worst blood-letting yet seen in the Texas Revolution, Castrillón yet stood atop the ammunition box, with arms folded, while "glaring down at his enemies," who desired his blood. He was soon riddled with bullets by the swarming Texians, who gave no thought of mercy to avenge the slaughters of March. With the heart of a true Irishman, Rusk's frantic efforts, including knocking away muskets pointed at the lone general and shouting "Don't shoot!" to save Castrillion's life, were in vain.[91]

Equally proud in the Spaniard and Conquistador tradition of battling against the odds like Castrillón, other Mexican officers, like Lieutenant Colonel Francisco Aguado, were engaged in other final acts of defiance that came at a frightfully high price. They "chose to die rather than turn over their swords" in surrender, wrote one saddened Mexican officer in his diary.[92]

All across the field of San Jacinto, Santa Anna's enlisted men continued to be dealt with in similar fashion, quickly dispatched without mercy or pity. William S. Taylor described how "we had no time nor opportunity for taking prisners [sic] so we shot them."[93] One of the most tragic Mexican soldado deaths during the blood-bath was witnessed by Sergeant Moses Bryan. He saw a young drummer boy with two broken legs, lying helpless and at the mercy of the Texians. When a vengeful Anglo-Celtic soldier pricked his body with his bayonet, the frightened boy cried out a desperate prayer that was ignored, "Hail Mary most pure! For God's sake, save my life!" But the enraged Texas soldier showed no mercy in the heat of the moment. He pulled out a pistol and "blew out the boy's brains."[94]

Two other young Mexican drummer boys were more fortunate amid the frenzy of butchery. In a rare display of mercy on the bloody field of San Jacinto, a compassionate Sergeant

Robert Goodloe literally fought off a number of his fellow Texians who were firmly intent on running the two Mexican boys through with their bayonets. Kentucky-born Colonel Sidney Sherman, who commanded the Texas cavalry, was nearby to intervene at the last second. So incensed were the Texians that the handsome colonel, just thirty and a dynamic, inspirational leader, was just narrowly able to not only help to save the lives of the helpless drummer boys, but also Goodloe himself from his own out-of-control comrades in the melee.[95]

An experienced officer at age forty-three and a dependable member of Santa Anna's staff, Colonel Delgado described the horror, writing how this "horrid slaughter [was] carried on all over the prairie by the blood-thirsty usurpers."[96]

Emily evidently remained either in the rear or safely in Santa Anna's tent, if she was ever there, instead of running outside, where she could have been killed amid the projectiles flying across the field. By this time nothing could control the enraged Texians and United States volunteers, who fully satisfied their bloodlust and vengeance to a degree not seen at any other time in the Texas Revolution. Clearly, the risk for Emily was considerable at this time, especially in view of her dark complexion. On a field covered with sulphurous smoke and rising clouds of dust, Emily could be mistaken for a Mexican. In the words of one Texas soldier, incensed like his revenge-seeking comrades, he was fully convinced, and swore that "if Jesus Christ were to come down from heaven and order me to quit shooting Santanistas, I wouldn't do it, sir!"[97]

These words were not an example of hyperbole. Along the north bank of Peggy's Lake some 500 yards to the Mexican encampment's south and rear, the Texas soldiers were so enraged that at least "one or two" soldaderas, those unsung, faithful, and stoic women who long supported the Mexican fighting men, were killed this afternoon, receiving shots in the head, or the coup de grace. Another unfortunate Mexican woman was sabered through the breast by a vengeful Texas officer, Major John Forbes, who had been born in the port of Cork, in south Ireland. Only recently a respected judge of the Nacogdoches Municipality in east Texas, Forbes served as the aide-de-camp to Houston and commissary general of the Texas Army.

Tragically, for this Mexican woman on this fatal day for the future of Mexico, Forbes was only "anxious to bloody his sword" at San Jacinto. Therefore, he killed one or two Mexican women on this hellish afternoon, when passions reached fever-pitch and swirled out of control.[98] Emily evidently had not encountered Captain Forbes in the confusion. She might well have saved herself by remaining under whatever convenient cover she could find amid the heightened savagery that shocked even the victors.

During the confused chaos of the fighting at the Alamo, one African American woman was killed when she made the mistake of racing out of her sleeping quarters into a hail of bullets amid the half-light of early morning. Travis' young slave Joe told the story to a newspaper correspondent who then published the native Alabamian's account in his newspaper: "Only one of the Negroes—a woman—who was found lying dead between two guns, Joe supposes she ran out in her fright, and was killed by a chance shot."[99] Other African Americans at the Alamo were more fortunate than this young black woman, who panicked on the cool morning of March 6, 1836, and was fatally cut down in consequence. Interestingly, a Texan wrote in a letter that was published in the *Commercial Bulletin*, New Orleans, Louisiana, on April 11, 1836, how Joe, "a negro boy, the servant of Col. Travis, whose life was spared—probably in consideration of his kindred blood" to mixed-race Mexicans.[100]

Emily very likely saved herself from harm during the attack by simply keeping her head, not panicking, and remaining stationary out of harm's way. If Emily had been indeed "closeted" as claimed by a single source and remained in a secure location in or around Santa

Anna's headquarters and even his tent, then this prudent decision to remain stationary might have saved her life during the battle. Houston, who had three horses shot from under him and was wounded in the foot, early lost control of his men. Emily D. West most likely was discovered after the fighting ended in the Mexican encampment by Captain Isaac N. Moreland, who commanded one of the "Twin Sisters" that had advanced during the attack in the line's center as flying artillery. Along with other Texian officers, Moreland returned to the Mexican encampment with a wagon to gather Santa Anna's personal effects from his large headquarters tent.[101]

During this afternoon in hell, Emily almost certainly saved herself by remaining calm and stationary, not following her initial instincts to take flight during the height of battle. Fleeing rearward might well have been fatal, with Texians killing almost anything that moved. Indeed, the worst slaughter of the Texas Revolution—far exceeding anything witnessed during the Alamo's blood-letting—occurred behind the Mexican encampment at Peggy's Lake, the natural obstacle that blocked the soldados' route of flight through the brushy woodlands south of Santa Anna's camp. One Texian soldier described how the Mexicans were "driven into the water, and the rifles ceased not their crack while an object [or Mexican heads] appeared above its surface."[102]

Here, along with a lengthy, concentrated line of his fellow soldiers, Private William Foster, who had taken a good firing position along the muddy north bank of the dark waters of Peggy's Lake, described: "I sat there and shot them until my ammunition gave out. Then I turned the butt end of my musket and started knocking them in the head."[103]

At this point, the surreal slaughter was so murderously thorough that hundreds of soldados would not live to tell the tale of one of Mexico's darkest hours. Barely a dozen of Santa Anna's men escaped the massacre to rejoin the bulk of the Mexican Army that eventually retired below the Rio Grande. One of these fortunate souls who escaped the fierce Texian rage this afternoon was a young drummer boy, evidently fleet of foot or just plain lucky. Fair game as if he was a mature, veteran fighting man, twelve-year-old Luis Espinosa was a member of the slaughtered Guerrero Battalion, which had held the far right flank of Santa Anna's line. These men suddenly found themselves even more trapped between the San Jacinto River on the right and Peggy's Lake to their rear than any other unit. But Our Lady of Guadalupe smiled upon young Luis on the plain of San Jacinto. He was the only member of his ill-fated battalion to escape the massacre.[104]

For ample good reason, the few Mexican survivors who later rejoined the main army "all agreed concerning the diabolism of the Texan soldiers," wrote one eye-witness with considerable understatement. "Each one regarded his escape as a miracle." One of the fortunate non-combatants who safely reached the main body of Mexican forces was a Mexican woman who had been wounded in the thigh when the Texians' wrath reached a fever-pitch, but who somehow struggled onward to rejoin her countrymen and tell of San Jacinto's horrors.[105]

Whenever Emily finally emerged from where she was undoubtedly hidden at the height of Houston's attack, what she now saw around her was a scene from hell itself. The gory plain of San Jacinto was a nightmarish killing field, especially along Peggy's Lake. As one shocked Texas soldier, who was sickened by the slaughter, wrote: "The sight was horrible. Here lying in clusters—there scattered singly—the ground was strewed with dead men, dead horses, guns, bayonets, swords, drums, trumpets—some shattered and broken—books, papers, sandals, and caps—the chaos of a routed army, was strewed upon the ground—in a confusion which the imagination cannot conceive—and which the natural eye must behold, to be convinced of the reality."[106]

William Zuber described the surreal horror that greeted Emily's eyes, as she viewed the sickening carnage that she could never have imagined before, not even in her worst nightmare: "The slain Mexicans were a ghastly sight. As their [number of dead] equaled that of our army, our men could not bury them."[107] Of the hundreds of Mexican dead and almost out of a sense of guilt for his murder, only brave General Castrillón, the heroic man of compassion and gentlemanly dignity, was at least granted a decent burial on the nearby ranch, on Buffalo Bayou and just northwest of the San Jacinto killing ground, of the Yucatan-born Lorenzo de Zavala, the Texas government's interim vice president and Santa Anna's former friend.[108] Thanks to the blazing Texas sun and the summer-like heat of the Gulf Coastal Plain, one of Houston's men described how in a short time, "The faces of most of the [Mexican] dead were as black as negroes."[109]

More than 600 Mexican dead lay sprawled across the blood-splattered field of San Jacinto, ensuring a good many widows and orphans across Mexico. An unknown Mexican officer had written a most prophetic entry into his diary during the spring of 1836 that now applied to the hundreds of Santa Anna's unfortunate soldados: "Better to die than to give up the most beautiful territory" known as Texas.[110] After looking over the killing ground, Morgan wrote in a letter, "The enemy were routed & drove into the lake—& butchered for 10 miles in almost every direction. Not less than 600 could have been kild as many or more prisoners."[111]

Hardly able to believe either the extent of his success or the sheer brutality of his men once unleashed with bayonets and Bowie knives, Houston reported that 630 Mexicans were killed. This figure was more than three times the number of defenders—Texians, United States volunteers, and Tejanos—killed at the Alamo, while fewer than 30 of Houston's men were either killed or wounded on fateful April 21. Representing a remarkable disparity that was only explained by way of a massacre, the disproportionate number of fatalities indicated the ugly truth of what had really happened at San Jacinto on that terrible afternoon.[112]

Because of the destruction of Vince's Bridge, behind the Mexican encampment and across Buffalo Bayou, by Deaf Smith and his scouts, including the free black Hendrick Arnold, and as ordered by Houston to ensure that Santa Anna received no additional reinforcements after Cos' arrival, few Mexicans escaped the slaughter to rejoin General Filísola's main body. Even Santa Anna's attempted escape and panicked flight on horseback was thwarted. He was captured on April 22, wearing old slave clothing taken from an abandoned slave cabin on the Vince Plantation on the night of April 21 as a disguise, placed over his fine linen shirt.

Santa Anna was shortly recognized by Major Lorenzo Zavala, Jr., the interim vice president's son whose family Emily D. West knew so well from the long journey to Texas. As fate would have it, a dejected Santa Anna was turned over to the custody of John Forbes, the officer who had brutally sabered the Mexican woman, who found herself in the wrong place at the wrong time at San Jacinto.

Despite many angry Texians calling for an immediate lynching of Mexico's president, Santa Anna was allowed to live thanks to Houston, who had been wounded in the left ankle by a bullet. Houston was demonstrating more wisdom than graciousness; Santa Anna traded his life for a guarantee of Texas independence from Mexico.

After agreeing to Houston's demands, Santa Anna was allowed to return to his magnificent silk campaign tent, where supposedly his intoxicating tryst with Emily had taken place, after it was set-up on April 23 near Houston's own headquarters tent. Santa Anna, at his personal request to Houston, was allowed to smoke opium to blot out the magnitude of the San Jacinto disaster, the slaughter of his men, and the greatest humiliation of his life.[113] Colonel Almonte survived unscathed by the "somewhat beserk Texans," and his fate continued to be intertwined with that of Emily D. West at San Jacinto, since he led his cavalrymen into New Washington. He saved a good many Mexican lives and brought an end to the slaughter by leading the survivors of the Guerrero Battalion, consisting of around 250 men, to Houston for a formal surrender.[114]

Not long thereafter and like Houston, Morgan demonstrated compassion at a most turbulent time, when so many other unruly Texians called for vengeance. After the Mexican prisoners were removed from the body-strewn field, Morgan, now a colonel in the Texas Army, safeguarded Santa Anna and his captured Mexicans on Galveston Island. As he wrote in a letter that displayed his rather remarkable self-control and sense of humanitarianism on the field of San Jacinto toward the Mexican leader, whom he should have yet wanted to destroy like so many others, Morgan never forgot how "Almonte [was the one] who brought Genl. Santa Ana to N[ew] W[ashington] to burn me out .... Yet but for me he would have been assassinated after the Battle of San Jacinto! I saved his life, which he is not aware of to this day!" All in all, this incident revealed an amazing display of decency toward a Mexican leader, whom Morgan believed had destroyed his New Washington dream and made his wife and children homeless and terrified refugees during the "Runaway Scrape."[115]

As could be expected, people across the United States gloated over Santa Anna's capture and decisive defeat at San Jacinto, praising Anglo-Celtic superiority and God's favor. A waggish article in the *Boston Times*, as quoted in *The Herald* of New York City, celebrated Houston for "capturing Santa Anna up a tree. Even the great Crockett could hardly have done better."[116]

While hundreds of bodies of dead Mexican officers and soldiers, yet wearing religious medals and crucifixes given them by loving family members before they marched north into Texas, lay unburied and left rotting on the field of San Jacinto to be torn apart by hogs, wolves, and dogs in the weeks ahead, Houston became one of America's greatest and most celebrated heroes. As printed in the pages of *The Herald*: "Sam Houston will henceforth take his rank, side by side, with the great men of the earth, either in ancient or modern times."[117]

San Jacinto was no ordinary clash of arms, because it was one of the most decisive battles in American history. However, the battle of San Jacinto fit neatly into an established pattern in other ways. It was only a continuation of a historic pattern of genocide, which became part of the overall process of conquest and westward expansion. In this bloody formula that had existed since the colonial period, indigenous people had to be removed by force by Americans (or Texians in this case) from a land that was coveted by these newest conquistadors in the name of Manifest Destiny.

Such was the case during the atrocious slaughters of the Creek War, when the Red Stick Creeks were massacred at places like the Indian village of Tallushatchee in today's Alabama. Here, in early November 1813 and to avenge the Fort Mims massacre, Jackson's vengeful troops showed no mercy and "shot them like dogs," wrote David Crockett of the slaughter that was faithfully replayed with a bloody thoroughness at San Jacinto.

And finally during the decisive showdown at Horseshoe Bend in mid–Alabama during March 1814, Red Stick resistance was broken forever, ending in a slaughter of hundreds of more Indians, who were trapped by a deep body of water like Santa Anna's ill-fated soldados when their escape was effectively blocked at Peggy's Lake. Of course, Santa Anna has been widely denounced for generations of Americans because of his no quarter policy, sanctioned by the Mexican Congress, at the Alamo and Goliad, while American soldiers, including regulars during the Creek War, employed an equally brutal no quarter policy at Tallushatchee, Horseshoe Bend, and San Jacinto, which has been largely overlooked and almost never emphasized.

In a symbolic continuum, some of Houston's Creek War veterans played key combat roles at San Jacinto. As a young United States lieutenant of a regular regiment, Houston had fallen wounded in the bold frontal attack at Horseshoe Bend on the Indian breastwork—more of a European-like defensive structure than a traditional feature of Native American warfare in America—and won Jackson's lasting admiration and respect. As seen in Jackson's slaughters of the Creeks at Tallushatchee and Horseshoe Bend, two distinct cultures had collided at San Jacinto in a winner-take-all struggle to determine which one would dominate the land of Texas with the same predictable horrific results: a massacre of hundreds of young men and boys, who died for what they believed right in defending their own homeland and internally-torn republic against an expansionist tide of Americans intoxicated by the heady promise of Manifest Destiny's blessings and the great dream of making Texas their own. In many ways, therefore, what happened at San Jacinto was an inevitable clash of arms because it actually represented the southwest extension of one of the greatest migrations in history: the relentless march of the Anglo-Celtic people in conquering and populating an entire continent all the way to the Pacific. Texas had just happened to lie in the path of the relentless march of a popular movement of the American people that first began during the colonial period.[118]

In spectacular fashion, Texas was won on April 21, 1836, in what historian Frederick Merk described as "one of the strangest of the world's important battles."[119] But this gifted historian would have been convinced that the battle of San Jacinto was even stranger had he been aware of the fact that the "Yellow Rose of Texas" myth proclaimed that one of the world's most decisive battles was determined by an alleged sexual liaison between Santa Anna and a slave woman named Emily.[120]

In an April 26 letter, Houston spread the almost unbelievable good news of the miracle of San Jacinto to the people of Texas, along with some sound advice now that the vast agricultural paradise known as Texas had been won from Mexico: "Tell our friends of the news, and that we have beaten the enemy. Generals Santa Anna and Cos were taken, and one General [Castrillón] slain.... Tell them to come on, and let the people plant corn."[121]

Houston had no need to implore such united action from the people of Texas, because the year's new crops, especially cotton and not corn, had already been planted by thousands of farmers and planters across Texas, while the men, almost all United States volunteers, had died at the Alamo and Goliad for the want of timely assistance of the Texas colonists, who remained on their farms and safely out of harm's way.[122]

Chapter VIII

Popular Myth-making and the Creation of "The Yellow Rose of Texas"

Both the American Revolution and the Texas Revolution, separated by barely a half century, shared a seemingly endless number of analogies, primarily because both struggles against the centralized authority of their respective mother countries stemmed from oppressions and abuses more hypothetical than real, despite propaganda that proclaimed otherwise. And neither people's revolution could have been won without sizeable intervention from outside sources: the American colonists won their struggle for liberty thanks in no small part to the timely 1778 French Treaty of Alliance and the Texians in 1836 by way of the massive support from the United States, including the flood of volunteers, who were even more pro-Texas independence than many Texian colonists.[1]

And in both cases, a romanticized creation myth was necessary to forge a national identity. Romantic national sagas were necessary and created to explain the moral basis and righteousness of the birth of these two mostly Protestant republics. And in both cases, what was created was the mythology of righteous God-fearing revolutionaries who were battling purely for an abstract principle (liberty) against decadent evil oppressors in a morality play. So the British became oppressors and villains in the romanticized story of America's first revolution, and then the Mexicans, and especially Santa Anna, likewise came to symbolize evil, to explain the success of the 1835–1836 revolution, which one modern Texas historian has called the "Texian Iliad."

In his classic work *Founding Myths: Stories That Hide Our Patriotic Past*, Ray Raphael emphasized how only a few chosen women—representative of the overall contributions of women in the story of America's birth—have been included in the revolutionary experience's romanticization. He explained that Americans and historians needed a representative female heroine in the telling of the dramatic story of a new nation's creation, rising like a phoenix from the fires of violent revolution.

In regard to the American Revolution, however, Raphael emphasized how historical facts and primary documentation have gotten in the way of the romance, fiction, and myth: "How nice it would be to discover a true heroine of the American Revolution. We have tried Betsy Ross, the woman who supposedly made the first American flag, but that story is now discredited. We would like to celebrate Deborah Sampson, who dressed as a man to enlist in the army, but if truth be told, some female soldiers were unjustly drummed out to the 'whore's march' once their identity was discovered. Our preferred heroine, if we could find her, would have braved enemy fire in a famous battle—dressed as a woman, not a man."[2]

Raphael questioned the validity of America's most popular revolutionary female image, but recognized that the role of women "has a legitimate place in the story of our nation's birth [but] Molly Pitcher does not. This conjured heroine is no more than a male fantasy: a woman who serves men but can also fight tough. She does not adequately represent the female presence in the Revolutionary War. The problem is, nobody can. Women's contributions, however real and important, cannot readily be revealed through heroic, martial stories, for they were marked by drudgery, not high drama. We prefer to imagine otherwise."[3]

Much more than the United States, revolutionary France celebrated the role of women, which was far more widespread than in America's struggle for liberty, because the radical revolutionary ideology, including women's equality and full rights as citizens, contrasted sharply with the conservative ideology (that excluded women from obtaining full rights) of the American Revolution. The French Revolution promised full inclusion of women—along with mulattoes and blacks—into the mainstream of French society in regard to equal and universal rights of a new revolutionary egalitarian social order. Women served as revered allegorical figures, such as the goddess liberty, that represented equality and freedom for all people, regardless of gender or race. The French Revolutionary Republic was represented by and bestowed with the female name of Marianne, who was the inspirational patroness of the revolution.[4]

But in fact, Marianne was an icon and not a real person.[5] Not unlike the French Revolution's mythical Marianne, no myth involving a woman has been greater than that of "The Yellow Rose of Texas" in yet another revolution in the New World. Thanks to the eager embrace and uncritical acceptance of "The Yellow Rose of Texas" myth, and later the brief Bollaert reference as factual, and not just a colorful, popular story of the day, the myth-creating process was clearly evident when Michener wrote about Emily and San Jacinto with such vivid prose and an over-active imagination that seamlessly wove fact and fiction together: "Immortality was visited upon the least likely participant in the battle. Emily Morgan, who had diverted General Santa Anna's attention with kama sutra–like antics in his headquarters tent that hot afternoon just before the charge of the Texans, became celebrated in song as 'The Yellow Rose of Texas' and few who sang it in romantic settings realize that they were serenading the memory of a mulatto slave."[6]

But in fact no evidence has been found on either side of the United States–Mexico border to connect "Emily" of San Jacinto fame with "The Yellow Rose of Texas" in any way, shape, or form. Historian James Crisp concluded, "Despite the utter lack of evidence that this song had anything to do with the woman who was soon being called 'The Maid of Morgan's Point,' a lot of people added up two and two and got five: the mulatto maid *must* have been a slave (and therefore taken the name of her master), and she *must* have been 'The Yellow Rose of Texas.'"[7] Crisp, a traditional Texas historian, concluded, "There might be more to this story than myth."[8]

Much like the American Revolution's celebrated Molly Pitcher, who was a creation of male fantasy and national myth-making, the story of "Emily" at San Jacinto was in fact just another Texas creation story myth whose alleged seductive and sexual role with Santa Anna at San Jacinto was based upon fiction and fantasy. Like the young United States, so the new Texas republic needed a female heroine in its creation myth, and Emily has fulfilled this cultural and societal requirement. Consequently, Emily Morgan as "The Yellow Rose of Texas" was little more than a folk heroine spawned from the fertile imaginations of myth-creators, especially popular writers, historians, and journalists, who were almost exclusively male.

The old adage has certainly applied that this most colorful of stories was simply just too good to be true. After all, few stories could have been created that were either more titillating, sexually-charged, or dramatic than that of a lone and allegedly patriotic woman of African descent altering the course of American history and the destiny of Texas in a decisive moment with her sexual skills, beauty, and seductiveness to render a much feared opponent—no less than the "Napoleon of the West"—incapable of resisting an attacking force, when the fate of two neighboring republics were at stake.

Historians and writers have evidently assumed that perhaps the best explanation of how Houston, if he was indeed the authentic author of the Emily reference, learned of the alleged Emily and Santa Anna liaison was from Emily herself by way of her employer, Colonel James Morgan, who presented the story to Houston. Based upon the alleged Houston letter in Bollaert's possession, they have assumed that because Emily was his "slave," then she would have openly described her San Jacinto experiences, including the alleged liaison, to Morgan. But, of course, Emily D. West was not a slave.

This scenario even appeared probable for a number of reasons, or so it seemed at first glance. After leaving his assignment at Galveston Island, where he impressed slaves, men and women, to erect fortifications and helped to transport fleeing citizens off the Texas mainland to the primary refugee camp on Galveston Island, Colonel Morgan, along with interim vice president Zavala, planned to proceed aboard the steamboat *Cayuga* up the wide, brown waters of Buffalo Bayou to reach Harrisburg. At this time, Morgan was yet unaware that the battle of San Jacinto had been fought. Morgan was now concerned about the fate of New Washington, including his hotel. On the way to Harrisburg and before moving up the San Jacinto River to gain Buffalo Bayou, the *Cayuga* stopped at what little remained of New Washington, which now lay in smoldering ruins.

With sadness, Colonel Morgan inspected the charred ruins of his once-fine plantation, the hotel where Emily had worked, and all that he had created and built up with so much effort and high hopes as the manager and Texas agent of the New Washington Association. Here, his servants—including evidently Emily D. West, who had returned to her place of employment by this time since she was bound to the one-year contract and had nowhere else to go—informed Morgan of Houston's dramatic victory.

Without her "free papers" that had been lost of the field of San Jacinto, Emily needed to show a connection to her place of employment to avoid enslavement.

Hereafter, Emily was in a most disadvantageous position of having to prove that she was a free woman without her free papers. This sad journey back to a destroyed New Washington provided Morgan and others of his party with the first news that he had heard of the battle. After the battle of San Jacinto and in order to leave a gory field covered with more than 500 dead who went unburied, Emily had only to travel around a dozen miles south from San Jacinto back to New Washington, where she had first encountered Colonel Almonte's cavalrymen on April 16.

Emily had to immediately depart the presence of Houston's Army, which was filled with a good many slave-owners or aspiring slave-owners and cotton planters, and as soon as possible. Now her own fellow Americans and not the Mexicans or Santa Anna posed the greatest threat to Emily, especially after the decisive victory was won at San Jacinto. Emily was just another dark-skinned woman among a larger number of dark-skinned women—the lower class, or peasants of Indian descent, soldaderas, who were the faithful wives, lovers, and family members of their fighting men, and who continued the ancient role of the Aztec women, known as the auianime, who had long accompanied unmarried warriors to war—on the field of San Jacinto.

Unlike the Mexicans, the Texian victors possessed the ability to enslave her with impunity because Emily no longer possessed her "free" papers, especially when away from Morgan, who could have verified her free status. The longtime beacon of freedom for escaped Texas slaves, Matamoros, on the south bank of the Rio Grande and nestled in Mexico's northeast corner not far from the gulf, was too far at some 350 miles south for Emily to make the dangerous attempt over no man's land.

Of course, what has never been explained was that if the story of "The Yellow Rose of Texas" was true according to the Bollaert reference and the enduring myth, then how might the story have been relayed, if at all? If the alleged Houston letter was indeed authentic, then Emily might have told Houston personally at San Jacinto of her alleged sexual connection to Santa Anna. But this was a most unlikely and improbable scenario. Might Houston have learned of Emily's role only two days the fighting on April 23, when Colonel Morgan, if Emily had informed him of the alleged incident, conferred with the wounded commander-in-chief, whose mobility was limited because of his ankle wound? In Morgan's own words from a letter: "I visited the field of battle a day or two after the fight which Commenced 8 miles above N[ew] W[ashington]."[9]

Another possibility existed. After the battle, the victors were presented ample opportunity to learn about what had really happened not only at San Jacinto but also at the Alamo. Through an interpreter, Sergeant George M. Dolson, Colonel Morgan interrogated captured Mexican officers now imprisoned on Galveston Island under Morgan's supervision. From San Jacinto, Morgan had escorted hundreds of Mexican prisoners to the coast and confinement. He served as the commander of Galveston Island, Texas, from March 20, 1836, to April 1, 1837, which included guarding the San Jacinto prisoners.

Because Morgan was unable to speak fluent Spanish, Dolson "employed a considerable part of my time interpreting Spanish for Colonel James Morgan, commander of this station," wrote Dolson in a July 19, 1836, letter from Camp Travis on Galveston Island. Under these circumstances, perhaps the Emily Morgan mythical story—as opposed to the real Emily D. West story—was either first learned or supported by prisoners' own statements about Santa Anna and Emily. Hoping to win favor, Mexican prisoners spoke openly and freely about details of the slaughter at the Alamo, including Crockett's death.[10]

But these possible scenarios are all speculation. What is most significant has been the fact that no primary documentation or record exists, or has been found, of the alleged Santa Anna and Emily tryst and "The Yellow Rose of Texas" story in any contemporary sources, before the alleged Houston letter that was not written in the decade of the 1830s. The alleged Houston letter was written around 1842, or more than half a decade after the battle of San Jacinto. It is highly suspect under these circumstances, as Bollaert showed by its non-inclusion into his work. Clearly, had Emily indeed played such a key role in Houston's victory at San Jacinto as alleged, then this contribution certainly would have been documented by the Texians who fought at San Jacinto immediately after the battle and long before the following decade.[11]

As emphasized by historians and writers, one source of evidence that has long served to bolster the mythical Emily as the "Yellow Rose of Texas" has been the general assumption—without any serious investigation—that Mexican historians themselves were well aware of Santa Anna's beautiful "quadroon mistress" during the Texas Campaign. While the propaganda of the sexual abuse of Anglo women by Santa Anna's men to generate sympathy and support from the United States, no solid evidence or primary documentation has been found to support this widely-accepted, popular view that American historians and writers have so often embellished to give credence to "The Yellow Rose of Texas" story, or myth in this case.

Quite simply, these writers have merely employed their own personal and cultural bias, faulty belief systems, and imaginative thinking to create a shaky foundation for the validity of the alleged Emily-Santa Anna liaison. They have then supported their speculative sensationalism by adding the unsubstantiated assumption that Mexican historians have corroborated the story of "Yellow Rose of Texas." Supposedly, Mexican historians have long known about the seductress Emily who contributed to Santa Anna's dramatic fall from grace at San Jacinto.[12]

However, such was not the case. The best known Mexican accounts, including the de la Pena memoir, have contained no mention or even hint of a beautiful, or ugly for that matter, slave woman in Santa Anna's tent at the most critical moment. Indeed, "no Mexican reports of Emily exist. Colonel José Enrique de la Peña, Ramon Martinez Caro, and others who criticized the Mexican leader would surely have added an afternoon tryst to the list of his shortcomings if one had taken place."[13]

If the Texans had in fact learned of Emily D. West and Santa Anna sexual connection immediately after the battle on April 21, then the Mexicans surely would have heard and written about the same story as well. Santa Anna's own officers possessed powerful motivations to have written about the alleged tryst for a host of political and personal reasons, especially in regard to the post-war blame game. But no Mexican records, memoirs, or documentation exist of Emily or the alleged carnal liaison between a slave woman and their commander-in-chief. In striking contrast, Santa Anna's phony marriage to the Tejano teen at San Antonio was widely known by both officers and enlisted men and well-publicized by his enemies, who used the incident to attack the generalísimo's character and integrity.[14]

Therefore, the most definitive biography of Santa Anna, *Santa Anna of Mexico*, published in 2007 by Will Fowler, addresses the issue of "The Yellow Rose of Texas" in the San Jacinto chapter only briefly in an endnote. Knowing that he was dealing with a myth, Fowler merely wrote how Santa Anna (and any Mexican officers and latter-day historians) failed to "mention any encounter with the beautiful and captivating mulatta Emily West Morgan, the mythical 'Yellow Rose of Texas,' who according to Texas lore seduced Santa Anna near New Washington and cunningly led him into the trap of San Jacinto."[15]

Quite simply, the "Yellow Rose of Texas" was exclusively a myth created, embellished, and supported solely north of the Rio Grande River by Texans and Americans, and mostly from males, for mostly popular consumption, humorous amusement, and bawdy entertainment.[16]

Today's most knowledgeable and respected historian in the United States of primary Mexican documents about the Texas Revolution, Roger Borroel, of East Chicago, Indiana, who has spent a lengthy, distinguished career in discovering and translating a large number of Mexican documents, responded when asked if any Mexican sources ever mentioned the liaison, "The answer to your question is no; there are NO Mexican writers who mention such a thing. It is entirely an American myth."[17]

Not only was the alleged Santa Anna–Emily tryst at San Jacinto a norteamericano myth but also the general assumption that the famed "Yellow Rose of Texas" was a dazzling, Latin-looking beauty with long dark hair. The portrayal of Emily as a voluptuous, light-skinned, mulatto beauty has endured to this day. This stereotypical physical appearance of Emily was a product of the fertile imaginations of white males, adhering to their standards of beauty.

The fabrication of Emily's Latina-like appearance was not unlike the popular tale that Santa Anna raced from his headquarters tent without his pants: a ridiculous and comical situation explained by popular American writers as resulting from the irresistible appeal of Emily's many alleged charms that, of course, had no end. The bawdy humor found in the much-related story that Santa Anna was caught by surprise when only in "his silken drawers" has been used as indisputable evidence by historians and writers that he was not only a boob but also engaged in sexual activity with Emily instead of having been asleep in his tent and in a partial state of dress. No evidence exists that either was true.[18]

How important was the battle of San Jacinto in the course of American and world history? This is a most valid question, because the battle's importance in part explains why the myth of "The Yellow Rose of Texas" was created. Placing the April 21 clash of arms in the proper historical perspective, one popular Houston biographer wrote: "San Jacinto was not only a remarkable feat of arms in which a small army from a province of some thirty-five thousand people had defeated a superior force from a nation of eight million. The battle altered politics and geography of America in the most profound ways. The role of the United States as a great power in the western hemisphere was solidified, and all or part of six states was carved out of the vast amount of territory that was soon gained from Mexico, nearly a million square miles."[19]

The stirring words inscribed at the base of the battle monument at the San Jacinto battlefield perhaps said it best: "Measured by its results, San Jacinto was one of the decisive battles of the world. The freedom of Texas from Mexico won here led to annexation and to the Mexican War, resulting in the acquisition by the United States of the states of Texas, New Mexico, Arizona, Nevada, California, Utah, and parts of Colorado, Wyoming, Kansas, and Oklahoma. Almost one-third of the present area of the American nation, nearly a million square miles, changed sovereignty."[20]

Placing the blame of Santa Anna's decisive loss of the battle of San Jacinto and Texas primarily on the alleged sexuality of a lowly woman of color has not only overlooked all the facts that made Mexican defeat all but inevitable, but also has stretched the limits of gullibility, credibility, and probability, because it relies on a single source, the Bollaert reference, which cannot be supported by any other primary sources in Texas, the United States, or Mexico. If Santa Anna was in fact with an alluring women in his headquarters tent at San Jacinto, then it was more likely with a Mexican mistress and not Emily, who probably never set foot in Santa Anna's headquarters tent and most likely remained in the encampment's rear with other African American laundresses, both slave and free, because most of the army's self-sacrificing soldaderas were left behind during the rapid pursuit of the refugee Texas government in flight.[21]

And if Emily was so ravishingly beautiful and seductive in accordance to "The Yellow Rose of Texas" myth, then she certainly would have been noticed by Houston's men at San Jacinto. Emily's alleged beauty would have fueled more motivation for one of Houston's men to gain a fortune by selling Emily, who would go to the highest bidder, into slavery. Emily's alleged beauty would have garnered a vast sum of money in the New Orleans market.

Forced entry into slavery was the unfortunate fate of other free blacks who had been indentured to work in Texas at the same time that Emily herself migrated to Texas as an indentured servant. In a letter and without displaying a hint of sympathy to his friend Samuel Swartwout, Morgan wrote of the tragedy of free black citizens of Great Britain (the British West Indies) who had found themselves (like Emily) in the wrong place and the wrong time in a newly-established slave-owning republic: "An English agent [arrived] to look up some West India Negroes from Barbados that were brought here [to Texas] in 1835 & left—supposed to have been sold [into slavery] in Texas. They were just Inden[tured] apprentices

[for] 7 years—Were sold no longer than for the time they were bound to serve—Yet possibly some of them many find a longer servitude as a part of them are in Louisiana and 'tis said!" Emily D. West had narrowly missed the most cruel of all fates, after Houston's men won their amazing success at San Jacinto.[22]

In the years after the Battle of San Jacinto, slaves represented an even more sizeable investment, source of economic security, and a ready source of capital investment. Therefore, when economic times become especially tough in the infant Texas Republic that had been devastated by the war, Morgan, like other Texans, resorted to a source of ready cash, when he sold one Negro to meet $600, half of a note due for payment.[23]

Even Sam Houston's own mother, the iron-willed Elizabeth, when Sam was yet a youth, had been forced to sell the family's slaves in an estate sale to liquidate assents and pay off debts, after her husband, Samuel, died in 1806. To raise cash, this remarkable, self-sufficient and independent woman (in some ways more formidable than old Sam in his prime) sold the family's thirteen-year-old male slave, two adult female slaves, and two small children.[24]

Given the situation and the loss of her "free papers," consequently, the distinct possibility existed that Emily had initially found safety on the field of San Jacinto with non–Texians from the United States, especially those from the North. These men, yet wearing United States regular uniforms, were officially listed as "deserters" on the books, but in fact they were zealous volunteers for the cause of Texas from General Edmund P. Gaines' army. These well-armed volunteers in blue United States uniforms included a good many northern-born men and perhaps even a number of abolitionists, who would have looked out for the welfare of a lone free black woman on her own and in a most compromised situation without her "free papers."

Not long before the showdown at San Jacinto, around 300 of Gaines' United States regulars had been covertly transferred to Houston's army, bolstering its ranks in timely fashion with well-trained and experienced fighting men. A United States regular from Emily's own native New England, perhaps even Connecticut or her hometown of New Haven, might have saved her from a cruel enslavement amid the chaos of the battle of San Jacinto and its immediate aftermath.[25]

This danger of suddenly losing her freedom forever was very real for Emily as the result of Houston's victory at San Jacinto, which was also a victory for slavery. Only a few years before, "an old Frenchmen" near the Texas border was murdered in cold blood by a lawless band for the express purpose of gaining possession of his mulatto wife and the couple's "several quadroon children." The unfortunate wife and offspring of the Frenchmen were then carried into Texas. Here, once on Texas soil, the surviving four family members, who spoke little English, were then sold on the auction block to the highest bidder to reap a fortune for the murderers and kidnappers.[26]

Forgotten Explanation

Because of the single Bollaert reference, the entire "Yellow Rose of Texas" story has been based upon the simple assumption and premise that the "Emily" of the myth was one of Morgan's slaves, when in fact the real Emily D. West was a free woman from the northeast. When Emily's possible role is viewed within the context of its proper historical setting—as a free woman—the story can be interpreted and understood from a point of view that comes much closer to the truth of what really happened and exactly why.

The possibility exists that the tryst story came from Emily herself in an effort to save herself. What has been most forgotten about the Emily D. West story was the fact that the rout of Santa Anna's forces at San Jacinto was the worst case scenario for her, because she was a woman of color who had lost her free papers on the battlefield. An undisciplined and ever-individualistic frontier army that now represented a newly-established slave-owning republic had just defeated a Mexican force which had freed African Americans across Texas. In stark contrast to Santa Anna and the soldados from Mexico who liberated slaves, the victors had fought in part not only to preserve slavery but also to ensure its permanent entrenchment as a cornerstone of the new Texas republic.

Emily suddenly found herself in the midst of a throng of unruly Texas soldiers, both officers and enlisted men, who either already owned slaves, or aspired to own slaves one day in the future, as emphasized by historians as Frederick Merk.

Houston's soldiers had won a dramatic victory for slavery and its future expansion in Texas. The Texas Constitution of 1836 had already proclaimed that slave-owners could no longer emancipate their slaves, even if they were his own sons or daughters by slave women, without the official approval of the Texas Congress or unless they were taken out of the new slave republic. She was now on her own. Emily was not only far from home but also from supportive northern abolitionists like Jocelyn, or her employer Morgan on Galveston Island. They were absent from the field of San Jacinto and unable to back up her story that seemed highly unlikely. At this time, few, if any, whites believed the words of a black person. Consequently, Emily had never been more vulnerable nor closer to becoming a slave than during the chaos after the battle of San Jacinto.

If Emily spun the story herself, she would have not only averted a life of slavery but also was on her way to becoming a folk heroine and true Texas patriot in the future: an artful, clever means to evading slavery and one that revealed her intelligence and skill in escaping the worst of all fates. Therefore, the possibility exists that Emily might have told this most colorful of stories to Houston to save herself. Yet again, there is no supporting evidence, however.

Had it been the case, she would have first told this incredible story to Captain Moreland. He was the one who first saw her at San Jacinto, and perhaps even around Santa Anna's headquarters tent, when he and others had been assigned to loading up Santa Anna's personal baggage. With so many compelling reasons to do so, Emily then could have spun this most colorful and bawdy of stories, which was even flattering in emphasizing the president of Mexico's lust that had allegedly caused him to literally lose his military sense, to gain favor, because of her now questionable status after she had lost her free papers.

This fanciful story might have then spread to the men in the ranks, becoming a soldier's story that made the rounds of the Texian encampment after the battle of San Jacinto, and all the way to Houston himself. Indeed, a private soldier wrote the oddly worded account that indicated his misuse of the word "voluptuousness" rather than "sensualness," by writing how "much of our success was due to Santa Anna's voluptuousness" at San Jacinto.

But another factor lay at the heart of "The Yellow Rose of Texas" myth. Houston's soldiers did not have the cultural values or military tradition of women serving with the army on active campaigning, like the fighting men of Mexico in regard to the respected soldadera tradition. Consequently, they assumed that the women in Santa Anna's encampment were there for sexual purposes. To demonize the enemy by the time of Santa Anna's invasion and contrary to the facts and all existing evidence, the Texians and United States propagandists painted the Mexicans in terms of dark-skinned sexual predators and rapists, who even despoiled lily-white virgins of unquestionable purity, to rally support to the cause.

Of course, such intelligence and colorful soldier stories would have eventually reached the ears of General Houston, who loved bawdy stories in the frontier tradition. Houston then evidently passed the tale along to Bollaert, who was not gullible enough to include an unbelievable, improbable story in his narrative. As in any military establishment and especially an army in the field, such generally unflattering gossip about a leader, especially if of a sexual nature and if about an opponent, often circulated in the lowest ranks. But such gossip seldom made it into the writings—either letters or memoirs—because of the day's Victorian values and sensitivities.

The possible spread of gossip of a sexual nature among the Texians was not unlike the popular soldier gossip about George Armstrong Custer. Despite being a married man, Custer was thought to have had a long-running sexual relationship with a young Indian woman named Mo-nah-se-tah, fathering a male child. She was the pampered daughter of Chief Little Rock. The attractive young woman, with long black hair and a beautiful face, was captured at the village at the Washita, where her father was killed by the attack of Custer's Seventh Cavalry troopers on a bitterly-cold November 27, 1868. Camp gossip existed for years that Custer enjoyed a lasting, if not loving, relationship with this young Cheyenne woman, even though he was yet madly in love, like an infatuated schoolboy, with his wife, Elizabeth Bacon, or Libbie.

Even though Houston allegedly wrote the passage about Emily's tryst role at San Jacinto, he included one key word of extreme importance that has been generally ignored, "probably." Houston's use of the word "probably" most likely indicated that the liaison tale was merely an old soldier's story, which was little more than camp gossip. Or perhaps the liaison story was created among the legion of Houston haters, who desired to taint his leadership at San Jacinto by emphasizing that a black woman was more responsible for the victory than their commander. As Houston allegedly wrote and as revealed in the Bollaert reference: "The Battle of San Jacinto was probably lost to the Mexicans, owing to the influence of a Mulatta Girl (Emily)."[27]

But what seldom has been asked was why in the world would Houston, the leader of one of the biggest routs in American history, repeat a common soldier's story and camp gossip that largely negated his own generalship and skill? After all, the Emily myth has clearly trivialized and minimized Houston's brilliant tactics—a case of masterful timing—that proved decisive, placing more credit for victory on the ample curves and allure of an alleged beautiful black woman. Quite likely, Houston became amused with this most colorful, humorous, and sensational of stories like everyone else, and then simply passed it along to Bollaert for his own private enjoyment, knowing that the erudite Englishman would not take it seriously. Why else would Houston bestow recognition to an obscure slave woman named "Emily" rather than himself and his masterful tactics for winning the most important battle in the Texas history?

Most of all, "The Yellow Rose of Texas" was almost the most amusing and colorful story that possibly could be devised, involving spicy interracial, or forbidden, sex and a proverbial tale of how a powerful man—especially a detested opponent who was then transformed into a scorned object of even greater ridicule, if that was possible, by the telling of the tale—was brought down by the lures and guile of an attractive woman. The myth of "The Yellow Rose of Texas" was in essence a frontier cautionary tale like the Bible's Samson and Delilah story.

Houston could relate with the Emily story in many ways. As the powerful governor of Tennessee, he himself had been brought down by a woman. The young, pretty woman who destroyed Houston's political career and personal life was Eliza Allen, whom he married back in Nashville, Tennessee, in 1829. Houston was disgraced by a divorce not long after he was married.

Then the most admired governor became little more than a running bawdy joke, that focused on his lack of sexual prowess, across the West. This personal fiasco and scandal in the governor's mansion in Nashville eventually led to Houston's flight to Texas to escape the shame and embarrassment and to embark upon a new start in life. Most significant of all, the forgotten reason for the collapse of Houston's marriage was because of crossing racial boundaries—by her, not him. He discovered that his young wife had sex with a male slave.

Houston very likely found some deep-seated personal satisfaction, comfort, and solace in this sensational, colorful story of Santa Anna having foolishly fallen victim to a black female's wiles at San Jacinto. This only increased the likelihood of him perpetuating this most amusing of all tales, including to Bollaert in the early 1840s.[28]

Houston was disliked among the army's ranks in Texas. He was even blamed for deliberately allowing the Alamo garrison, which contained chief political rivals, to be extinguished for his own gain. This widely-believed rumor at the time had some substance in fact. Then, Houston was sharply condemned for withdrawing his amateur army almost all the way to the border of Louisiana, leaving defenseless families unprotected across Texas and allowing Santa Anna to sweep the land of Anglo-Celtic settlement and civilization like an avenging angel.

Therefore, in what could be called a mutiny of sorts, the army's junior officers and enlisted men had taken charge of the San Jacinto Campaign. They had literally forced Houston to march upon Santa Anna's vanguard at San Jacinto by making the key decision on their own. Therefore, Houston was so detested by his fellow Texians that many people were fully convinced that his wounding at San Jacinto resulted from fratricide. By placing the key to the San Jacinto victory upon the sexual guile and finesse of an attractive black woman, anti–Houston Texians found yet another way of minimizing Houston's success in winning the most decisive battle of the war.[29]

Another strong psychological factor also existed among the Anglo-Celts for the ready acceptance and spread of the Santa Anna–Emily liaison story. Across an America struggling with its internal racial demons that had allowed deep fissures to crack open in an increasingly fragile society during the mid–1830s, the fear of widespread amalgamation among whites, both North and South, was rampant. Americans, especially Southerners, were overly concerned that northern abolitionists, like Jocelyn, were determined to "mulattoize" America and overturn the so-called "natural" order of American society and the racial caste system. Almost a hysterical paranoia unseen in more racially enlightened nations like Mexico or Spain, this had become a national obsession in both North and South by the mid–1830s, including in Texas.

Exemplifying a central contradiction in a nation that was supposedly dedicated to universal liberty, white citizens of even northern cities, like Cincinnati, Ohio, blamed Southerners for the many mulattoes in their midst. But in fact most people of mixed race heritage had been born north of the Ohio River (in Ohio) and not in the South. Indeed, the heaviest racial mixing between black and white was a more dominant feature of the Upper South instead of the Deep South. This widespread racial mixing led to a sharp backlash among northern whites, who felt that the social order and their world was threatened.

The primary catalyst for the activation of the mob riots that raged through New York City's streets in 1834 and 1835, which had almost certainly convinced Emily to depart the city and migrate to Texas in late 1835, had been the fear that the northern abolitionists were promoting racial mixing between free blacks and whites to overthrow America's social order. This fear about racial mixing disguised the fact that miscegenation had been long occurring wherever and wherever black and white met in America and from the beginning, going back to the 1600s.

In many ways, the story of the alleged Santa Anna and Emily tryst symbolized the greatest fears among Anglo-Celts of Texas on two levels: the spread of racial intermixing that would threaten the very foundation of their fragile, slave-owning society, and then the threat of the uniting of blacks and Mexicans to wage holy war of vengeance upon the Texian people in 1835–1836.[30]

Clearly, a wide range of divergent factors coincided to create, fuel and promote the mythical Emily Morgan, fusing together a unique blend of stereotypes, misconceptions, and fantasies that led to the development of a composite tale of romanticized fabrication and myth, which has been supported only by Bollaert's single reference. Indeed, almost a cultural inheritance, the longtime, widespread perception among white males—then and today—of black women as nothing more than highly-sexualized and sensual beings only worthy of exploitation as sex objects because of their alleged inherent inferiority has long served as a central foundation of "The Yellow Rose of Texas" mythology. Therefore, according to popular perceptions based upon race, the mythical Emily fulfilled her expected traditional and stereotypical sexual role much like Santa Anna, also considered a racial inferior in the xenophobic Anglo mind, who fell from grace because of his cultural, biological and racial deficiencies.

As commonly portrayed in a morality play in which he fell victim to his libido as much as Houston's hard-charging Texians, Santa Anna was conquered by a superior Anglo-Celtic rationality, discipline, and intelligence, which prevailed in Darwinian-like fashion to bring decisive victory on the field of San Jacinto. For Texians who had fought in part because Mexican troops had been viewed as a sexual threat to their wives and daughters, nothing could possibly have greater appeal or more lasting amusement than the story of how Mexico's detested president had lost Texas, because of his fateful decision to go to bed with a black woman: a racial and morality transgression that demonstrated an alleged white superiority over both blacks and Mexicans as represented by the Emily–Santa Anna union.

According to "The Yellow Rose of Texas" myth, both Santa Anna, as a Mexican male, and Emily, as an African America female, displayed the stereotypical shortcomings of character, heritage, and race: the scenario most expected and believed by whites to support racial beliefs and to demonstrate superiority. Therefore, the real Emily was transformed by the myth—as much racial as historical—into just another lower class, immoral, and dark-skinned women, who fulfilled white expectations of the stereotype of the promiscuous black Jezebel-like role that was distinguished by an unthinking sensualness, sexuality, and immorality: the alleged proof of a lower form of animal-life behavior compared to superior, noble, and heroic Anglo-Celts. In "The Yellow Rose of Texas" myth, Santa Anna became as much of a fallen man as Emily became a fallen woman to the delight of whites, who saw their racial beliefs confirmed in dramatic fashion.

The battle of San Jacinto within the larger context of race was described by the editor of *The Herald* of New York City: "Victory, after a hard contest, settles on the side of intelligence, liberty, courage, resolution, and the noble Anglo-Saxon race."[31] Even the racial concepts of Manifest Destiny likewise led to the creation of the "Yellow Rose of Texas" myth and even bestowed added credibility to the single Bollaert reference and the dual demeaning of Santa Anna's character (Mexican) and Emily's character (black) to provide representative examples of alleged inferior beings who were doomed by God (part of the patriotic religion of Manifest Destiny), biology, and nature. Therefore, according to these concepts, Santa Anna was only the victim of the twin flaws of a lack of intelligent foresight and excessive sensuality at the wrong place and wrong time.

Such common beliefs have long provided largely race-based explanations to rationalize and prove Anglo-Celtic superiority by way of the dramatic victory at San Jacinto and disproportionately low losses among Houston's men on April 21, 1836, without mentioning the real explanation of massacre, while demonstrating the alleged inferiority of two people of color in a momentous situation of extreme importance: the dark legacy of San Jacinto.[32]

In this endless process of myth-making, Emily's identify as a proud, free black woman has been misrepresented. Like the stereotypical black Jezebel, Emily has been depicted as lacking in character and moral substance. She has been portrayed as a loose women "of dubious virtue" and with sexual wiles and skills befitting an experienced, hardened prostitute. Ironically, in many ways, the battle of San Jacinto itself has almost emerged as of secondary importance in the popular imagination thanks to the excessive focus on the sensationalism and sexual aspects of the story of "The Yellow Rose of Texas." The story has been twisted and distorted far beyond all existing evidence and sexualized to an extreme degree. What was created was a mythical story that has been focused on the actions of a black woman, which predictably has "degenerated into a lewd anecdote of sexual indiscretion" on Santa Anna's part, leading to his downfall on April 21, 1936.[33]

Emily's common portrayal as seductress and sex object, based on the single Bollaert reference, has struck a nerve with some African Americans, especially women. Black women are only too familiar with how popular American culture and historical writing have portrayed blacks, and certainly women, in a most negative light. In an article appearing just after the 159th anniversary of the battle of San Jacinto, writer Darrell Flint in the *San Antonio Express-News* deplored the stereotypical portrayal of Emily as nothing more than "a lady of pleasure." Flint saw that the negative stereotypes of Emily as sexual object and symbol of black immorality, if not debauchery, smacked of racism, because these long-existing stereotypical portrayals were in fact embellished primarily by the fertile imaginations of mostly white male historians, writers and journalists with relatively little knowledge of the black experience.[34]

But, to the present day, the most consistent, enduring, and greatest fuel—besides racial stereotypes—for the alleged tryst between Emily and Santa Anna has been a pervasive hatred for Santa Anna by seemingly one and all, including historians, in both Mexico and the United States. Santa Anna has been portrayed in the worst possible light without a single redeeming quality worthy of note. A 2002 Santa Anna biography by a distinguished academic in the United States has been titled *Santa Anna: A Curse Upon Mexico*. Mirroring the common views of Mexican historians, this respected American scholar concluded how Santa Anna on his own "prevented Mexico for all time from developing into a world power."[35]

In the more balanced biography, Will Fowler perhaps placed the overall image of Santa Anna in a proper historical perspective: "Santa Anna remains to this day the leader all Mexicans (and Texans) love to hate. He was demonized by Mexicans who wanted a scapegoat for losing the Mexican-American War and by Americans who needed a hate figure to justify their military involvement in Mexico."[36]

But a bemused Fowler, who realistically weighed the many obstacles in embarking upon the task of writing the most non-biased account of the generalísimo's life, made an even more revealing observation by explaining how Santa Anna's "vilification has been so thorough and effective that the process of deconstructing the numerous lies that have been told about him takes time. Only by going back to the primary sources does one begin to appreciate the extent to which Santa Anna's life has been misrepresented."[37]

In much the same way, so the story of the alleged tryst between Emily and Santa Anna that supposedly altered the course of battle of San Jacinto and American history in such dramatic fashion can be identified as nothing more than the most enduring of the Texas creation story myths and Texas tall tales. Because Santa Anna has been endlessly represented by way of a "recurrent depiction as a womanizer" of the worst stripe, this view has long created an uncritical acceptance of the mythical Santa Anna–Emily liaison because it so neatly fit the pervasive stereotype without close scrutiny.[38]

Three popular and enduring Anglo-centric myths have developed to explain Santa Anna's folly at San Jacinto and to rationalize the stunning magnitude of his crushing defeat on April 21. As can be expected, these explanations have focused on the most negative stereotypical aspects of black women and Santa Anna: 1) not placing pickets to guard his encampment or making adequate defensive preparations to protect his position, 2) Santa Anna was in an opium stupor at the time of Houston's attack, and 3) Santa Anna was having sex with Emily in his headquarters tent when Houston unexpectedly struck on the afternoon of April 21. Of these three most commonly accepted explanations for Santa Anna's defeat at San Jacinto, the myth of "The Yellow Rose of Texas" has evolved into the most famous. But the most reliable evidence and documentation has indicated that none of these three explanations for Santa Anna's defeat were true at San Jacinto.[39]

In truth, Santa Anna had made himself vulnerable partly because he was actually too conscientious as a general, just before Houston's attack. He had spent much of the warm, sun-drenched morning of April 21 in supervising the creation of makeshift defenses, setting out pickets in their proper positions, and in making personal reconnaissances in surveying Houston's position. All of these efforts were directed at safeguarding the Mexican encampment. All in all, Santa Anna had sufficiently "burned his energy," which caused his retirement to his tent in a state of exhaustion, especially after he had been up the entire previous night in performing his required duties as a commander. Most of all, Santa Anna was yet more of a career soldier than a politician.[40]

Widespread anti–Houston sentiment also played a role in bolstering the ready acceptance of the "Yellow Rose of Texas" myth to minimize the overall quality of Houston's already much-criticized generalship, despite the one-sided success that he won on April 21. In the annals of history, few generals who ever won such a complete or decisive battle to ensure a new nation's independence have been more thoroughly censured and criticized, especially by his own political and military leaders and even common soldiers in his army's ranks than Houston in regard to the San Jacinto Campaign. The words of President Burnet represented a common sentiment: "Sam Houston has been generally acclaimed the hero of San Jacinto. No fiction of the novelist is farther from the truth. Houston was the only man on the battlefield who deserved censure. The army regarded him as a military fop, and the citizens were disgusted at his miserable imbecility."[41]

But most of all, the overwhelming evidence of what really happened at San Jacinto has not been able to halt the steady evolution of a Texan legend. The widespread acceptance and popularity of the ever-growing legend of the "Yellow Rose of Texas," based upon the single Bollaert reference, has been due to its fascinating core elements that have created a cautionary tale of hubris, interracial sex, and a powerful fallen man that affected one of the most important battles ever fought on the North American continent.

Perhaps no single story could have been fabricated to more thoroughly demean the Mexican character or Santa Anna, not only as a man but also as a general. According to the myth, not only was Santa Anna outsmarted by Houston and the Anglo-Celts, but also by an African American woman.

As a cautionary tale, Emily's mythical role as a loose woman and temptress and Santa Anna's fall from grace by way of her sexual wiles and voluptuous body fit neatly into some of the central mythologies and creation stories of western civilization, including Biblical tales. Foremost among these Biblical analogies were the stories about a conniving, seductive Eve in the Garden of Eden, who brought about Adam's and man's moral fall from God's loving graces. The equally cautionary tale about Samson and Delilah was also analogous. In both cases, an artful, beautiful woman, or a temptress, was responsible for orchestrating the downfall of a highly-elevated man.

The story was also created by myth-makers because it provided a cautionary tale of the high price that had to be paid, if strict race relations and unwritten racial rules and boundaries were not maintained in a land where large numbers of blacks lived in the midst of whites. Therefore, the story of the Santa Anna–Emily tryst was fostered in part to reinforce and promote (traditional and conservative) racial and social values and white society's expectations in regard to maintaining the rigid status quo of segregation and racial boundaries by demonstrating the folly of engaging in intimate personal and sexual relations with people of color and the inevitable high cost that had to be paid for such egregious violations.[42]

Helping to set the stage for the widespread acceptance of the Santa Anna–Emily liaison myth, the early history of the cinematic Alamo, where core Texas Revolutionary myths were not only created but embellished and distorted, was marred by racist depictions of raping Mexicans in a striking parallel to David W. Griffith's portrayal of blacks, whom he painted as lusting for white women, in his *The Birth of a Nation* (1915). Anti-black and anti–Mexican themes and stereotypes in movies and writings of the Texas Revolution predominated for decades, taking the place of the earlier anti–Catholic themes that were already deeply embedded in American history and culture. And, of course, Santa Anna always has been depicted as the epitome of evil, fulfilling a host of racial stereotypes while representing the Mexican nation in general. As early as 1915 and exploiting a common and popular theme of "The Yellow Rose of Texas" myth, a title card for the film *Martyrs of the Alamo* (1915) described Santa Anna as an "inveterate drug fiend noted for his shameful orgies."[43] Without even mentioning the gross distortions, especially in racial terms, on a scale seldom seen even in the history of cinema dominated by artistic license, author Frank Thompson correctly concluded, "As history, nearly every Alamo film is worthless."[44]

In the end, both the image of Santa Anna, as fallen man, and Emily, as loose, hypersexual black women and the mythical Jezebel, were equally tarnished by the alleged liaison in the headquarters tent. In contrast, Anglo-Celtic women of Texas—like in the South in general—were placed on lofty pedestals of virtue largely because of racial, societal, and cultural reasons. White historians and writers have portrayed white Texian females, especially Mrs. Susanna Dickinson, the wife of Captain Almeron Dickinson, in a heroic light, despite facts to the contrary. Susanna was transformed into a Texas heroine and a symbol of Anglo female virtue and dignity. What has been overlooked was the fact that not only Susanna but also her daughter became prostitutes when economic times were difficult after the Texas Revolution. Therefore, this revered white Texas heroine, long portrayed in myth as asexual, noble and virtuous, proved immoral in the end. This was not the case with the allegedly immoral, loose ethnic woman, the mythical black Jezebel, named Emily, who never became a prostitute. A close look at the lives of these two women not only mocks but also reverses the core racial, cultural, and gender assumptions that have long supported the two most popular myths regarding the two leading female figures of the Texas Revolution and the Texas creation myth.[45]

More revealing evidence that the Santa Anna–Emily alleged tryst was nothing but a historical hoax and Texas tall tale can be seen from the lack of primary documentation at the time. No primary evidence, especially letters from the men (Mexican, Texian, Tejano or United States volunteer) of San Jacinto, has been found about the "Yellow Rose of Texas" story in the entire decade of the 1830s. In fact, nothing exists at all in regard to primary evidence or documentation, before the single and obscure Bollaert reference that suddenly appeared seemingly out of thin air in the early 1840s.

And most revealing because the Emily of tryst fame was allegedly owned by James Morgan, the many lengthy, informative letters written by Morgan, the agent and manager of the New Washington Association who was Emily's employer, to Samuel Swartwout in 1836 never mentioned anything about the alleged liaison. This is a most glaring, but revealing, omission because Morgan's letters even presented intimate details about the battle of San Jacinto and even the eventual fate of Santa Anna's headquarters tent, which was sent to Swartwout by Morgan as a trophy of Houston's decisive victory. But nothing in Morgan's detailed letters gave any mention or even a hint of either Emily, or the alleged liaison, which was supposed to have occurred in the very tent dispatched by water to Swartwout and all the way to New York City. And, most significant, if this alleged tryst had occurred at all, then Morgan certainly would have learned of it and almost certainly passed such information along to this close friend Swartwout. Such information would have made Santa Anna's tent of true historical significance rather than a mere curiosity.[46]

But perhaps the best evidence that the Emily D. West story was nothing more than a myth was the fact that she was eventually forced to leave Texas because she could be enslaved (even if her free status was verified after she lost her free papers at San Jacinto) because of the anti–free black laws of the Texas Constitution. If Emily had in fact played such a key role in ensuring the most decisive victory in Texas history at San Jacinto, then she almost certainly would have enjoyed an elevated status among Texians. Emily would have certainly been allowed to remain in Texas without threat of enslavement, if she was indeed the fabled folk heroine as alleged. Almost certainly, a community, county, or city in Texas would have been named in her honor, if Emily had been an authentic heroine of the battle of San Jacinto.

In the end, the anti-free black laws of the Texas Congress denied Emily permission to remain in Texas after her one-year contract expired on October 25, 1836. Clearly, Emily D. West only became a heroine long after the Texas Revolution and as a result of the myth-making of Emily that emerged in the mid–Twentieth Century. According to all available evidence, she certainly did not enjoy any acknowledgment or any kind of recognition when she lived in Texas after the battle of San Jacinto: evidence that indicated that the story of the "Yellow Rose of Texas" had not been yet created or known at this time.[47]

Quite simply, not enough sufficient primary evidence of any kind or on any level can be found to support the alleged tryst between Emily D. West and Santa Anna that supposedly changed the course of history. Practically everything about the alleged liaison at San Jacinto has been either the result of fabrication, speculation, or embellishment, including perhaps even the most specific single, brief reference allegedly from Houston. Only a single, highly questionable source, that no longer exists today, even hints of a possible tryst with an "Emily" without a last name. And this obscure, short paragraph in the Bollaert account was deliberately placed outside the narrative by the author, because he considered what was in fact the tallest of Texas tall tales as simply too questionable or unreliable. Therefore, this obscure paragraph was only used by the scholarly editors as merely a footnote in the 1956 edited version of the Bollaert manuscript, because they knew that the alleged liaison could not be corroborated with any known primary documentation. This brief reference was penned by Bollaert after the Englishman's trip to Texas that lasted from the summer of 1842 to 1844. The alleged incident was chronicled by him for the first time on July 6, 1842, more than six years after the battle of San Jacinto. This is the only direct reference to the supposedly history-changing liaison.

Bollaert's short paragraph about the alleged incident, he said, "was given to me by" Houston by way of a letter at some unknown time. Then Bollaert allegedly wrote out the paragraph verbatim from the alleged Houston letter, but he failed to include it in his narrative. But that letter either does not exist today and has not been discovered by anyone, if it ever existed at all.

Most revealing, the master storyteller Bollaert failed to elaborate upon any details about the Emily story in narrative form in his published work. He himself sincerely doubted either the source or the truthfulness of the sensational tryst story, despite Bollaert's obvious interest in the battle that determined the destiny of Texas on April 21, 1836. The gossipy, undocumented nature of the Bollaert reference also revealed why the first editors of Bollaert's work included it only in a footnote, as if only an afterthought. Perhaps most damaging to the story's credibility was the fact that Bollaert was most of all a colorful storyteller and notorious gossip rather than a critical or serious historian. He knew a good story when he heard one, but yet Bollaert neglected to write at length about perhaps the most important and juicy historical incident that he probably ever learned about in his life, because Bollaert himself obviously did not believe the story and it was never published.

Of course, what cannot be denied was that the "Yellow Rose of Texas" was certainly a good story, even by Texas tall tale standards, second to none. In fact, no one in all Texas, including the historian and scholarly community, knew anything about the Emily–Santa Anna tryst story until the University of Oklahoma Press published *William Bollaert's Texas* in 1956, consisting of Bollaert's papers. Published for the first time, these papers were housed at the Newberry Library, Chicago, Illinois, and were forgotten by the historian community until the book's publication.

Most revealing, the most important details of the alleged Houston letter were simply wrong: (1) that Emily was a slave, and, (2) that she was owned by James Morgan, and (3) that her name was Emily Morgan, because neither free blacks nor employees (like Emily D. West) took an employer's last name. Only slaves took a master's surname. In addition, the Bollaert account has been the only source that described Emily as being of mixed blood, or a "Mulatta Girl." At age 36 by early 1837, Emily D. West was certainly not a young "Girl" of nineteen as represented in the "Yellow Rose of Texas" myth and perhaps not even of black and white parentage—the mythical Emily of mulatto beauty—by this time. The real Emily was a mature, middle-aged and literate free women with an education and abolitionist leanings and sympathies. By the time of the dramatic showdown at San Jacinto, the worldly, jaded Houston was only around six years older than Emily. In addition, Emily was a common name among free black women in Harris County, indicating that another African American woman besides Emily D. West perhaps might have been the subject in question at San Jacinto in regard to the alleged liaison.[48]

A host of other problems exist with the often unusual terminology used in the alleged Houston letter. It states the battle was only "probably" lost because of the alleged Santa Anna–Emily tryst, indicating a high degree of uncertainty in Houston's claim. And the description that "owing to the influence" of Emily, who was allegedly "closeted in the tent" of Santa Anna, might have had nothing whatever to do with sex.

If not sex, then what was the exact nature of this mysterious "influence" that drew Santa Anna's attention? Neither the alleged Houston letter nor the obscure Bollaert reference—allegedly one and the same—was revealing on this score. The letter seemed to be deliberately phrased in an ambiguous manner, because the humorous, bawdy story was actually only gossip created primarily for entertainment value, perhaps intended for Bollaert's Texan audience.

The wording of this artfully-written description has been structured to allow readers the maximum opportunity to utilize the fullness of their imaginations and existing anti-Latino, anti-black, and anti–Santa Anna stereotypes to envision the most sensational and sexually-titillating situation. Like the great horror film director Alfred Hitchcock, who knew the importance of allowing the audience the maximum opportunity to employ their imaginations to creatively envision a graphic horror scene beyond what could be depicted on film for the greatest possible shock value, the writer of this short paragraph—like the storyteller that Bollaert was—gave the reader a chance to fill in the gaps.

But the most significant discrepancy in the alleged Houston letter, supposedly copied verbatim by Bollaert, can be found in the spelling of Santa Anna's name. In this undated letter, Santa Anna's name has been oddly misspelled "Santana" by the president of Texas: a strange misspelling by Houston, whose treaties that guaranteed Texas independence were signed with Santa Anna, with the Mexican president. The fact that one president, who had some fluency in Spanish, would not have known the correct spelling of another president, with whom he dealt closely in an important way after the battle of San Jacinto, is inexplicable.

However, a March 11, 1836, Houston letter to James Walker Fannin in the A. J. Houston Collection at the Texas State Library and Archives in Austin, Texas, has revealed that Sam Houston had repeatedly spelled the generalísimo's name the same way, as "Gen. St Anna" and not "Santana." Houston's letter from Gonzales was written in haste, indicating the need for abbreviation, however. Other letters, written with time not nearly as urgent, penned by Houston during the Texas Revolution have revealed his more proper and full usage of the name, "Santa Anna." Such serious discrepancies in the Bollaert account suggest a forged Houston letter, because Bollaert copied it verbatim, that has served as the primary basis of the liaison myth.[49]

Bollaert spelled Santa Anna as "Santana" in other entries in his work, such as in his journal entries on August 1842. In an August 21, 1842, letter, Bollaert described in regard to the ill-fated Santa Fe Expedition how "Santana had time to give his orders and prepare for defense against them."[50] Such evidence in part has indicated that Bollaert himself, and not Houston, was in fact the sole author of the now famous paragraph that has served as the basis for the tryst and the "Yellow Rose of Texas" myth, and that this paragraph was not taken, as alleged, and copied verbatim by Bollaert from a Houston letter.

In addition, the word "mulatta," as revealed in the alleged Houston letter, was a Spanish and Catholic term—actually spelled "mulata"—and not a common Anglo-Celtic term in Texas during this period. The common Spanish and Mexican definition of "mulata" was as follows: "From European and black, a mulata is born." In fact, the term "mulatta" had been commonly used by people in Eighteenth Century Mexico, especially the Spanish. Therefore, the usage of the term "mulata" would have been highly unlikely by the former governor of Tennessee, who was of Scotch-Irish heritage, a Presbyterian with an Upper South upbringing, and a relative newcomer to Texas. Again, as a sophisticated world traveler and a fluent Spanish-speaker with a keen eye for the nuances of other lands and people of different races, especially because most of his travels were in Spanish lands. Englishman Bollaert would have been more likely than Houston to use the word "mulatta." This fact certainly raises additional doubts about the letter's authenticity and authorship, providing more evidence that it was fabricated by Bollaert and not written by Houston.[51]

In addition, this Emily passage was included only as an attachment in Bollaert's manuscript and was labeled by the Englishman as "a copy of an unpublished letter written by General Houston to a friend after this extraordinary battle." First and foremost, who was the so-called "friend"? The name of this mysterious friend has remained unknown to this day. Not only was the letter unpublished, but it has disappeared without a trace. Most importantly, Houston's alleged words also indicated that what he related was simply not first-hand information and therefore not accurate information, but gained from another source or sources that are yet unknown. If actually conveyed from Houston himself, the entire basis of the allegedly Santa Anna–Emily liaison at San Jacinto most likely was only second-hand information, or, quite simply, gossip from an unidentified source.

All in all, a good many things about this alleged Houston letter simply do not ring true, make sense, or seem logical. If Houston wrote it, he was mistaken about some of the most important and essential facts that cannot be denied, such as Emily's status as a free person and not a slave. No former military commander whose fame was primarily based upon a decisive battlefield victory of such supreme strategic importance that it altered the course of nations would have minimized his own generalship by bestowing even more recognition for the one-sided success at San Jacinto not on himself but an obscure black woman who was only a slave.

The only way that Houston would have given such noteworthy recognition to an obscure slave "girl" of African heritage at the expense of his own lofty reputation as the revered "George Washington of Texas" was if he knew that the story was untrue and only for amusement: a Texas tall tale.[52] Indeed, why would Houston give such information damaging to his own ability and reputation to a British writer, who hailed from what was seen as a predator nation that had been America's longtime enemy and rival? At this time, the average American's hatred toward England was stronger than toward any other nation.

In addition, Bollaert would not have been able to tell an authentic Houston signature from a fake, if in fact the letter had been signed at all with Houston's name. What also has been forgotten by historians was that the alleged Houston letter was written in the early 1840s at the height of the avalanche of political attacks on Houston's conduct, strategic and tactical thinking, and leadership ability during the San Jacinto Campaign. No one hated Houston more than the republic's first president, Burnet. With an aggressive newspaper campaign in which he leveled very personal charges of alcoholism and even cowardice on the transplanted Tennessean, Burnet especially attacked Houston's generalship on all levels. Outright lies and slander dominated the vicious political campaign between Houston and Burnet, when Houston sought a second term as the republic's president, which he won in September 1841.

Perhaps Burnet actually wrote the alleged Houston letter to disparage the former general, whose greatest fame rested upon his decisive victory at San Jacinto, which in the "history of war does not furnish a parallel," by bestowing more recognition for his amazing success

VIII. Popular Myth-making and the Creation of "The Yellow Rose of Texas"   213

on the raw sexuality of an obscure slave woman named Emily rather than Houston's masterful blend of tactics and timing that were little short of brilliant.[53]

If the supposed Emily–Santa Anna tryst were true, then might the alleged Houston letter, written more than a half decade after the battle of San Jacinto, have confused the names of people of color? Morgan was already a slave-owner by time of the Texas Revolution. After San Jacinto, Morgan's wife gained two female slaves—Mary Jane and Sally Ann—from the will of James Routh, who had lived on Galveston Bay, Harris County, near Clopper's, or Morgan's, Point. These two black female slaves were young adults, because the will stipulated that Sylvia's younger children, including a girl named Emily who was around age nine, was to remain with their mother. Perhaps more than Emily, it was one of these women who were engaged in the alleged tryst with Santa Anna, if it occurred at all, because they later became members of Morgan's household (or Morgan's slaves) after the battle. At the time that the letter was written, the writer might well have assumed that they were Morgan's slaves at the time of the battle.

These two young black women remained with the Morgan family for years, because the will stipulated that freedom was to be granted to them only when they reached the age of twenty-one. Therefore, when the alleged Houston letter was written in the early 1840s, Mary Jane and Sally Ann were Morgan's slaves. Because Routh's will was paternalistic and benevolent—including bestowing more than 300 acres to Sylvia and some education to the children—for the time, this situation almost certainly indicated that Sylvia had been the master's longtime sexual partner and that the children were probably his own offspring. Therefore, of course, the children would have been mulattos. And if one of the names had been confused in relating the tryst story, then perhaps one of Sylvia's daughters was in fact the mysterious Texas "Mulatta Girl (Emily) belonging to Colonel Morgan" and not the free black woman named Emily D. West from the northeast. But this is only speculation.[54]

By early 1838 after having patched up their personal differences, Morgan and Houston became close friends. The hero of San Jacinto even stayed with Morgan at Clopper's Point, after their feud ended not long after victory at San Jacinto. At this time and thereafter during visits by "The Raven," Morgan might have told Houston about a mulatto "Girl" named Emily—a person who would have been a correct fit in regard to age, status, and ownership (Morgan's slave) and perhaps even closer in color (lighter from her father) than Emily D. West, who was older, free not slave, and perhaps not even a mulatto. In this probable, but forgotten, scenario, Houston wrote his letter around 1842 based upon this information from Morgan that would have been accurate in regard to one of Routh's daughters and not the free black woman from New England named Emily D. West. Therefore, in this speculative and improbable scenario, the Houston letter might have been in fact accurate and factual.[55]

If the alleged Houston letter was indeed authentic and the facts were correct, then the possibility existed that one of Routh's daughters was the real "Yellow Rose of Texas," and not Emily D. West. There might have been a real Emily Morgan after all, but not Emily D. West. And, if Santa Anna took her to bed in his headquarters tent on the warm afternoon of April 21, then she also might have been a ravishing young beauty after all: a scenario that was closer to the enduring myth of "The Yellow Rose of Texas" than the tale of Emily D. West.

So quite possibly, and for the sake of speculation, the real "Yellow Rose of Texas" was not Emily D. West, but an entirely different person. If Santa Anna was actually engaged in any sensual activity in his headquarters tent, then it was most likely with a young Mexican mistress, as during the siege of the Alamo, and perhaps one of the officers' wives or girlfriends, who accompanied him during the latter stages of the San Jacinto Campaign, and stayed in his headquarters tent for carnal purposes.[56]

Morgan's and Bollaert's Forgotten Hidden Agenda

Very likely the authentic source of the alleged Houston letter, supposedly copied verbatim by Bollaert in the margin of a page in his original manuscript, was either Morgan himself or even a collaborative effort between Morgan and Bollaert, because of a strong vested interest in promoting New Washington. Since becoming the head agent in Texas for the grand investment scheme and speculative effort known as the New Washington Association, Morgan's most important priority was to somehow put New Washington on the map. Therefore, he attempted to promote the site of New Washington and its extensive land-holdings by almost every conceivable way and by every possible angle, including by claiming that the association's lands were considered the best in all Texas and that the promising site of New Washington would be the ideal location for the greatest city of Texas and the republic's capital in the future.

Most of all, Morgan was a savvy speculator, promoter, and businessman, and the future of the New Washington Association and the entire success of this grandiose speculative venture and his investor friends and the company's stockholders was based in large part upon his own ability to successfully promote New Washington, especially as the best location of the Texas capital. After Texas won its independence, the key to getting the site of New Washington known across Texas, especially to leading politicians and the people of Texas, would have been by way of a savvy promotional campaign to put New Washington on the map. If New Washington could only be sufficiently publicized to people across Texas, then Morgan and his New York investors, especially Swartwout, were convinced that New Washington could become the greatest and most magnificent city in Texas, to rival not only New Orleans, but also New York City.

Therefore, quite likely under these circumstances, Morgan himself created this most colorful and unforgettable bawdy tale of the Emily–Santa Anna tryst in the hope that it would draw new attention to the town and help to transform the obscure backwater of New Washington, which had been destroyed by the war and needed to be resurrected into a historically significant place, because one of its own "citizens" had played a key role in ensuring that Mexico would lose Texas. With Houston's remarkable victory yet almost incomprehensible after the Texians had suffered so many reversals, this colorful tryst story explained what was not fully understood: exactly how and why Santa Anna was so easily and quickly defeated in the most important battle in Texas history.

Morgan could have developed no more colorful, sensational story than Santa Anna having engaged in illicit sex with a black female at the exact moment that Houston launched his counterattack to catch the generalísimo by surprise. Such a tantalizing and titillating bombshell would certainly have given widespread recognition to a growth-stunted New Washington, which was yet struggling to survive in its remote location, especially after it had been destroyed on Santa Anna's orders in April 1836.

Therefore, when Bollaert visited New Washington as early as 1842 and then later to enjoy Morgan's legendary Southern-style hospitality—fine food, and ample drinks in the Southern planter class tradition—he very likely heard of the Emily story for the first time.

Perhaps it was Morgan, an experienced promoter and propagandist, and well-known for having written anti–Houston letters for publication in newspapers, which had caused the temporary rift between the two men, who wrote the mysterious paragraph and attributed it to Houston to garner publicity for the rebuilding of New Washington. Most significant, such recognition would help to attract settlers and jumpstart the entrepreneurial enterprise in a last-ditch attempt to transform a dying backwater dream into a successful community and perhaps even a great city. Morgan and his closest friends and fellow investors had already placed everything on the high stakes bet—and lost thanks to the war—that their grand future visions would become realized. Therefore, the Emily–Santa Anna story might have been concocted by Morgan in a final bid to gain recognition for New Washington, or accept the painful, undeniable reality of a failed enterprise, wasted fortunes, and broken dreams.[57]

Morgan's distinct flair for salesmanship was evident not long after the Alamo's fall. He was the first businessman in Texas who sought to exploit the news of Crockett's death at the Alamo. By April 5, less than a month after the tragic death of the popular Tennessean, now a lamented national martyr, Morgan had already formulated plans for the creation of "the new town of Crockett that he means to lay out" near Galveston Bay.[58]

Or Morgan might have picked up the story of the alleged Emily–Santa Anna liaison from the gossip growing and spreading about the most remarkable victory in Texas history. After all, a good many "tales abounded along the gulf coast, in hotels, bordellos, and barrooms, and exaggerated battlefield accounts of individual heroism were common in the months and years following the Battle of San Jacinto." The inevitable process of transforming a dramatic historical event of extreme importance into mythology had already begun.[59]

After all, Morgan only had to link his own name—which represented his New Washington Association investors and the speculative company—and that of Emily (and then with Houston) to the colorful story to create a sensational legend that he hoped could make New Washington world-famous, and better known than the nearby fast-growing town of Houston, which had been named in honor of San Jacinto's victor: a possible explanation as to why the alleged Houston letter so thoroughly minimized the general's leadership and tactical skill in achieving such a complete victory at San Jacinto by making the unbridled sexuality of a slave woman more responsible for winning the battle than even the best efforts of the "George Washington of Texas."

Bollaert also had a vested interest in New Washington's success. Like Morgan, especially after New Washington had been destroyed by Santa Anna's troops, Bollaert was seemingly always in need of money, not to mention recognition and acclaim for his writing. He had not become the financially-successful writer that he so desired to be by 1842.

Like almost everyone else who journeyed to Texas with high hopes, Bollaert had set his sights on a future prosperous life in Texas far from his rainy, overcast isle, and this meant investing as a speculator to gain prosperity, respectability and status: all things that this class-conscious, but hard-luck, Englishman coveted. After gaining admission to the Texas bar and joining the infant Texas Navy of the young republic, Bollaert seemingly had a bright future ahead, until Texas' annexation by the United States drew closer, a move made in part to eliminate Great Britain's ambitions for Texas and ensure the United States' continued expansion and commercial development. However, if Great Britain prevailed, a new "career as promoter and land agent, and in time as representative of English commercial capital, might open for him" in Texas to restore him to fame and fortune.

Both Morgan and Bollaert had based their futures upon land speculation in regard to the vast holdings of the New Washington Association. Therefore, both men engaged in a round of active political maneuvering to promote the New Washington Association, conversing and associating with the leading men of Texas, befriending them. All the while, they promoted themselves, their personal interests, and the speculative land schemes of the New Washington Association. Morgan naturally targeted Houston, cultivating him and repeatedly emphasizing that New Washington was the best possible site for the future capital of Texas.

However, Bollaert suddenly departed Texas in July 1844 when his Texas dreams failed to materialize, going broke after his speculative ambitions were crushed by hard times. He was forced to borrow money to pay for the return trip to England. Bollaert reached his native homeland on the Atlantic's other side "without a dollar." Bollaert, consequently, never finished his most ambitious writing projects or his planned future books about Texas. He had nearly a dozen Texas-related articles published in journals and magazines, but Bollaert never published or elaborated upon the Emily–Santa Anna tryst story.[60]

Chapter IX

Emily After the Fiery Storm at San Jacinto

One of the great myths of traditional patriarchal cultures, including American, since time immemorial was that women were the weaker sex, marked by not only physical but also spiritual, intellectual, and moral inferiority. Therefore, society's expectations for Nineteenth Century American women were extremely low, and especially for women of color. The life of Emily D. West, in part because she hailed from a matriarchal black society and culture of West Africa that served as the core foundation for the survival of not only the slave family and community but also the free black community, demonstrated the fallacy of these common negative stereotypes about women, both black and white.

A greater sexual equality stemming from the overall black experience, in which more women served as household heads; the traditional features of a matriarchal society, which in general produced less passivity and less dependence upon men; and the supreme importance of the black female as the head of the family thanks to slavery and its effects ensured the survival of the black family, while creating resilient, enterprising, and ambitious young women like Emily. Emily's life can be viewed as very much embodying a lifelong struggle against the dual oppressions of racism and sexism. And in this struggle, she not only survived but also rose up to overcome obstacles and challenges in the North and in Texas during wartime.[1]

Emily stayed with Colonel Isaac N. Moreland and his family at their home at some point after the battle of San Jacinto. More so than Colonel Morgan, who owned slaves and hailed from the South, Colonel Moreland was an open-minded, enlightened man, who only belatedly embraced war as the only option. No fire-eater, he had originally advocated a conservative approach to the crisis with Mexico, calling for Texans to obey Mexican laws less than six months before the Texas Revolution's outbreak. After first meeting her—perhaps even finding her hidden in some relatively safe place since she had been unhurt during the battle—on the field of San Jacinto, he felt empathy toward this free black woman, who was now on her own and far from family and friends. While later serving as a chief justice in Houston, Moreland remained sympathetic toward free blacks. In this role, he signed all the petitions submitted to Congress for free blacks to remain in Texas. Therefore, Moreland was now Emily's best white friend and supporter in Texas.

As a respected member of a slave-owning society that was comparable to that of the Deep South, Moreland's relative enlightenment in regard to matters of race explained why he took Emily into his home at some point after the battle of San Jacinto. Most significant, he also was protecting her from any hard-hearted Texans who would have enslaved Emily, if they discovered she was without her "free" papers, which she had lost at San Jacinto. Ironically, Santa Anna's crushing defeat at San Jacinto, which had been celebrated across Texas, had imperiled Emily to a degree that she had never known before in her life. Therefore, she desperately needed a protector, a benevolent hand. Fortunately for Emily, this proved to be Moreland.[2]

The considerable risk now posed to Emily, when without her "free" papers, represented the typical plight of other free blacks across Texas. Indeed, Houston's stunning victory at San Jacinto had been won over military forces that freed enslaved African Americans across Texas, and had been viewed, including by Emily, as a liberating force. Slavery became more entrenched then ever before. All liberal Mexican laws in regard to slaves had been swept away with the winning of Texas independence and in accordance with the laws of the Texas Constitution created in early March 1836.

Other than the destruction of New Washington, yet another possible reason why Emily left Morgan and joined Moreland and his family was because Morgan might well have displayed an ugly side that was in keeping with his slave-holding tendencies and Southern upbringing. He had been raised in a slave-owning family in the Upper South, and he was considered "rich, but unpopular" at this time. And at least one author has even emphasized a dark past for Morgan as a slave trader and an abuser of slaves, including women.

Therefore, some evidence has revealed that Morgan might have viewed any black woman, including even free persons of color, as little more than a slave available for exploitation. If so, then Emily departed Morgan's tight, if not oppressive, grip to gain the safety and support of a more enlightened and fair-minded individual in Moreland. Quite simply, with her liberty at stake, she might have known, or sensed, that Morgan might try to keep her in Texas as a slave. Such a situation would have explained why Moreland became Emily's protector.

Indeed, when the old planter Routh died in the summer of 1837, Morgan's wife gained the two daughters of free black woman Sylvia Routh, according to Routh's will, of which Morgan acted as one of two executors. Morgan was shocked to discover that a proud and independent Sylvia was defiant to him and his instructions, evidently because he refused to acknowledge her free status and independence. An angry Morgan, displaying the darker and less kind side of his nature, appealed to the chief justice of Harris County, requesting confinement of the free-thinking, outspoken Sylvia as punishment. As could be expected, the chief justice, also a Texas slave-owner, promptly ordered this defiant free black woman hauled off to the county jail. And when another one of Routh's African Americans, Jim, who also had been freed by Routh, likewise displayed insubordination toward Morgan, the free black man was also thrown into jail.[3] Emily almost certainly viewed Morgan as a threat.

Even before the climactic showdown at San Jacinto, it was not uncommon for recently freed black persons in Harris County to be treated as slaves by Texians. In Harris County and not far from Clopper's Point, William Vance's slave woman, Sally, was set free upon her master's death and as stipulated in his September 7, 1834, will. However, Sally was kept in bondage as a slave by Allen Vance, who was the will's executor. Such sinister developments so close to where she resided in Harris County also indicated that Emily's free status was not at all safe by remaining either with Morgan or in Harris County, where slavery was the law of the land, thanks to Houston's victory at San Jacinto. Sally was forced to file a lawsuit to win back her freedom and "right to liberty."[4]

The distinct possibility also existed that Morgan might have been the real sexual abuser of Emily rather than Santa Anna. Author Carmen Goldthwaite emphasized that Morgan was a slave-owner "with a penchant for choosing mulattos" for his own personal and sexual pleasure: a Southern planter tradition that had been transferred across the Sabine. If so, then such a situation also explained why Emily was not long with Morgan, whose less humanitarian side had evidently risen to the fore, perhaps because of the war's stresses (especially the burning down of New Washington) and brutalities, after the battle of San Jacinto.[5]

Clearly, if a free Emily D. West had indeed played the vital role in paving the way to Houston's victory at the battle of San Jacinto by seducing Santa Anna as claimed by the romantic legend, and if she had told Morgan, then would not Morgan have been more sympathetic not only to her but also to other free blacks? Would not Morgan have been more tolerant if he had known that a free black woman—whom he himself had hired and worked with at New Washington—had made a decisive victory at San Jacinto possible?

Fortunately for her in a Texas that had created a permanent place for slavery that was guaranteed by Houston's success at San Jacinto, Emily could not have found a better benefactor than Moreland. He stayed true to his humanitarian principles and beliefs. Emily first met the Georgia-born Moreland, who had migrated to Texas in 1834, on the field of San Jacinto. Immediately after the battle, Moreland might well have protected Emily from enslavement by slave-owning Texians, because Moreland lingered on the battlefield with an assigned detail to secure Santa Anna's personal effects after the fighting ended, while Morgan had only reached the field of San Jacinto on April 23: a crucial two-day period when Emily was especially vulnerable without her free papers. Moreland, as a promising captain of Houston's artillery corps, became so upset about the breakdown of discipline and looting of the Mexican encampment, evidently including the taking of Santa Anna's headquarters tent as a trophy, that he personally reported the fact to General Houston, who respected the native Georgian as a man and leader.

If so, then this situation might in part explain why and how Moreland first encountered Emily and then became her guardian and closest white male friend. After all, he was destined to present a positive character endorsement and emphasize her free status in order for Emily D. West to successfully secure her passport to finally leave Texas, when Moreland was a Harris County judge in the summer of 1837, after he left the army. Most likely, the compassionate Moreland rescued Emily from enslavement during the confused aftermath of the battle of San Jacinto. Moreland's intervention could not have been more crucial. At this time, free blacks in Texas were only safe if they had a white man, preferably one of social standing, to protect and speak for them as a personal guardian.

An inspirational leader and friend of Houston, a man of compassion, and perhaps even a closet abolitionist in the midst of a robust empire for slavery, Moreland had joined the Texas Revolution in October 1835. He then served in the siege of San Antonio before the city's capture in December 1835. And he assisted in raising a volunteer company in a belated attempt to relieve the doomed Alamo garrison, before becoming second-in-command of Houston's only artillery, the two light-weight guns known as the "Twin Sisters," at San Jacinto. Moreland, the oldest and most capable Texas artillery officer present on the field by the time of the showdown at San Jacinto, commanded one of these barking guns that had been cast in Cincinnati, Ohio.[6]

Emily's work at New Washington ended when the town was burned to the ground in April 1836. However, the expiration of Emily's one-year contract with Morgan and the New Washington Association came on October 25, 1836, or almost exactly six months after the battle of San Jacinto. In legal terms, Emily was no longer bound by any ties to Texas. She was now free to depart. Emily did not sign up for another term as housekeeper at New Washington because a new hotel had not been built by this time and money was scarce for Morgan and his New Washington Association investors, who had lost almost everything in the war. New Washington had yet to be resurrected, even though the dream of a future great city remained ever-present in the minds of Morgan, Swartwout and so many New Yorkers: in the end, a vain, futile hope for all of the wealthy New York City investors, who envisioned fantastic profits once New Washington turned into a boom town. Plans had been made for New Washington's resurrection but the necessary funds and labor were lacking in the aftermath of a destructive and cruel war that had ravaged Texas.

Emily faced serious obstacles in her desire to depart a land devoted to enslavement. In addition, Emily might have been denied permission to remain on Texas soil, if she so desired, although very unlikely, by slave-owning congressional members, who looked unkindly on the presence of free blacks in Texas after the battle of San Jacinto. The 1836 Constitution required all free blacks to gain permission from Congress to remain on Texas soil. Evidently, this permission had been denied to Emily after October 25, 1836, if she applied for it at all. Worst of all, in legal terms, any failure of a free black to gain permission from Congress to remain on Texas soil paved the way for eventual enslavement.[7]

Emily, at age thirty-six and having had more than enough of revolution, life-threatening trouble and upheaval in Texas, economic hard times, and threats to her freedom, now simply wanted to return home to either New Haven or New York City. Such a desire also might well have indicated that she either had children or family, perhaps a husband, back East. If so, then she may have saved some money from her four-month term of service at the New Washington Hotel. Since the hotel was burned down by Santa Anna's soldiers, she was unable to fulfill her contractual obligation to work a full year for payment of $100, even if she had so desired. If she was paid for four months of work, it was around $30.

Most likely, the chaos of war and New Washington's destruction resulted in nonpayment, because Morgan was out of funds and economic times—heavy debts from the revolutionary struggle and no immediate annexation by the United States to lift the financial burden—for the infant republic were rough: perhaps another reason that caused the split between Emily and Morgan which required Moreland's intervention.[8]

In the summer of 1837 while the "skeletons of the dead yet cover[ed] the plain" of San Jacinto, Emily made her first legal attempt to leave Texas. She officially requested a passport from the Texas government for her return back to New York City with Colonel Moreland's assistance. The enlightened Moreland was now a crony of Houston and a respected magistrate in the bustling new town of Houston. He also practiced law in Houston with David Gouverneur Burnet.

Moreland, later a chief justice of Harris County, penned a personal reference letter in her passport application to verify Emily's upright character. Emily was most fortunate to have an influential, highly-respected white citizen endorse her good character and assist this free black woman for no gain on his part. Moreland refuted any dark stains on Emily's character or background, and emphasized her good standing, which was earlier verified when Morgan had signed her up in New York City for work at New Washington in late October 1835.

In truth and as Moreland verified in the application for her passport, Emily D. West was of outstanding character. Contrary to the myth of the conniving whore of "The Yellow Rose of Texas" myth, she was perhaps very religious in the strict New England Congregationalist tradition, reflecting her New Haven upbringing and the teachings of the northern abolitionists, especially Jocelyn.

All existing evidence, therefore, indicates that Emily was not the kind of woman who would have willingly engaged in an affair or tryst with Santa Anna, or the type who might have resorted to prostitution at the price of her dignity and self-esteem. In the West, especially during hard economic times, prostitution was often an irresistible lure and relatively safe haven for hard-luck frontier women, especially those women without families, husbands, or male providers (such as Emily had), to help them survive a harsh frontier environment.

Emily refused the option of taking the easy route of prostitution in the growing city of nearby Houston, despite her impoverished plight and uncertain status. After all, the prospect of being a free prostitute in a whorehouse, where food and shelter was provided, was perhaps a preferable fate to a lifetime of slavery in a cotton fields of Texas. Therefore, Emily D. West fit in between the two most common stereotypes of women in the West, the sinful "spoiled dove," who wallowed in debauchery, and the virtuous "Madonna of the Prairies," who embodied saint-like traits that were more mythical than real.

The fact that Morgan never wrote a character reference for Emily's passport application to depart Texas was most revealing. She had been under his employment at New Washington and knew him longer than Moreland. Moreland was more liberal and enlightened in racial matters than Morgan, who might have desired Emily for either a sexual partner or slave, or both.

In his reference letter, Moreland described to the Texas secretary of state, who had been appointed by Houston to that elevated office in early 1837, Tennessee-born Robert Anderson Irion in Austin, that he had first encountered Emily in April 1836. This first meeting was most likely on the field of San Jacinto. Houston had recently courted Irion's wife, Anna Raguet, before her marriage. Houston wrote to her about his victory at San Jacinto and even sent a wreath to her from the battlefield. Of course, he made no mention of the alleged Santa Anna–Emily liaison. But Houston's new-won fame and recognition set him on another course in life, and an ardent pursuit of his future wife, Margaret Lea, whom he married in May 1840. He advised his good friend Dr. Irion, a distinguished graduate of Transylvania University, Lexington, Kentucky, to pursue pretty Anna Raguet, which Irion did with zeal.

Most importantly, in his letter of application, Moreland emphasized Emily's free status in order for her to secure a passport: "The bearer of this, Emily D. West, has been since my first acquaintance with her in April of [18] 36 a free women. She emigrated to this country with Col. James Morgan from the state of New York in September [December] of [18]35 and is now anxious to return and wishes a passport [and] I believe myself that she is entitled to one." Moreland emphasized that Emily was most "anxious" to return her native state.

Moreland added a final note: "Her free papers were lost at San Jacinto as I am informed [by her] and believe in April [21, 18] 36." Of course, this would have been the most favorable possible time for Moreland to have mentioned any seductive role (that would have made her a Texas patriot in accordance to "The Yellow Rose of Texas" myth) that Emily might have played toward the victory at San Jacinto. Moreland's mentioning nothing at all in this regard constitutes some of the most convincing evidence that the much-touted liaison between Santa Anna and Emily never occurred in the first place.

After Moreland wrote her character reference, he described in writing how Emily "requested me to give for her this note to you" in order to enhance her chances for obtaining a passport. This effort not only revealed Emily's intelligence, savvy, and resourcefulness in having the influential Moreland initiate this effort, but also provided one of the best indications of just how desperate Emily was to leave Texas as soon as possible.

By this time, Emily was in dire need of assistance because she had not yet retrieved her "free" papers which had been lost on the field of San Jacinto on April 21. Demonstrating his strong sympathy for free people of color, Moreland later signed every one of the five petitions—including one for a free black woman named Ann Tucker and one for Diana Leonard, the New Haven native who had journeyed to Texas with Emily after signing up to work at New Washington with Morgan—which were eventually submitted to Congress by free blacks from Harris County to remain safely in Texas.

Thanks to her own ideas and Moreland's efforts, Emily was shortly granted a passport, issued by the infant Texas Republic, to depart Texas. With her passport in hand and having taken a legal step that few other free blacks, especially women, elected to take, Emily was more than ready leave the scenes of so much strife. Emily now prepared to return to New York City. She had seen enough war for a lifetime, especially after the slaughter that she had witnessed to her horror at San Jacinto.[9]

Emily's plans to leave to Texas came just in time. In the future, New Washington was to fade away into even greater obscurity, while the vibrant city of Houston mushroomed. Like all other eastern investors of the New Washington Association and not unlike Emily's own personal dream of beginning a fulfilling new life in Texas, Morgan could hardly believe that his gamble that New Washington would eventually become a great city was lost forever: "Houston growing up like magic…. But for Almonte N[ew] W[ashington] wo'd have been that spot!"[10]

In a May 3, 1837, letter to Swartwout, Morgan concluded gloomily that while the upstart Houston had become a boom town, New Washington continued to be distinguished by a glaring lack of activity and progress, "remaining in all its primitive loveliness" and "loneliness [as] nothing doing there now."[11] A discouraged Morgan planned to resign as the agent of the New Washington Association: "I think the N[ew]. W[ashington]. A[ssocation]. can do without me any longer."[12] What New Washington now needed for a dramatic resurgence was the arrival of a railroad line, as emphasized by Morgan, linking it to Houston and the outside world, but even that dream failed to materialize. Quite simply, progress and development had already passed New Washington by.[13]

For reasons apart from the death of the once-bright, entrepreneurial dream of New Washington and economic hard times for the bankrupt, troubled Republic of Texas, Emily needed to depart the newly-established Republic of Texas forever. Quite simply, "the Lone Star," or Texas, was now "an independent white republic" based upon slavery. With abolitionist Mexico and its military forced out of Texas after the battle of San Jacinto thanks to Santa Anna's coerced orders to withdraw, the peculiar institution in Texas was now guaranteed to prosper like the slave regimes that made the vast cotton lands of Mississippi, Alabama, and Georgia so productive and lucrative. Houston's amazing victory at San Jacinto ensured that the harsh laws enacted by the early March 1836 Texas Constitution went into effect to protect slavery in Texas as never before.

Thousands of enslaved black women, men, and children were brought into Texas by the flood of migrants from the South each year following Houston's improbable success at San Jacinto. In a rare moment of renewed optimism, Morgan was excited about Texas' future prospects as a slave empire and a vast land of cotton, writing in a 1841 letter: "Times appear a little more Cheering—only to think of 30,000 Negroes brought into Texas within the last 12 months!" Morgan's words reflected the belief that slavery and cotton cultivation were the keys to the development and future prosperity of the young republic. Morgan's pro-slavery stance also can explain why Emily clashed with her former employer and escaped his presence after the battle of San Jacinto.

From around 5,000 slaves working in Texas, mostly in the cotton fields, when Emily arrived in December 1835, more than 12,000 slaves were counted in 1840. And because of Texas' rich soil, ample sunshine, plentiful rainfall, and ideal climate for growing staples, especially cotton, the future prosperity of Texas based upon a system of plantation slavery seemed boundless.[14]

After the roar of San Jacinto's guns ceased to echo across the humid coastal plain, Texas became far less safe for a free person of color like Emily, especially one without her "free" papers. Even free black soldiers who fought beside their white Texian comrades in Houston's charge, like Hendrick Arnold, who had long enjoyed full and equal rights as a Mexican citizen before the Texas Revolution, were no longer entirely safe in the land, where they had only recently risked their lives to save Texas from Mexico's grasp.

As early as January 5, 1836, just two months before the signing of the Texas Declaration of Independence, the ordinance of the General Council of the Texas provisional government had recognized the status of free blacks. But the new Texas constitution required free African Americans to officially gain permission from Congress to remain on Texas soil. Of course, if permission was denied, then every free black would be forced out of Texas or risked enslavement, including if they failed to request permission because they simply had no knowledge of the new law.[15]

Fortunately for Emily, an enlightened Moreland, an educated man ahead of his time, had come to her rescue in her greatest hour of need. And this effort was just in time with slavery permanently established in legal terms, sweeping away the vestiges of Mexico's liberal guarantees and full equality for blacks. Clearly, Emily had to flee Texas as soon as possible, because free blacks were viewed by Texan slave-owners as simply too risky to remain on Texas soil. Free blacks, including Emily, were seen as a most unwelcome presence, because they allegedly were a dangerous influence—by way of example—upon slaves, who saw for themselves the blessings of free status for people of color.

With a free Mexico located just across the Rio Grande and with white Texians, especially along the Gulf Coastal Plain, living in the midst of a large slave population, the free black presence in Texas had to be eventually eliminated. While the new Texas constitution and laws allowed for free blacks, especially those men of African (and also often white) heritage who served in the struggle for independence, in revolutionary Texas to maintain their lofty free status, the die had been cast for the future.

Therefore, the new Texas government limited future immigration of free blacks, while setting restrictions upon and challenging the free status of those already there. The establishment of the new republic, which supposedly had been conceived in liberty, brought only a host of new threats and greater dangers for free blacks like Emily. According to the new 1836 Texas constitution, free persons of one-eighth black blood could neither own property nor vote, testify in court, or even intermarry with whites.

As Emily knew, conditions in Texas were only getting much worse for free blacks who stayed, especially after Houston left the presidency in late 1838. On February 5, 1840, less than five years after victory at San Jacinto, the Texas Congress, with the blessing of Georgia-born President Mirabeau Buonaparte Lamar, who fought at San Jacinto and represented the values of his Deep South homeland, passed a law requiring all free blacks to leave Texas by January 1, 1842. If they refused to depart Texas soil by the appointed legal deadline of less than two years, then these free blacks, including those who had supported or fought for Texas, would become slaves. President Sam Houston repealed the law later that year.[16]

Then, just before seceding from the Union, Texas, which had been conceived in violent revolution in the name of liberty, "reversed the tradition of English law" by legally making it possible for whites to re-enslave free blacks. Clearly, Emily's decision to depart Texas was a guarantee that she would enjoy the blessings of her free status for the rest of her life far away from Texas and a Deep South–like world dominated by slave-owners and slave interests.[17]

Leaving Texas

Much to her relief and on what must have been one of the happiest days of her life, Emily was officially granted her passport by the secretary of state of the Republic of Texas, Robert Irion, at a time when the law of the land was that "no free person of African descent ... shall be permitted to reside permanently in the republic," in the Texas Declaration of Independence.[18] Emily was now free to return to her northern homeland so far away. The sparkling San Jacinto victory that led to Texas' independence had brought neither rights nor equality to people of color. Houston's victory had an entirely different meaning to Emily and other free blacks compared to white Texians.

In the summer of 1837, Emily D. West boarded another schooner than the *Flash*, that had brought her to Texas in December 1835. By this time, the journey to Texas must have seemed like a lifetime ago for Emily, after what she had seen and been through in this untamed land called Tejas during not only a civil war but also a revolution. As might be expected under the circumstances, Emily was elated about the prospect of leaving Texas, where seemingly endless conflict, the horrors of war, dangers from nature—hurricanes or animals, including man-eating alligators that made settlers, black or white, disappear forever—and man, especially raiding Indians and pro-slavery Texians, posed ever-present threats for a free black woman on her own.

And Mexico, refusing to accept Santa Anna's coerced promises and treaties, yet wanted to regain its former province and reverse the Texas Revolution's gains reaped by the audacity of the Texian colonists and so many United States volunteers, ensuring years of future warfare and additional military invasions of Texas from deep inside Mexico. Texas was caught between a vengeful enemy to the south, Mexico, and another ruthless enemy to the north and west, Indians, especially the wide-ranging Comanche. Emily herself likewise would have been stranded between the omnipresent threat of hostile Indians and slave-owners, if she had remained in Texas to tempt fate once again as in the past.

After Lorenzo Zavala's November 15, 1836, death from pneumonia after his small boat turned over in Buffalo Bayou's rough waters, amid a raging "blue norther," his wife also decided to forsake a hard-luck, risky life in Texas. In March 1837, she departed on the *Flash*, which took her back to her native New York, where she had been born in the Albany area. Lorenzo Zavala never saw his native Yucatan again. His wife left behind his lonely grave situated along the brown waters of Buffalo Bayou. During the hopeful journey to Texas in late 1835, Emily had cared for the three Zavala children. It seems a degree of mutual affection between this free black woman and the Zavala family endured.[19]

In a candid letter not meant for publication, James Morgan wrote of Mrs. Zavala's departure. In his March 3, 1837, letter to his good friend Swartwout, Morgan revealed his twin obsessions with wealth generated from successful cotton production and the captivating young widow with an enchanting beauty: "great Cotton & Corn Crops may be expected next year .... Mrs. Zavala goes on in *Flash*. V[ice] P[resident Mirabeau Buonaparte] Lamar has gone up there to settle some business with her before she goes about a 11 L[eague land] grant. Tis *whispered* he has some *other business* with her [but this is] *conjecture* only. I expect them both down today in S. Boat Laura. Lamar is a fine fellow & well deserving [of] any woman [but] I hardly think Mrs. Z. has ever thought about such an affair yet."[20]

Morgan casually spread somewhat scandalous gossip about the new Texas Republic's vice president, who was a real Southern gentleman from the planter class of the Deep South, while mentioning nothing about the alleged Santa Anna–Emily tryst at San Jacinto. Lamar had been born on a magnificent plantation named Fairfield, where cotton and slaves were abundant, which was located near Milledgeville, Georgia. The former editor of the *Columbus Enquirer* of Columbus, Georgia, with soaring political ambitions, Lamar had lost his beloved wife, Tabitha Jordan, in August 1830 when she died of tuberculosis.[21]

More out of necessity than choice since he was himself a widower, Lamar was an ardent pursuer of pretty women, especially widows. Ruggedly handsome and with a prominent square jaw, Lamar was a force to be reckoned with by a recent widow. As could be expected, attractive, wealthy widows were Lamar's targets of choice, revealing his desire to establish a long-term relationship and to make a suitable match. When Stephen Fuller Austin's cousin, Mary Austin Holley, who had been born in New Haven, Connecticut, like Emily D. West, visited Texas in the fall of 1837, Lamar eagerly sought the attentions of the refined relative of a man whom he greatly admired. The finely-educated, aristocratic Lamar, who "looked as French as his name," desired a new wife, and applied his charm to Mary with heavy doses.

The cultured and esteemed head of the Philosophical Society of Texas, he had tired of the dreary bachelor's life at the popular Brazoria Inn and boardinghouse, a longtime "center for [those] seeking Texas's independence," operated by Jane Long, who was the widow of Dr. James Long, one of the most diehard revolutionaries in Texas.[22]

With no fanfare and largely unnoticed in the summer of 1837, Emily D. West finally departed Texas, where so many of her hopes and dreams had died, thanks to the winds of war that had descended upon New Washington with a vengeance. Upon leaving Texas, what might have been some of Emily D. West's thoughts, when she finally embarked on the long journey back up the East Coast through the Atlantic's waters back to New York City, after her strange personal odyssey in Texas that she would never forget? What was she thinking about when the double-masted schooner sailed slowly out to sea under summer skies and then pushed beyond sight of the green, tree-lined Texas mainland and string of lengthy barrier islands, which disappeared in the distance, likely much to Emily's joy?

The sense of relief for Emily must have been great by this time. After all, Emily had survived the most risky and dangerous period of her life when only attempting to make a living in Texas. Emily almost certainly knew that she would never return to the troubled, seemingly-cursed, but picturesque land that had briefly been her home. Here, slavery thrived and the Texas cotton fields, that brought so much misery to blacks but wealth to whites, spanned to the horizon. She certainly felt fortunate to have gotten out alive. Best of all, Emily surely took comfort in the fact that she had not been enslaved like so many of her people on Texas soil.

While departing Texas for the last time and trying hard to forget the war's horrors, Emily would never forgot the natural beauty of Clopper's Point and the verdant gulf coast. But she would certainly not miss the turmoil, strife, and dangers of an untamed land seemingly blessed by God in bounty, but cursed by man's folly. Not only would Emily never again see Texas, but also she would never again witness the sickening and haunting sight—something that she could never forget—of men, women, and children working in the cotton fields under a broiling Texas sun. Even while aboard the vessel when sailing toward its ultimate destination of New York City, she was yet wracked by the searing memory of the horrors that she had seen both on and off the battlefield, and they were equally disturbing for a northern woman of compassion and faith.

In one of the strangest of the seemingly endless ironies of Texas history, Santa Anna's silk headquarters tent had been transported aboard the *Flash*. In truth, this was probably Emily's closest connection to the famous tent, where she supposedly unleashed the sexual beast in the middle-aged Santa Anna and allegedly set the stage for Houston's successful attack. Santa Anna's tent was sent by Morgan, proud of what his fellow Texians had achieved at San Jacinto, as a most memorable war "trophy of the valor of our brethren in Texas" to Swartwout aboard the *Flash*. It is not known, but Emily probably had no idea that the tent had become a precious Texas war trophy.

Most significant, Morgan made no mention of the alleged tryst between Santa Anna and Emily in this very tent during the lengthy correspondence, in which the tent was a subject more than once, between Morgan and Swartwout. In an April 20, 1837, letter to Morgan, Swartwout wrote to his friend who was the front man for the New Washington Association in Texas: "I must have thanked you for Santa Anna's Tent, which was recieved [*sic*] in due season [after the arrival of the *Flash* in New York harbor]. It is a great curiosity, and I mean, some day hence, to lend it, in your name to the Museum."[23]

Emily had plenty of good reason to feel thankful for having survived her time and a number of harrowing experiences in the midst of the Texas Revolution, which had swirled around her like a tornado. Even surviving the frontier experience was no small achievement for Emily, who was fortunate not to have been laid low by the prevalent ravages of disease that took a good many lives of Texians, especially along the Gulf Coast. Not even the "Father of Texas," Stephen F. Austin, had survived the omnipresent dangers. He had died of pneumonia only two days after Christmas 1836 at only age forty-three, while Emily was yet in Texas.

At this time, many Texian males who had been alive when Emily first arrived in December 1835 were now dead, having fallen in the struggle for Texas' independence. Hundreds of young Texian and United States volunteers had been consumed by the funeral pyres of the Alamo and Goliad. As William Fairfax Gray penned in his diary: "A great many widows here in Texas."[24]

Emily D. West had been living in Texas for only a year and a half, but she had witnessed some of the most stirring moments and dramatic events in Texas history. Even more, she had been both an observer and direct player in a number of unforgettable moments and dramatic scenes. And according to the mythology of "The Yellow Rose of Texas," this free African American women was alleged to have been at center stage in a key situation during the most decisive event of the Texas Revolution, the battle of San Jacinto.

In truth, when she finally departed Texas aboard the swift schooner, which was propelled by the fully-extended white canvas sails full of air from a soft breeze blowing east, Emily was not known for having done anything special or significant. She certainly was not a known or popular figure at this time in Texas or anywhere else. From all evidence, no knowledge or information existed about the alleged tryst between her and San Anna. Most of all, Emily was certainly no Texas heroine.

Therefore, when she left Texas forever in the summer of 1837, Emily D. West was just another black woman, almost invisible in the eyes of whites after the battle of San Jacinto. Therefore, Emily departed quietly, without notice and without fanfare. In the end, she was just another free black woman, among the relatively few free African American females in all Texas, who was neither noticed or acknowledged in any way by anyone in all of Texas. Quite simply, she had done nothing extraordinary, especially at San Jacinto, or worthy of notice, not even by her employer Morgan.

Nor was she acknowledged in the northeast or anywhere in the United States or Mexico for anything that she had done in either Texas or San Jacinto, especially on April 21, 1836. Once back in New York City after disembarking from the vessel, Emily simply emerged into the mainstream of the hustle and bustle of daily life. No one knows exactly what happened to Emily after her return to the vast urban sprawl that was New York City, which she reached in the early autumn of 1837. Perhaps Emily could now forget about the horrors of war and the worst of her experiences in Texas.[25]

Today we know more about the ultimate fate of the schooner *Flash*, which had earlier carried the news of Santa Anna's defeat at San Jacinto and the generalísimo's capture to New Orleans, than that of Emily D. West. Of course, this situation provided additional evidence that she had played no significant role at San Jacinto, because she was yet an unknown personage of absolute no popular recognition.

Indeed, while Morgan detailed the demise of the *Flash* in his May 3, 1837, letter from his beloved Orange Grove plantation to Swartwout in New York City, he continued to make no mention of Emily D. West, almost as if she never existed at all, even though he had brought her to Texas aboard the same vessel and she had worked under him for months. Most of all, Morgan wrote nothing about what would have been the most famous tryst in all Texas history. On the return trip from New York City the sad end of the *Flash* finally came when the "drunken vagabond" pilot stranded the vessel, sold off the cargo worth $12,000, collected a nice profit from his ill-gotten gains, and disappeared into the Spanish moss–draped woodlands and from the pages of history.[26]

After her dangerous, but unforgettable, sojourn on the unruly southwest frontier, Emily D. West now became just another face in the crowd. She was just another black woman passing by in the noisy streets, shopping at the busy marketplace, and living in the ill-heated dark brick tenements of the low rent district on Manhattan's Lower East Side, where generations of immigrants had been confined. In the end and as before she journeyed to Texas, Emily once again became an ordinary woman of color who was attempting to survive in a harsh urban world as best she could, largely because of nothing more than her race. But as a free and literate black woman of ability, she maintained a sense of pride and dignity, despite all of the adversity and challenges, thanks to her strong religious faith.

Very few, if any, people, black or white, in bustling New York City knew that she had once been a pioneer woman in the faraway Texas frontier and had been a firsthand eyewitness to one of the most important battles in American history. Emily D. West at least stood out in her own distinctive way of thinking. She was now very much changed because of where she had been, what she had accomplished, and the nature of her unique, harrowing experiences at a time when few people believed that a black woman possessed even an ounce of courage or resourcefulness, or an enterprising nature, especially on the western frontier.

It was most ironic that an obscure free black woman would thereafter be remembered by posterity—thanks to a single highly questionable, unverified reference to a mythical woman of color who allegedly caused Santa Anna to fall from grace at San Jacinto and lose all of Texas. But in fact what generations of Texans and Americans fell in love with and embraced as a genuine Texas folk heroine was not at all the real Emily D. West. Instead, they embraced the colorful myth of the "Yellow Rose of Texas," while forgetting all about the real person: the literate, ambitious, hard-working free black woman, who possessed the western pioneering spirit and an adventuresome nature that caused her to migrate to the Texas frontier far from her native New England and New York City antecedents and abolitionist connections. By this time, Emily was most of all a survivor of harrowing experiences and a good many close calls.

Quite simply, the myth of the "Yellow Rose of Texas" has thoroughly contradicted the truth that Emily was anything but a lowly, illiterate slave of master Morgan. And she was definitely not a person who would have assisted the Texas cause out of a so-called patriotic sense of duty in what was actually one of the great land grabs in history and to further the spread of slavery across Texas. Instead, she was a proud, independent, and free black woman who thought for herself and acted according to her principles and beliefs. And, most of all, she was decidedly against slavery and any cause or people that perpetuated it.

Therefore, to play her imaginary patriotic part as a Texas heroine on April 21, 1836, that became the core foundation of the Texas creation myth, the real Emily had to first lose her true identity, last name, free status, abolitionist connections, literacy, educational background, and even her African appearance and physical characteristics: the systematic erasing, silencing, and eradication of the authentic Emily D. West, which was literally a whitewashing of the authentic person, the free woman from the northeast. In one of the greatest ironies of the myth of "The Yellow Rose of Texas," the authentic story of the real Emily D. West, the actual free person of color, was actually more interesting and fascinating than the mythical Emily Morgan, the lowly slave who allegedly changed the course of Texas history with sex at San Jacinto.

Quite simply and despite the mysterious 58-word paragraph allegedly written by Houston, taken from an undated and non-extant letter, in the Bollaert Papers, the story of the alluring, beautiful "Yellow Rose of Texas" and how her alleged tryst with Santa Anna allowed Houston to surprise the Mexican Army and reap a decisive victory at San Jacinto has been one of the most popular, romantic, and colorful myths, based primarily on circumstantial evidence, rumor, and gossip, not only of the highly-romanticized Texas Revolution but also of Texas and American history.[27]

Epilogue

Unfortunately, practically nothing is known of Emily's life upon her return to the north, after her harrowing experiences on the Texas frontier in the midst of a violent revolution in which she was in peril more than once. She narrowly survived the Texas Revolution, in which so many United States volunteers had met tragic fates. This was no small accomplishment under the circumstances, especially for a black woman caught in the vortex of the largest and most important battle of the Texas Revolution.

After her return to the United States, Emily could also look back with pride on what she had learned and experienced during her risky sojourn in Texas, however. In her own personal odyssey to the distant western frontier just after the beginning of the Texas Revolution and then back again after the war's conclusion, Emily had come full circle by returning to everyday life and a relative quiet, mundane existence in New York City, from where she had departed with such high hopes for a new life and fresh start in the fall of 1835.[1]

Evidently, Emily yet had some family members back in New York City, and almost certainly abolitionist friends, black and white and associates of Jocelyn, whom she was probably eager to see after an absence of more than a year. Surely weary from her Texas adventure in the unruly southwest and a wartime environment, Emily returned home in a subtle and quiet personal triumph of sorts, basking in a measure of satisfaction and sense of accomplishment in regard to her memorable experiences. Emily had gained more experience and greater knowledge about the world and the people in it, now including Tejanos and Mexicans, whom she had not known before arriving in Texas. In a learning experience, she gained some empathy, insight, and understanding of these distinctive Latino people of a different culture and heritage.

And now upon returning to New York City, perhaps Emily D. West even had some money in her pocket from her around four months of work in New Washington. She had faithfully fulfilled her contractual obligations until New Washington had been burned down upon Santa Anna's orders, despite knowing that the war was heading her way. And, of course, Emily had grown a good deal wiser about a good many things, if not a bit world weary by this time. Several years after she departed the Texas frontier, the 1840 Census revealed that Emily was yet living in New York City that she now called home. Here, Emily became an anonymous figure in the midst of the large free black community of the bustling commercial city that offered a degree of economic opportunity, especially domestic work, to free black women.[2]

No one knows of what became of Emily D. West in the upcoming decades. But to be sure, no matter where she lived or went in her later years, Emily remembered her eventful days in Texas, as they had become a part of her very being. From that searing experience, Emily surely had gained and felt a sense of pride in what she had seen and endured in faraway Texas when swept by the horrors of war. She had lived to tell the tale—not of "The Yellow

Rose of Texas"—but a story of simple survival. In the years to come, Emily may have found the security and peace that had eluded her in Texas during one of the most eventful and turbulent periods of her life.

How would Emily D. West have reacted had she known that she was destined to become a popular Texas heroine and the sensational subject of one of the most colorful, romanticized, and fictionalized stories in all Texas history, the "Yellow Rose of Texas"? Would she be amused? Shocked and disgusted? The answer lies only in speculation, as the story and its spread in Texas was entirely unknown to her.

The alleged tryst was not documented by anyone in either Texas or Mexico, except more than ten decades later as an obscure 58-word footnote, created by the mid–Twentieth Century editors of *William Bollaert's Texas* and not part of Bollaert's narrative. This reference only appeared in *William Bollaert's Texas* after it was taken by the editors from an obscure reference written by Bollaert in the margin of a page in Bollaert's original, unpublished manuscript and not included in the original narrative. It was supposedly taken verbatim from an alleged Houston letter to a "friend," who was not even Bollaert, instead of originating from an original, detailed account written about by Bollaert, despite the fact that his livelihood, ambition, and reputation depended upon his being a fanciful storyteller. Therefore, apparently no one knew anything about the sensational story of the mysterious "Emily" for more than a century, not only because nothing was published about her until 1956, but also because the alleged liaison at San Jacinto existed in no other accounts, especially contemporary and primary sources on either side of the Rio Grande.[3]

Historian Jack Johnson was correct when he concluded that the story of the Santa Anna and Emily tryst, as revealed in the alleged Houston letter, was most likely only "an example of Houston's droll humor at the expense of a gullible Englishman," William Bollaert.[4] Therefore, this fine historian summarized quite correctly how the story of "The Yellow Rose of Texas" was just one of many colorful, "entertaining yarns" of Texas history.[5]

But a dark side of the legend existed, which in part explained its latter-day popularity and widespread acceptance. All in all, the myth has rested primarily upon a racial theme and long-existing racial stereotypes in American society, which were most infamously exhibited in blatant form in David W. Griffith's *The Birth of a Nation* (1915).[6]

The Santa Anna–Emily story became a Texas creation myth more than a century after the battle of San Jacinto. It came to life in large part because it was first a popular song—originally a jaunty tune sung by hardworking slaves toiling in the cotton fields and then resurrected as a mid–Nineteenth Century minstrel song played by black performers and later popularized by Mitch Miller in 1955, more than a full century later—and colorful, bawdy story and Texas tall tale that was almost certainly unknown to Emily in her lifetime. This woman who hated slavery with a passion could never have guessed that she would become the subject of what would become one of the most iconic songs in modern Texas and a popular heroine of a Texas in which slavery thrived. During her lifetime, Emily D. West almost certainly never heard some of the most famous words ever spoken in Texas history:

> There's a yellow girl in Texas
> That I'm going down to see
> No other darkies know her,
> No darkey, only me
> She cried so when I left her

> That it like to broke my heart,
> And if I only find her,
> We never more will part[7]

More than sixteen years after Emily departed Texas and sailed back to New York City, the first published lyrics of the popular song "The Yellow Rose of Texas" were published in *Christy's Plantation Melodies* by Edwin P. Christy in Philadelphia in 1853. He was the founder of the popular Christy Minstrels, which consisted of white performers in black-face playing slave songs to white audiences, who could not get enough of this form of popular entertainment. In performing "The Yellow Rose of Texas," a central theme of the Christy Minstrels was that of the love of a black man, or "darkey," for a beautiful mulatto woman with an abundance of white blood: the usual, traditional bestowing of white physical features and looks to a woman of African descent in a process that has long emphasized the stereotypical, white-based standards of feminine beauty in America in a process that has continued unabated to this day.

As deemed by America's predominate cultural values and traditional standards of feminine attractiveness, Emily was part of the typical process of the whitening of the black woman to conform to what was widely viewed as the epitome of beauty, at least in white eyes. Therefore, this legendary beauty, in which white blood and features dominated, was lavishly praised in song in glowing tributes to the light-hued beauty of the fair roses (mulatto women) of Alabama, Texas, Virginia, and Maryland. Indeed, the popular performers of Christy's Minstrels sang not only about "The Yellow Rose of Texas," but also "The Rose of Alabama," "The Rose of Baltimore," and "The Virginia Rose Bud"—perhaps the cynical meaning and sexual analogy (bud as equating to vagina) of the long mysterious, cryptic words that summarized the life of John Foster Kane, from the much later movie *Citizen Kane* emphasized.[8]

The traditional Southern-based analogy of beautiful mulatto women (after all these were the daughters of white fathers) to flowering roses was contained in the pages of the September 18, 1855, issue of the *San Antonio Herald*, San Antonio, Texas, which had become a thoroughly Southern city in regard to the culture and sentiment of the power elite during the antebellum period, thanks to Houston's victory at San Jacinto, but the reference was not complimentary. Reflecting popular beliefs in white American society, this passage mentioned "Colored ladies [who] were born to blush unseen" because of their dark hue but not "unsmelt," which was a racial slur in keeping with the day's common racial stereotypes.[9]

References of the popular analogies between mulatto women and the rose existed in Texas long before the antebellum period, extending all the way back to pioneering days on the Texas frontier. For instance, one early popular song sung by the slaves in the sun-baked cotton fields of Texas (and almost certainly also in the Deep South before these same slaves were brought into Texas) was then picked up by Austin's white colonists as early as 1827. Judge Robert Alpin Williams, one fiery independence-minded leader of revolutionary Texas, performed a minstrel show in San Felipe de Austin nearly a decade before the Texas Revolution. He sang a song that was comparable in many ways to "The Yellow Rose of Texas" tune in regard to describing a plaintive courtship between two African Americans and the beauty of an unforgettable black woman.[10]

But interestingly the love object of the 1827 song sung in the Texas settlements in the Brazos River country was not a mulatto beauty, but in fact, "Rose, Rose; coal black Rose."[11] This dark beauty, with traditional African features and non-white standards of beauty, was nothing like what the whites of Christy's Minstrels sang about in regard to the enchanting beauty of the light-hued "roses" from Alabama, Virginia, Maryland, and Texas. Clearly, to appeal to a white audience, Christy had simply imposed his own cultural and racial definition of feminine beauty when it came to black women. Of course, this traditional cultural standard of female beauty that prevailed across America was something that the white audience of the day (and today as well) could easily relate to and identify with, as Christy well knew.[12]

Therefore, as presented in the old slave song, a real and original dark-skinned beauty of the slave quarters of the South was significantly altered into a light-skinned beauty of popular myth, the famed "Yellow Rose of Texas." Not surprisingly, it was then all but inevitable that modern writers and historians, both men and women, since the 1950s, and the popular Mitch Miller song, "completely changed the meaning and origins of 'The Yellow Rose of Texas' and laid the foundation for one of the most enduring and sensational inaccuracies in Texas history."[13]

In many ways, the light-skinned Emily of romantic myth was needed to validate the Texas creation story, bestowing upon a war for slavery (the Texas Revolution) and a slave-owning republic and state (one that seceded from the Union and joined the Confederacy in February 1861) a measure of moral legitimacy instead of a dark moral stain, thanks to slavery and its tragic legacy. The beautiful, light-skinned Emily of "The Yellow Rose of Texas" myth also has an analogy in another beautiful woman, Helen of Troy, who was immortalized by Homer in the *Iliad*. Like the start of this ancient war of legend between the Greeks and the Trojans, Homer explained how Troy's ultimate destruction stemmed from the radiance of Helen's beauty.

Homer spoke most eloquently of a morality play and cautionary tale of the legendary immoral woman—even Helen deemed herself a "whore"—and the severe, if not inevitable, consequences of unrestrained sexual excesses that defied the accepted moral code. In this moralistic sense, and according to the myth, Emily was Mexico's Helen of Troy, who paved the way for Santa Anna's disaster at San Jacinto and the permanent loss of Texas, which then later led to the loss of one-half of Mexico's territory as the result of American victory in the Mexican–American War.[14]

It is not known whether Emily either knew about or attended a historic meeting of independent-minded women in the town of Seneca Falls, New York, on July 19–20, 1848, when Emily was age forty-seven. Writing words that Emily certainly would have been delighted to hear, the delegates of this women's rights convention, the first of its kind in the western world and known as the Seneca Falls Convention, which was attended by Frederick Douglass, proclaimed: "We hold these truths to be self-evident: that all men and women are created equal."[15]

Despite the severe limitations and restrictions that society and her own country, the land of her birth, had so fairly placed upon her, the twisting course of the remarkable life of Emily D. West has provided a timeless and inspirational example that is yet valid and most important today. Despite the seemingly insurmountable obstacles and oppressions that she faced in life, Emily was able to persevere through it all and survive with her dignity intact. In the end, this proud and free black woman was not defeated or destroyed. Instead of becoming a victim in life, Emily created and found a special meaning, beauty, and dignity in her life, despite all of the adversity that she faced with courage and strength of character.

Chapter Notes

Chapter I

1. James E. Crisp, *Sleuthing the Alamo: Davy Crockett's Last Stand, and Other Mysteries of the Texas Revolution* (Oxford: Oxford University Press, 2005), pp. 188–191; Holly Beachley Brear, *Inherit the Alamo: Myth and Ritual at an American Shrine* (Austin: University of Texas Press, 1995), pp. 45–49, 53–54; James Lutzweiler, "Emily D. West and the Yellow Prose of Texas: A Primer on Some Primary Documents and Their Doctoring," a paper presented at the 100th Anniversary of the Texas State Historical Association on 8 March 1997, New Haven Museum and Historical Society, New Haven, Connecticut.

2. James W. Loewen, *Lies Across America: What Our Historic Sties Get Wrong* (New York: Simon and Schuster, 2000), pp. 1–28.

3. William C. Davis, *Three Roads to the Alamo: The Lives and Fortunes of David Crockett, James Bowie, and William Barret Travis* (New York: Harper Collins, 1998), p. xi.

4. "Emily D. West," Handbook of Texas Online; Crisp, *Sleuthing the Alamo*, pp. 188–195; Brear, *Inherit the Alamo*, pp. 53–54; Lutzweiler, "Emily D. West and the Yellow Prose of Texas," New Haven Museum and Historical Society; Philip French, *Westerns* (New York: The Viking Press, 1973), pp. 18, 31, 157, 159; Phillip Thomas Tucker, *Exodus from the Alamo: The Anatomy of the Last Stand Myth* (Philadelphia: Casemate, 2010), pp. viii–343.

5. Randolph B. Campbell, *An Empire for Slavery: The Peculiar Institution in Texas, 1821–1865* (Baton Rouge: Louisiana State University Press, 1989), pp. 1–4; Lutzweiler, "Emily D. West and the Yellow Prose of Texas," New Haven Museum and Historical Society; French, *Westerns*, pp. 9–167.

6. Campbell, *An Empire for Slavery*, pp. 1–4; Trudier Harris, "'The Yellow Rose of Texas': A Different View," *Callaloo*, Vol. 20, No. 1 (Winter 1997), pp. 10–18; Brear, *Inherit the Alamo*, pp. 49–50; French, *Westerns*, pp. 14, 101–103.

7. Crisp, *Sleuthing the Alamo*, pp. 188–193; Trudier Harris, "'The Yellow Rose of Texas': A Different View," *Callaloo*, pp. 10–18; Campbell, *An Empire for Slavery*, pp. 1–230; Brear, *Inherit the Alamo*, pp. 49–50; Lutzweiler, "Emily D. West and the Yellow Prose of Texas," New Haven Museum and Historical Society; Robert L. Scheina, *Santa Anna: A Curse Upon Mexico* (Washington, D.C.: Brassey's, 2000), p. 30; J. M. Roberts, *A Short History of the World* (Oxford: Oxford University Press, 1993), pp. 375–376.

8. Denise McVea, *Making Myth of Emily: Emily West de Zavala and the Yellow Rose of Texas Legend* (San Antonio: Auris Books, 2006), pp. 1–176; Carmen Goldthwaite, "Emily D. West (Morgan), 'The Yellow Rose of Texas,'" in Glenda Riley and Richard W. Etulain, editors, *Wild Women of the Old West* (Golden, Colorado: Fulcrum, 2003), pp. 30–34, 40; "Emily D. West," The Handbook of Texas Online; Crisp, *Sleuthing the Alamo*, pp. 188–195; "Lorenzo D. Zavala," The Handbook of Texas Online; William Fairfax Gray, *Diary of Col. Wm. Fairfax Gray, From Virginia to Texas, 1835* (Houston: Fletcher Young, 1965), p. 132; Robert Austin Warner, *New Haven Negroes: A Social History* (New York: Arno Press and the New York Times, 1969), pp. xi–104; Eric Hinderaker and Peter C. Mancall, *At the Edge of Empire: The Backcountry in British North America* (Baltimore: John Hopkins University Press, 2003), pp. 81–84; Colin G. Calloway, *The American Revolution in Indian Country: Crisis and Diversity in Native American Communities* (Cambridge: Cambridge University Press, 1995), pp. 17, 129–130, 140–141; Bruce A. Glasrud and Merline Pitre, editors, *Black Women in Texas History* (College Station: Texas A&M University Press, 2008), p. 13–14; Brear, *Inherit the Alamo*, pp. 45, 49–50; Lutzweiler, "Emily D. West and the Yellow Prose of Texas," New Haven Museum and Historical Society; Sue Eakin and Joseph Logsdon, eds., *Twelve Years A Slave by Solomon Northup* (Baton Rouge: Louisiana State University Press, 1968), p. 4; Nancy Bonvillain, *The Mohawk* (Philadelphia: Chelsea House 2005), pp. 23, 53–57; Nell Irvin Painter, *Creating Black Americans: African-American History and its Meanings, 1619 to the Present* (Oxford: Oxford University Press, 2006), p. 59; Andrew Hacker, *Two Nations: Black and White, Separate, Hostile, Unequal* (New York: Ballantine, 1995), pp. 3–21.

9. Brear, *Inherit the Alamo*, pp. 45–47; Hacker, *Two Nations*, pp. 3–245.

10. W. Eugene Hollon, editor, *William Bollaert's Texas* (Norman: University of Oklahoma Press, 1989), pp. ix–xxvi, p. 108, note 24; Lutzweiler, "Emily D. West and the Yellow Prose of Texas," New Haven Museum and Historical Society; Lawrence Goldstone, *Dark Bargain: Slavery, Profits, and the Struggle for the Constitution* (New York: Walker, 2005), pp. 11–195; Stephen L. Hardin, *Texian Iliad: A Military History of the Texas Revolution* (Austin: University of Texas Press, 1994), p. 214; Hacker, *Two Nations*, pp. 3–245.

11. Rebecca Smith Lee, *Mary Austin Holley: A Biography* (Austin: University of Texas Press, 1962), pp. 4; "Stephen Fuller Austin," The Handbook of Texas Online; "Emily D. West," The Handbook of Texas Online.

12. Lee, *Mary Austin Holley*, p. 4; "Stephen Fuller Austin," The Handbook of Texas Online.

13. Warner, *New Haven Negroes*, pp. 1–4, 45–46; Lee, *Mary Austin Holley*, pp. 4, 6–7, 9, 25; Trevor Burnard, *Mastery, Tyranny, and Desire: Thomas Thistlewood and His Slaves in the Anglo-Jamaican World* (Chapel Hill: University of North Carolina Press, 2004), pp. 2–22, 42–43; *New York Times*, August 19, 1879; Milton Meltzer, *Slavery: A World History* (New York: Da Capo Press, 1993), pp. 157–159; John Demos, editor, *Remarkable Providences, 1600–1760* (New York: George Braziller, 1972), p. 14; Walter A. McDougall, *Promised Land, Crusader State: The American Encounter with the World Since 1776* (New York: Houghton Mifflin, 1997), p. 17; Goldstone, *Dark Bargain*, p. 79; Leonard L. Richards, *"Gentlemen of Property and Standing": Anti-Abolition Mobs in Jacksonian America* (Oxford: Oxford University Press, 1970), p. 50; Center Church on-the-Green, Archives of the First Church of Christ, New Haven, Connecticut; Eric Jaffe, *The King's Best Highway: The Lost History of the Boston Post Road, The Route That Made America* (New York: Scribner, 2010), pp. 4–8; Richard S. Dunn, *Sugar and Slaves: The Rise of the Planter Class in the English West Indies, 1624–1713* (New York: W. W. Norton, 1972), pp. 50, 84–223; Roberts, *A Short History of the World*, pp. 375–376; David S. Landes, *The Wealth and Poverty of Nations* (New York: W. W. Norton, 1998), pp. 119–120; *Texas Gazette*, San Felipe de Austin, Texas, January 23 and 30, 1830.

14. Warner, *New Haven Negroes*, pp. 4–5; Yale University authors, "The Story of Yale Abolitionists," *Yale, Slavery and Abolition* essay series, Yale University Library, New Haven, Connecticut; Michael Lee Lanning, *Defenders of Liberty: African Americans in the Revolutionary War* (New York: Citadel Press, 2000), p. 198.

15. W. Jeffrey Bolster, *Black Jacks: African American Seamen in the Age of Sail* (Cambridge: Harvard University Press, 1997), pp. 2–92.153–154.

16. Ibid., 153–154; Gary Zaboly, *American Colonial Ranger: The Northern Colonies, 1724–1764* (Oxford: Osprey, 2004), pp. 4–50; Thomas Fleming, *Liberty! The American Revolution* (New York: Viking, 1997), pp. 151–152, 302; John R. Cuneo, *Robert Rogers of the Rangers* (New York: Richardson and Steirman, 1987), pp. 17–137.

17. George Athan Billas, *General John Glover and his Marblehead Mariners* (New York: Henry Holt, 1960), pp. 3–15, 68–69, 96–109; Mark Puls, *Henry Knox: Visionary General of the American Revolution* (New York: Palgrave MacMillan, 2008), pp. 60, 74–75.

18. *Connecticut Gazette*, New London, Connecticut, September 7, 14, and 21, 1781; Charles Allyn, *Battle of Groton Heights, September 6, 1781* (Mystic: Seaport Autographs, 1999), pp. 10–172; *Maryland Gazette*, September 27 and October 4, 1781, Annapolis, Maryland; Warner, *New Haven Negroes*, p. 39; Mark Mayo Boatner III, *Encyclopedia of the American Revolution* (New York: David McKay, 1966), pp. 699–700; Bruce Chadwick, *George Washington's War* (Naperville: Sourcebooks, 2005), p. 468; Robert B. Edgerton, *Hidden Heroism: Black Soldiers in America's Wars* (Boulder: Westview Press, 2001), pp. 16–17.

19. Warner, *New Haven Negroes*, p. 39; "Return J. Meigs, Sr.," Wikipedia, internet.

20. Warner, *New Haven Negroes*, pp. 39–41; Ralph Ketcham, *From Colony to Country: The Revolution in American Thought 1750–1820* (New York: Macmillan, 1974), pp. 36–37, 268; John Keane, *Tom Paine: A Political Life* (Boston: Little, Brown, 1995), pp. 99–100, 192–196

21. Keane, *Tom Paine*, p. 99.

22. Ibid., p. 134.

23. Warner, *New Haven Negroes*, pp. v, xi, 5, 7, 40.

24. Ibid., pp. 10–11; Bolster, *Black Jacks*, pp. 102–117.

25. Warner, *New Haven Negroes*, p. 42.

Chapter II

1. "Emily D. West," The Handbook of Texas Online; Lee, *Mary Austin Holley*, pp. 4–7; Kenneth M. Stampp, *The Peculiar Institution: Slavery in the Ante-Bellum South* (New York: Vintage Books, 1956), pp. 74, 94, 258; Lee, *Mary Austin Holley*, pp. 6–7; Crisp, *Sleuthing the Alamo*, p. 193; New Haven Telephone Directories, 2007 and 2008, New Haven Library, New Haven, Connecticut; Linda Wolfe Keister, *The Complete Guide to African-American Baby Names* (New York: Penguin Group, 1998), p. 71; Lutzweiler, "Emily D. West and the Yellow Prose of Texas," New Haven Museum and Historical Society; Jaffe, *The King's Best Highway*, pp. 4–7; Lanning, *Defenders of Liberty*, pp. x–49, 60–119.

2. Warner, *New Haven Negroes*, p. 301.

3. Warner, *New Haven Negroes*, pp. 18, 27–31, 33–34, 196–198, 301; "Emily D. West," The Handbook of Texas Online; Lutzweiler, "Emily D. West and the Yellow Prose of Texas," New Haven Museum and Historical Society; Susanne Everett, *History of Slavery* (London: Bison Books, 1978), pp. 32–34.

4. Everett, *The History of Slavery*, p. 226.

5. Warner, *New Haven Negroes*, pp. 1,15, 19–24,

27, 31–32; The Hill (New Haven), Wikipedia, internet.

6. Winthrop D. Jordan, *The White Man's Burden: Historical Origins of Racism in the United States* (Oxford: Oxford University Press, 1974), pp. 88–98; Stampp, *The Peculiar Institution*, pp. 371–377; Paul Johnson, *A History of the Jews* (New York: Harper and Row, 1987), pp. 13–79.

7. Stampp, *The Peculiar Institution*, pp. 371–372.

8. Ibid.; Painter, *Creating Black Americans*, pp. 45–47; Nathan Irvin Huggins, *Black Odyssey: The Afro-American Ordeal in Slavery* (New York: Pantheon Books, 1977), pp. 72–73; Jordan, *The White Man's Burden*, p. 98; Frederick Merk, *History of the Westward Movement* (New York: Alfred A. Knopf, 1978), p. 280.

9. Jordan, *The White Man's Burden*, p. 98; George Whitefield, Christian Classics Ethereal Library, internet.

10. *New York Times*, New York, August 19, 1879; *The National Cyclopaedia of American Biography* (New York: James T. White, 1895), p. 326; "Emily D. West," The Handbook of Texas Online; Warner, *New Haven Negroes*, pp. 6–7, 46, 80, 196–198; Lutzweiler, "Emily D. West and the Yellow Prose of Texas," New Haven Museum and Historical Society.

11. *New York Times*, August 19, 1879; Crisp, *Sleuthing the Alamo*, p. 193; Warner, *New Haven Negroes*, pp. v, 6–7, 11, 46, 80, 107, 301; Yale University authors, "Simeon Jocelyn," *Yale, Slavery and Abolition* essay series, Yale University Library; Yale University authors, "The 'Negro' College," *Yale, Slavery and Abolition* essay series, Yale University Library; Center Church on-the-Green, Archives of the First Church of Christ, NH; Doris B. Townshend, Center Church historian, to author, October 24, 2008.

12. Warner, *New Haven Negroes*, pp. 28–29, 48, 80; Yale University authors, "Simeon Jocelyn," *Yale, Slavery and Abolition* essay series, Yale University Library; Center Church on-the-Green, Archives of the First Church of Christ, NH.

13. Herman Melville, *Moby-Dick* (New York: Barnes and Noble, 1993), p. 7.

14. Doris B. Townshend, Center Church historian, to author, October 24, 2008.

15. Lutzweiler, "Emily D. West and the Yellow Prose of Texas," New Haven Museum and Historical Society; *The National Cyclopaedia of American Biography*, p. 326; Lee, *Mary Austin Holley*, pp. 9, 25; Warner, *New Haven Negroes*, pp. 71–72, 80–85, 90, 92, 301; Yale University authors, "The Story of Yale Abolitionists," *Yale, Slavery and Abolition* essay series, Yale University Library; Crisp, *Sleuthing the Alamo*, pp. 193–194; "Emily D. West," The Handbook of Texas Online; Dunn, "One More Piece of the Puzzle," *The Compass Rose*; Roberts, *A Short History of the World*, p. 376.

16. *New York Times*, August 19, 1879.

17. "Emily D. West," The Handbook of Texas Online; Warner, *New Haven Negroes*, pp. 45–46.

18. "Trowbridge Square Historic District Study," The New Haven Preservation Trust, New Haven, Connecticut; Warner, *New Haven Negroes*, pp. 28–29, 31, 101; Demos, ed., *Remarkable Providences, 1600–1760*, p. 14; Roberts, *A Short History of the World*, p. 376.

19. Charles M. Wiltse, *The New Nation, 1800–1845* (New York: Hill and Wang, 1961), p. 158; Masur, *1831*, pp. 9–216.

20. Goldstone, *Dark Bargain*, pp. 16–195; Louis P. Masur, *1831*, pp. 22–23.

21. Masur, *1831*, pp. 9–216; *The National Cyclopaedia of American Biography*, p. 326; Yale University authors, "Simeon Jocelyn," *Yale, Slavery and Abolition* essay series, Yale University Library; "Trowbridge Square Historic District Study," the New Haven Preservation Trust; Yale University authors, "The 'Negro' College," *Yale, Slavery and Abolition* essay series, Yale University Library; Warner, *New Haven Negroes*, pp. 48, 53–54; Keane, *Tom Paine*, p. 92; Roberts, *A Short History of the World*, p. 376.

22. Yale University authors, "The 'Negro' College," *Yale, Slavery and Abolition* essay series, Yale University Library.

23. Ibid.; *The National Cyclopaedia of American Biography*, p. 326; Warner, *New Haven Negroes*, pp. 55–56; Masur, *1831*, pp. 26–27; Yale University authors, "Simeon Jocelyn," *Yale, Slavery and Abolition* essay series, Yale University Library.

24. *The Richmond Enquirer*, Richmond, Virginia, August 26, 30, September 2, 12, 20, 27, and October 4, 1831; *The Constitutional Whig*, Richmond, Virginia, September 26, 1831; *The Liberator*, Boston, Massachusetts, September 3 and 17 and October 1, 1831; *Maryland Gazette*, September 1, 1831; John B. Duff and Peter M. Mitchell, editors, *The Nat Turner Rebellion: The Historical Event and the Modern Controversy* (New York: Harper and Row, 1971), pp. 11–112; Henry Irving Tragle, *The Southampton Slave Revolt of 1831: A Compilation of Source Material, including the full text of the 'Confessions' of Nat Turner* (New York: Vintage Books, 1971), pp. 3–276; Warner, *New Haven Negroes*, pp. 55–57; Richards, *"Gentlemen of Property and Standing,"* pp. 37–38; *New York Times*, July 21, 1860; Masur, *1831*, pp. 22–36; Stephen B. Oates, *The Fires of Jubilee: Nat Turner's Fierce Rebellion* (New York: Harper and Row, 1975), pp. 69–143.

25. Duff and Mitchell, eds., *The Nat Turner Rebellion*, pp. 39–41.

26. Masur, *1831*, p. 30.

27. Ibid., pp. 10, 30–34.

28. *Connecticut Journal*, New Haven, Connecticut, October 11 and 21, 1831, and November 1, 1831; Richards, *"Gentlemen of Property and Standing,"* pp. 38–40.

29. Warner, *New Haven Negroes*, p. 64; David Buckley, *The Right to be Proud: A Brief Guide to Jamaican Heritage Sites* (Kingston: MAPCO Business Printers, 2005), p. 14; The Gleaner, *Geography and History of Jamaica* (Kingston: The Gleaner, 1995), pp. 92–93; J. H. Parry, Philip Sherlock, and Anthony Maingot, *A Short History of the West Indies* (New York:

St. Martin's Press, 1987), pp. 160–161; Roberts, *A Short History of the World*, p. 376.

30. Scot French, *The Rebellious Slave: Nat Turner in American Memory* (Boston: Houghton Mifflin, 2004), p. 71.

31. Ibid.

32. Yale University authors, "Colonization," *Yale, Slavery and Abolition*, essay series, Yale University Library.

33. Warner, *New Haven Negroes*, p. 73; Roberts, *A Short History of the World*, p. 376.

34. *The National Cyclopaedia of American Biography*, p. 326.

35. Warner, *New Haven Negroes*, p. 28–32; Yale University authors, "Simeon Jocelyn," *Yale, Slavery and Abolition* essay series, Yale University Library; "The Hill (New Haven)" Wikipedia; Lutzweiler, "Emily D. West and the Yellow Prose of Texas," New Haven Museum and Historical Society.

36. *New York Times*, August 19, 1879; Yale University authors, "Simeon Jocelyn," *Yale, Slavery and Abolition* essay series, Yale University Library.

37. *Amistad—"Give Us Free": A Celebration of the Film by Steven Spielberg* (New York: Newmarket Press, 1998), pp. 17–37; Warner, *New Haven Negroes*, pp. 66–68; Center Church on-the-Green, Archives of the First Church of Christ, New Haven; Karen Zeinert, *The Amistad Slave Revolt and American Abolition* (North Haven: Shoestring Press, 1997), pp. 1–89; Lutzweiler, "Emily D. West and the Yellow Prose of Texas," New Haven Museum and Historical Society.

38. Warner, *New Haven Negroes*, p. 73.

39. Yale University authors, "The Story of Yale Abolitionists," *Yale, Slavery and Abolition* essay series, Yale University Library.

40. Edgar J. McManus, *A History of Negro Slavery in New York* (Syracuse: Syracuse University Press, 1966), pp. 184–185; Warner, *New Haven Negroes*, pp. 45–46; Richards, "Gentlemen of Property and Standing," p. 40; Center Church on-the-Green, Archives of the First Church of Christ, New Haven; Jeff Dunn, "One More Piece of the Puzzle: Emily West in Special Collections," *The Compass Rose*, Vol. 19, No. 1 (Spring 2005); Lutzweiler, "Emily D. West and the Yellow Prose of Texas," New Haven Museum and Historical Society; Joseph J. Ellis, *Founding Brothers: The Revolutionary Generation* (New York: Vintage Books, 2000), pp. 22, 113.

41. "Emily D. West," The Handbook of Texas Online; Muir, "The Free Negro in Harris County, Texas," Southwestern Historical Quarterly Online, p. 5; Stephen L. Moore, *Eighteen Minutes: The Battle of San Jacinto and the Texas Independence Campaign* (Austin: Republic of Texas Press, 2004), pp. 237, 257; Riley and Etulain, eds., *Wild Women of the Old West*, p. 31; Dunn, "One More Piece of the Puzzle," *The Compass Rose*; Lutzweiler, "Emily D. West and the Yellow Prose of Texas," New Haven Museum and Historical Society; Doris Townshend, historian of Center Church, to author, October 24, 2008.

42. Eakin and Logsdon, editors, *Twelve Years a Slave by Solomon Northup*, pp. 4–23, 109–121.

43. Ernest Jerome Yancy, *Historical Lights of Liberia's Yesterday and Today* (New York: Herman Jaffe, 1954), pp. 14, 17–57; "Emily D. West," The Handbook of Texas Online; Warner, *New Haven Negroes*, p. 42; Roberts, *A Short History of the World*, p. 376.

44. Alwyn Barr, *Black Texans: A History of African Americans in Texas, 1528–1995* (Norman: University of Texas Press, 1973), pp. 5–6; Wiltze, *The New Nation*, pp. 157–158.

45. Herbert Asbury, *The Gangs of New York: An Informal History of the Underworld* (New York: Thunder's Mouth Press, 1998), pp. xii–xv, 5–10; "Emily D. West," The Handbook of Texas Online; Richards, "Gentlemen of Property and Standing," p. 154; Tyler Anbinder, *Five Points* (New York: Penguin Group, 2002), pp. 1–36; Lutzweiler, "Emily D. West and the Yellow Prose of Texas," New Haven Museum and Historical Society.

46. McManus, *A History of Negro Slavery in New York*, pp. 1–178; Anbinder, *Five Points*, pp. 9, 11, 16; Everett, *History of Slavery*, pp. 32–33.

47. *New York Times*, August 19, 1879; Warner, *New Haven Negroes*, pp. 65, 93; Yale University authors, "Simeon Jocelyn," *Yale, Slavery and Abolition* essay series, Yale University Library; Anbinder, *Five Points*, pp. 1–36.

48. Anbinder, *Five Points*, pp. 35–36.

49. Richards, "Gentlemen of Property and Standing," pp. 3–15.

50. Yale University authors, "Simeon Jocelyn," *Yale, Slavery and Abolition* essay series, Yale University Library; McManus, *A History of Negro Slavery in New York*, pp. 186–188; Richards, "Gentlemen of Property and Standing," pp. 30, 41–49, 113–122, 150–170; Anbinder, *Five Points*, 7–13, 23–26; Lutzweiler, "Emily D. West and the Yellow Prose of Texas," New Haven Museum and Historical Society; Johnson, *A History of the Jews*, pp. 113–116, 206–207, 217–229.

51. Richards, "Gentlemen of Property and Standing," pp. 16–19, 23, 25, 29–30; Anbinder, *Five Points*, pp. 23–26.

52. Richards, "Gentlemen of Property and Standing," pp. 50–81.

53. *New York Times*, December 15, 1907.

54. McManus, *A History of Negro Slavery in New York*, pp. 188–196; Buddy Levy, *American Legend: The Real-Life Adventures of David Crockett* (New York: Berkley Books, 2005), pp. 227–233; Riley and Etulain, eds., *Wild Women of the Old West*, p. 31; Anbinder, *Five Points*, pp. 35–36; Painter, *Creating Black Americans*, p. 72.

55. Masur, *1831*, pp. 25–26; Riley and Etulain, eds., *Wild Women of the Old West*, p. 31.

56. Masur, *1831*, pp. 35–38.

57. Ibid., p. 42; Riley and Etulain, eds., *Wild Women of the Old West*, p. 31; "Emily D. West," The Handbook of Texas Online.

58. Levy, *American Legend*, pp. 232–233; "Emily

D. West," The Handbook of Texas Online; Anbinder, *Five Points*, 2, 26–27; William Jay, *A View of the Action of the Federal Government, in Behalf of Slavery* (Miami: Mnemosyne, 1969), p. 20; Goldstone, *Dark Bargain*, pp. 1–195; Eakin and Logsdon, *Twelve Years a Slave by Solomon Northup*, pp. 4–23; Painter, *Creating Black America*, pp. 71–73, 84–89.

59. Jean Zimmerman, *The Women of the House: How a Colonial She-Merchant Built a Mansion, a Fortune, And a Dynasty* (New York: Harcourt, 2006), pp. 4–338.

60. Painter, *Creating Black Americans*, p. 95; "Emily D. West," The Handbook of Texas Online.

61. Lee, *Mary Austin Holley*, pp. 3–4, 38–254.

62. Ibid., p. 217.

63. Ibid.

64. Ibid., p. 219.

65. Ibid., p. 220.

66. Ibid., pp. 220–222.

67. Ibid., pp. 223–224, 229, 235.

68. Ibid., p. 233.

69. Ibid., p. 265.

Chapter III

1. Everett, *History of Slavery*, p. 226; Charlotte Forten Grimke (1837–1914), National Women's History Museum, internet; Painter, *Creating Black Americans*, p. 75.

2. Charlotte Forten Grimke (1837–1914), National Women's History Museum, internet; White, *Ar'n't I a Woman?*, pp. 157–160.

3. White; *Ar'n't I a Woman?*, p. 158.

4. Ibid., p. 160.

5. *New York Times*, August 19, 1879; Lee, *Mary Austin Holley*, pp. 4–7; "Morgan's Point, Texas," The Handbook of Texas Online; Muir, "The Free Negro in Harris County, Texas," Southwestern Historical Quarterly Online, p. 5; Crisp, *Sleuthing the Alamo*, pp. 192–193; Bass and Brunson, eds., *Fragile Empires, pp. xx–xxi, xxiii*; McVea, *Making Myth of Emily*, pp. 30, 127; "New Washington Association," The Handbook of Texas Online; Memorials and Petitions, petition of Diana Leonard, December 14, 1840, Texas State Library and Archives Commission, Austin, Texas; McVea, *Making Myth of Emily*, pp. 60–61, 66–71, 107–108, 112–116, 122; Riley and Etulain, eds., *Wild Women of the Old West*, pp. 30–32, 34; Painter, *Creating Black America*, pp. 71–72; Victor H. Treat, "William Goyens: Free Negro Entrepreneur," in Alwyn Barr and Robert A. Calvert, *Black Leaders, Texans for Their Times* (Austin: Texas State Historical Association, 1981), pp. 21, 24, 28; Alwyn Barr, *Black Texans: A History of African Americans in Texas, 1528–1995* (Norman: University of Oklahoma Press, 1996), pp. 3–4; Dunn, "One More Piece of the Puzzle," *The Compass Rose*; Anbinder, Five Points, pp. 1–2, 4, 10–17, 32; Lutzweiler, "Emily D. West and the Yellow Prose of Texas," New Haven Museum and Historical Society; Eakin and Logsdon, *Twelve Years a Slave by Solomon Northup*, pp. 4–23. "Greenbury Logan," Texas Black History Preservation Project: Documenting the Complete African American Experience in Texas, internet; David Barry Gaspar and David Patrick Geggus, *A Turbulent Time and the French Revolution and the Great Caribbean* (Bloomington: Indiana University Press, 1997), p. 214; "James Morgan," The Handbook of Texas Online; Roberts, *A Short History of the World*, p. 376; Randolph B. Campbell, *The Laws of Slavery in Texas* (Austin: University of Texas Press, 2010), pp. 3, 21–22; John Edward Weems with Jane Weems, *Dream of Empire: A History of the Republic of Texas, 1836–1846* (New York: Barnes and Noble, 1995), p. 12; "Emily D. West," The Handbook of Texas Online.

6. *New Bedford Mercury*, New Bedford, Massachusetts, November 20, 1835.

7. "New Washington Association," The Handbook of Texas Online.

8. "Emily D. West," The Handbook of Texas Online; Crystal Saee Ragsdale, *Women and Children of the Alamo* (Austin: State House Press, 1994), pp. 56–63; Lutzweiler, "Emily D. West and the Yellow Prose of Texas," New Haven Museum and Historical Society.

9. Lutzweiler, "Emily D. West and the Yellow Prose of Texas," New Haven Museum and Historical Society.

10. Ibid.; Painter, *Creating Black Americans*, pp. 72, 75; "James Morgan," The Handbook of Texas Online, internet; Eastern Argus, Portland, Maine, May 3, 1836; "New Washington Association," The Handbook of Texas Online.

11. Everett, *History of Slavery*, p. 226; Painter, *Creating Black Americans*, p. 75; "James Morgan," The Handbook of Texas Online.

12. "James Morgan," The Handbook of Texas Online; Lutzweiler, "Emily D. West and the Yellow Prose of Texas," New Haven Museum and Historical Society; Campbell, ed., *The Laws of Slavery in Texas*, p. 3.

13. Painter, *Creating Black Americans*, p. 70.

14. Richards, *"Gentlemen of Property and Standing,"* p. 22; Warner, *New Haven Negroes*, pp. 48–51, 83; Riley and Etulain, eds., *Wild Women of the Old West*, p. 31; Lutzweiler, "Emily D. West and the Yellow Prose of Texas," New Haven Museum and Historical Society; Painter, *Creating Black Americans*, p. 74.

15. Warner, *New Haven Negroes*, pp. 82–84, 92; Masur, *1831*, pp. 25–27, 31; Riley and Etulain, eds., *Wild Women of the Old West*, p. 31; "Emily D. West," The Handbook of Texas Online; Painter, *Creating Black Americans*, pp. 9–10.

16. Hardin, *Texian Iliad*, pp. 11–13; Fleming, *Liberty!*, pp. 109–120; Jane Bradfield, *Rx Take One Cannon* (Shiner: Patrick J. Wagner, 1981), pp. ix–xi, 20–25; Masur, *1831*, pp. 37–38, 42; Bass and Brunson, eds., *Fragile Empires*, pp. xxi–12, 65; Riley and Etulain, eds., *Wild Women of the Old West*, p. 31; Lutzweiler, "Emily D. West and the Yellow Prose of Texas," New

Haven Museum and Historical Society; Frederick Merk, *History of the Westward Movement* (New York: Alfred A. Knopf, 1978), pp. 125–275; Daughters of the Republic of Texas, *The Alamo, Long Barrack Museum* (Dallas: Taylor, 1986), p. 19; Ragsdale, *Women and Children of the Alamo*, pp. 56–57.

17. Paul D. Lack, *The Texas Revolutionary Experience, A Political and Social History, 1835–1836* (College Station: Texas A&M Press, 1992), pp. 238–244; Everett, *History of Slavery*, pp. 163; "Cotton Culture," The Handbook of Texas Online; Campbell, *An Empire for Slavery*, pp. 35–49.

18. Lack, *The Texas Revolutionary Experience*, p. 148; Everett, *History of Slavery*, p. 163; Fleming, *Liberty!*, pp. 71–74, 76; Daughters of the Republic of Texas, *The Alamo*, pp. 19–20.

19. Barr, *Black Texans*, p. 6; Bob Boyd, *The Texas Revolution: A Day-by-Day Account* (San Angelo: San Angelo Standard Times, 1986), p. 9; Bill Walraven and Marjorie K. Walraven, *The Magnificent Barbarians: Little Told Stories of the Texas Revolution* (Austin: Eakin Press, 1993), p. 151–152; Campbell, *An Empire for Slavery*, pp. 35–49; "Emily D. West," The Handbook of Texas Online; Fleming, *Liberty!*, pp. 71, 74; Daughters of the Republic of Texas, *The Alamo: Long Barrack Museum* (Dallas: Taylor, 1986), p. 21; Lack, *The Texas Revolutionary Experience*, pp. 238–244; "Benjamin Rush Milam," The Handbook of Texas Online.

20. Barr, *Black Texans*, pp. 4, 6; *Houston Telegraph*, Houston, Texas, March 28, 1837; *The Floridian*, Pensacola, Texas, May 13, 1837; Alwyn Barr, *Texans in Revolt: The Battle for San Antonio, 1835* (Austin: University of Texas Press, 1990), pp. 17–18, 42, 45–66; "Erastus Smith," The Handbook of Texas Online; "Emily D. West," The Handbook of Texas Online; Walraven and Walraven, *The Magnificent Barbarians*, pp. 152–153; Lack, *The Texas Revolutionary Experience*, p. 248; "Hendrick Arnold," The Handbook of Texas Online; "Greenbury Logan," Texas Black History Preservation Project, Documenting the Complete African American Experience in Texas, internet; Daughters of the Republic of Texas, *The Alamo*, pp. 21–22, 50; "Benjamin Rush Milam," The Handbook of Texas Online.

21. "Emily D. West," The Handbook of Texas Online; *Texas Gazette*, January 23 and 30, 1830; Campbell, *An Empire for Slavery*, pp. 1–4, 10–208; Goldstone, *Dark Bargain*, p. 20; Merk, *History of the Westward Movement*, pp. 196–273; Campbell, ed., *The Laws of Slavery in Texas*, p. 3; *Houston Telegraph*, Houston, Texas, March 28, 1837; *The Floridian*, May 13, 1837.

22. Barr, *Black Texans*, p. 17; Masur, *1831*, p. 57.

23. Campbell, *An Empire for Slavery*, pp. 19–24; Lutzweiler, "Emily D. West and the Yellow Prose of Texas," New Haven Museum and Historical Society; David Nevin, *The Texans* (New York: Time-Life Books, 1975), pp. 32–32, 225.

24. Campbell, *An Empire for Slavery*, p. 24.

25. Sean M. Kelley, *Los Brazos de Dios: A Plantation Society in the Texas Borderlands, 1821–1865* (Baton Rouge: Louisiana State University Press, 2010), p. 74; "Robert McAlpin Williamson," The Handbook of Texas Online.

26. Painter, *Creating Black Americans*, pp. 89–90.

27. Campbell, *An Empire for Slavery*, p. 25; Andrew Burstein, *The Passions of Andrew Jackson* (New York: Alfred A. Knopf, 2003), pp. 225–226; T. R. Fehrenbach, *Lone Star: A History of Texas and the Texans* (New York: Da Capo Press, 2000), p. 165; Clarence Lusane, *The Black History of the White House* (San Francisco: City Lights Books, 2011) p. 149.

28. Lusane, *The Black History of the White House*, pp. 149–150.

29. Lack, *The Texas Revolutionary Experience*, p. 240; Campbell, *An Empire for Slavery*, 35–49.

30. Lack, *The Texas Revolutionary Experience*, pp. 240–241; Huffines, *Blood of Noble Men*, p. 2; *Richmond Enquirer*, Richmond, Virginia, January 10, 1837; *Democratic Free Press*, Detroit, Michigan, November 9, 1836; Jack Jackson, editor, *Almonte's Texas: Juan N. Almonte's 1834 Inspection, Secret Report and Role in the 1836 Campaign* (Austin: Texas State Historical Association, 2005), p. 40.

31. Jackson, ed., *Almonte's Texas*, p. 40.

32. Ibid.

33. Ibid.

34. Ibid., p. 257.

35. Will Fowler, *Santa Anna of Mexico* (Lincoln: University of Nebraska Press, 2007), pp. 174–175, 182–183; Campbell, *An Empire for Slavery*, pp. 40–41.

36. Jack Jackson, editor, *Texas by Terán: The Diary Kept by General Manuel de Mier y Terán on His 1828 Inspection of Texas* (Austin: University of Texas Press, 2000), p. 96.

37. "Emily D. West," The Handbook of Texas Online; Stampp, *The Peculiar Institution*, pp. 94, 258; Lutzweiler, "Emily D. West and the Yellow Prose of Texas," New Haven Museum and Historical Society.

38. Kelley, *Los Brazos de Dios*, p. 97.

39. Ibid.; Jack Jackson, ed., *Texas by Terán*, pp. 144–145.

40. Jack C. Ramsey, Jr., *Texas Sinners and Revolutionaries: Jane Long and Her Fellow Conspirators* (Plano: Republic of Texas Press, 2001), p. 71.

41. "Emily D. West," The Handbook of Texas Online.

42. Catherine Squires, *African Americans and the Media* (Cambridge: Polity Press, 2009), p. 23.

Chapter IV

1. Memorials and Petitions, petition of Diana Leonard, December 14, 1840, Texas State Library and Archives Commission, Austin, Texas; Lutzweiler, "Emily D. West and the Yellow Prose of Texas," New Haven Museum and Historical Society; "Emily D. West," The Handbook of Texas Online; McVea, *Making Myth of Emily*, p. 116; Muir, "The Free Negro in

Harris County, Texas," *Southwestern Historical Quarterly Online*, p. 5; Marshall De Bruhl, *The Sword of San Jacinto: A Life of Sam Houston* (New York: Random House, 1993), p. 203; Riley and Etulain, eds., *Wild Women of the Old West*, pp. xiv, 29–31, 33; Bass and Brunson, eds., *Fragile Empires*, pp. xx–xxi; Dunn, "One More Piece of the Puzzle," *The Compass Rose*; "James Morgan," The Handbook of Texas Online; Painter, *Creating Black Americans*, p. 90; *Eastern Argus*, May 31, 1836.

2. Mrs. Brigadier Gen. Egbert L. Viele, *Following the Drum* (Austin: Steck-Vaughn, 1968), pp. vii, 47.

3. "Emily D. West," The Handbook of Texas Online; McVea, *Making Myth of Emily*, pp. 87, 89, 91, 101, 107–108, 116; "New Washington Association," The Handbook of Texas Online; Riley and Etulain, eds., *Wild Women of the Old West*, pp. 31, 33; "James Morgan," The Handbook of Texas Online; *Eastern Argus*, May 31, 1836; Ramon Eduardo Ruiz, *Mexico: Why a Few Are Rich and the People Poor* (Berkeley: University of California Press, 2010), pp. 60–61.

4. *Richmond Enquirer*, April 5, 1836.

5. Gray, *Diary of Col. Wm. Fairfax Gray*, pp. 1, 120.

6. *Maryland Gazette*, Annapolis, Maryland, March 17, 24 and April 7 and 21, 1836; John K. Mahon, *History of the Second Seminole War, 1835–1842* (Gainesville: University of Florida Press, 1967), pp. 21, 25, 104–106; Bruce Edward Twyman, *The Black Seminole Legacy and North American Politics, 1693–1845* (Washington, D.C.: Howard University Press, 1999), pp. 7–20, 115–140; Woodburne Potter, *The War in Florida* (Baltimore: Lewis and Coleman, 1836), pp. 105–106, 117–118; "Emily D. West," The Handbook of Texas Online; Riley and Etulain, eds., *Wild Women of the Old West*, pp. 31, 33; Kenneth C. Davis, *A Nation Rising: Untold Tales of Flawed Founders, Fallen Heroes, and Forgotten Fighters from America's Hidden Past* (New York: HarperCollins, 2010), pp. 169–171; David Barry Gaspar and David Patrick Geggus, editors, *A Turbulent Time: The French Revolution and the Greater Caribbean* (Bloomington: Indiana University Press, 1997), pp. 166–171; Gray, *Diary of Col. Wm. Fairfax Gray*, p. 72.

7. *Albany Evening Journal*, Albany, New York, March 25, 1836.

8. City of La Porte, Texas, Chamber of Commerce, La Porte, Texas; Jackson, ed., *Texas by Terán*, pp. 10, 14, 21–27; "Morgan's Point, Texas," The Handbook of Texas Online; Bass and Brunson, eds., *Fragile Empires*, pp. xxiv, page 8, note 6, page 24, note 1, page 51, and page 58, note 5, and page 67 and 71; Riley and Etulain, eds., *Wild Women of the Old West*, 32–33; *Eastern Argus*, May 31, 1836; Dunn, "One More Piece of the Puzzle," *The Compass Rose*; "James Morgan," The Handbook of Texas Online; Paul Horgan, *Lamy of Santa Fe* (New York: Farrar, Straus and Giroux, 1980), p. 94; Viele, *Following the Drum*, pp. 78–79; "New Washington Association," The Handbook of Texas Online; Nevin, *The Texans*, pp. 36, 180.

9. Smithwick, Noah, *The Evolution of a State, or Recollections of Old Texas Days* (Austin: University of Texas Press, 1983) pp. ix, xiii, 5; Kelly, *Los Brazos de Dios*, p. 14.

10. *Morning Courier and New York Enquirer*, New York, New York, June 9, 1836.

11. Smithwick, *The Evolution of a State*, p. 5.

12. Smithwick, *The Evolution of a State*, p. 5.

13. Weems and Weems, *Dream of Empire*, p. 91; "Clear Creek (Fort Bend County)," The Handbook of Texas Online.

14. Kelley, *Los Brazos de Dios*, pp. 49–51.

15. William A. Fletcher, *Rebel Private: Front and Rear, Memoirs of a Confederate Soldier* (New York: Meridian Books, 1997), pp. 1–2.

16. Jackson, ed., *Almonte's Texas*, p. 184.

17. Donna Wyatt Howell, compiler, *I Was a Slave: True Life Stories Dictated by Former American Slaves in the 1930s* (Washington, D.C.: American Legacy Books, 2000), p. 13.

18. Ibid., p. 51.

19. *Pennsylvania Freeman*, Philadelphia, Pennsylvania, November 5, 1836.

20. Weems and Weems, *Dream of Empire*, p. 49.

21. Jackson, ed., *Texas by Terán*, pp. 2–4, 57, 100–101.

22. Jack Jackson, editor, *Almonte's Texas: Juan N. Almonte's 1834 Inspection, Secret Report and Role in the 1836 Campaign* (Austin: Texas State Historical Association, 2005), pp. 249–250.

23. Gray, *Diary of Col. Wm. Fairfax Gray*, p. 72.

24. "Kian," The Handbook of Texas Online; Kiamata Long, "'Kian,' Slave, Personal Maid for Jane Long," Texas Black History Preservation Project, Documenting the Complete African American Experience in Texas, internet; Ramsey, *Texas Sinners and Revolutionaries: Jane Long and Her Fellow Conspirators*, pp. 2–27, 249, 253–254; Jackson, ed., *Almonte's Texas*, p. 19.

25. Bass and Brunson, eds., *Fragile Empires*, pp. xxi, xxiii–xxiv; Robin Lane Fox, *Alexander the Great* (New York: Penguin Books, 1986), pp. 66, 197–198; Demos, ed., *Remarkable Providences, 1600–1760*, p. 14; Gray, *Diary of Col. Wm. Fairfax Gray*, p. 72; "Morgan's Point, Texas," The Handbook of Texas Online; Michael Wood, *In the Footsteps of Alexander the Great* (Los Angeles, University of California Press, 2001), pp. 82–83; Dunn, "One More Piece of the Puzzle," *The Compass Rose*; "James Morgan," The Handbook of Texas Online; Kelley, *Los Brazos de Dios*, pp. 14, 17, 27.

26. Bass and Brunson, eds., *Fragile Empires*, p. 51; Riley and Etulain, eds., *Wild Women of the Old West*, p. 33.

27. Jackson, ed., *Almonte's Texas*, pp. 334–336; Weems and Weems, *Dream of Empire*, pp. 12–13.

28. Lee, *Mary Austin Holley*, p. 241.

29. Bass and Brunson, eds., *Fragile Empires*, pp. 61, 73.

30. Ibid., p. 85; "James Morgan," The Handbook of Texas Online.

31. Graham Davis, *Land! Irish Pioneers in Mexican and Revolutionary Texas* (College Station: Texas

A&M University Press, 2002), p. 9; Riley and Etulain, *Wild Women of the Old West*, pp. 32, 34–35; Smithwick, *The Evolution of a State*, pp. 5, 49; "John Joseph Linn," The Handbook of Texas Online; *New Hampshire Sentinel*, Keene, New Hampshire, May 19, 1836; Gary S. Zaboly, *An Altar for Their Sons: The Alamo and the Texas Revolution in Contemporary Newspaper Accounts* (Buffalo Gap: State House Press, 2011), pp. 131–132; *Albany Evening Journal*, March 25, 1836; Ramsey, *Texas Sinners and Revolutionaries*, p. 74; Weems and Weems, *Dream of Empire*, pp. 19–20.

32. Gray, *Diary of Col. Wm. Fairfax Gray*, p. 93.
33. Jackson, ed., *Almonte's Texas*, p. 268.
34. Jackson, ed., *Almonte's Texas*, p. 232.
35. *Commercial Bulletin and Missouri Literary Register*, St. Louis, Missouri, June 15, 1835; "New Washington Association," The Handbook of Texas Online.
36. Weems and Weems, *Dream of Empire*, p. 12.
37. Davis, *Land!*, p. 10.
38. *New York Times*, December 15, 1907; James Atkins Shackford, *David Crockett, The Man and the Legend* (Lincoln: University of Nebraska Press, 1986), pp. 204–215, 232–235.
39. Jackson, ed., *Texas by Terán*, p. 45.
40. Ibid.; Bass and Brunson, eds., *Fragile Empires*, p. 215; "New Washington Association," The Handbook of Texas Online.
41. Julie Roy Jeffrey, *Frontier Women: The Trans-Mississippi West, 1840–1880* (New York: Hill and Wang, 1979), pp. xi–9; Ramsey, *Texas Sinners and Revolutionaries*, pp. 50–51; "Emily D. West," The Handbook of Texas Online; Muir, "The Free Negro in Harris County, Texas," Southwestern Historical Quarterly Online, pp. 4; Riley and Etulain, eds., *Wild Women of the Old West*, p. 31; Sally Roesch Wagner, editor, *Daughters of Dakota: A Sampler of Stories from the South Dakota Pioneers Daughters Collection*, Vol. 1 (Yankton: Daughters of Dakota, 1989), pp. xiii–xvi; Kelley, *Los Brazos de Dios*, p. 60.
42. Weems and Weems, *Dream of Empire*, pp. 44–45; "Harriet A. Moore Page Potter Ames," The Handbook of Texas Online.
43. Jackson, ed., *Almonte's Texas*, p. 224.
44. Gray, *Diary of Col. Wm. Fairfax Gray*, p. 212.
45. Jackson, ed., *Almonte's Texas*, p. 246.
46. *The New Orleans Bee*, New Orleans, Louisiana, June 10, 1836; Timothy M. Matovina, *The Alamo Remembered: Tejano Accounts and Perspectives* (Austin: University of Texas Press, 1995), pp. 1–119; C. T. Smith, *An Historical Geography of Western Europe Before 1800* (New York: Frederick A. Praeger, 1969), p. 252; *San Antonio Daily Express*, San Antonio, Texas, July 26, 1888; Reuben Rendon Lozano, *Vivia Tejas: The Story of the Tejanos, the Mexican-born Patriots of the Texas Revolution* (San Antonio: Alamo Press, 1985), pp. 1–80; *Dallas Morning News*, February 21, 1897; Lack, *The Texas Revolutionary Experience*, pp. 183–207; "John Joseph Linn," The Handbook of Texas Online; David Nicolle, *The Moors: The Islamic West, 7th–15th Centuries, AD* (Oxford: Osprey, 2001), p. 7; Ragsdale, *Women and Children of the Alamo*, p. 5; *Baltimore Gazette and Daily Advertiser*, Baltimore, Maryland, December 22, 1836; Ragsdale, *The Women and Children of the Alamo*, pp. 27, 30–33; Donovan, *The Blood of Heroes*, p. 299; Jackson, *Alamo Legacy*, pp. 121–122; Kelley, *Los Brazos de Dios*, pp.14–17, 22, 60; Gray, *Diary of Col. Wm. Fairfax Gray*, p. 165.
47. Smithwick, *The Evolution of a State*, p. 18.
48. Ibid.; "Philip Dimmitt," The Handbook of Texas Online.
49. Thomas Lloyd Miller, *The Public Lands of Texas, 1519–1970* (Norman: University of Oklahoma Press, 1972), p. 17.
50. Smithwick, *The Evolution of a State*, p. 18.
51. Gray, *Diary of Col. Wm. Fairfax Gray*, p. 89.
52. Jackson, ed., *Almonte's Texas*, p. 223.
53. Gray, *Diary of Col. Wm. Fairfax Gray*, p. 93.
54. Ibid., p. 94.
55. Ragsdale, *The Women and Men of the Alamo*, p. xiii.
56. Smithwick, *The Evolution of a State*, pp. 9–10.
57. Ibid., 9–10, 14; Glasrud and Pitre, eds., *Black Women in Texas History*, p. 17; Jackson, ed., *Texas by Terán*, p. 70; "Emily D. West," The Handbook of Texas Online; Muir, "The Free Negro in Harris County, Texas," Southwestern Historical Quarterly Online, p. 5; Riley and Etulain, eds., *Wild Women of the Old West*, p. 31; Ragsdale, *Women and Children of the Alamo*, p. xiii; Ragsdale, *Woman and Children of the Alamo*, pp. 5, 41, 42–44.
58. Campbell, *An Empire for Slavery*, p. 70.
59. "Claiborne West," The Handbook of Texas Online; Daughters of the Republic of Texas, *The Alamo*, p. 18; *Farmer's Cabinet*, Amherst, New Hampshire, April 4, 1836.
60. Gray, *Diary of Col. Wm. Fairfax Gray*, p. 166.
61. Herman L. Bennett, *Africans in Colonial Mexico: Absolution, Christianity, and Afro-Creole Consciousness, 1570–1640* (Bloomington: Indiana University Press, 2003), pp. 1–125; Barr, *Black Texans*, pp. v–5; Glasrud and Pitre, eds., *Black Women in Texas History*, pp. 13–14; Muir, "The Free Negro in Harris County, Texas," Southwestern Historical Quarterly Online, p. 23, note 57; Riley and Etulain, eds., *Wild Women of the Old West*, p. 31; Everett, *History of Slavery*, p. 32; John A. Crow, *Spain: The Root and the Flower* (Berkeley: University of California Press, 2005), pp. 42–50; Nicolle, *The Moors*, pp. 3–8.
62. *Houston Telegraph*, Houston, Texas, March 28, 1837; "Hendrick Arnold," The Handbook of Texas Online.
63. Smithwick, *The Evolution of a State*, p. 163.
64. Ibid.
65. Ibid.
66. Ibid.
67. Jackson, ed., *Texas by Terán*, p. 118.
68. Kelley, *Los Brazos de Dios*, pp. 62–64; "Varner-Hogg Plantation State Historical Park," The Handbook of Texas Online.
69. Kelley, *Los Brazos de Dios*, p. 62.
70. Smithwick, *The Evolution of a State*, p. 9; Painter, *Creating Black Americans*, pp. 44–47;

Stampp, *The Peculiar Institution: Slavery in the Ante-Bellum South*, pp. 368–377;

71. Smithwick, *The Evolution of a State*, pp. 24–25, 28; "Jesse G. Thompson," The Handbook of Texas History Online.

72. Smithwick, *The Evolution of a State*, p. 28; "East Columbia, Tx," The Handbook of Texas Online; "Zeno Philips," The Handbook of Texas Online.

73. Osceola Plantation, Brazoport Archaeological Society, Brazoport, Texas.

74. Muir, "The Free Negro in Harris County, Texas," Southwestern Historical Quarterly Online, pp. 2, 6, 9–10; "Husk, Zilpha," The Handbook of Texas Online.

75. Lee, *Mary Austin Holley*, pp. 253–254, 293; Kelley, *Los Brazos de Dios*, p. 94.

76. Barr and Calvert, eds., *Black Leaders: Texans for Their Times*, pp. 19–39; "William Goyens," The Handbook of Texas Online; Ragsdale, *Women and Children of the Alamo*, p. xi; Weems and Weems, *Dream of Empire*, p. 60.

77. Barr, *Black Texans*, p. 32; *Daily National Intelligencer*, Washington, D.C., December 7, 1829; Campbell, *An Empire for Slavery*, p. 41; Muir, "The Free Negro in Harris County, Texas," Southwestern Historical Quarterly Online, p. 5; "Emily D. West," The Handbook of Texas Online; "Hendrick Arnold," The Handbook of Texas Online; Barr and Calvert, eds., *Blacks Leaders*, pp. 19–39.

78. Glasrud and Pitre, eds., *Black Women in Texas History*, p. 45; Riley and Etulain, eds., *Wild Women of the Old West*, p. 32; "James Morgan," The Handbook of Texas Online.

79. Campbell, *An Empire for Slavery*, pp. 156–176; Glasrud and Pitre, eds., *Black Women in Texas History*, pp. 16–17, 19–29, 118–160; George P. Rawick, *From Sundown to Sunup: The Making of the Slave Community* (Westport: Greenwood, 1972), pp. xix–93; Riley and Etulain, eds., *Wild Women of the Old West*, p. 31; Painter, *Creating Black Americans*, pp. 84–103; "William B. Travis," The Handbook of Texas Online; "Husk, Zilpha," The Handbook of Texas Online.

80. Smithwick, *The Evolution of a State*, p. 48.

81. Ibid., p. 40.

82. Ibid., p. 49.

83. Ibid., p. 49; "Robert McAlpin Williamson," The Handbook of Texas Online; Jackson, ed., *Almonte's Texas*, pp. 80, 345–346; "War Party," The Handbook of Texas Online.

84. White, *Ar'n't I a Woman*, p. 118.

85. Ibid., pp. 118–160.

86. Jeffrey, *Frontier Women*, pp. xii–xiii, 3–4, 201–204.

87. Ibid., p. 203.

88. Warner, *New Haven Negroes*, pp. 79–80.

89. Nancy Rubin, *Isabella of Castile: The First Renaissance Queen* (New York: St. Martin's Press, 1991), pp. 2–3, 197–297.

90. Gayle C. Shirley, *More Than Petticoats: Remarkable Colorado Women* (Helena: Morris, 2002), pp. 1–8.

91. Ibid.; Lack, *The Texas Revolutionary Experience*, pp. 239–240; Hardin, *Texian Iliad*, pp. 89–102; "James Morgan," The Handbook of Texas Online.

92. Lack, *The Texas Revolutionary Experience*, pp. 241–243; "Emily D. West," The Handbook of Texas Online.

93. Lack, *The Texas Revolutionary Experience*, p. 244.

94. Jackson, ed., *Texas by Terán*, p. 101.

95. Scheina, *Santa Anna*, p. 30; Weems and Weems, *Dream of Empire*, p. 65.

96. Campbell, ed., *The Laws of Slavery in Texas*, p. 8.

97. Jackson, ed., *Texas by Terán*, pp. 177, 179.

98. *The Telegraph and Texas Register*, January 23, 1836.

99. Lack, *The Texas Revolutionary Experience*, p. 244.

100. *Richmond Enquirer*, September 2, 1836.

101. Jackson, ed., *Almonte's Texas*, pp. 12, 336, 351–352, 374.

102. Campbell, ed., *The Laws of Slavery in Texas*, pp. 52–53, 57; Lack, *The Texas Revolutionary Experience*, pp. 250–252.

103. Campbell, *An Empire for Slavery*, p. 35.

104. Susanne Starling, *Land Is the Cry! Warren Angus Ferris, Pioneer Surveyor and Founder of Dallas County* (Austin: Texas State Historical Association, 1988), pp. 42–45.

105. *The Telegraph and Texas Register*, March 5, 1836.

Chapter V

1. Gray, *Diary of Col. Wm. Fairfax Gray*, p. 111.

2. Ibid.

3. Scheina, *Santa Anna*, pp. 5, 24, 26–28; Paul Johnson, *Napoleon: A Life* (New York: Penguin Books, 2006), pp. 49–72; *Missouri Argus*, St. Louis, Missouri, August 26, 1836.

4. *Jamestown Journal*, Jamestown, New York, July 29, 1841.

5. "Typescript Diary of Major John P. Gaines," Journal and Diaries, 1846, Missouri Historical Society, St. Louis, Missouri.

6. *The Telegraph and Texas Register*, January 23, 1836; "James Neill Clinton," The Handbook of Texas Online.

7. Hardin, *Texian Iliad*, pp. 111, 117.

8. *The Telegraph and Texas Register*, January 23, 1836; John Holmes Jenkins, editor, *Recollections of Early Texas* (Austin: University of Texas Press, 1987), pp. 25–26; Stephen L. Moore, *Savage Frontier: Rangers, Riflemen, and Indian Wars in Texas* (Plano: Republic of Texas Press, 2002), Vol. 1, pp. 24–29.

9. Gray, *Diary of Col. Wm. Fairfax Gray*, pp. 114–115, 117.

10. Jackson, ed., *Almonte's Texas*, pp. 364–365.

11. Mark Derr, *The Frontiersman: The Real Life and the Many Legends of Davy Crockett* (New York: William Morrow, 1993), p. 185; *National Intelligencer*,

Washington, D.C., April 30, 1836; *Commonwealth*, Frankfort, Kentucky, May 25, 1936; *Commercial Bulletin*, New Orleans, Louisiana, April 11, 1836; *Memphis Enquirer*, Memphis, Tennessee, April 12, 1836; Clifford Hopewell, *James Bowie, Texas Fighting Man: A Biography* (Austin: Eakin Press, 1994), p. 119; Walraven and Walraven, *The Magnificent Barbarians*, p. 154; Campbell, *An Empire for Slavery*, p. 31; Barr, *Black Texans*, p. 6; Todd Hansen, editor, *The Alamo Reader: A Study in History* (Mechancisburg: Stackpole Books, 2003), pp. 462–463; *Philadelphia Public Ledger*, Philadelphia, Pennsylvania, October 22, 1846.

12. *Baltimore Gazette and Daily Advertiser*, September 7, 1833.
13. *The New York Herald*, New York, New York, June 23, 1836.
14. *Arkansas Gazette*, Little Rock, Arkansas, March 29, 1836.
15. Gray, *Diary of Col. Wm. Fairfax Gray*, pp. 118, 120.
16. *The New York Herald*, June 25, 1836.
17. *El Mosquito Mexicano*, Mexico City, Mexico, March 18, 1836.
18. "James Bowie," The Handbook of Texas Online; *St. Louis Republican*, November 18, 1888.
19. Smithwick, *The Evolution of a State*, p. 97.
20. *Dallas Weekly Herald*, June 8, 1867.
21. *The Telegraph and Texas Register*, March 12, 1836.
22. Gray, *Diary of Col. Wm. Fairfax Gray*, p. 124.
23. Scheina, *Santa Anna*, pp. 28–29; Hardin, *Texian Iliad*, pp. 127–149.
24. Jerry J. Gaddy, *Texas in Revolt: Contemporary Newspaper Accounts of the Texas Revolution* (Fort Collins: Old Army Press, 1973), p. 14.
25. *Floridian and Advocate*, Tallahassee, Florida, April 30, 1836.
26. Gaddy, *Texas in Revolt*, pp. 77–79.
27. *The Telegraph and Texas Register*, March 24, 1836; Walraven and Walraven, *The Magnificent Barbarians*, p. 153.
28. Bill Groneman, *Alamo Defenders, A Genealogy: The People and Their Words* (Austin: Eakin Press, 1990), pp. 64–65; Hansen, ed., *The Alamo Reader*, p. 82; Scheina, *Santa Anna*, p. 30; Hardin, *Texian Iliad*, p.
29. *Telegraph and Texas Register*, August 26, 1837.
30. *St. Louis Republic*, November 18, 1888; Jackson, ed., *Almonte's Texas*, pp. 336, 376; Bill Groneman, *Eyewitness to the Alamo* (Plano: Republic of Texas Press, 1996), p. 174; Tucker, *Exodus from the Alamo*, pp. 279–281; Stephen L. Moore, *Savage Frontier: Rangers, Riflemen, and Indian Wars in Texas, 1835–1837*, Vol. 1 (Republic of Texas Press, 2002), pp. 3, 31, 98–100; John Myers, *The Alamo* (New York: Bantam Books, 1966), pp. 154, 159; Ragsdale, *Women and Children of the Alamo*, p. 56.
31. Groneman, *Eyewitness to the Alamo*, p. 186.
32. *Frankfort Commonwealth*, Frankfort, Kentucky, May 25, 1836; Jackson, ed., *Almonte's Texas*, p. 376.
33. *Telegraph and Texas Register*, August 26, 1837.

34. Ibid., October 11, 1836; New Orleans Bee, March 28, 1836, *San Antonio Express*, March 14, 1878; *Arkansas Gazette*, April 12, 1836; Donovan, *The Blood of Heroes*, pp. 300–302; Jackson, ed., *Almonte's Texas*, p. 376.
35. Ragsdale, *The Women and Children of the Alamo*, pp. 5–6, 36.
36. *Philadelphia Public Ledger*, Philadelphia, Pennsylvania, October 22, 1846; Ragsdale, *The Women and Children of the Alamo*, p. 36; Hopewell, *James Bowie*, p. 119.
37. Groneman, *Eyewitness to the Alamo*, p. 180.
38. McVea, *Making Myth of Emily*, p. 123; *The Telegraph and Texas Register*, May 27, 1837; Ramsey, *Texas Sinners and Revolutionaries*, p. 106.
39. Groneman, *Alamo Defenders*, pp. 4–123; Scheina, *Santa Anna*, p. 30.
40. Merk, *History of the Westward Movement*, p. 273.
41. Hardin, *Texian Iliad*, p. 156; Groneman, *Alamo Defenders*, pp. 4–124; "New Orleans Greys," The Handbook of Texas Online.
42. *Supplemento al Diario del Gobierno*, Mexico City, Mexico, March 21, 1836.
43. *New Orleans Bee*, April 20, 1836.
44. Nicolle, *The Moors*, p. 21; Walter Lord, *A Time to Stand: A Chronicle of the Valiant Battle of the Alamo* (New York: Bonanza Books, 1987), p. 212; Zaboly, *An Altar for Their Sons*, p. 4; David A. Clary, *Eagles and Empire: The United States, Mexico, and the Struggle for a Continent* (New York: Bantam Books, 2009), pp. 368–374.
45. "New Washington Association," The Handbook of Texas Online; Fleming, *Liberty!*, pp. 253–255.
46. Gaddy, *Texas in Revolt*, p. 47.
47. *National Banner and Nashville Whig*, Nashville, Tennessee, May 30, 1836.
48. Jenkins, ed., *Recollections of Early Texas*, pp. xvii, 35–36, note 3.
49. Gray, *Diary of Col. Wm. Fairfax Gray*, p. 127.
50. Ibid., pp. 128–129
51. Ibid., p. 130; "Jesse B. Badgett," The Handbook of Texas Online; Goodrich, "Benjamin Briggs," The Handbook of Texas Online; "Jesse Grimes," The Handbook of Texas Online.
52. "Albert Calvin Grimes," The Handbook of Texas Online; "John Calvin Goodrich," The Handbook of Texas Online.
53. John H. Jenkins, editor, *Papers of the Texas Revolution* (10 vols., Austin: Presidial Press, 1973), Vol. 5, pp. 81–82.
54. Ibid.
55. Gray, *Diary of Col. Wm. Fairfax Gray*, p. 131.

Chapter VI

1. Crawford, ed., *The Eagle*, p. 52.
2. *New Hampshire Gazette*, Portsmouth, New Hampshire, October 12, 1813; Jackson, ed., *Almonte's Texas*, p. 390; *Universal Gazette*, Washington, D.C.,

June 11, 1813; *New Orleans Bee*, April 20, 1836; Bruhl, *Sword of San Jacinto*, p. 188; Scheina, *Santa Anna*, pp. 6, 30; *The Herald*, New York, New York, June 27, 1836; Donovan, *The Blood of Heroes*, p. 309.

3. *The Herald*, New York, May 3, and 8, 1836; Lack, *The Texas Revolutionary Experience*, p. 248; Hardin, *The Alamo 1836*, pp. 52–69, 73; *New Orleans Bee*, April 20, 1836; Carmen, trans. and ed., *With Santa Anna in Texas*, pp. 81–82; Jackson, ed., *Almonte's Texas*, pp. 389, 392; Hardin, *Texian Iliad*, p. 179; Barr, *Black Texans*, p. 6; "José Urrea," The Handbook of Texas Online; Peter Allen, "Texas Black History Preservation Project: Documenting the Complete African American Experience in Texas," internet; Donovan, *The Blood of Heroes*, pp. 305, 309–310, 313–317, 319; "Georgia Battalion," The Handbook of Texas Online.

4. Donovan, *The Blood of Heroes*, pp. 294–296, 317.

5. Chartier and Enss, *She Wore a Yellow Ribbon*, pp. 1–12; "Nashville Battalion," The Handbook of Texas Online.

6. *Mercantile Advertiser and New York Advocate*, New York, New York June 29, 1836.

7. *New Orleans Bee*, March 16, 1836.

8. Donovan, *The Blood of Heroes*, p. 320.

9. Ibid., pp. 320–321.

10. *Maryland Gazette*, May 12, 1836; Hardin, *The Alamo 1836*, pp. 69, 72–73; Moore, *Eighteen Minutes*, pp. 134, 136, 138; *Richmond Enquirer*, June 14, 1836; Donovan, *The Blood of Heroes*, p. 322; Jackson, ed., *Texas by Terán*, pp. 144–145; Gray, *Diary of Col. Wm. Fairfax Gray*, pp. 134–136, 142.

11. Jeff Long, *Duel of Eagles: The Mexican and U.S. Fight for the Alamo* (New York: William Morrow, 1990), pp. 296–301; Hardin, *The Alamo 1836*, pp. 72–73; Donovan, *The Blood of Heroes*, p. 322.

12. Scheina, *Santa Anna*, p. 31; Jackson, ed., *Almonte's Texas*, pp. 324, 358–359.

13. *Richmond Enquirer*, June 14, 1836; Richard G. Santos, *Santa Anna's Campaign Against Texas, 1835–1836* (Waco, Texas: Texian Press, 1968), pp. 86–87, 90; Hardin, *The Alamo 1836*, pp. 72–73; Donovan, *The Blood of Heroes*, p. 322.

14. Santos, *Santa Anna's Campaign Against Texas, 1835–1836*, p. 90; Carmen, trans. and ed., *With Santa Anna in Texas*, p. 95; Scheina, *Santa Anna*, p. 31; Donovan, *The Blood of Heroes*, pp. 322–323.

15. Gregg J. Dimmick, *Sea of Mud: The Retreat of the Mexican Army After San Jacinto: An Archeological Investigation* (Austin: Texas State Historical Association, 2004), p. 8; Carmen, trans. and ed., *With Santa Anna in Texas*, pp. 97; Scheina, *Santa Anna*, pp. 30–32; Donovan, *The Blood of Heroes*, pp. 309–310; Gray, *Diary of Col. Wm. Fairfax Gray* p. 146.

16. Carmen, trans. and ed., *With Santa Anna in Texas*, pp. 65–81, 95; *Mercantile Advertiser and New York Advocate*, June 29, 1836; Santos, *Santa Anna's Campaign Against Texas, 1835–1836*, pp. 36, 86–87, 97; Hardin, *The Alamo 1836*, pp. 69, 72–73; Caesar, *The Conquest of Gaul* (New York: Penguin Books, 1982), p. 93; Scheina, *Santa Anna*, pp. 30–32.

17. *Richmond Enquirer*, May 3, 1836.

18. *Nashville Banner and Nashville Whig*, Nashville, Tennessee, April 11, 1836.

19. *Richmond Enquirer*, May 3, 1836

20. *Nashville Banner and Nashville Whig*, April 11, 1836.

21. Gray, *Diary of Col. Wm. Fairfax Gray*, p. 142.

22. Ibid., p. 143.

23. Ibid., p. 144.

24. Ibid., pp. 144–145.

25. Ibid., p. 145.

26. Weems and Weems, *Dream of Empire*, p. 87.

27. Gray, *Diary of Col. Wm. Fairfax Gray*, pp. 151–153.

28. Weems and Weems, *Dream of Empire*, pp. 87–88; "Harriet A. Moore Page Potter Ames," The Handbook of Texas Online; Gray, *Diary of Col. Wm. Fairfax Gray*, p. 153

29. Gray, *Diary of Col. Wm. Fairfax Gray*, p. 153.

30. Weems and Weems, *Dream of Empire*, p. 88; "Twin Sisters," The Handbook of Texas Online.

31. Gray, *Diary of Col. Wm. Fairfax Gray*, p. 153.

32. Donovan, *The Blood of Heroes*, pp. 325–326.

33. Carmen, trans. and ed., *With Santa Anna in Texas*, p. 102.

34. Santos, *Santa Anna's Campaign Against Texas, 1835–1836*, pp. 92–94; Hardin, *The Alamo 1836*, pp. 68–69, 72; Jackson, ed., *Almonte's Texas*, p. 400; Scheina, *Santa Anna*, p. 31; Dimmick, *Sea of Mud*, pp. 29–30; DeBuhl, *Sword of San Jacinto*, p. 193; Campbell, *An Empire for Slavery*, pp. 14, 82; Hardin, *Texian Iliad*, p. 118; Hardin, *The Alamo 1836*, p. 73; Moore, *Eighteen Minutes*, pp. 139–140, 205.

35. Judith Ewell and William H. Beezley, *The Human Tradition in Latin America* (Wilmington: Scholarly Resources, 1991), pp. 7–16.

36. *Baltimore Gazette and Daily Advertiser*, April 30, 1836.

37. Gray, *Diary of Col. Wm. Fairfax Gray*, p. 168.

38. Santos, *Santa Anna's Campaign Against Texas, 1835–1836*, p. 95; Dimmick, *Sea of Mud*, pp. 29–30; Hardin, *The Alamo 1836*, pp. 73, 76; Moore, *Eighteen Minutes*, pp. 187, 205; Albert A. Nofi, *The Alamo and the Texas War for Independence, September 30, 1835–April 21, 1836* (Conshohocken: Combined Books, 1992), pp. 58–59; Felix Markham, *Napoleon* (New York: Penguin Books, 1963), pp. 164–170.

39. Donovan, *The Blood of Heroes*, p. 327.

40. Jackson, ed., *Almonte's Texas*, p. 400; Pohl, *The Battle of San Jacinto*, pp. 20–21; Hardin, *The Alamo 1836*, pp. 72–73; Moore, *Eighteen Minutes*, pp. 140, 179, 187.

41. *Richmond Enquirer*, May 3, 1836.

42. Jackson, ed., *Almonte's Texas*, p. 365.

43. *The Herald*, March 7 and April 28, 1836; "James Morgan," The Handbook of Texas Online.

44. *Richmond Enquirer*, May 3, 1836.

45. *The Herald*, March 7 and April 28, 1836, March 10, 1836.

46. *Richmond Enquirer*, May 3, 1936.

47. Perry, ed. and trans., *With Santa Anna in Texas*, p. 81.

48. *The Herald*, April 23, 1836; Hardin, *The Alamo 1836*, p. 72; Jackson, *Alamo Legacy*, pp. 148–149; Zaboly, *An Altar for Their Sons*, pp. 131–132; *Richmond Enquirer*, May 2, 1836; *Baltimore Gazette and Daily Advertiser*, April 30, 1836.
49. Jackson, ed., *Almonte's Texas*, pp. 358, 375.
50. Pedro Delgado, "The Battle of San Jacinto," The McArdle Notebooks, Texas State Library and Archives Commission, Austin, Texas; Scheina, *Santa Anna*, p. 30; Howell, compiler, *I Was a Slave*, p. 56.
51. Lack, *The Texas Revolutionary Experience*, p. 249; Gray, *Diary of Col. Wm. Fairfax Gray*, p. 157.
52. Gray, *Diary of Col. Wm. Fairfax Gray*, p. 155.
53. Santos, *Santa Anna's Campaign Against Texas*, p. 97.
54. Donovan, *The Blood of Heroes*, p. 327.
55. Moore, *Eighteen Minutes*, pp. 218–230; Jackson, ed., *Almonte's Texas*, p. 404; Nofi, *The Alamo*, p. 146; Hardin, *Texian Iliad*, p. 191; Donovan, *The Blood of Heroes*, pp. 323–324.
56. Long, *Duel of Eagles*, pp. 303–305; Hardin, *The Alamo 1836*, pp. 72–73; Moore, *Eighteen Minutes*, pp. 206–209; Scheina, *Santa Anna*, p. 30; *Baltimore Gazette and Daily Advocate*, April 30, 1836; Gray, *Diary of Col. Wm. Fairfax Gray*, pp. 152, 168.
57. Bill Groneman, *Eyewitness to the Alamo* (Plano: Republic of Texas Press, 1996), pp. 145, 147; Ron Jackson, *Alamo Legacy: Alamo Descendants Remember the Alamo* (Austin: Eakin Press, 1997), p. 117; Tucker, *Exodus From the Alamo*, pp. 330–331.
58. Carmen, trans. and ed., *With Santa Anna in Texas*, pp. 81–82.
59. *New Orleans Bee*, April 11, 1836.
60. *Richmond Enquirer*, May 3 and June 14, 1836; Campbell, ed., *The Laws of Slavery in Texas*, p. 8; Jackson, ed., *Almonte's Texas*, pp. 12–18, 358, 388; *Democratic Free Press*, Detroit, Michigan, November 9, 1836; "David Gouveneur Burnet," The Handbook of Texas Online; Hannah Este Burnet, Texas Historical Markers on Waymarking.com, internet; De Bruhl, *The Sword of San Jacinto*, pp. 199–200, 281; Riley and Etulain, eds., *Wild Women of the Old West*, pp. 31, 33, 35–36; Hardin, *Texian Iliad*, pp. 188, 101, 191; Alan C. Huffines, *Blood of Noble Men: The Alamo Battle and Siege* (Austin: Eakin Press, 1999), p. 2; McVea, *Making Myth of Emily*, pp. 138, 156; Moore, *Eighteen Minutes*, pp. 219–220, 230–232; "Emily D. West," The Handbook of Texas Online; "James Morgan," The Handbook of Texas Online; Nofi, *The Alamo*, p. 79; Scheina, *Santa Anna*, p. 30; *New Orleans Bee*, April 11, 1836; "New Washington Association," The Handbook of Texas Online; Donovan, *The Blood of Heroes*, p. 323, 328; Gray, *Diary of Col. Wm. Fairfax Gray*, pp. 144–145, 164, 210; Hubert Herring, *A History of Latin America, From Beginnings to the Present* (New York: Alfred A. Knopf, 1968), pp. 296, 303–304.
61. *Richmond Enquirer*, June 14, 1836; Jackson, ed., *Almonte's Texas*, p. 358; Herring, *A History of Latin America*, p. 250.
62. Campbell, ed., *The Laws of Slavery in Texas*, p. 8; Jackson, ed., *Almonte's Texas*, pp. 12–18, 223; Herring, *A History of Latin America*, p. 250.
63. *Richmond Enquirer*, January 10, 1837; *Galveston News*, Galveston, Texas, February 3, 1881; Jackson, ed., *Almonte's Texas*, pp. 223, 351–352, 358–360, 374, 376, 404; Jack Johnson, "Santa Anna's 1836 Campaign, Was It Directed Toward Ethnic Cleansings?" *The Journal of South Texas* (Spring 2002), Vol. 15, No. 1, p. 12.
64. *The Herald*, June 10, 1836; Riley and Etulain, eds., *Wild Women of the Old West*, pp. 32, 37; Edward L. Miller, *New Orleans and the Texas Revolution* (College Station: Texas A&M University Press, 2004), p. 198; *New Orleans Bee*, March 28, 1836; Jackson, *Almonte's Texas*, pp. 12–33, 97, 123, 138, 160, 213, 220, 223, 358, 376, 389, 404, 406; "New Washington Association," The Handbook of Texas Online; Gray, *Diary of Col. Wm. Fairfax Gray*, p. 157; "Twin Sisters," The Handbook of Texas Online; Hardin, *Texian Iliad*, p. 188; Bass and Brunson, eds., *Fragile Empires*, pp. xxii–xxiii, 10, 181; McVea, *Making Myth of Emily*, p. 136; Delgado, "The Battle of San Jacinto," Texas State Library and Archives Commission; Moore, *Eighteen Minutes*, pp. 231–233; Nofi, *The Alamo*, pp. 79, 206; "James Morgan," The Handbook of Texas Online; Donovan, *The Blood of Heroes*, p. 300, 328; "Texas Navy," The Handbook of Texas Online; Weems and Weems, *Dream of Empire*, p. 88.
65. Bass and Brunson, eds., *Fragile Empires*, p. 31; Jackson, ed., *Almonte's Texas*, pp. 389, 404, 406; *Democratic Free Press*, November 9, 1836; Moore, *Eighteen Minutes*, pp. 219–220, 236–237; "James Morgan," The Handbook of Texas Online; Nofi, *The Alamo*, p. 146.
66. "James Morgan," The Handbook of Texas Online; Gray, *Diary of Col. Wm. Fairfax Gray*, p. 153.
67. *Democratic Free Press*, Detroit, Michigan, September 7, 1836; Lack, *The Texas Revolutionary Experience*, pp. 228, 249; McVea, *Making Myth of Emily*, p.134; Moore, *Eighteen Minutes*, p. 249; Riley and Etulain, eds., *Wild Women of the Old West*, p. 36; "James Morgan," The Handbook of Texas Online; *Richmond Enquirer*, June 10, 1836; "Thomas Jefferson Rusk," The Handbook of Texas Online.
68. McVea, *Making Myth of Emily*, pp. 138, 156; Hollon, ed., *William Bollaert's Texas*, p. 14.
69. Roberts and Olsen, *A Line in the Sand*, p. 143.
70. Bass and Brunson, eds., *Fragile Empires*, p. xxiii.
71. Ibid., p. 7; "James Morgan," The Handbook of Texas Online; "New Washington Association," The Handbook of Texas Online.
72. Moore, *Eighteen Minutes*, pp. 235–236; Nofi, *The Alamo*, p. 146; *Niles' Weekly Register*, Baltimore, Maryland, June 25, 1836; Gaddy, *Texas in Revolt*, p. 8.
73. Crawford, ed., *The Eagle*, pp. 49–50; Scheina, *Santa Anna*, pp. 26–31.
74. Fowler, *Santa Anna of Mexico*, pp. 174–175; Scheina, *Santa Anna*, p. 30.
75. Memorials and Petitions, petition of Diana Leonard, December 14, 1840, Texas State Library and Archives Commission, Austin, Texas; Delgado, "The Battle of San Jacinto," McArdle Notebooks, Texas

State Library and Archives Commission; *1877 Disestablishments: Telegraph and Texas Register* (Memphis: Books LLC, 2010), pp. 25–28; "Emily D. West," The Handbook of Texas Online; Muir, "The Free Negro in Harris County, Texas," *Southwestern Historical Quarterly Online*, p. 5; McVea, *Making Myth of Emily*, p. 136; Moore, *Eighteen Minutes*, pp. 219, 236–237, 257; Riley and Etulain, eds., *Wild Women of the Old West*, pp. 31, 36; Dunn, "One More Piece of the Puzzle," *The Compass Rose*; *Telegraph and Texas Register*; Nofi, *The Alamo*, p. 146; Nevin, *The Texans*, p. 160.

76. Lack, *The Texas Revolutionary Experience*, p. 249; Gray, *Diary of Col. Wm. Fairfax Gray*, pp. 155, 164.

77. Lack, *The Texas Revolutionary Experience*, p. 249; Scheina, *Santa Anna*, p. 30.

78. Donovan, *The Blood of Heroes*, p. 309; Riley and Etulain, eds., *Wild Women of the Old West*, pp. 31–32; Jackson, ed., *Almonte's Texas*, pp. 334–335, 358, 375–376, 385; *Nashville Banner and Nashville Whig*, April 11, 1836; *El Mosquito Mexicano*, Mexico City, September 30, 1836; Elizabeth Salas, *Soldaderas in the Mexican Military* (Austin: University of Texas Press, 2006), pp. ix–30; *Richmond Enquirer*, July 1, 1836; *Democratic Free Press*, November 9, 1836; Long, *Duel of Eagles*, p. 306; William L. Shea and Earl J. Hess, *Pea Ridge: Civil War Campaign in the West* (Chapel Hill: University of North Carolina Press, 1992), pp. 301–303; David Nevin, *Sherman's March: Atlanta to the Sea* (Alexandra: Time-Life Books, 1986), pp. 56–59; Perry, ed. and trans., *With Santa Anna in Texas*, p. 104; Campbell, *An Empire for Slavery*, p. 180; John Charles Chasteen, *Born in Blood and Fire: A Concise History of Latin America* (New York: W. W. Norton, 2001), pp. 53–57; "Emily D. West," The Handbook of Texas Online; Scheina, *Santa Anna*, p. 30; Crisp, *Sleuthing the Alamo*, pp. 190–191; Elizabeth B. Custer, *Tenting on the Plains: General Custer in Kansas and Texas* (New York: Barnes and Noble, 2006), pp. 7–14; *Portland Advertiser*, Portland, Maine, May 3, 1836; *Philadelphia Public Ledger*, Philadelphia, Pennsylvania, May 31, 1836; Roberts, *A Short History of the World*, p. 376; Weems and Weems, *Dream of Empire*, p. 69; Rubin, *Isabella of Spain*, p. 3; Jackson, *Alamo Legacy*, pp. 144–145; Nofi, *The Alamo*, pp. 146, 193–194; Iris Chang, *The Rape of Nanking: The Forgotten Holocaust of World War II* (New York: Basic Books, 1997), pp. 49–53, 89–96; Ragsdale, *The Woman and Children of the Alamo*, p. xiii; Campbell, ed., *The Laws of Slavery in Texas*, p. 8; George Seldes, compiler, *The Great Thoughts* (New York: Ballantine Books, 1985), p. 114.

79. Jacques Soustelle, *Daily Life of the Aztecs on the Eve of the Spanish Conquest* (Stanford: Stanford University Press, 1961), pp. xiii, 46–47, 54–55, 135, 184–185.

80. Ibid., p. 184.

81. Donovan, *The Blood of Heroes*, pp. 316, 376; Scheina, *Santa Anna*, p. 5; Ragsdale, *The Women and Children of the Alamo*, p. xiii.

82. *Phoenix Civilian*, Cumberland, Maryland, February 2, 1836.

83. *Pennsylvania Freeman*, November 5, 1836; Hammond Innes, *The Conquistadors* (New York: Alfred A. Knopf, 1969), pp. 12–193; Jackson, *Alamo Legacy*, pp. 16; Hardin, *Texian Iliad*, p. 101.

84. Ann Fears Crawford, editor, *The Eagle: The Autobiography of Santa Anna* (Austin: State House Press, 1988), pp. ix, xi–xii; Santa Anna Will, Roger Borroel Collection, East Chicago, Indiana; Perry, ed. and trans., *With Santa Anna in Texas*, pp. 104, 109; Long, *Duel of Eagles*, p. 152; "Emily D. West," The Handbook of Texas Online; Scheina, *Santa Anna*, pp. 14, 30; Stampp, *The Peculiar Institution*, pp. 350–361; Crisp, *Sleuthing the Alamo*, pp. 190–191; Salas, *Soldaderas in the Mexican Military*, pp. ix–30.

85. Huffines, *Blood of Noble Men*, p. 50; Brear, *Inherit the Alamo*, p. 54; Scheina, *Santa Anna*, p. 24.

86. *Texas Mute Ranger*, April 1882, John Salmon Ford Papers, Center for American History, Austin, Texas.

87. Ibid.; Brear, *Inherit the Alamo*, p. 54.

88. Jackson, ed., *Almonte's Texas*, p. 376; Donovan, *The Blood of Heroes*, p. 326.

89. Huffines, *Blood of Noble Men*, p. 11; Harris, "'The Yellow Rose of Texas.' A Different Cultural View," *Callaloo*, p. 9; De Bruhl, *The Sword of San Jacinto*, pp. 95–106; Scheina, *Santa Anna*, p. 14; Fowler, *Santa Anna of Mexico*, p. 92; *Niles' Weekly Register*, June 25, 1836; *New Hampshire Gazette*, Portsmouth, New Hampshire, March 30, 1829.

90. *San Antonio Express*, July 19, 1907.

91. De Bruhl, *The Sword of San Jacinto*, pp. 98, 103, 108, 119, 194.

92. Ramsey, *Texas Sinners and Revolutionaries*, p. 37.

93. *New Hampshire Gazette*, March 30, 1829; Ramsey, *Texas Sinners and Revolutionaries*, pp. 61–63.

94. Fowler, *Santa Anna of Mexico*, pp. 8–17; *Niles' Weekly Register*, June 25, 1836; Ramsey, *Texas Sinners and Revolutionaries*, p. 64.

95. Jerry J. Gaddy, *Texas in Revolt, Contemporary Newspaper Account of the Texas Revolution* (Fort Collins: Old Army Press, 1973), p. 91.

96. *Richmond Enquirer*, June 14, 1836.

97. Perry, trans. and ed., *With Santa Anna in Texas*, p. 125.

98. Riley and Etulain, eds., *Wild Women of the Old West*, p. 37; Donovan, *The Blood of Heroes*, p. 326.

99. Nevin, *The Texans*, p. 128.

100. Moore, *Eighteen Minutes*, pp. 233–235; Donovan, *The Blood of Heroes*, p. 324; Edwin P. Hoyt, *The Alamo: An Illustrated History* (Dallas: Taylor, 1999), p. 148.

101. Hardin, *Texian Iliad*, pp. 191, 199–200; De Bruhl, *Sword of San Jacinto*, p. 201; Hardin, *The Alamo 1836*, pp. 76, 79; Nofi, *The Alamo*, p. 146.

102. Hardin, *Texian Iliad*, pp. 191, 217; De Bruhl, *Sword of San Jacinto*, p. 205; Nofi, *The Alamo*, p. 146.

103. Delgado, "The Battle of San Jacinto," The McArdle Notebooks, Texas State Library and Archives Commission; Pohl, *The Battle of San Jacinto*, pp. 15–16; Nofi, *The Alamo*, p. 146.

104. Pohl, *The Battle of San Jacinto*, pp. 15–16; Donovan, *The Blood of Heroes*, p. 326.
105. Pohl, *The Battle of San Jacinto*, pp. 15–16; Hardin, *Texian Iliad*, pp. 191, 200.
106. Bass and Brunson, eds., *Fragile Empires*, p. 10.
107. Hardin, *Texian Iliad*, p. 191; *New Hampshire Gazette*, March 30, 1829; McVea, *Making Myth of Emily*, pp. 116, 118–119; "Emily D. West," The Handbook of Texas Online; "Lorenzo de Zavala," The Handbook of Texas Online; Gray, *Diary of William Fairfax Gray*, pp. 120, 145, 164.
108. Gaddy, *Texas in Revolt*, p. 70.

Chapter VII

1. Gaddy, *Texas in Revolt*, p. 75.
2. *The Floridian*, May 13, 1837; Hardin, *The Alamo 1836*, p. 79; Pohl, *The Battle of San Jacinto*, p. 24; Hardin, *Texian Iliad*, pp. 191, 199; Moore, *Eighteen Minutes*, pp. 237–240, 247–248; *Memphis Enquirer*, Memphis, Tennessee, August 26, 1837; Donovan, *The Blood of Heroes*, pp. 324–325; *Houston Telegraph*, March 28, 1837; Hoyt, *The Alamo*, pp. 148, 152; Gray, *Diary of Col. Wm. Fairfax Gray*, p. 145.
3. Hardin, *Texian Iliad*, p. 191.
4. Gray, *Diary of Col. Wm. Fairfax Gray*, p. 146.
5. Moore, *Eighteen Minutes*, pp. 236–237, 257; Riley and Etulain, eds., *Wild Women of the Old West*, p. 31; Dunn, "One More Piece of the Puzzle," *The Compass Rose*; Hardin, *Texian Iliad*, pp. 199–200; Donovan, *The Blood of Heroes*, p. 328.
6. Santos, *Santa Anna's Campaign Against Texas*, pp. 97–99; Long, *Duel of Eagles*, pp. 307–308; De Bruhl, *The Sword of San Jacinto*, pp. 128, 205; Hoyt, *The Alamo*, pp. 148–150; Pohl, *The Battle of San Jacinto*, p. 28; Hardin, *Texian Iliad*, pp. 200–202; *Richmond Enquirer*, June 10, 1836; Moore, *Eighteen Minutes*, pp. 236, 258–270; Riley and Etulain, eds., *Wild Women of the Old West*, p. 37; Nofi, *The Alamo*, p. 146; *Commercial Bulletin and Missouri Literacy Register*, St. Louis, Missouri, June 15, 1835; Scheina, *Santa Anna*, pp. 6, 24; Donovan, *The Blood of Heroes*, pp. 325, 328–329; Weems and Weems, *Dream of Empire*, p. 87.
7. Hollon, ed., *William Bollaert's Texas*, p. 108; Nofi, *The Alamo*, p. 149.
8. *Baltimore Gazette and Daily Advertiser*, Baltimore, Maryland, June 11, 1836.
9. Delgado, "The Battle of San Jacinto," The McArdle Notebooks, Texas State Library and Archives Commission; De Bruhl, *The Sword of San Jacinto*, pp. 202–205; Hardin, *The Alamo 1836*, p. 79; "Emily D. West," The Handbook of Texas Online; McVea, *Making Myth of Emily*, pp. 116, 118; Pohl, *The Battle of San Jacinto*, p. 21; Fowler, *Santa Anna of Mexico*, p. 170; Hardin, *Texian Iliad*, p. 189; Moore, *Eighteen Minutes*, pp. 152–153, 201, 263–268; Weems and Weems, *Dream of Empire*, p. 88; Donovan, *The Blood of Heroes*, p. 325.
10. Hardin, *The Alamo 1836*, pp. 79–80; Moore, *Eighteen Minutes*, pp. 236, 263–282; Hoyt, *The Alamo*, p. 151.
11. Pohl, *The Battle of San Jacinto*, p. 31; Moore, *Eighteen Minutes*, p. 236.
12. *Texas Mute Ranger*, April 1882, Ford Papers, Center for American History; Scheina, *Santa Anna*, pp. 14, 44; "Emily D. West," The Handbook of Texas Online; Fowler, *Santa Anna of Mexico*, pp. 92, 166; Huffines, *Blood of Noble Men*, p. 57; Hollon, ed., *William Bollaert's Texas*, p. 108, note 24; Stampp, *The Peculiar Institution*, pp. 350–361; Crisp, *Sleuthing the Alamo*, pp. 189–191.
13. Memorials and Petitions, petition of Diana Leonard, December 14, 1840, Texas State Library and Archives Commission, Austin, Texas; Walraven and Walraven, *The Magnificent Barbarians*, pp. 156–157; Muir, "The Free Negro in Harris County, Texas," Southwestern Historical Quarterly Online, p. 5; Crisp, *Sleuthing the Alamo*, p. 192; McVea, *Making Myth of Emily*, p. 19; Moore, *Eighteen Minutes*, p. 162; Hollon, ed., *William Bollaert's Texas*, p. 108, note 24; Nofi, *The Alamo*, pp. 194–195.
14. Perry, ed. and trans., *With Santa Anna in Texas*, pp. 104–105; *Wisconsin Democrat*, Madison, Wisconsin, May 8, 1847; Zaboly, *An Altar for Their Sons*, p. 291.
15. *Texas Mute Ranger*, April 1882, Ford Papers, Center for American History; Salas, *Soldaderas*, p. 29; Kelley, *Los Brazos de Dios*, pp. 99.
16. Barr, *Black Texans*, pp. 28–29, 31; Campbell, *An Empire for Slavery*, p. 180; Kelley, *Los Brazos de Dios*, p. 99.
17. Delgado, "The Battle of San Jacinto," The McArdle Notebooks, Texas State Library and Archives Commission; Hardin, *The Alamo 1836*, pp. 37, 39, 47; Dimmick, *Sea of Mud*, p. 22–23; Fowler, *Santa Anna of Mexico*, p. 171; Moore, *Eighteen Minutes*, p. 292; Nofi, *The Alamo*, pp. 193–194; Jackson, *Alamo Legacy*, p. 16.
18. *Richmond Enquirer*, June 14, 1836; *Niles' Register*, February 6, 1836.
19. Dimmick, *Sea of Mud*, p. 23; Moore, *Eighteen Minutes*, p. 292.
20. Perry, trans. and ed., *With Santa Anna in Texas*, pp. 26, 81, 98; Daughters of the Republic of Texas, *The Alamo*, p. 49.
21. Jackson, *Alamo Legacy*, p. 149.
22. Pohl, *The Battle of San Jacinto*, p. 24.
23. Moore, *Eighteen Minutes*, pp. 292–293; 301–302.
24. Perry, ed. and trans., *With Santa Anna in Texas*, pp. 130–131; Donovan, *The Blood of Heroes*, p. 327.
25. Delgado, "The Battle of San Jacinto," McArdle Notebooks, Texas State Library and Archives Commission; Hoyt, *The Alamo*, p. 150.
26. William C. Davis, *Lone Star Rising: The Revolutionary Birth of the Texas Republic* (New York: The Free Press, 2004), pp. 268–269; Brands, *Lone Star Nation: How a Ragged Army of Volunteers Won the Battle for Texas Independence* (New York: Doubleday, 2004), pp. 448–449; Gaddy, *Texas in Revolt*, p. 93; Hardin, *Texian Iliad*, p. 209.

27. Brands, *Lone Star Nation*, p. 448.
28. Pohl, *The Battle of San Jacinto*, p. 36; Fowler, *Santa Anna of Mexico*, p. 171; Hardin, *Texian Iliad*, p. 209.
29. Moore, *Eighteen Minutes*, p. 309; Donovan, *The Blood of Heroes*, p. 305; "Thomas Jefferson Rusk," The Handbook of Texas Online; Hoyt, *The Alamo*, p. 151.
30. McVea, *Making Myth of Emily*, p. 23; Crisp, *Sleuthing the Alamo*, pp. 190–191.
31. McVea, *Making Myth of Emily*, pp. 22–23, 136; *Philadelphia Public Ledger*, Philadelphia, Pennsylvania, May 21, 1836; *Portland Advertiser*, Portland, Maine, May 3, 1836; Roger Borroel, East Chicago, Indiana, to author, February 15, 2008, and April 9 and 11, 2012; Crisp, *Sleuthing the Alamo*, pp. 190–191.
32. Scheina, *Santa Anna*, p. 14; Donovan, *The Blood of Heroes*, p. 328; "Copano, Tx," The Handbook of Texas Online.
33. *National Gazette*, Philadephia, Pennsylvania, June 11, 1836; Delgado, "The Battle of San Jacinto," The McArdle Notebooks, Texas State Library and Archives Commission; Bernard Chevallier, *Napoleon* (Memphis: Lithograph, 1993), p. 146; Riley and Etulain, eds., *Wild Women of the Old West*, p. 37; Nofi, *The Alamo*, p. 150; Hoyt, *The Alamo*, p. 150; Scheina, *Santa Anna*, pp. 5–6, 24; Nicolle, *The Moors*, p. 10.
34. Perry, ed. and trans., *With Santa Anna in Texas*, pp. 61–62.
35. *The Telegraph and Texas Register*, January 2, 1836.
36. McVea, *Making Myth of Emily*, p. 140.
37. *National Gazette*, June 11, 1836; Crawford, ed., *The Eagle*, p. 54; Scheina, *Santa Anna*, p. 32; Daughters of the Republic of Texas, *The Alamo*, pp. 22, 49; Pieter Geyl, *Napoleon: For and Against* (Middlesex: Penguin Books, 1976), pp. 25–33.
38. *National Gazette*, June 11, 1836; Crawford, ed., *The Eagle*, pp. xi, 54; Roger Borroel, translator and editor, *Field Reports of the Mexican Army During the Texan War of 1836*, Vol. 8 (East Chicago, Indiana: La Villita, 2007), p. 14; De Bruhl, *Sword of San Jacinto*, p. 213; McVea, *Making Myth of Emily*, p. 140; Moore, *Eighteen Minutes*, p. 316; Scheina, *Santa Anna*, p. 32; Nofi, *The Alamo*, p. 150; Donovan, *The Blood of Heroes*, pp. 332, 334.
39. Delgado, "The Battle of San Jacinto," The McArdle Notebooks, Texas State Library and Archives Commission; Donovan, *The Blood of Heroes*, pp. 332, 334; *National Gazette*, June 11, 1836; Scheina, *Santa Anna*, p. 32.
40. De Bruhl, *Sword of San Jacinto*, p. 208; Crisp, *Sleuthing the Alamo*, pp. 188–191.
41. *National Gazette*, June 11, 1836; Nofi, *The Alamo*, p. 154; Donovan, *The Blood of Heroes*, pp. 332, 334.
42. Fowler, *Santa Anna of Mexico*, pp. 171–172; *National Gazette*, June 11, 1836; Moore, *Eighteen Minutes*, p. 287; Scheina, *Santa Anna*, pp. 31–32; Nofi, *The Alamo*, p. 150; Donovan, *The Blood of Heroes*, pp. 332, 334.

43. Scheina, *Santa Anna*, p. 32.
44. Ibid., pp. 14, 44; *New York Herald*, July 14, 1836.
45. De Bruhl, *Sword of San Jacinto*, p. 212; Hollon, ed., *William Bollaert's Texas*, p. 108, note 24; Nofi, *The Alamo*, pp. 154, 159
46. James A. Michener, *The Eagle and The Raven* (Austin: State House Press, 1990), p. 160; *National Gazette*, June 11, 1836.
47. James A. Michener, *Texas* (New York: Random House, 1985), p. 409.
48. Ibid.; Catherine Squires, *African Americans and the Media* (Cambridge: Polity Press, 2009), pp. 25, 34; Andrew Hacker, *Two Nations: Black and White, Separate, Hostile, Unequal* (New York: Ballantine, 1995) p. 67.
49. De Bruhl, *Sword of San Jacinto*, p. 208; Crawford, ed., *The Eagle*, p. 55; Hollon, ed., *William Bollaert's Texas*, p. 108, note 24; Nofi, *The Alamo*, p. 159.
50. Crawford, *The Eagle*, pp. ix, xii.
51. De Bruhl, *Sword of San Jacinto*, pp. 193–194, 212; Nofi, *The Alamo*, p. 159; "James Hazard Perry," The Handbook of Texas Online.
52. De Bruhl, *Sword of San Jacinto*, p. 193–194, 197, 212; Moore, *Eighteen Minutes*, pp. 66, 192, 329, 334–335; Nofi, *The Alamo*, p. 159; Donovan, *The Blood of Heroes*, p. 323.
53. Donovan, *The Blood of Heroes*, p. 331.
54. *National Gazette*, June 11, 1836; Crawford, ed., *The Eagle*, p. xi; Moore, *Eighteen Minutes*, pp. 368–369, 411; Perry, ed. and trans., *With Santa Anna in Texas*, p. 104; Riley and Etulain, eds., *Wild Women of the Old West*, p. 37; Hollon, ed., *William Bollaert's Texas*, p. 108, note 24; Nofi, *The Alamo*, p. 150; Scheina, *Santa Anna*, p. 32; Donovan, *The Blood of Heroes*, pp. 332, 334.
55. Ramon Eduardo Ruiz, *Mexico: Why a Few Are Rich and the People Poor* (Berkeley: University of California Press, 2010), p. 61.
56. Fowler, *Santa Anna of Mexico*, pp. ix–x, 174–175; Lack, *The Texas Revolutionary Experience*, p. 244; James Lockhart and Stuart B. Schwartz, *Early Latin America: A History of Colonial Spanish America and Brazil* (Cambridge: Cambridge University Press, 1997), pp. 315–321, 342; Chasteen, *Born in Blood and Fire*, pp. 53–57; Scheina, *Santa Anna*, pp. 24, 30; F. G. Hourtoulle, *Austerlitz: The Empire at its Zenith* (Paris: Histoire and Collections, 2003), pp. 39–41; Johnson, *Napoleon*, pp. 58–59.
57. Fowler, *Santa Anna of Mexico*, pp. 182–184; Scheina, *Santa Anna*, p. 30.
58. Fowler, *Santa Anna*, pp. ix–x; Daughters of the Republic of Texas, *The Alamo: Long Barrack Museum*, p. 49; Santos, *Santa Anna's Campaign Against Texas*, p. 13–14; Gaddy, *Texas in Revolt*, p. 14; D. A. Brading, *Mexican Phoenix, Our Lady of Guadalupe: Image and Tradition Across Five Centuries* (Cambridge: Cambridge University Press, 2001), pp. 54–242; Scheina, *Santa Anna*, pp. 23–25, 30, 33.
59. Moore, *Eighteen Minutes*, p. 370; *Niles' Weekly Register*, June 25, 1836; Perry, ed. and trans., *With*

Santa Anna in Texas, p. 104; Jackson, ed., *Almonte's Texas*, p. 376; Riley and Etulain, eds., *Wild Women of the Old West*, p. 37; Felix Markham, *Napoleon* (New York: Penguin Books, 1963), pp. 30–31, 72–73; Kent Biffle, "Details Emerge on Legendary Yellow Rose," *The Dallas Morning News*, Dallas, Texas, April 9, 2007; Fowler, *Santa Anna of Mexico*, p. 92; Huffines, *Blood of Noble Men*, p. 57; Hollon, ed., *William Bollaert's Texas*, p. 108, note 24; Crisp, *Sleuthing the Alamo*, p. 194; Donovan, *The Blood of Heroes*, pp. 300, 332, 334; Scheina, *Santa Anna*, pp. 14, 31–32, 44; Ragsdale, *Women and Children of the Alamo*, pp. 56, 62.

60. Riley and Etulain, eds., *Wild Women of the Old West*, p. 39; Salas, *Soldaderas*, p. 29; Dunn, "One More Piece of the Puzzle," *The Compass Rose*; Hollon, ed., *William Bollaert's Texas*, p. 108, note 24; Crisp, *Sleuthing the Alamo*, p. 194.

61. Delgado, "The Battle of San Jacinto," The McArdle Notebooks, Texas State Library and Archives Commission; *National Gazette*, June 11, 1836; Fowler, *Santa Anna of Mexico*, pp. 170–172; McVea, *Making Myth of Emily*, pp. 12–14, 17, 21–22, 25–26; Nofi, *The Alamo*, p. 156; Scheina, *Santa Anna*, p. 32; Daughters of the Republic of Texas, *The Alamo*, p. 49; Hoyt, *The Alamo*, p. 153; Donovan, *The Blood of Heroes*, pp. 205, 284, 332, 334. 375.

62. *National Gazette*, June 11, 1836.

63. Ibid.

64. Elsa Larralde, *The Land and People of Mexico* (New York: J. B. Lippincott, 1964), p. 75.

65. Ibid., pp. 75–76.

66. Perry, ed. and trans., *With Santa Anna in Texas*, pp. 130–131; Crisp, *Sleuthing the Alamo*, p. 194.

67. Perry, ed. and trans., *With Santa Anna in Texas*, p. 169.

68. Dimmick, *Sea of Mud*, p. 327.

69. Smithwick, *The Evolution of a State*, p. 99.

70. Fowler, *Santa Anna of Mexico*, pp. 171–172; Moore, *Eighteen Minutes*, p. 287; Scheina, *Santa Anna*, p. 32; Donovan, *The Blood of Heroes*, pp. 332, 334.

71. Delgado, "The Battle of San Jacinto," The McArdle Notebooks, Texas State Library and Archives Commission; Dimmick, *Sea of Mud*, p. 7; Scheina, *Santa Anna*, p. 32; Donovan, *The Blood of Heroes*, pp. 332, 334.

72. Donovan, *The Blood of Heroes*, pp. 332, 334; Scheina, *Santa Anna*, p. 32.

73. Delgado, "The Battle of San Jacinto," The McArdle Notebooks, Texas State Library and Archives Commission; De Bruhl, *Sword of San Jacinto*, p. 208; Moore, *Eighteen Minutes*, pp. xiv, 283; Hollon, ed., *William Bollaert's Texas*, p. 108, note 24; Donovan, *The Blood of Heroes*, pp. 332, 334; Scheina, *Santa Anna*, p. 32.

74. Delgado, "The Battle of San Jacinto," The McArdle Notebooks, Texas State Library and Archives Commission; Davis, *Lone Star Rising*, pp. 268–269; Fehrenbach, *Lone Star*, pp. 230–231; Fowler, *Santa Anna of Mexico*, p. 170; Brands, *Lone Star Nation*, pp. 448–449; Hoyt, *The Alamo*, pp. 154–155; Pohl, *The Battle of San Jacinto*, pp. 36–37; Moore, *Eighteen Minutes*, pp. xix, 286, 294, 324–325; Scheina, *Santa Anna*, p. 32; Nofi, *The Alamo*, p. 150; Jackson, *Alamo Legacy*, pp. 148–150; Barr, *Black Texans*, p. 6; "Dick the Drummer," The Handbook of Texas Online; "Dick the Drummer at the Battle of San Jacinto," Texas Black History Preservation Project, Documenting the Complete African American Experience in Texas, internet; Hoyt, *The Alamo*, p. 150; Donovan, *The Blood of Heroes*, pp. 331–332, 334

75. Barr, *Black Texans*, p. 6; Dick the Drummer at the Battle of San Jacinto, Texas Black History Preservation Project, Documenting the Complete African American Experience in Texas, internet; Barr, *Texans in Revolt*, pp. 17–18; Walraven and Walraven, *The Magnificent Barbarians*, pp. 152–153; Moore, *Eighteen Minutes*, pp. xvii, 299–300, 316–317, 324–325; Barr, *Black Texans*, p. 6; Hoyt, *The Alamo*, p. 156; "Dick the Drummer," The Handbook of Texas Online; Donovan, *The Blood of Heroes*, p. 332.

76. Perry, ed. and trans., *With Santa Anna in Texas*, p. 127; Hoyt, *The Alamo*, p. 156; Moore, *Eighteen Minutes*, pp. 294, 316–318, 324–325.

77. *Maryland Gazette*, May 26, 1836; *National Gazette*, June 11, 1836; Perry, ed. and trans., *With Santa Anna in Texas*, p. 127; Jackson, ed., *Almonte's Texas*, p. 375; Fowler, *Santa Anna of Mexico*, pp. 171–172; Moore, *Eighteen Minutes*, pp. 316–318, 328–329; Nofi, *The Alamo*, pp. 154–156; Scheina, *Santa Anna*, p. 32; Hoyt, *The Alamo*, pp. 155–156; Hardin, *Texian Iliad*, p. 99; Donovan, *The Blood of Heroes*, pp. 332, 334.

78. Perry, ed. and trans., *With Santa Anna in Texas*, p. 127.

79. Delgado, "The Battle of San Jacinto," The McArdle Notebooks, Texas State Library and Archives Commission; Moore, *Eighteen Minutes*, p. 236. List of Mexican Officers Taken Prisoner, "The Battle of San Jacinto Notebook," The McArdle Notebooks, Texas State Library and Archives Commission; Moore, *Eighteen Minutes*, pp. 329, 329, 335, 371–372, 377; McVea, *Making Myth of Emily*, pp. 20–21, 25; Brear, *Inherit the Alamo*, p. 46; Hollon, ed., *William Bollaert's Texas*, p. 108, note 24; Hoyt, *The Alamo*, pp. 156–157; Scheina, *Santa Anna*, p. 32; Donovan, *The Blood of Heroes*, pp. 332, 334.

80. Moore, *Eighteen Minutes*, pp. 329, 334–335; Hoyt, *The Alamo*, p. 156; Brear, *Inherit the Alamo*, p. 46; Hollon, ed., *William Bollaert's Texas*, p. 108, note 24.

81. Michener, *Texas*, pp. 409–410; Brear, *Inherit the Alamo*, p. 46; Moore, *Eighteen Minutes*, pp. 329, 334–335; Hollon, ed., *William Bollaert's Texas*, p. 108, note 24; Crisp, *Sleuthing the Alamo*, pp. 189–191.

82. Moore, *Eighteen Minutes*, p. 329–330, 334–335; Brear, *Inherit the Alamo*, p. 46; "Walter Payne Lane," The Handbook of Texas Online.

83. Moore, *Eighteen Minutes*, p. 337; Hoyt, *The Alamo*, p. 159; List of Mexican Officers Taken Prisoner, "Battle of San Jacinto Notebook," The McArdle

Notebooks, Texas State Library and Archives Commission.
84. Long, *Duel of Eagles*, p. 313; Moore, *Eighteen Minutes*, pp. 344–357.
85. Donovan, *Blood of Heroes*, p. 334.
86. *The Herald*, June 13, 1836; Dimmick, *Sea of Mud*, p. 10; Long, *Duel of Eagles*, p. 313; Moore, *Eighteen Minutes*, p. 344; Nofi, *The Alamo*, pp. 193–194.
87. *National Gazette*, June 11, 1836.
88. Ibid.; Perry, ed. and trans., *With Santa Anna in Texas*, p. 127; Fowler, *Santa Anna of Mexico*, pp. 171–172.
89. *New Orleans Bee*, May 11, 1836.
90. *The Herald*, June 13, 1836.
91. Jackson, ed., *Almonte's Texas*, p. 375; Long, *Duel of Eagles*, p. 313; Moore, *Eighteen Minutes*, pp. 329, 334–336; Nofi, *The Alamo*, pp. 154–156; Hoyt, *The Alamo*, pp. 153, 159, 162.
92. Dimmick, *Sea of Mud*, p. 327; List of Mexican Officers Killed at San Jacinto, "The Battle of San Jacinto Notebook," The McArdle Notebooks, Texas State Library and Archives Commission.
93. William S. Taylor Account, The McArdle Notebooks, Texas State Library and Archives Commission, Austin, Texas.
94. Long, *Duel of Eagles*, p. 314.
95. Moore, *Eighteen Minutes*, p. 360.
96. Delgado, "The Battle of San Jacinto," The McArdle Notebooks, Texas State Library and Archives Commission; List of Mexican Officers Taken Prisoner, "Battle of San Jacinto Notebook," The McArdle Notebooks, Texas State Library and Archives Commission.
97. Long, *Duel of Eagles*, p. 313.
98. Moore, *Eighteen Minutes*, pp. 350–353; Donovan, *The Blood of Heroes*, p. 336; "John Forbes," The Handbook of Texas Online.
99. *Commonwealth*, Frankfort, Kentucky, May 25, 1836.
100. *Commercial Bulletin*, April 11, 1836.
101. Moore, *Eighteen Minutes*, pp. 370, 384; "Emily D. West," The Handbook of Texas Online; Hollon, ed., *William Bollaert's Texas*, p. 108, note 24; "Isaac N. Moreland," The Handbook of Texas Online; Donovan, *The Blood of Heroes*, pp. 332–333; Weems and Weems, *Dream of Empire*, p. 88.
102. *The Herald*, June 13, 1836; Moore, *Eighteen Minutes*, pp. 344–357.
103. Long, *Duel of Eagles*, p. 314.
104. *Morning Courier and New York Enquirer*, New York, New York, July 9, 1836; *The Herald*, June 13, 1836; Dimmick, *Sea of Mud*, p. 25; .
105. Dimmick, *Sea of Mud*, pp. 25–26.
106. *The Herald*, June 13, 1836.
107. Moore, *Eighteen Minutes*, p. 392.
108. Ibid., pp. 389–390; Jackson, ed., *Almonte's Texas*, p. 375; Gray, *Diary of Col. Wm. Fairfax Gray*, pp. 120, 134.
109. *Richmond Enquirer*, June 14, 1836.
110. Dimmick, *Sea of Mud*, p. 331; Moore, *Eighteen Minutes*, p. 364.
111. Bass and Brunson, eds., *Fragile Empires*, p. 7.
112. Moore, *Eighteen Minutes*, p. 364.
113. *New Orleans Bee*, May 11, 1836; *Richmond Enquirer*, June 10, 1836; Zaboly, *An Altar for Their Sons*, p. 337; De Bruhl, *Sword of San Jacinto*, p. 213; Moore, *Eighteen Minutes*, pp. 300, 339, 350–352, 372, 380–382, 389; Donovan, *The Blood of Heroes*, p. 334.
114. Jackson, ed., *Almonte's Texas*, p. 407; "Emily D. West," The Handbook of Texas Online.
115. Bass and Brunson, eds., *Fragile Empires*, p. 191; Riley and Etulain, eds., *Wild Women of the Old West*, p. 39.
116. *The Herald*, June 15, 1836.
117. Ibid., June 10, 1836.
118. Robert V. Remini, *Andrew Jackson and His Indian Wars* (New York: Penguin Books, 2001), pp. 63–64, 75–79; Ward Churchill, *A Little Matter of Genocide: Holocaust and Denial in the Americas, 1492 to the Present* (San Francisco: City Lights Books, 1997), pp. 186, 215–216; Fowler, *Santa Anna of Mexico*, pp. ix–x, xix; DeBruhl, *Sword of San Jacinto*, pp. 42–44; Merk, *History of the Westward Movement* (New York: Alfred A. Knopf, 1978), p. xv, 274–275.
119. Merk, *History of the Westward Movement*, p. 275.
120. Crisp, *Sleuthing the Alamo*, pp. 189–191.
121. Gaddy, *Texas in Revolt*, p. 87.
122. Fehrenbach, *Lone Star*, p. 201; *Texas Republican*, March 2, 1836; *Telegraph and Texas Register*, February 27, 1836;

Chapter VIII

1. Merk, *History of the Westward Movement*, pp. 274–275; Fleming, *Liberty!*, pp. 271–274; Hardin, *Texian Iliad*, pp. 105–106.
2. Ray Raphael, *Founding Myths, Stories that Hide Our Patriotic Past* (New York: MJF Books, 2004), p. 27; Hardin, *Texian Iliad*, pp. xi–xiii, 184–185; Crisp, *Sleuthing the Alamo*, pp. 190–191.
3. Raphael, *Founding Myths*, pp. 43–44.
4. Sara E. Melzer and Leslie W. Rabine, *Rebel Daughters, Women and the French Revolution* (New York: Oxford University Press, 1992), pp. 3–32, 102–116.
5. Ibid., p. 30.
6. Ibid., pp. 28–31; Michener, *Texas*, p. 418; Hollon, ed., *William Bollaert's Texas*, p. 108, note 24; Crisp, *Sleuthing the Alamo*, pp. 189–194.
7. Crisp, *Sleuthing the Alamo*, p. 190.
8. Ibid., p. 194.
9. Moore, *Eighteen Minutes*, p. 389; "Emily D. West," The Handbook of Texas Online; Bass and Brunson, eds., *Fragile Empires*, p. 7; McVea, *Making Myth of Emily*, pp. 31–34; Lack, *The Texas Revolutionary Experience*, pp. 228, 249; Hollon, ed., *William Bollaert's Texas*, p. 108, note 24; Crisp, *Sleuthing the Alamo*, pp. 189–191; "New Washington Association," The Handbook of Texas Online; Merk, *History of the Westward Movement*, p. 273; Gaddy, *Texas in Revolt*,

p. 8; Soustelle, *Daily Life of the Aztecs*, pp. 46, 184; Kelley, *Los Brazos de Dios*, p. 99.

10. Jackson, ed., *Almonte's Texas*, p. 415; *Democratic Free Press*, September 7, 1836; Bill Groneman, *Defense of a Legend: Crockett and the de la Peña Diary* (Plano: Republic of Texas Press, 1994), pp. 56–58.

11. Hollon, ed., *William Bollaert's Texas*, p. 108, note 24; Lutzweiler, "Emily D. West and the Yellow Prose of Texas," New Haven Museum and Historical Society; Crisp, *Sleuthing the Alamo*, p. 190.

12. Jackson, ed., *Almonte's Texas*, p. 377; McVea, *Making Myth of Emily*, pp. 21–23; Hollon, ed., *William Bollaert's Texas*, p. 108, note 24.

13. Walraven and Walraven, *The Magnificent Barbarians*, p. 157.

14. Fowler, *Santa Anna of Mexico*, pp. 166–167; Huffines, *Blood of Noble Men*, p. 57.

15. Fowler, *Santa Anna of Mexico*, p. 425, note 37.

16. McVea, *Making Myth of Emily*, p. 22; Crisp, *Sleuthing the Alamo*, p. 190.

17. Roger Borroel, East Chicago, Indiana, to author, February 15, 2008.

18. McVea, *Making Myth of Emily*, pp. 23–26, 143; Delgado, The Battle of San Jacinto Notebook, The McArdle Notebooks, Texas State Library and Archives Commission; Brear, *Inherit the Alamo*, p. 46.

19. De Bruhl, *Sword of San Jacinto*, pp. 218–219; Hollon, ed., *William Bollaert's Texas*, p. 108, note 24; Crisp, *Sleuthing the Alamo*, pp. 189–191; Donovan, *The Blood of Heroes*, p. 327.

20. Pohl, *The Battle of San Jacinto*, p. 48.

21. Hollon, ed., *William Bollaert's Texas*, p. 108, note 24; Crisp, *Sleuthing the Alamo*, pp. 189–190; Donovan, *The Blood of Heroes*, p. 327.

22. Bass and Brunson, *Fragile Empires*, p. 97.

23. Ibid., p. 318.

24. Ramsey, *Texas Sinners and Revolutionaries*, p. 36.

25. Gaddy, *Texas in Revolt*, p. 78; Hardin, *Texian Iliad*, pp. 177, 208–209; Smithwick, *The Evolution of a State*, p. 93.

26. Smithwick, *The Evolution of a State*, p. 64.

27. Jackson, ed., *Almonte's Texas*, p. 377; Lutzweiler, "Emily D. West and the Yellow Prose of Texas," New Haven Museum and Historical Society; Crisp, *Sleuthing the Alamo*, pp. 189–191; Muir, "The Free Negro in Harris County, Texas," Southwestern Historical Quarterly Online, p. 8; Moore, *Eighteen Minutes*, pp. 370, 415; McVea, *Making Myth of Emily*, p. 20; Riley and Etulain, eds., *Wild Women of the Old West*, pp. 37, 39; Jay Monaghan, *Custer: The Life of General George Armstrong Custer* (Lincoln: University of Nebraska Press, 1971), pp. 315–324, 327–328 and 328 note; Salas, *Soldaderas*, p. 29; Hollon, ed., *William Bollaert's Texas*, p. 108, note 24; "Emily D. West," The Handbook of Texas Online; Scheina, *Santa Anna*, p. 30; John Koster, "Plural Wives and the Plains Indians," *Wild West* (June 2012), p. 44; Merk, *History of the Westward Movement*, p. 273; Weems and Weems, *Dream of Empire*, p. 69; Soustelle, *Daily Life of the Aztecs*, pp. 46, 184.

28. *New Hampshire Gazette*, March 30, 1829; De Bruhl, *The Sword of San Jacinto*, pp. 97–104.

29. Moore, *Eighteen Minutes*, pp. 223–310, 417; Shackford, *David Crockett*, pp. 224–227; "Emily D. West," The Handbook of Texas Online; Nofi, *The Alamo*, p. 152; Donovan, *The Blood of Heroes*, p. 324.

30. Richards, "Gentlemen of Property and Standing," pp. 42–166, note 70, p. 122; Warner, *New Haven Negroes*, pp. 58; Gaddy, *Texas in Revolt*, pp. 77–78.

31. *The Herald*, May 19, 1836; Hollon, ed., *William Bollaert's Texas*, p. 108, note 24; Crisp, *Sleuthing the Alamo*, pp. 190–191; White, *Ar'n't I a Woman*, pp. 28–33; Weems and Weems, *Dream of Empire*, p. 69.

32. Crisp, *Sleuthing the Alamo*, pp. 190–191; Hollon, ed., *William Bollaert's Texas*, p. 108, note 24; White, *Ar'n't I a Woman*, pp. 28–33; Merk, *History of the Westward Movement*, pp. 263–275; Donovan, *The Blood of Heroes*, p. 327.

33. McVea, *Making Myth of Emily*, p. 26; Hollon, ed., *William Bollaert's Texas*, p. 108, note 24; Lutzweiler, "Emily D. West and the Yellow Prose of Texas," New Haven Museum and Historical Society; Crisp, *Sleuthing the Alamo*, pp. 190–191; White, *Ar'n't I a Woman*, pp. 28–33; Johnnydad, "The Yellow Rose of Texas, She was the Sweetest Gal You'll Ever Know," July 10, 2010, Wikinut, internet.

34. Darrell Flint, "Our Yellow Rose isn't blighted," *San Antonio Express-News*, April 25, 1995; Hollon, ed., *William Bollaert's Texas*, p. 108, note 24.

35. Scheina, *Santa Anna*, p. 90.

36. Will Fowler, *Santa Anna of Mexico* (Lincoln: University of Nebraska Press, 2007), p. ix.

37. Ibid., p. x.

38. Ibid., p. xxi; Donovan, *The Blood of Heroes*, p. 327.

39. Fowler, *Santa Anna of Mexico*, pp. ix–xxi, 171; Pohl, *The Battle of San Jacinto*, p. 36; De Bruhl, *Sword of San Jacinto*, p. 208; Moore, *Eighteen Minutes*, p. 329; Crisp, *Sleuthing the Alamo*, pp. 189–191.

40. Fowler, *Santa Anna of Mexico*, pp. 171–172; Donovan, *The Blood of Heroes*, pp. 332.

41. Pohl, *The Battle of San Jacinto*, p. 73.

42. Brear, *Inherit the Alamo*, pp. 48–53.

43. Frank Thompson, *The Alamo: A Cultural History* (Dallas: Taylor Trade, 2001), 149–154; Crisp, *Sleuthing the Alamo*, p. 154–155.

44. Thompson, *The Alamo*, p. 147.

45. Jordan, *White Man's Burden*, pp. 69–86, Brear, *Inherit the Alamo*, pp. 60–62; Crisp, *Sleuthing the Alamo*, pp. 189–191; White, *Ar'n't I a Woman?*, pp. 29–33.

46. Bass and Brunson, eds., *Fragile Empires*, pp. 1–355; Hollon, ed., *William Bollaert's Texas*, p. 108, note 24; Crisp, *Sleuthing the Alamo*, pp. 190–191.

47. Muir, "The Free Negro in Harris County, Texas," Southwestern Historical Quarterly Online, p. 3; "Emily D. West," The Handbook of Texas Online; Crisp, *Sleuthing the Alamo*, pp. 189–101.

48. Lutzweiler, "Emily D. West and the Yellow Prose of Texas," New Haven Museum and Historical

Society; Crisp, *Sleuthing the Alamo*, pp. 189–191, 194; Muir, "The Free Negro in Harris County, Texas," Southwestern Historical Quarterly Online, pp. 2, 6, 9; McVea, *Making Myth of Emily*, pp. 27–30, "Emily D. West," The Handbook of Texas Online; Brear, *Inherit the Alamo*, p. 45; De Bruhl, *Sword of San Jacinto*, p. 16; Dunn, "One More Piece of the Puzzle," *The Compass Rose*; Hollon, ed., *William Bolleart's Texas*, p. 108, note 24.

49. Lutzweiler, "Emily D. West and the Yellow Prose of Texas," New Haven Museum and Historical Society; Hollon, ed., *William Bollaert's Texas*, pp. x, 108, note 24; Samuel Houston to James W. Fannin, March 11, 1836, A. J. Houston Collection, Texas State Library and Archives, Austin, Texas; Hansen, ed., *The Alamo Reader*, pp. 519–520; Dunn, "One More Piece of the Puzzle," *The Compass Rose*; White, *Ar'n't I a Woman?*, pp. 29–33.

50. Hollon, ed., *William Bollaert's Texas*, pp. 108 note 24, 128, 131.

51. Ibid., pp. xviii–xxi, 43 note 16, 108 note 24; Lutzweiler, "Emily D. West and the Yellow Prose of Texas"; Ilona Katzew, *Casta Painting* (New Haven: Yale University Press, 2004), pp. 49, 91, 117–118, 181; De Bruhl, *The Sword of San Jacinto*, pp. 7–8.

52. McVea, *Making Myth of Emily*, pp. 31–35; Dunn, "One More Piece of the Puzzle," *The Compass Rose*; Hollon, ed., *William Bollaert's Texas*, pp. x, 108 note 24.

53. De Bruhl, *Sword of San Jacinto*, pp. 280–283; *Jackson Mississippian*, Jackson, Mississippi, May 6, 1836.

54. Muir, "The Free Negro in Harris County, Texas," Southwestern Historical Quarterly Online, pp. 2, 9–10; Crisp, *Sleuthing the Alamo*, p. 189; McVea, *Making Myth of Emily*, pp. 27–28, 127; Hollon, ed., *William Bollaert's Texas*, p. 108, note 24.

55. Bass and Brunson, eds., *Fragile Empires*, pp. 29–30, 63, 134–135; Crisp, *Sleuthing the Alamo*, pp. 189–190; Hollon, ed., *William Bollaert's Texas*, p. 108, note 24.

56. Riley and Etulain, eds., *Wild Women of the Old West*, pp. 37, 39; Hollon, ed., *William Bollaert's Texas*, p. 108, note 24; Crisp, *Sleuthing the Alamo*, pp. 189–191.

57. Hollon, ed., *William Bollaert's Texas*, pp. xvii–xxvi, 108, note 24; Riley and Etulain, eds., *Wild Women of the Old West*, pp. 41–42; Bass and Brunson, eds., *Fragile Empires*, pp. xx–342.

58. Gray, *Diary of Col. Wm. Fairfax Gray*, p. 153.

59. Riley and Etulain, eds., *Wild Women of the Old West*, pp. 41–43; "Emily D. West," The Handbook of Texas Online.

60. Hollon, ed., *William Bollaert's Texas*, pp. xvii–xxvi, 108 note 24, 132; Bass and Brunson, eds., *Fragile Empires*, pp. xx–342.

Chapter IX

1. Antonia Fraser, *The Weaker Vessel* (New York: Alfred A. Knopf, 1984), pp. 1–6; "Emily D. West," The Handbook of Texas Online; White, *Ar'n't I a Woman?*, pp. 154–160.

2. McVea, *Making Myth of Emily*, p. 127; *Richmond Enquirer*, July 1, 1836; "Emily D. West," The Handbook of Texas Online; Muir, "The Free Negro in Harris County, Texas," Southwestern Historical Quarterly Online, pp. 4; Bass and Brunson, eds., *Fragile Empires*, p. 7; Moore, *Eighteen Minutes*, p. 370; "Isaac N. Moreland," The Handbook of Texas Online.

3. Muir, "The Free Negro in Harris County, Texas, Southwestern Historical Quarterly Online, pp. 9–10; McVea, *Making Myth of Emily*, p. 127; Riley and Etulain, eds., *Wild Women of the Old West*, p. 29; Campbell, ed., *The Laws of Slavery in Texas*, pp. 52–53, 57; Gray, *Diary of Col. Wm. Fairfax Gray*, p. 147.

4. Muir, "The Free Negro in Harris County, Texas," Southwestern Historical Quarterly Online, pp. 11–12.

5. Riley and Etulain, eds., *Wild Women of the Old West*, p. 29.

6. Moore, *Eighteen Minutes*, pp. 91–92, 85, 200–201, 213, 263, 276, 290, 313, 336, 370; "Emily D. West," The Handbook of Texas Online; Bass and Brunson, eds., *Fragile Empires*, p. 7; McVea, *Making Myth of Emily*, p. 142; Moore, *Eighteen Minutes*, pp. 341, 415–416, 436; Barr and Calvert, eds., *Black Leaders, Texans for their Times*, p. 30; "Isaac N. Moreland," The Handbook of Texas Online; "Twin Sisters," The Handbook of Texas Online.

7. Muir, "The Free Negro in Harris County, Texas," Southwestern Historical Quarterly Online, p. 3; "Emily D. West," The Handbook of Texas Online; Bass and Brunson, eds., *Fragile Empires*, pp. xxiii, 42–45.

8. "Emily D. West," The Handbook of Texas Online; Bass and Brunson, eds., *Fragile Empires*, pp. 36, 43–44, 66, 97–98. 102–103; Gray, *Diary of Col. Wm. Fairfax Gray*, p. 219.

9. Passport of Emily D. West, Texas State Library and Archives Commission, Austin, Texas; "Emily D. West," The Handbook of Texas Online; *Morning Courier and New York Enquirer*, New York, New York, July 9, 1836; Crisp, *Sleuthing the Alamo*, p. 191; Bass and Brunson, eds., *Fragile Empires*, pp. xxiii–xxiv; Muir, "The Free Negro in Harris County, Texas," Southwestern Historical Quarterly Online, pp. 3–4; McVea, *Making Myth of Emily*, pp. 35, 171, 173; Long, *Duel of Eagles*, p. 339; Hansen, ed., *The Alamo Reader*, p. 56; Memorials and Petitions, petition of Diana Leonard, December 14, 1840, Texas State Library and Archives, Austin, Texas; "Robert Anderson Irion," The Handbook of Texas Online; Moore, *Eighteen Minutes*, p. 370; De Bruhl, *Sword of San Jacinto*, pp. 224, 259, 281–282, 364–366; Lutzweiler, "Emily D. West and the Yellow Prose of Texas," New Haven Museum and Historical Society; Patricia Smith Prather and Jane Clements Monday, *From Slave to Statesman: The Legacy of Joshua Houston, Servant to Sam Houston* (Denton: University of North Texas Press, 1993), pp. 9, 17–18; *St. Louis Republic*, St. Louis, Missouri, November 18, 1888; *Galveston News*, Galveston, Texas, February 3, 1881; "Isaac N. Moreland," The Handbook

of Texas Online; Shirley, *More than Petticoats*, pp. ix–x; "David Gouverneur Burnet," The Handbook of Texas Online.
  10. Bass and Brunson, eds., *Fragile Empires*, p. 65.
  11. Ibid., pp. 43–44.
  12. Ibid., pp. 43–44.
  13. Ibid., p. 44.
  14. Campbell, *An Empire for Slavery*, pp. 50–66; Bass and Brunson, eds., *Fragile Empires*, pp. 42–43, 120; Campbell, ed., *The Laws of Slavery in Texas*, pp. 52, 57; Ronald White, *What Is America? A Short History of the New World Order* (New York: Da Capo Press, 2008), p. 150.
  15. Muir, "The Free Negro in Harris County, Texas," Southwestern Historical Quarterly Online; p. 3; Campbell, ed., *The Laws of Slavery in Texas*, p. 118; Crisp, *Sleuthing the Alamo*, p. 189.
  16. Glasrud and Pitre, *Black Women in Texas History*, pp. 14–15; Barr, *Black Texans*, pp. 3–12; Muir, "The Free Negro in Harris County, Texas," Southwestern Historical Quarterly Online, p. 3; McVea, *Making Myth of Emily*, p. 35; Campbell, ed., *The Laws of Slavery in Texas*, p. 66.
  17. Muir, "The Free Negro in Harris County, Texas," Southwestern Historical Quarterly Online, p. 17.
  18. "Emily D. West," The Handbook of Texas Online; McVea, *Making Myth of Emily*, p. 125.
  19. *Morning Courier and New York Enquirer*, July 9, 1836; Bass and Brunson, eds., *Fragile Empires*, pp. 34–36; McVea, *Making Myth of Emily*, pp. 35–36, 38, 85, 168–169, 174; Brands, *Long Star Nation*, pp. 466, 486–493; Riley and Etulain, eds., *Wild Women of the Old West*, pp. 33, 40; "Lorenzo de Zavala," The Handbook of Texas Online; "Emily D. West," The Handbook of Texas Online.
  20. Bass and Brunson, eds., *Fragile Empires*, pp. 35–36.
  21. Ibid.; "Mirabeau Buonaparte Lamar," The Handbook of Texas Online; Ramsey, *Texas Sinners and Revolutionaries*, pp. 53–56.
  22. Lee, *Mary Austin Holley*, pp. 291–292; Ramsey, *Texas Sinners and Revolutionaries*, pp. 55, 74–75, 253–254; "Emily D. West," The Handbook of Texas Online.
  23. Bass and Brunson, eds., *Fragile Empires*, pp. 27, 41; Crisp, *Sleuthing the Alamo*, pp. 189–190.
  24. Gray, *Diary of Col. Wm. Fairfax Gray*, p. 224.
  25. Bass and Brunson, eds., *Fragile Empires*, p. 41; Riley and Etulain, eds., *Wild Women of the Old West*, p. 40; Crisp, *Sleuthing the Alamo*, pp. 189–193; "Emily D. West," The Handbook of Texas Online.
  26. Gaddy, *Texas in Revolt*, p. 89; Bass and Brunson, eds., *Fragile Empires*, pp. 43, 45.
  27. Hollon, ed., *William Bollaert's Texas*, p. 108, note 24; Crisp, *Sleuthing the Alamo*, pp. 189–193; "Emily D. West," The Handbook of Texas Online.

Epilogue

  1. Riley and Etulain, eds., *Wild Women of the Old West*, p. 40; "Emily D. West," The Handbook of Texas Online.
  2. Riley and Etulain, eds., *Wild Women of the Old West*, p. 40.
  3. Hollen, ed., *William Bollaert's Texas*, pp. ix–xxvi, 108, note 24; Lutzweiler, "Emily D. West and the Yellow Prose of Texas," New Haven Museum and Historical Society; Crisp, *Sleuthing the Alamo*, pp. 189–191.
  4. Jackson, ed., *Almonte's Texas*, p. 406.
  5. Ibid.
  6. Roberts and Olson, *A Line in the Sand*, p. 218.
  7. "Yellow Rose of Texas," The Handbook of Texas Online; Crisp, *Sleuthing the Alamo*, p. 190.
  8. "Yellow Rose of Texas," The Handbook of Texas Online.
  9. *San Antonio Herald*, San Antonio, Texas, September 18, 1855; Larry P. Knight, "Defending the Unnecessary: Slavery in San Antonio in the 1850s," *Journal of South Texas* (Spring 2002), Vol. 15, No. 1, pp. 57–58.
  10. Crisp, *Sleuthing the Alamo*, p. 190; Yellow Rose of Texas, The Handbook of Texas Online.
  11. Smithwick, *The Evolution of a State*, p. 49.
  12. Ibid.; "Yellow Rose of Texas," The Handbook of Texas Online.
  13. "Yellow Rose of Texas," The Handbook of Texas Online.
  14. Ibid.; Crisp, *Sleuthing the Alamo*, pp. 189–191; Thomas Cahill, *Sailing The Wine-Dark Sea: Why the Greeks Matter* (New York: Anchor Books, 2004), pp. 18, 30–31.
  15. George Seldes, *The Great Thoughts* (New York: Ballantine Books, 1985), p. 457.

Bibliography

Manuscripts

Center Church on-the-Green, Archives of the First Church of Christ, New Haven, CT.

Delgado, Pedro. "The Battle of San Jacinto," The McArdle Notebooks, Texas State Library and Archives Commission, Austin, TX.

Houston, Samuel, to James W. Fannin, March 11, 1836. A. J. Houston Collection, Texas State Library and Archives, Austin, TX.

List of Mexican Officers Taken Prisoner, "The Battle of San Jacinto Notebook." The McArdle Notebooks, Texas State Library and Archives Commission, Austin, TX.

Lutzweiler, James. "Emily D. West and the Yellow Prose of Texas: A Primer on Some Primary Documents and Their Doctoring." Paper presented at the 100th anniversary of the Texas State Historical Association, 8 March 1997, New Haven Museum and Historical Society, New Haven, CT.

Memorials and Petitions, petition of Diana Leonard, December 14, 1849, Texas State Library and Archives Commission, Austin, TX.

Passport of Emily D. West, Texas State Library and Archives Commission, Austin, TX.

Santa Anna, Antonio de López. Roger Borroel Collection, East Chicago, IN.

Taylor, William S., Account. The McArdle Notebooks, Texas State Library and Archives Commission, Austin, TX.

Texas Mute Ranger, 1882. John Salmon Ford papers, Center for American History, Austin, TX.

"Trowbridge Square Historic District Study." New Haven Preservation Trust, New Haven, CT.

"Typescript Diary of Major John P. Gaines." Journal and Diaries, 1846, Missouri Historical Society, St. Louis, MO.

Yale University authors, "Colonization," *Yale, Slavery and Abolition* essay series, Yale University Library, New Haven, CT.

Yale University authors, "The 'Negro' College," *Yale, Slavery and Abolition* essay series, Yale University Library, New Haven, CT.

Yale University authors, "Simeon Jocelyn," *Yale, Slavery and Abolition* essay series, Yale University Library, New Haven, CT.

Yale University authors, "The Story of Yale Abolitionists," *Yale, Slavery and Abolition* essay series, Yale University Library, New Haven, CT.

Newspapers

Albany Evening Journal, Albany, NY.
Arkansas Gazette, Little Rock, AR.
Baltimore Gazette and Daily Advertiser, Baltimore, MD.
Commercial Bulletin, New Orleans, LA.
Commercial Bulletin and Missouri Literary Register, St. Louis, MO.
Commonwealth, Frankfort, KY.
Connecticut Gazette, New London, CT.
Connecticut Journal, New Haven, CT.
The Constitutional Whig, Richmond, VA.
Daily National Intelligencer, Washington, D.C.
Dallas Daily Weekly, Dallas, TX.
Dallas Morning News, Dallas, TX.
Democratic Free Press, Detroit, MI.
Eastern Argus, Portland, ME.
El Mosquito Mexicano, Mexico City, Mexico.
Farmer's Cabinet, Amherst, NH.
The Floridian, Pensacola, FL.
Floridian and Advocate, Tallahassee, FL.
Frankfort Commonwealth, Frankfort, KY.
Galveston News, Galveston, TX.
The Herald, New York, NY.
Houston Telegraph, Houston, TX.
Jackson Mississippian, Jackson, MS.
Jamestown Journal, Jamestown, NY.
The Liberator, Boston, MA.
Maryland Gazette, Annapolis, MD.
Memphis Enquirer, Memphis, TN.
Mercantile Advertiser and New York Advocate, New York, NY.

Missouri Argus, St. Louis, MO.
Morning Courier and New York Enquirer, New York, NY.
Nashville Banner and Nashville Whig, Nashville, TN.
National Banner and Nashville Whig, Nashville, TN.
National Gazette, Philadelphia, PA.
National Intelligencer, Washington, D.C.
New Bedford Mercury, New Bedford, MA.
New Hampshire Gazette, Portsmouth, NH.
New Hampshire Sentinel, Keene, NH.
The New Orleans Bee, New Orleans, LA.
The New York Herald, New York, NY.
New York Times, New York, NY.
Niles' Weekly Register, Baltimore, MD
Pennsylvania Freeman, Philadelphia, PA.
Philadelphia Public Ledger, Philadelphia, PA.
Phoenix Civilian, Cumberland, MD.
Portland Advertiser, Portland, OR.
Richmond Enquirer, Richmond, VA.
St. Louis Republic, St. Louis, MO.
San Antonio Daily Express, San Antonio, TX.
San Antonio Express-News, San Antonio, TX.
San Antonio Herald, San Antonio, TX.
Supplemento al Diario del Gobierno, Mexico City, Mexico.
The Telegraph and Texas Register, San Felipe de Austin, TX.
Texas Gazette, San Felipe de Austin, TX.
Universal Gazette, Washington, D.C.
Wisconsin Democrat, Madison, WI.

Books and Articles

Allen, Peter. "Texas Black History Preservation Project, Documenting the Complete African American Experience in Texas." Internet.
Allyn, Charles. *Battle of Groton Heights, September 6, 1781*. Mystic, CT: Seaport Autographs, 1999.
"Ames, Harriett A. Moore Page Potter." The Handbook of Texas Online. Internet. http://www.tshaonline.org/handbook/online/articles/fam03.
Amistad—"Give Us Free": A Celebration of the Film by Steven Spielberg. New York: Newmarket Press, 1998.
Anbinder, Tyler. *Five Points*. New York: Penguin Group, 2002.
"Arnold, Henrick." The Handbook of Texas Online. Internet. http://www.tshaonline.org/handbook/online/articles/far15.
Asbury, Herbert. *The Gangs of New York: An Informal History of the Underworld*. New York: Thunder's Mouth Press, 1998.
"Austin, Stephen Fuller." The Handbook of Texas Online. Internet. http://www.tshaonline.org/handbook/online/articles/fau14.

"Badgett, Jesse B." The Handbook of Texas Online. Internet. http://www.tshaonline.org/handbook/online/articles/fba04.
Barr, Alwyn. *Black Texans: A History of African Americans in Texas, 1528–1995*. Norman: University of Oklahoma Press, 1973.
_____. *Texans in Revolt: The Battle for San Antonio, 1835*. Austin: University of Texas Press, 1990.
_____, and Robert A. Calvert, eds. *Black Leaders: Texans for Their Times*. Austin: Texas State Historical Association, 1981.
Bennett, Herman L. *Africans in Colonial Mexico: Absolution, Christianity, and Afro-Creole Consciousness, 1570–1640*. Bloomington: Indiana University Press, 2003.
Billas, George Athan. *General John Glover and his Marblehead Mariners*. New York: Henry Holt, 1960.
Boatner, Mark Mayo, III. *Encyclopedia of the American Revolution*. New York: David McKay, 1966.
Bolster, W. Jeffrey. *Black Jacks: African-American Seamen in the Age of Sail*. Cambridge: Harvard University Press, 1997.
Bonvillain, Nancy. *The Mohawk*. Philadelphia: Chelsea House, 2005.
"Bowie, James." The Handbook of Texas Online. Internet. https://www.tshaonline.org/handbook/online/articles/fbo45.
Boyd, Bob. *The Texas Revolution: A Day-by-Day Account*. San Angelo, TX: San Angelo Standard Times, 1986.
Bradfield, Jane. *Rx Take One Cannon*. Shiner, TX: Patrick J. Wagner Research, 1981.
Brading, D. A. *Mexican Phoenix: Our Lady of Guadalupe; Image and Tradition Across Five Centuries*. Cambridge: Cambridge University Press, 2001.
Brands, H. W. *Lone Star Nation: How a Ragged Army of Volunteers Won the Battle for Texas Independence*. New York: Doubleday, 2004.
Brear, Holly Beachley. *Inherit the Alamo: Myth and Ritual at an American Shrine*. Oxford: Oxford University Press, 2005.
Buckley, David. *The Right to Be Proud: A Brief Guide to Jamaican Heritage Sites*. Kingston: MAPCO Business Printers, 2005.
Burnard, Trevor. *Mastery, Tyranny, and Desire, Thomas Thistlewood and his Slaves in the Anglo-Jamaican World*. Chapel Hill: University of North Carolina Press, 2004.
"Burnet, David Gouverneur." The Handbook of Texas Online. Internet. http://www.tshaonline.org/handbook/online/articles/fbu46.
Burnet, Hannah Este. Texas Historical Markers. Waymarking.com. Internet. http://www.waymarking.com/waymarks/WM2189_Hannah_Este_Burnet.

Burstein, Andrew. *The Passions of Andrew Jackson.* New York: Alfred A. Knopf, 2003.

Caesar. *The Conquest of Gaul.* New York: Penguin Books, 1982.

Cahill, Thomas. *Sailing the Wine-Dark Sea: Why the Greeks Matter.* New York: Anchor Books, 2004.

Calloway, Colin G. *The American Revolution in Indian Country: Crisis and Diversity in Native American Communities.* Cambridge: Cambridge University Press, 1995.

Campbell, Randolph B. *An Empire for Slavery: The Peculiar Institution in Texas.* Baton Rouge: Louisiana State University Press, 1989.

Campbell, Randolph B. *The Laws of Slavery in Texas.* Austin: University of Texas Press, 2010.

Carmen, Perry, trans. *With Santa Anna in Texas: A Personal Narrative of the Revolution.* College Station: Texas A&M University Press, 1975.

Chadwick, Bruce. *George Washington's War.* Naperville: Sourcebooks, 2005.

Chang, Iris. *The Rape of Nanking: The Forgotten Holocaust of World War II.* New York: Basic Books, 1997.

Chartier, JoAnn, and Chris Enss. *She Wore a Yellow Ribbon: Soldiers and Patriots of the Western Frontier.* Boulder: TwoDot, 2004.

Chasteen, Charles. *Born in Blood and Fire: A Concise History of Latin America.* New York: W. W. Norton, 2001.

Chevallier, Bernard. *Napoleon.* Memphis: Lithograph, 1993.

Churchill, Ward. *A Little Matter of Genocide, Holocaust and Denial in the Americas, 1492 to the Present.* San Francisco: City Lights, 1997.

City of La Porte, TX, Chamber of Commerce.

Clary, David A. *Eagles and Empire: The United States, Mexico, and the Struggle for a Continent.* New York: Bantam Books, 2009.

"Clear Creek (Fort Bend County)." The Handbook of Texas Online. Internet. http://www.tshaonline.org/handbook/online/articles/rbcex.

"Cotton Culture." The Handbook of Texas Online. Internet. http://www.tshaonline.org/handbook/online/articles/afc03.

Crawford, Ann Fears, ed. *The Eagle: The Autobiography of Santa Anna.* Austin: State House Press, 1988.

Crisp, James E. *Sleuthing the Alamo: Davy Crockett's Last Stand, and other Mysteries of the Texas Revolution.* Oxford: Oxford University Press, 2005.

Crow, John A. *Spain: The Root and the Flower.* Berkeley: University of California, 2005.

Cuneo, John R. *Robert Rogers of the Rangers.* New York: Richardson and Steirman, 1987.

Custer, Elizabeth B. *Tenting on the Plains: General Custer in Kansas and Texas.* New York: Barnes and Noble, 2006.

Daughters of the Republic of Texas. *The Alamo: Long Barrack Museum.* Dallas, TX: Taylor, 1986.

Davis, Graham. *Land! Irish Pioneers in Mexican and Revolutionary Texas.* College Station: Texas A&M University Press, 2002.

Davis, Kenneth C. *A Nation Rising: Untold Tales of Flawed Founders, Fallen Heroes, and Forgotten Fighters from America's Hidden Past.* New York: HarperCollins, 2010.

Davis, William C. *Lone Star Rising: The Revolutionary Birth of the Texas Republic.* New York: The Free Press, 2004.

_____. *Three Roads to the Alamo: The Lives and Fortunes of David Crockett, James Bowie, and William Barret Travis.* New York: Harper Collins Publishers, 1998.

De Bruhl, Marshall. *The Sword of San Jacinto: A Life of Sam Houston.* New York: Random House, 1993.

Demos, John, ed. *Remarkable Providences, 1600–1780.* New York: George Braziller, 1972.

Derr, Mark. *The Frontiersman: The Real Life and the Many Legends of Davy Crockett.* New York: William Morrow, 1993.

"Dick the Drummer." The Handbook of Texas Online. Internet. http://www.tshaonline.org/handbook/online/articles/fdi44.

Dimmick, Gregg J. *Sea of Mud: The Retreat of the Mexican Army after San Jacinto: An Archeological Investigation.* Austin: Texas State Historical Association, 2004.

Donovan, James. *The Blood of Heroes.* New York: Little, Brown, 2012.

Duff, John B., and Peter M. Mitchell, eds. *The Nat Turner Rebellion: The Historical Event and the Modern Controversy.* New York: Harper and Rows, 1971.

Dunn, Jeff. "One More Piece of the Puzzle: Emily West in Special Collections," *The Compass Rose,* Vol. 19, No. 1 (Spring 2005).

Dunn, Richard S. *Sugar and Slaves: The Rise of the Planter Class in the English West Indies, 1624–1713.* New York: W. W. Norton, 1972.

Eakin, Sue, and Joseph Logsdon, eds. *Twelve Years a Slave by Solomon Northup.* Baton Rouge: Louisiana State University Press, 1968.

"East Columbia, TX." The Handbook of Texas Online. Internet. http://www.tshaonline.org/handbook/online/articles/hne02.

Edgerton, Robert B. *Hidden Heroism: Black Soldiers in America's Wars.* Boulder, CO: Westview Press, 2001.

1887 Disestablishments: Telegraph and Texas Register. Memphis: Books LLC, 2010.

Ellis, Joseph J. *Founding Brothers: The Revolutionary Generation.* New York: Vintage Books, 2000.

Everett, Susanne. *History of Slavery.* London: Bison Books, 1978.

Ewell, Judith, and William H. Beezley. *The Human Tradition in Latin America*. Wilmington, DE: Scholarly Resources, 1991.

Fehrenbach, T. R. *Lone Star: A History of Texas and the Texans*. New York: Da Capo, 2000.

Fleming, Thomas. *Liberty! The American Revolution*. New York: Viking, 1997.

Fletcher, William A. *Rebel Private: Front and Rear, Memoirs of a Confederate Soldier*. New York: Meridian, 1997.

Fowler, Will. *Santa Anna of Mexico*. Lincoln: University of Nebraska Press, 2007.

Fox, Robin Lane. *Alexander the Great*. New York: Penguin, 1986.

Fraser, Antonia. *The Weaker Vessel*. New York: Alfred A. Knopf, 1984.

French, Philip. *Westerns*. New York: Viking, 1973.

French, Scot. *The Rebellious Slave: Nat Turner in American Memory*. Boston: Houghton Mifflin, 2004.

Gaddy, Jerry J. *Texas in Revolt: Contemporary Newspaper Accounts of the Texas Revolution*. Fort Collins: Old Army Press, 1973.

Gaspar, David Barry, and David Patrick Geggus. *A Turbulent Time: The French Revolution and the Great Caribbean*. Bloomington: Indiana University Press, 1997.

"Georgia Battalion." The Handbook of Texas Online. Internet. http://www.tshaonline.org/handbook/online/articles/qjg01.

Geyl, Pieter. *Napoleon: For and Against*. Middlesex: Penguin, 1976.

Glasrud, Bruce A., and Pitre Merline, eds. *Black Women in Texas History*. College Station: Texas A&M University Press, 2008.

The Gleaner. *Geography and History of Jamaica*. Kingston: Gleaner, 1995.

Goldstone, Lawrence. *Dark Bargain: Slavery, Profits, and the Struggle for the Constitution*. New York: Walker, 2005.

"Goodrich, Benjamin Briggs." The Handbook of Texas Online. Internet. http://www.tshaonline.org/handbook/online/articles/fgo12.

Gray, William Fairfax. *Diary of Col. Wm. Fairfax Gray, From Virginia to Texas, 1835*. Houston: Fletcher Young, 1965.

"Greenbury Logan." Texas Black History Preservation Project, Documenting the Complete African American Experience in Texas. Internet. http://www.tbhpp.org/logan.html.

"Grimes, Albert Calvin." The Handbook of Texas Online. http://www.tshaonline.org/handbook/online/articles/fgram.

"Grimes, Jesse." The Handbook of Texas Online. Internet. http://www.tshaonline.org/handbook/online/articles/fgr67.

"Grimke, Charlotte Forten." National Women's History Museum. Internet. http://www.nwhm.org/education-resources/biography/biographies/charlotte-forten-grimke/.

Groneman, Bill. *Alamo Defenders, a Genealogy: The People and Their Words*. Austin: Eakin Press, 1990.

_____. *Defense of a Legend: Crockett and the de la Peña Diary*. Plano: Republic of Texas Press, 1994.

_____. *Eyewitness to the Alamo*. Plano: Republic of Texas Press, 1996.

Hacker, Andrew. *Two Nations, Black and White, Separate, Hostile, Unequal*. New York: Ballantine Books, 1995.

Hanson, Todd, editor. *The Alamo Reader: A Study in History*. Mechanicsburg, PA: Stackpole Books, 2003.

Hardin, Stephen L. *The Alamo 1836: Santa Anna's Texas Campaign*. Oxford: Osprey, 2001.

_____. *Texian Iliad: A Military History of the Texas Revolution*. Austin: University of Texas Press, 1994.

Harris, Trudier. "'The Yellow Rose of Texas': A Different View." *Callaloo*, Vol. 20, No. 1 (Winter 1997).

Herring, Hubert. *A History of Latin America, From Beginnings to the Present*. New York: Alfred A. Knopf, 1968.

"The Hill (New Haven)." Wikipedia. Internet. http://en.wikipedia.org/wiki/The_Hill_(New_Haven).

Hinderaker, Eric, and Peter C. Mancall, *The Edge of Empire: The Backcountry in British North America*. Baltimore, MD: Johns Hopkins University Press, 2003.

Hollen, W. Eugene, ed. *William Bollaert's Texas*. Norman: University of Oklahoma Press, 1989.

Hopewell, Clifford. *James Bowie, Texas Fighting Man: A Biography*. Austin: Eakin Press, 1994.

Horgan, Paul. *Lamy of Santa Fe*. New York: Farrar, Straus and Giroux, 1980.

Hourtoulle, F. G. *Austerlitz: The Empire at Its Zenith*. Paris: Histoire and Collections, 2003.

Howell, Donna Wyatt, compiler. *I Was a Slave: True Life Stories Dictated by Former American Slaves in the 1930s*. Washington, D.C.: American Legacy Books, 2000.

Hoyt, Edwin P. *The Alamo: An Illustrated History*. Dallas, TX: Taylor, 1999.

Huffines, Alan C. *Blood of Noble Men: The Alamo Battle and Siege*. Austin: Eakin Press, 1999.

Huggins, Nathan Irvin. *Black Odyssey: The Afro-American Ordeal in Slavery*. New York: Pantheon, 1977.

"Hust, Zilpha," The Handbook of Texas Online.

Innes, Hammond. *The Conquistadors*. New York: Alfred A. Knopf, 1969.

"Irion, Robert Anderson." The Handbook of Texas Online. Internet. http://www.tshaonline.org/handbook/online/articles/fir04.

Jackson, Jack, ed. *Almonte's Texas: Juan N. Almonte's 1834 Inspection, Secret Report and Role in the 1836 Campaign.* Austin: Texas State Historical Association, 2005.

_____, ed. *Texas by Terán: The Diary Kept by General Manuel de Mier y Terán on His 1828 Inspection of Texas.* Austin: University of Texas Press, 2000.

Jackson, Ron. *Alamo Legacy: Alamo Descendants Remember the Alamo.* Austin: Eakin Press, 1997.

Jaffe, Eric. *The King's Best Highway: The Lost History of the Boston Post Road, The Route that Made America.* New York: Scribner, 2010.

Jay, William. *A View of the Action of the Federal Government, in Behalf of Slavery.* Miami, FL: Mnemosyne, 1969.

Jeffrey, Julie Roy. *Frontier Women: The Trans-Mississippi West, 1840–1880.* New York: Hill and Wang, 1979.

Jenkins, John Holmes, ed. *Papers of the Texas Revolution.* 10 vols., Austin, TX: Presidial, 1973.

_____, ed. *Recollections of Early Texas.* Austin: University of Texas Press, 1987.

Johnnydod. "The Yellow Rose of Texas, She Was the Sweetest Gal You'll Ever Know," July 10, 2010, Wikinut. Internet. http://guides.wikinut.com/The-Yellow-Rose-of-Texas%2C-she-WAS-the-sweetest-gal-you-ll-ever-know./cse9hgrw/.

Johnson, Jack. "Santa Anna's 1836 Campaign: Was It Directed toward Ethnic Cleansings?" *Journal of South Texas* (Spring 2002).

Johnson, Paul. *A History of the Jews.* New York: Harper and Row, 1987.

_____. *Napoleon: A Life.* New York: Penguin, 2006.

Jordan, Winthrop D. *The White Man's Burden: Historical Origins of Racism in the United States.* Oxford: Oxford University Press.

Katzew, Iiona. *Casta Painting.* New Haven, CT: Yale University Press, 2004.

Keane, John. *Tom Paine: A Political Life.* Boston: Little, Brown, 1995.

Keister, Linda Wolfe. *The Complete Guide to African-American Baby Names.* New York: Penguin Group, 1998.

Kelley, Sean M. *Los Brazos De Dios: A Plantation Society in the Texas Borderlands, 1821–1865.* Baton Rouge: Louisiana State University Press, 2010.

Ketcham, Ralph. *From Colony to Country: The Revolution in American Though 1750–1820.* New York: Macmillan, 1974.

"Kiamata Long, 'Kian.'" Slave, Personal Maid for Jane Long," Texas Black History Preservation Project. Internet. http://www.tbhpp.org/kian.html.

"Kian." The Handbook of Texas Online. Internet. http://www.tshaonline.org/handbook/online/articles/fki01.

Knight, Larry P. "Defending the Unnecessary: Slavery in San Antonio in the 1850s," *Journal of South Texas* (Spring 2002).

Koster, John. "Plural Wives and the Plains Indians." *Wild West* (June 2012).

Lack, Paul D. *The Texas Revolutionary Experience: A Political and Social History, 1835–1836.* College Station: Texas A&M Press, 1992.

"Lamar, Mirabeau Buonaparte." The Handbook of Texas Online. Internet. http://www.tshaonline.org/handbook/online/articles/fla15.

Landes, David S. *The Wealth and Poverty of Nations.* New York: W. W. Norton, 1998.

"Lane, Walter Paye." The Handbook of Texas Online. Internet. http://www.tshaonline.org/handbook/online/articles/fla28.

Lanning, Michael Lee. *Defenders of Liberty: African Americans in the Revolutionary War.* New York: Citadel Press, 2000.

Larralde, Elsa. *The Land and People of Mexico.* New York: J. B. Lippincott, 1964.

Lee, Rebecca Smith. *Mary Austin Holley: A Biography.* Austin: University of Texas Press, 1962.

Levy, Buddy. *American Legend: The Real-Life Adventures of David Crockett.* New York: Berkley Books, 2005.

"Linn, John Joseph." The Handbook of Texas Online. Internet. http://www.tshaonline.org/handbook/online/articles/fli12.

Lockhart, James, and Stuart B. Schwartz. *Early Latin America: A History of Colonial Spanish America and Brazil.* Cambridge: Cambridge University Press, 1997.

Loewen, James W. *Lies Across America: What Our Historic Sites Get Wrong.* New York: Simon and Schuster, 2000.

"Logan, Greenbury." The Handbook of Texas Online. Internet. http://www.tshaonline.org/handbook/online/articles/flo04

Long, Jeff. *Duel of Eagles: The Mexican and U.S. Fight for the Alamo.* New York: William Morrow, 1990.

Lord, Walter. *A Time to Stand: A Chronicle of the Valiant Battle of the Alamo.* New York: Bonanza, 1987.

Lozano, Reuben Rendon. *Viva Tejas: The Story of the Tejanos, the Mexican-born Patriots of the Texas Revolution.* San Antonio: Alamo Press, 1985.

Lusane, Clarence. *The Black History of the White House.* San Francisco: City Lights, 2011.

Mahon, John K. *History of the Second Seminole War, 1835–1842.* Gainesville: University of Florida Press, 1967.

Markham, Felix. *Napoleon.* New York: Penguin Books, 1963.

Matovina, Timothy M. *The Alamo Remembered: Tejano Accounts and Perspectives.* Austin: University of Texas Press, 1995.

McDougall, Walter A. *Promised Land, Crusader State: The American Encounter with the World Since 1776*. New York: Houghton Mifflin, 1997.

McVea, Denise. *Making Myth of Emily: Emily West de Zavala and the Yellow Rose of Texas Legend*. San Antonio, TX: Auris Books, 2006.

"Meigs, Return J., Sr." Wikipedia. Internet. http://en.wikipedia.org/wiki/Return_J._Meigs,_Sr..

Meltzer, Milton. *Slavery: A World History*. New York: Da Capo Press, 1993.

Meltzer, Sara E., and Leslie W. Rabine. *Rebel Daughters: Women and the French Revolution*. New York: Oxford University Press, 1992.

Melville, Herman. *Moby-Dick*. New York: Barnes and Noble, 1993.

Merk, Frederick. *History of the Westward Movement*. New York: Alfred A. Knopf, 1978.

Michener, James A. *Texas*. New York: Random House, 1985.

"Milam, Benjamin Rush." The Handbook of Texas Online. Internet. http://www.tshaonline.org/handbook/online/articles/fmi03.

Miller, Edward L. *New Orleans and the Texas Revolution*. College Station: Texas A&M University Press, 2004.

Miller, Thomas Lloyd. *The Public Lands of Texas, 1519–1970*. Norman: University of Oklahoma Press, 1972.

Monaghan, Jay. *Custer: The Life of General George Armstrong Custer*. Lincoln: University of Nebraska Press, 1971.

Moore, Stephen L. *Eighteen Minutes: The Battle of San Jacinto and the Texas Independence Campaign*. Austin: Republic of Texas Press, 2004.

_____. *Savage Frontier: Rangers, Riflemen, and Indian Wars in Texas*. 2 vols., Plano: Republic of Texas Press, 2002.

"Moreland, Isaac N." The Handbook of Texas Online. Internet. http://www.tshaonline.org/handbook/online/articles/fmo43.

"Morgan, James." The Handbook of Texas Online. Internet. http://www.tshaonline.org/handbook/online/articles/fmo50.

"Morgan's Point, Texas." The Handbook of Texas Online. Internet. http://www.tshaonline.org/handbook/online/articles/hlm89.

Muir, Andrew Forest. "The Free Negro in Harris County, Texas." Southwestern Historical Quarterly Online.

Myers, John Meyers. *The Alamo*. New York: Bantam Books, 1966.

The National Cyclopaedia of American Biography. New York: James T. White, 1895.

"Neill, James Clinton." The Handbook of Texas Online. Internet. http://www.tshaonline.org/handbook/online/articles/fne11.

Nevin, David. *Sherman's March: Atlanta to the Sea*. Alexandria, VA: Time-Life Books, 1986.

_____. *The Texans*. New York: Time-Life Books, 1975.

New Haven, Connecticut, Telephone Directories, 2007 and 2008, New Haven, CT, Library.

"New Orleans Greys." The Handbook of Texas Online. Internet. http://www.tshaonline.org/handbook/online/articles/qjn02.

"New Washington Association," The Handbook of Texas Online. Internet. http://www.tshaonline.org/handbook/online/articles/ufn01.

Nicolle, David. *The Moors: The Islamic West, 7th–15th Centuries, AD*. Oxford: Osprey, 2001.

Nofi, Albert A. *The Alamo and the Texas War for Independence, September 39, 1835–April 21, 1836*. Conshohocken: Combined Books, 1992.

Oates, Stephen B. *The Fires of Jubilee: Nat Turner's Fierce Rebellion*. New York: Harper and Row, 1975.

Painter, Nell Irvin. *Creating Black Americans: African-American History and Its Meanings, 1619 to the Present*. Oxford: Oxford University Press, 2006.

Parry, J. H., Philip Sherlock, and Anthony Maingot. *A Short History of the West Indies*. New York: St. Martin's Press, 1987.

"Philips, Zeno." The Handbook of Texas Online. Internet. http://www.tshaonline.org/handbook/online/articles/fph05.

Pohl, James W. *The Battle of San Jacinto*. Austin: Texas State Historical Association, 1989.

Potter, Woodburne. *The War in Florida*. Baltimore, MD: Lewis and Coleman, 1836.

Prather, Patricia Smith, and Jane Clements Monday. *From Slave to Statesman: The Legacy of Joshua Houston, Servant to Sam Houston*. Denton: University of North Texas Press, 1993.

Puls, Mark. *Henry Knox: Visionary General of the American Revolution*. New York: Palgrave MacMillan, 2008.

Ragsdale, Crystal Saee. *Women and Children of the Alamo*. Austin, TX: State House Press, 1994.

Ramsey, Jack C., Jr. *Texas Sinners and Revolutionaries: Jane Long and Her Fellow Conspirators*. Plano: Republic of Texas Press, 2001.

Raphael, Ray. *Founding Myths: Stories That Hide Our Patriotic Past*. New York: MJF Books, 2004.

Rawick, George P. *From Sundown to Sunup: The Making of the Slave Community*. Westport, CT: Greenwood, 1872.

Remini, Robert V. *Andrew Jackson and His Indian Wars*. New York: Penguin Books, 2001.

Richards, Leonard L. *"Gentlemen of Property and Standing": Anti-Abolition Mobs in Jacksonian America*. Oxford: Oxford University Press, 1970.

Riley, Glenda, and Richard W. Etulain, eds. *Wild Women of the Old West*. Golden: Fulcrum, 2003.

Roberts, J. M. *A Short History of the World*. Oxford: Oxford University Press, 1993.

Roberts, Randy, and James S. Olsen. *A Line in the Sand: The Alamo in Blood and Memory.* New York: The Free Press, 2001.

Rubin, Nancy. *Isabella of Castle: The First Renaissance Queen.* New York: St. Martin's Press, 1991.

Ruiz, Ramon Eduardo. *Mexico: Why a Few Are Rich and the People Poor.* Berkeley: University of California Press, 2010.

"Rusk, Thomas Jefferson." The Handbook of Texas Online. Internet. http://www.tshaonline.org/handbook/online/articles/fru16.

Salas, Elizabeth. *Soldaderas in the Mexican Military.* Austin: University of Texas Press, 2006.

Santos, Richard G. *Santa Anna's Campaign against Texas, 1835–1836.* Waco: Texian Press, 1968.

Scheina, Robert L. *Santa Anna: A Curse Upon Mexico.* Washington, D.C.: Brassey's, 2000.

Seldes, George, comp. *The Great Thoughts.* New York: Ballantine, 1985.

Shackford, James Atkins. *David Crockett: The Man and the Legend.* Lincoln: University of Nebraska Press, 1986.

Shea, William L., and Earl J. Hess. *Pea Ridge: Civil War Campaign in the West.* Chapel Hill: University of North Carolina Press, 1992.

Shirley, Gayle C. *More Than Petticoats: Remarkable Colorado Women.* Helena, MT: Morris, 2002.

Smith, C. T. *An Historical Geography of Western Europe Before 1800.* New York: Frederick A. Praeger, 1969.

"Smith, Erastus." The Handbook of Texas Online. Internet. http://www.tshaonline.org/handbook/online/articles/fsmac/.

Smithwick, Noah. *The Evolution of a State, or Recollections of Old Texas Days.* Austin: University of Texas Press, 1983.

Soustelle, Jacques. *Daily Life of the Aztecs on the Eve of the Spanish Conquest.* Stanford: Stanford University Press, 1961.

Squires, Catherine. *African Americans and the Media.* Cambridge: Polity Press, 2009.

Stampp, Kenneth M. *The Peculiar Institution: Slavery in the Ante-Bellum South.* New York: Vintage, 1956.

Starling, Susanne. *Land Is the Cry!, Warren Angus Ferris, Pioneer Surveyor and Founder of Dallas County.* Austin: Texas State Historical Association, 1988.

"Texas Navy." The Handbook of Texas Online. Internet. https://www.tshaonline.org/handbook/online/articles/qjt02.

Thompson, Frank. *The Alamo: A Cultural History.* Dallas, TX: Taylor Trade, 2001.

"Thompson, Jesse G." The Handbook of Texas Online. Internet. http://www.tshaonline.org/handbook/online/articles/fth61.

Tragle, Henry Irving. *The Southampton Slave Revolt of 1831: A Compilation of Source Material, including the full text of the 'Confessions' of Nat Turner.* New York: Vintage Books, 1971.

"Travis, William Barrett." The Handbook of Texas Online. Internet. http://www.tshaonline.org/handbook/online/articles/ftr03.

Tucker, Phillip Thomas. *Exodus from the Alamo: The Anatomy of the Last Stand Myth.* Philadelphia: Casemate, 2010.

"Twin Sisters." The Handbook of Texas Online. Internet. http://www.tshaonline.org/handbook/online/articles/qvt01.

Twyman, Bruce Edward. *The Black Seminole Legacy and North American Politics, 1693–1845.* Washington, D.C.: Howard University Press, 1999.

"Urrea, José de." The Handbook of Texas Online. Internet. http://www.tshaonline.org/handbook/online/articles/fur02.

"Varner-Hogg Plantation State Historical Park." The Handbook of Texas Online. Internet. http://www.tshaonline.org/handbook/online/articles/ghv01.

Viele, Mrs. Brigadier Gen. Egbert L. *Following the Drum.* Austin, TX: Steck-Vaughn, 1968.

Wagner, Sally Roesch. *Daughters of Dakota: A Sampler of Stores from the South Dakota Pioneers Daughters Collection,* Vol 1. Yankton: Daughters of Dakota, 1989.

"War Party." The Handbook of Texas Online. Internet. http://www.tshaonline.org/handbook/online/articles/waw02.

Warner, Robert Austin. *New Haven Negroes: A Social History.* New York: Arno Press and the New York Times, 1969.

Weems, John Edward, and Jane Weems. *Dream of Empire: A History of the Republic of Texas, 1836–1846.* New York: Barnes and Noble, 1995.

"West, Claiborne." The Handbook of Texas Online. Internet. http://www.tshaonline.org/handbook/online/articles/fwe30.

"West, Emily D." The Handbook of Texas Online. Internet. http://www.tshaonline.org/handbook/online/articles/fwe41.

White, Deborah Gray. *Ar'n't I a Woman: Female Slaves in the Plantation South.* New York: W. W. Norton, 1999.

White, Ronald. *What Is America? A Short History of the New World Order.* New York: Da Capo Press, 2008.

Whitefield, George. Christian Classics Ethereal Library. Internet.

"Williamson, Robert McAlpin," The Handbook of Texas Online. Internet. http://www.tshaonline.org/handbook/online/articles/fwi42.

Wiltse, Charles M. *The New Nation, 1800–1845.* New York: Hill and Wang, 1961.

Wood, Michael. *In the Footsteps of Alexander the Great.* Los Angeles: University of California Press, 2001.

Yancy, Ernest Jerome. *Historical Lights of Liberia's Yesterday and Today*. New York: Herman Jaffe, 1954.

"Yellow Rose of Texas." The Handbook of Texas Online. Internet. http://www.tshaonline.org/handbook/online/articles/xey01.

Zaboly, Gary. *An Altar for Their Sons: The Alamo and the Texas Revolution in Contemporary Newspaper Accounts*. Buffalo Gap, TX: State House Press, 2011.

_____. *American Colonial Ranger: The Northern Colonies, 1724–1764*. Oxford: Osprey, 2004.

"Zavala, Lorenzo de." The Handbook of Texas Online. Internet. http://www.tshaonline.org/handbook/online/articles/fza05.

Zeinert, Karen. *The Amistad Slave Revolt and American Abolition*. North Haven, CT: Shoestring Press, 1997.

Zimmerman, Jean. *The Women of the House: How a Colonial She-Merchant Built a Mansion, a Fortune, and a Dynasty*. New York: Harcourt, 2006.

Correspondence

Roger Borroel, East Chicago, IN, to the author, February 15, 2008, and April 9 and 11, 2012.

Doris B. Townshend, Center Church historian, New Haven, CT, to the author, October 24, 2008.

Index

Adeline 103
African Americans 7, 9–11, 16–17, 30–31, 37–43, 46–47, 49, 51, 53–55, 59, 69, 74, 79, 95, 106, 109, 143, 149–150, 154, 164, 177, 181, 190, 202, 205, 218, 223, 231
African Ecclesiastical Society 42
African Improvement Society 43
African Sabbath School 42
Aguado, Francisco 159
Aguirre, Marcial 180
Alabama 71, 77, 82, 115, 120, 125, 222, 231
Alameda 139–140
Alamo 9, 12, 14, 19, 20, 22, 67, 70, 71, 89, 91, 96, 102, 111–118, 120–121, 123–126, 130, 133, 137, 139, 145–146, 147, 149, 152, 154, 156–157, 160–162, 164, 167–9, 178, 188, 190–192, 194, 197, 206, 215, 226; blacks at 115–116
The Alamo 20–21
Alavéz, Francita 125–126
Alavéz, Telesforo 126
Albany, New York 24
Alexander the Great 88
Alexandria 88
Allen, Peter 125
Allen, Richard 125
Almonte, Brígida 141
Almonte, Juan Nepomuceno 75–76, 87, 91, 95, 97, 109, 113, 116, 135, 137–138, 141–145, 148–150, 166, 186, 193
Alsbury, Horatio Alexander 96, 181
Alvarado 155
American Anti-Slavery Society 40, 48
American Colonization Society 55
American Revolution 24, 26–30, 31–32, 34, 56–57, 71, 115, 184, 195–196; blacks in 30–32, 34
American Society of Free Persons of Colour 44
"America's Schoolteacher" 27
Amistad 52
Amistad Committee 51, 53
Anahuac 66, 79
Andrews, Joseph 156
Angel of Goliad 126
Angelina 116
Angola 99
Antislavery Association 43

Aragon 107
Arkansas 102, 155
Army of Operations 22, 108
Arnold, Benedict 31
Arnold, Hendrick 72–73, 101, 185, 223
Arnold, Rachel 102
Arrelo, Daniel 101
Arrendondo, Joaquín de 122
Attucks, Crispus 71
Austin, Archibald 26
Austin, Elijah 26–7, 34–35, 63, 66
Austin, Mary 35
Austin, Moses 63
Austin, Stephen Fuller 7, 26, 63, 66, 89, 91, 93, 101, 103, 226
Aztec 24, 99, 153–154

Bachiller, Miguel 160
Bagdad 166
Bahamas 172
Baldwin, Ebenezer 31
Baltimore 24, 80
Barbados 28, 200
Barrera, Melchora 154–155, 165
Bass, Sandy 125
Bastrop 101, 120
Bell, Josiah Hugh 102
Bercerra, Francisco 154
Bettie 112, 166
Bible 12
The Birth of a Nation 208, 230
Bivens, Hester 110
Bolivar Peninsula 83
Bolivar Point 83, 87
Bollaert, William 11–13, 15, 25–26, 163, 172, 176, 179, 180–181, 195–198, 201, 203–6, 210–212, 214–6, 228, 230
Bonaparte, Josephine 179
Bonaparte, Napoleon 111, 135, 138, 154, 158, 170–171, 177–178, 188
Borroel, Roger 199
Boston 6, 27, 44, 59
Boston Massacre 71
Bowery 55
Bowie, James 9, 17, 19, 20, 96, 112–114, 116, 120, 166

Bowie, Ursula 114
Brazoria 132
Brazos River 63, 65, 74, 77, 86, 90, 93, 95, 102–104, 106, 110, 120–121, 127–129, 132, 134–135
Bringas, Juan 188
Briscoe, Andrew 120
British 24, 30–31
Brown, Clara 107–108
Brown, Eliza 151
Bryan, Moses 189
Buffalo, New York 100
Buffalo Bayou 19, 81, 129, 131, 134, 138
Burnet, David G. 137–138, 141–142, 145–7, 149, 175, 207, 212, 220
Butler, Ruth Lapham 25

Caesar 82, 130
Cajun 96
Camp Travis 146, 198
Canada 23, 30, 166
Canary Islands 96
Canterbury 50
Canton, China 27
Carey, William R. 121
Caribbean 16, 28
Castile 100
Castrillón, Manuel Fernández 154, 173, 180, 186, 189, 192, 194
Catholic Church 124
Catholics 15, 27, 97, 104, 107, 124, 145, 153–155, 156, 168, 173, 178, 208, 211
Cayuga 132–133, 197
Center Congregational Church 31, 40–41, 46, 52–53
Céspedes, Manuel 186
Chapultepec Castle 119
Charleston 81
Charlottesville 75
Chicago 11, 210
China 27, 34, 55
Chocolate 98
Christy, Edward 231
Christy's Minstrels 231
Christy's Plantation Melodies 231
Cincinnati 133, 164, 204
Cinque 52
Citizen Kane 231
"City on a Hill" 27, 89
Civil War 151
Clarissa 74
Clay, Cassius 53
Clopper, Joseph Chambers 84
Clopper's Point 65, 83–84, 88–89, 91, 93, 103, 132, 141, 146, 203, 218, 225
Coats, M. 101
Cold War 20
Coleto Creek 124
Colonization Society 68
Colorado 107
Columbia 102
Columbus 124

Columbus, Christopher 107
Columbus Enquirer 225
"Come and Take It" 70
Commercial Bulletin 190
Concepción, battle of 73
Concord 34
Congo 99
Congress, Mexico 13
Congress, United States 12
Connecticut 10, 14, 21, 26, 28–32, 34, 36, 50, 53, 54, 56, 67, 93, 99
Connecticut River 27
Constitution, United States 25, 45
Convention of the Free People of Colour 45
Cooper, George 54, 79, 143, 148, 161
Copano Bay 125, 170
Cork, Ireland 190
Cortéz 156
Cos, Martín Perfecto 71–72, 108, 138, 163–164, 165, 167–169, 186, 188, 192, 194
Cotton Gin 28–29
The Cotton Plant 74
County Cork, Ireland 187
"Cradle of Texas Liberty" 19
Crandall, Prudence 15, 115, 120, 193
Creek 82, 130
Creek War 193
Crockett, David 9, 12–14, 17, 19–20, 60–62, 91, 112, 189, 198, 215
Cuba 16, 52, 86, 180
Curbelo, María de Jesús 96
Custer, Elizabeth 203
Custer, George Armstrong 151, 203

Dade, Francis L. 82
Dade Massacre 82
Davis, William C. 20
De Bruhl, Marshall 182
Declaration of Independence, Texas 187–188, 190, 223–224
Declaration of Independence, United States 29, 31, 33–34, 57
Delaware River 30
Delgado, Pedro 168, 172
Delilah 12, 203, 208
Demopolis 120
Depression of 1837 61
De Sauque, Francis L. 115
De Tocqueville, Alexis 62
Dick 184
Dickinson, Almeron 70, 116, 143, 208
Dickinson, Susanna 67, 70, 116, 123, 143–144, 149, 178–179, 208
Dimmick, Gregg 187
Dimmitt, Philip 97
District of Columbia 62
Dolson, George M. 198
Douglas, Frederick 152, 232
Drouett, Nicholas 55
Durango 123
Durham 26

Durham Boats 30
Dutch 56, 62

East Chicago 199
East Feliciana 60
Edward, David 91
Edwards, Jonathan 31
Egypt 88, 91, 179
El Camino Real 104, 123
El Indio 153
Eliza Jane 107
"Empire State of the South" 21
England 28, 46, 51
Espinosa, Luis 189, 191
Esteban 100
Europe 55, 59, 90, 111, 113, 171, 188

Fannin, James Walker 114–115, 124–127, 188, 211
"Father of Texas" 26
Female Humane Society 43
Ferdinand, King 107
Ferris, Charles 110
Fifty-Fourth Massachusetts Infantry 31
Filísola, Vincente 133, 135, 137–138, 160, 162–163, 165, 192
"First Hero of the Texas Revolution" 72
Five Points 55–59, 62, 66, 70, 82
Flash 24, 67, 79–83, 119, 132, 141–143, 145–146, 164, 224–227
Fletcher, William A. 86
Flores, "Old Gasper" 97
Florida 66–67, 81–82, 115
Forbes, John 190
Ford, John 20
Fort Defiance 124
Fort Griswold 31
Fort Mims 193
Fort Wagner 31
Forten, Charlotte 64, 68
Forten, James, Jr. 64
Foster, William 19
Founding Myths 195
Fourteenth Massachusetts Continental Infantry 30
Fowler, Will 199, 206
Framingham 71
France 66, 100
Franklin Square 43
Fredericksburg 97
French Alliance 195
French and Indian War 30, 34
French Revolution 196

Gaines, Edmund 127, 201
Gallic Wars 182
Galveston 87
Galveston Bay 63, 65–66, 73, 83–86, 88, 90–91, 103, 122, 129, 135, 138–139, 141, 144, 162, 213
Galveston Bay and Texas Land Company 79, 163
Galveston Island 83, 86, 132, 137, 142–143, 146–49, 161, 193
Gaona, Antonio 123

García, Doña Inés 155, 165, 173
Garrison, William Lloyd 43–45, 47, 50–51, 55, 59, 61, 69, 177
Gay, Thomas 110
"George Washington of Texas" 212, 215
Georgia 81–82, 103–104, 121–122, 219, 225
Georgia Battalion 124
Germany 107
Gladstone, Lawrence 25
Glover, John 30
Goldthwaithe, Carmen 218
Goliad 71–72, 113–115, 124–125, 128, 130, 133, 137, 147, 157, 160–161, 164, 169, 188, 194, 226
Goliad Massacre 124–126
Gonzales 70–71, 104, 116, 123–124, 127, 144, 148
Goodlove, Robert 190
Goodrich, Benjamin Briggs 121
Goodson, Edmund 121
Goodson, John 121
Goyens, William 103–104
Gradual Emancipation Act 32
Gradual Manumission Act 57
Grant, James 114
Graves, Emily 105
Gray, William Fairfax 81, 87, 90, 95, 97–98, 111–114, 120–121, 131—133, 135, 137, 140, 146, 161, 226
Great Awakening 31, 37
Great Britain 22, 24–25, 29, 31, 46, 51, 54, 60, 200, 215
Griffin-Viele, Teresa 80
Griffith, D. W. 208, 230
Grimes, Albert Calvin 121
Groce, Jared Ellison 77, 87, 127–128, 130, 133–134
Groton Heights, battle of 30
Guadalupe River 70, 97, 124
Guerrero, Vicente 75, 109
Guinea 35, 56
Gulf of Mexico 65, 68, 72, 83, 85, 89, 108, 123, 146, 156–157, 164

Haiti 49
Hamilton, Alexander 53
Hamilton, Thomas 60
Hamlet, Violet 101
Hardin, Stephen 14–15
Harrell, Celia 66
Harris, Benjamin 116, 166
Harrisburg 129, 131, 134–138, 144–145, 147, 149, 157–158, 160–162, 164, 197
Hartford 32
Havana 52, 180, 186
Helen of Troy 232
Hell's Kitchen 55
Hemings, Sally 13, 75
Hendrick, María 101
The Herald 136, 193, 205
Hitchcock, Alfred 211
Hollon, W. Eugene 25
Holly, Martin Austin 63–64, 225
Hollywood 9, 21

"Home of the Yellow Rose of Texas" 19
Horseshoe Bend 130, 193–194
Houston, Elizabeth Allen 155, 201
Houston, Sam 7, 9–15, 17, 19, 23, 117, 123–124, 126–139, 142, 147, 155–176, 181–186, 188, 190–194, 197–198, 200–204, 207–217, 223, 230–231
Hudson River 24
Humphreys, David 31
Huntsville 125
Husk, Emily 103
Husk, Zilpha 103

Illinois 11, 50
Industrial Revolution 51
Ireland 190
Irish 12, 55–56, 70, 75, 80
Iron, Robert Anderson 221, 224
Iroquoia 24
Iroquois Confederacy 24
Iroquois League 24
Isabella, Queen 107

Jackson, Andrew 75, 82, 112, 127, 177, 194
Jacobs, Harriet 75
Jalapa 153
Jamaica 28, 32, 37, 46, 50
Jameson, Green B. 114
Jefferson, Thomas 13, 29, 75, 100, 137
Jenkins, John Holland 120
Jerusalem 49
Jesup, Thomas Sidney 82
Jews 37, 59
Jocelyn, Nathaniel 38–39, 43, 52, 54
Jocelyn, Simeon S. 38–54, 57–58, 65, 67–68, 74–76, 93, 202, 204, 220
Joe 115–117, 190
John 115
Johnson, Francis White 72
Jones, John R. 110
Juana 96

Kane, John Foster 231
Karnes, Henry 160–161
Kendall, George W. 111
Kentucky 190
Kiamata (also Kian or Ki) 87
King Cotton 22
Kosciuszko 68, 119, 145
Koscuiszko, Thaddeus 119

La Bahia 124, 160
La Porte 19, 88
Lafitte, Jean 87
Lake Michigan 11
Lamar, Mirabeau B. 223, 225
Lane, Walter Payne 187
Lazo, María Luisa 97
Lea, Margaret 221
Leavitt, Joshua 58
Ledyard, William 31

Leonard, Diana 54, 66, 79, 148, 150, 165, 272
Lexington 34
Lexington Green 70
"Lexington of the Texas Revolution" 70
The Liberator 44, 51
Liberia 55
Liberian Hotel 36
Lies Across America 97
Lila 103
Lindsey, Mary 104
Linn, John Joseph 90–91, 97
Little Rock, Chief 203
Livingston, Philip 56
Locke, John 31
Loewen, James W. 20
Logan, Greensbury B. 65, 73
Long, James 8, 87
Long, Jane Herbert Wilkinson 8, 87, 90, 93
Long, Jeff 188
Long Island 26, 52
Long Island, Battle of 309
Long Island Sound 27, 38, 43
Louisiana 16, 54, 60, 65, 70, 74, 86, 99, 103, 123, 127–128, 132, 161–1672, 175, 178–179, 190
The Louisiana Advertiser 120
Louisiana Territory 100
Lucy 103
Lundy, Benjamin 55, 65
Lutzweiler, Jim 11
Lynchburg 129, 160–161, 162, 164
Lynch's Ferry 129, 131, 157–158, 161–163

Macon 124
The Man Who Shot Liberty Valance 20–21
Manhattan 55–57
Manifest Destiny 10, 21, 128, 193–194, 205
Manumission Society 57
Marblehead 30
Marianne (French Revolutionary Republic) 196
Marshall 55
Marshall, Adeline 86
Maryland 8, 24, 53–54, 56, 80, 87, 231
Massachusetts 26–27, 30, 42, 71
Massachusetts Bay Company 26, 43, 89
Matagorda 120
Matamoros 11, 166–167
Mayan 24, 72, 99
McCulloch, Samuel, Jr. 71–72
McCulloch, Samuel, Sr. 71–72
McFarland, Fanny 93
McFarland, William 93
Medina, Battle of 122
Meigs, Return Jonathan 31
Melton, Eliel 96
Melville, Herman 42
Merk, Frederick 117
Methodism 38, 125
Mexican-American War 7, 9, 55, 119, 200, 232
Mexican Congress 147, 194
Mexican Constitution 64
Mexico City 55, 70–71, 76–77, 82, 87, 91, 95, 100–

101, 108, 113, 116–117, 119, 124, 128, 133–134, 141, 147, 153–154, 158, 160, 169, 170, 188–189
Michener, James A. 174
Michigan 101
Middleton 36
Milam, Benjamin Rush 72
Mill River 27
Milledgeville 124, 225
Miller, Mitch 230, 232
Miller, William Parsons 125
Minon, José Vincente 154
Mississippi 162, 222
Missouri 65, 96, 116
Mobile 136
Moby Dick 42
Montego Bay 50
Montgomery, William 31
Monticello 13, 29, 75
Moorish battle flags 119
Moors 100, 107, 156
Morales, Rafael 137, 168
Moreland, Isaac C. 191, 217–223
Morelos, José María 109, 142–143
Morgan, Celia Gordon 150
Morgan, Emily 8, 10–1, 14–15, 20–22, 165, 187, 196, 198
Morgan, James 8, 10, 25, 54, 65–68, 74, 77, 80, 83–84, 87–88, 91, 99, 103, 105, 132–133, 136–137, 141–142, 145–150, 161–162, 164, 192–193, 197–198, 200, 201, 209, 213–213, 217, 219–222, 224
Morgan's Point 65, 84, 90, 103, 106, 164, 196, 213
Mose 102
"Mother of Texas" 8, 87
Mount Pleasant 36
Mount Vernon 30
Muldroon, Michael 91

Nacogdoches 96, 98, 103, 123, 130, 136, 161, 190
Nantucket 42
Nashville 120, 125, 155, 204
Nashville Battalion 125
Nassau 122
Natchez 87
National Banner and Nashville Whig 170
National Gazette 180
Navarro, Juana 96, 116
Navarro, Gertrudis 118
Navarro Family 116
Neale, William 166
Neches River 89, 112, 128
Neill, James Clinton 112
New Amsterdam 56, 62
New Canaan 65
New England 8, 10, 11, 22, 24, 26, 29–32, 35, 37–38, 50, 53–54, 65, 107, 201, 213
New England Anti-Slavery Society 51
New Guinea 35–36
New Hampshire 30
New Haven 10, 11, 15–16, 23–24, 26–29, 31–59, 61–63, 65, 67–69, 79, 82, 89, 92, 99, 106, 148, 151, 161, 201

New Haven Arms Company 29
New Haven Colonization Society 33
New Haven Theology 39
New Jerusalem 26, 43
New Kentucky 139
New Liberia 35–36, 43–44, 50
New London 26, 30
New Netherlands 56
New Orleans 63, 82, 86, 88–89, 93–94, 105, 108–109, 119–120, 132, 136–137, 143, 145, 164, 184, 190, 214, 227
New Orleans Greys 117, 119
New Spain 99–100
New Washington 5, 24, 65–69, 77, 80, 82–83, 86–91, 93–94, 98, 101–109, 115, 119, 122, 124–126, 128–129, 131–132, 135–136, 138–141, 146–149, 151–152, 154, 156–157, 160, 162–163, 165, 193, 197, 199, 214–215, 218–219, 221–222, 226, 229
New Washington Association 24, 65–67, 79–80, 82, 84, 88–89, 91, 119, 132, 137, 140, 142, 144, 146–147, 150, 158, 162–163, 197, 209, 214–216, 219, 220, 222
New York Anti-Slavery Society 51
New York City 15–16, 22, 24, 26, 30, 35, 40, 53–62, 65–67, 77, 79, 82, 84, 88–91, 93, 99, 106, 132, 136, 140, 148, 158, 161, 165, 193, 205, 214, 214, 220, 222, 225–237, 231
New York Daily Advertiser 156
New York Manumission Society 53
Newberry Library 210
Nofi, Albert A. 173
North Carolina 66, 81, 85, 103, 112
Northrup, Mintus 54
Northrup, Solomon 23, 54, 64

Orozimbo Plantation 103
Osceola 82
Ouinnipiac River 27
Our Lady of Guadalupe 152–153, 168, 178, 191
Oxford 38

Pacific 7, 10
Page, Harriet Moore 93–95, 132
Page, Solomon 93–95, 132
Paine, Thomas 31–32, 45
Paris 80, 179
"Patrick Henry of Texas" 106
Patton, Columbus R. 102
Patton, St. Clair 102
Patton, William 102
Peace and Benevolent Society of African Americans 69
Peggy's Lake 163, 189, 191, 193
Peña, José Enrique de la 13–14, 129–130, 133, 153, 156, 166, 168, 171, 181, 186, 199
Pennington, James 53
Pequot 26
Pérez, Alejo 96
Perry, Emily Austin 103
Perry, James Aeneas 103
Perry, James Hazard 175

Philadelphia 31–32, 45, 46, 48, 53, 64, 66, 115, 125, 180, 231
Philadelphia Slave Market 45
Philips, Zeno 102–103
Philipse, Hardenbroeck 62
Pickett, George Edward 119
Pickett's Charge 119
Platt, Frederick 68
Point Bolivar 83
Portilla, José Nicolás de la 153, 168
Potomac River 30, 71
Poverty Square 36
Powell, Elizabeth 135
Presidio la Bahia 72
Puritan 24, 26–27
Puss 101–102

Rabia, Santiago 151
Rains, Eda 86
Raphael, Ray 195
Rappahannock River 97, 111
Raquet, Anna 221
The Raven 213
Reconquista 107, 178
Red River 21, 54
Religion and the True Principles of Morality 78
Republic of Mexico 64–65, 69, 81, 101, 109, 177
Republic of Texas 10, 19, 87, 117, 140
Rhode Island 54
Rice, C. C. 164
Richmond Enquirer 136
Rightor, Nicholas 84
Rightor's Point 83
Rio Bravo 11
Rio Grande River 11, 71, 75, 100, 112, 166, 191, 198–199, 223, 230
Ripley, Eleazar 126
Ripley, Henry 126
Roberts, Abraham 139
Robertson, Sterling C. 85
Robinson, James W. 109
Rogers, Robert 30
Rogers, Tiana 12, 155
Rogers' Rangers 30
Rome 95
Rose of Alabama 231
Rose of Baltimore 231
Ross, Betsey 195
Routh, Emily 103, 218
Routh, Jones 103, 213, 218
Routh, Sylvia 218
Rubicon 67
"Runaway Scrape" 137, 193
Rusk, Thomas J. 137, 146, 170, 176, 189

Sabine River 8, 16, 21, 68, 70–72, 74, 79, 89, 100, 102, 104, 123, 127–128, 130, 133–134, 139, 161, 219
St. Augustine 81
Saint-Domingue (Haiti) 108
St. James Parish 50
St. Phillips African Episcopal Church 59
Saltillo 114, 167
Sampson, Deborah 195
Samson (Biblical) 12, 203, 208
San Antonio de Béxar 20, 65, 70, 71–73, 76, 84, 96–97, 104, 108, 111, 114–116, 119, 122–125, 128, 137, 149, 152, 154–156, 178, 219
San Antonio Express 155
San Antonio Express News 206
San Antonio Herald 231
San Felipe de Austin 62, 74, 77, 86, 89, 93, 95, 103, 105–106, 112, 116, 123–124, 129, 133–135, 137, 148, 166, 231
San Fernando Church 114
San Jacinto 7–14, 16, 19–22, 24–25, 67, 104, 106, 117, 120, 156, 159, 163–169, 171–193, 196–198, 200–202, 205, 210–212, 215, 217–228, 230, 232
San Jacinto Bay 83, 164
San Jacinto River 65, 83, 89, 129, 131, 157, 162–163, 168, 197
San Luis Potosí 125
Sandifer, Marmaduke D. 74
Sands, Harriet Newell 101
Santa Anna, Antonio López de 8–13, 19, 22–23, 25–26, 66, 71, 73–75, 80–81, 96, 104, 106, 108–109, 111, 110, 112–117, 119, 122–142, 144, 147–150–188, 190–215
Santa Anna: A Curse Upon Mexico 206
Santa Anna of Mexico 199
Savannah 81
Scheina, Robert L. 181
Schultz, Charles 60
Scotch Irish 30, 166
Scotland 91
Scottish Highlanders 66
Scottish Highlands 66
Second Seminole War 81–82
Seguín, Juan N. 96, 170
Seminole 82
Seneca 232
Seneca Falls 232
Sharpe, Sam 50
Sherman, Sidney 190
Sierra Leone 52
Slave Revolt 104–105
Smith, Erastus "Deaf" 72, 101, 160, 185, 192
Smith, John William 96
Smith, Juanita 101
Smithwick, Noah 55, 97–98, 101, 105–106, 181
Society for the Relief of Female Professors of Religion 43
Sodom Hill 36–37, 50
Soldaderas 152–153, 184
Soustelle, Jacques 153
South Carolina 31, 75, 81, 86, 146, 181
Southampton County 48–50
Spireworth School 51, 53
Spireworth Square 43
Stephens, Thomas 73
Stewart, Maria 77–78
Supreme Court 52

Swartwout, Samuel 66, 89, 91, 141, 145, 149, 158, 200, 209, 220, 222, 226

Tallahassee 115
Tampa 82
Tappan, Arthur 40, 45–46, 50–51, 58–60
Tappan, Lewis 44–46, 51, 58
Taylor, Nathaniel 39–40
Taylor, William S. 189
Tejano 7, 9–10, 15, 19, 21, 89, 95–98, 104, 107, 114, 116, 122, 147, 154, 165, 168, 172, 184, 192, 299
Tejas 7, 10, 16, 64, 84, 91, 96, 98, 100, 129
The Telegraph and Texas Register 110, 116, 138, 148–149, 161
Temple Street Church 40, 42, 44, 54
Tennessee 61, 85, 116, 120, 125, 133, 155, 168–169, 212
Terán, Manuel de Mier y 76, 87, 91
Texas Congress 209, 217, 220, 222–223
Texas Constitution 209, 222–223
Texas Declaration of Independence 81, 96, 99
Texas Republic 9, 66, 73, 80, 104, 131, 141, 146, 148, 202, 222, 232
Texas Sesquicentennial 9
Texian Iliad 14
Thames River 30
Thompson, Frank 209
Thompson, Isaac 43, 51
Thompson, Jesse G. 102
Three Roads to the Alamo 20
Tornel, José María 110
Travis, William B. 9, 12, 17, 19–20, 105, 112, 114–117, 120, 161, 188, 190
Treat, James 66
Trenton 30
Trinity Bay 66, 79, 84
Trinity River 83–84, 89, 120
Tritton, Lois 53
Trowbridge Square 37, 43, 46, 52
Truth, Peter 68
Truth, Sojourner 68
Turner, Frederick Jackson 106
Turner, Nat 48–50
Tuskegee Institute 45
"Twin Sisters" 132, 145, 164, 189, 191, 219

Ulster Province 30
United African Society 42
Urrea, Juan José 114, 123–126, 128

Van Buren, Martin 58, 60
Vance, William 218
Varner, Martin 102
Vera Cruz 99, 111, 156, 170
Vera Cruz Lancers 134, 158
Vera Cruz Province 135, 147, 153, 157
Vermont 54

Victoria 124, 126
Victoria Guadalupe 126
Village of Spireworth 43–44, 46
Virgin of Guadalupe 98
Virginia 30, 48–49, 75, 77, 125, 134, 151, 231
Virginia Rose Bud 231
Visigoths 100, 107, 151

War of 1812 32, 72, 126
Ward, William 124
Washington, George 30–31, 75
Washington, D.C. 12, 23, 54, 81, 88, 112, 115, 177
Washington-on-the-Brazos 81, 99, 113–114, 117, 120–121, 123, 127
Washita 203
Waterloo 14
Wayne, John 20
Webber, John F. 101–102
Webster, Noah 27, 42
Wesley, John 38
West, Claiborne 99
West, Emily D. 7–17, 19–25, 33–39, 42–46, 50, 52–62, 64–71, 73–95, 98–99, 101–110, 117, 119, 121, 125–126, 128–129, 131–132, 135–136, 138–145, 148–154, 156–159, 161, 164–166, 170, 173–182, 184, 186–187, 190–192, 195, 198–224, 232
West, "Sawyer" 99
West Point 119, 175
Wharton, William H. 75
White, Deborah Gray 106
Whitefield, George 38
Whitney, Eli 28–29
William Bollaert's Texas 25, 210, 230
Williams, Ezekiel 70
Williamson, Robert McAlpin 74, 106, 231
Willis 165
Wilmington 81
Wilson 134
Winthrop, John 27–28, 43, 88
Wyatt, Peyton S. 125

Yale College 27–29, 35–40, 42, 45–48, 52, 58
Yellow Rose of Texas 7–12, 14–16, 19–20, 23, 34, 106, 141, 165, 170, 179, 182, 187, 194, 196, 198–199, 200–203, 205–208, 211, 213, 220–221, 226, 228, 230–232
Yellowstone 134
Yucatan 80–81, 131, 192, 224

Zapadores 129
Zavala, Lorenzo de 23–24, 66, 80–81, 121, 131, 133, 138, 140–141, 157–160, 197, 224
Zavala, Lorenzo de, Jr. 192
Zavala, Miranda West de 23–24, 80–81, 131, 141, 143, 224–225
Zuber, William 192

www.ingramcontent.com/pod-product-compliance
Ingram Content Group UK Ltd.
Pitfield, Milton Keynes, MK11 3LW, UK
UKHW050538150426
5217IPUK00026B/1987